THE CULTURAL CONTEXT OF INFANCY

VOLUME 2

Multicultural and Interdisciplinary Approaches to Parent–Infant Relations

edited by

J. Kevin Nugent
University of Massachusetts
at Amherst
and Harvard Medical School

Barry M. Lester
Brown University/Bradley
and Women and Infant's Hospitals

T. Berry Brazelton
Children's Hospital, Boston
and Harvard Medical School

ABLEX PUBLISHING CORPORATION
NORWOOD, NEW JERSEY

155.422
C968
v.2

Library of Congress Cataloging-in-Publication Data
(Revised for volume 2)

The Cultural context of infancy.

  Includes bibliographies and indexes.
  Contents: v. 1. Biology, culture, and infant development — v.   2. Multicultural and interdisciplinary approaches to parent-infant relations.
  1. Infants—Development.   2. Individual differences.
I. Nugent, J. Kevin.   II. Lester, Barry M.
RJ134.C85   1989   155.4'22   88-26059
ISBN 0-89391-627-7 (v. 2)

Ablex Publishing Corporation
355 Chestnut Street
Norwood, New Jersey 07648

Contents

iii

Series Preface

J. Kevin Nugent

*Univ. of Massachusetts at Amherst
and Children's Hospital
Harvard Medical School*

In the year 1626, Thomas Nugent, an Irish farmer living at Coolamber near Mullingar in Westmeath, was cutting turf when he came upon a pair of giant antlers. "They were the only wonder of those halcyon days because of their prodigious largeness", Sir William Piers wrote of their discovery in 1682. When they were cleaned and erected on Mr. Nugent's wall "they were no less than twelve feet in length and the palms out of which the smallest horns branched, were as broad as the targets, which in those days men of the blade used to wear" (Piers, p. 52). Though Thomas Nugent did not realize it, the antlers were in fact, the horns of the extinct Giant Irish Elk.

The Giant Irish Elk was the largest deer that ever lived and his antlers have never been exceeded. Their size seem all the more impressive as paleontologist Stephen J. Gould points out, when we recognize they were grown and re-grown annually (Gould, 1977). The giant deer evolved during the glacial period of the last few million years but became extinct in Ireland about 11,000 years ago. The question that has engaged scientists ever since has been why the giant deer became extinct. The most popular explanation has been that the giant antlers were an example of overspecialization and that the Elk, weighed down by the excessive weight, became defenseless and died out. However, recent studies have shown that in fact there is a strong positive correlation between antler size and body size in the Irish Elk, so that the original overspecialization argument for its extinction must be rejected. Why then did the giant deer become extinct? The consensus among paleontologists today is that the Irish Elk flourished in Ireland for only a brief warm period of 1000 years, but was unable to adapt to the cold epoch that followed (Gould, 1977). Extinction became the fate of the giant deer because they were unable to adapt to the changing conditions of climate.

For man on the other hand, it is his biological plasticity and his capacity for adaptation over a wide range of environments that has constituted his success as a species. Unlike the ill-fated Irish Elk who was locked into his environment, man has been able to transform his environment in order to meet his survival needs. In the end it is his capacity for material culture that has enabled the human species to forge new and unique adaptations in every corner of the globe.

The range and variety of the different expressions of adaptation is nowhere more evident than in the diverse ways in which societies protect, nurture, and educate their young. Although parenthood is a universal phenomenon, patterns of child-rearing are highly variable across the human species. Over the last fifty years, anthropologists have documented the diversity of child-rearing practices in different cultures and have consistently demonstrated the degree to which the environments of infancy and early childhood are shaped by cultural values and practices (e.g., LeVine, 1980; Whiting & Whiting, 1975; and Whiting & Edwards, 1988). In a parallel but complementary tradition, cross-cultural studies in psychology have shown that differences exist in newborn behavior among cultural groups around the world. While the basic organizational processes in infancy are universal, it is argued, the range and form of these adaptations are shaped by the demands of each particular culture (Lester & Brazelton, 1982).

However, despite this growing comparative tradition, it must be acknowledged that much of our contemporary knowledge of child development is the product of Western cultural history (Bronfenbrenner, Kessel, Kessen, & White, 1986). Kessen and Cahan (1986) in their review of the history of psychology also conclude that child development as a scientific endeavor has been a predominately North-American-European enterprise and as such could be characterized as a narrow and essentially local tradition. Given the narrow database, there is a growing awareness that the empirical findings of child development cannot be generalized to most of the world's children today.

The overarching goal of this series therefore is to add to the database of research in infant development by describing the developmental processes of infancy over a wide range of cultural and social environments. By presenting multiple alternative examples of the context of infant development, our goal is to stimulate continued discussion on the ways in which biological, social, and cultural factors influence the course of human development from the beginning. Specifically, the goals of the series are: (1) to assemble reports of original empirical research on infancy from different countries around the world, (2) to present this material from a variety of disciplinary perspectives, (3) to document the use of the Neonatal Behavioral Assessment Scale (NBAS) as a research tool in different cultural settings, and (4) to ultimately examine the relationship between biology, culture, and infant development by documenting different neonatal environments and child-care practices in different cultures. Finally, we hope that these studies will not only extend the depth and richness of the existing canon of infancy research but because of the diversity of settings will challenge our core assumptions about infancy on the one hand and our beliefs about the nature of child development itself on the other.

References

Bronfenbrenner, U., Kessel, F., Kessen, F., & White, S. (1986). Toward a critical social history of developmental psychology. *American Psychologist, 41* (11), 1218–1230.

Gould, S. J. (1977). *Ever since Darwin.* New York: Norton.

Kessen, W., & Cahan, E. (1986). A century of psychology: From subject to object to agent. *American Scientist, 74,* 640–650.

Lester, B. M., & Brazelton, T. B. (1982). Cross-cultural assessment of neonatal behaviors. In D. Wagner & H. Stevenson (Eds.), *Cultural perspectives on child development.* San Francisco: Freeman and Co.

LeVine, R. A. (1980). A cross-cultural perspective on parenting. In M. Fantini & R. Cardenas (Eds.), *Parenting in a multicultural society.* New York: Longman.

Piers, Sir W. (1981). *A chronological description of the county of Westmeath, 1682.* Naas: Meath Archeological and Historical Publications.

Whiting, B. W., & Edwards, C. P. (1988). *Children of different worlds: The formation of social behavior.* Cambridge, MA: Harvard University Press.

Whiting, B. B., & Whiting, J. W. M. (1975). *Children of six cultures: A psychocultural analysis.* Cambridge, MA: Harvard University Press.

Foreword
The Role of Culture in Brain Organization, Child Development, and Parenting

E. Z. Tronick
and
Gilda A. Morelli

The chapters in this volume present the reader with a varied set of studies on the relations between newborn behavioral organization, parenting, and culture. It is striking to us that, despite the diversity of these studies' settings and of the researchers' backgrounds, there is an underlying perspective that unifies the different works and helps create a more integrated picture of the factors shaping development.

This perspective promotes the view that development can only be understood by studying the interplay of infant characteristics, including biological and temperamental factors, and parenting practices that are shaped by sociocultural and ecological factors. It is a complex, transactional perspective; scholars who adopt it are faced with the difficult task of taking into account the multiplicity of factors affecting development while not losing sight of the issues under study. For example, examining the relation of infant behavior and culture while considering ecological factors is extremely difficult because these factors come from radically different domains. One solution to the challenges posed is provided by recent theorizing about brain development that allows us to integrate these factors into a more unified model.

The transactional position, which is a radical shift from the perspective that sees sociocultural experiences as modifying only what the brain learns or stores, argues that structural as well as functional characteristics of the brain are modified by culturally shaped pre- and postnatal experiences. In the following passage, pediatric neurologist Heinz Prechtl clearly expresses this view:

> The effects of the selective pressure on the pre-programmed maturation of the nervous system [and related changes in behavior] should not be considered without taking into account the influence of the caregiver. There is an inevitable process of matching between the offspring and care-giver through mutual influences. Put differently, the young will only survive and grow and develop properly if the mothering and nursing repertory of the care-giver is precisely adapted to the properties of the young and vice versa. . . . [Thus] our interest shifts from the seemingly limited [behavioral] abilities of the young organism to their astonishing competence to cope with a large variety of specific demands of internal regulation as well as adaptation and responsiveness to environmental features. (Connelly & Prechtl, 1981, p. 199)

Prechtl's position is broad; nonetheless, he is very specific that nonneurological factors such as "mothering and nursing repertory," and caregiver's and infant's behavioral characteristics, are among the primary forces shaping the organization of the infant's brain. The interdependence of biology and culture is clear; to the extent that culture modifies caregiving (e.g., mothering) and the co-regulation of caregiver and infant behavior, then to that extent does culture affect the developing brain. Culture and infant behavior now take their rightful place in a transactional perspective alongside biological factors (e.g., nutrition, deprivation, toxic insults, drug exposure, ecological stresses) that are known to affect features of the brain. Indeed, each of these factors can be seen to be involved in a dynamic developmental process of transactions between the organization of the infant's brain and behavior, and the parenting the infant receives.

The studies in this volume attend to the organization of infant behavior and parenting as they are modified by culture. While the description of culture is approached in many different ways (e.g., interviews with informants, historical records, literature reviews), the Brazelton Neonatal Behavioral Assessment Scale (BNBAS) is used in each of the studies for assessing the organization of the infant's behavior.

The BNBAS presents us with two simultaneous views of the infant. One view looks "inward" and evaluates the status of the infant's central nervous system by assessing the functional organization of the infant's behavior. The second view looks "outward" at the impact of the infant's behavior on the behavior of its caregivers. The quantified characterization of the infant's neural and behavioral repertoire is the type of information required by Prechtl to understand the relation among behavior, brain development, and culture. Moreover, the use of the BNBAS by all of the researchers provides a unifying methodological theme. This is effective strategy for the volume because it helps bridge the research described in the different chapters.

We have developed a model, the caregiver-child strategy model, that is useful in framing our understanding of the chapters in this volume. While this model is sharply focused on child-caregiver interactions and the strategies child and caregiver develop to manage their interactions, it also maintains a background focus on parenting practices as embedded within the sociocultural and ecological system. The caregiver-child strategy model views the child and the caretaker as having proximal and distal goals. The child's proximal goals are to regulate internal physiologic, behavioral and affective states and, at the same time, engage the social and physical world. The child's distal goals are survival, growth and development, and eventual reproductive success, economic self-sufficiency and the acquisition of culturally appropriate behaviors.

To accomplish these goals children use what we have termed resource acquisition strategies. These strategies are the set of regulatory physiologic and behavioral processes for maintaining internal regulation, instrumental behaviors for acquiring resources from the inanimate environment and, most centrally, communicative behaviors for modifying caregiver activities in order to procure psychological and physical resources. The organization of the infant's basic resource acquisition strategy is what is assessed by the BNBAS. The behaviors making up these elemental strategies include self-comforting, orientation, and alertness, facial expressions, vocalizations and gestures. With development, the infant's resource acquisition strategies will be elaborated, most uniquely, into a univesal culture-specific form—speech—which, as argued by Vygotsky, will serve as a form of self-regulation and communication.

Caretakers have proximal and distal goals that are similar but not identical to their offspring's goals. They also have strategies, called caretaker investment strategies, for achieving these goals (see LeVine, 1977, for a discussion of these strategies). While caregiver investment strategies necessarily include Prechtl's maternal and nursing behaviors, their most fundamental characteristic is the capacity of the caregiver to understand and act on the child's communicative displays in culturally appropriate ways. These child and caregiver strategies are reciprocal adaptive processes that assure the accomplishment of the caretaker and and offspring's success. Essentially, their mutual adaptation is a communicative process because without communication there can be no effective regulation between the child's resource acquisition strategy and the parental investment strategy.

Strategies vary among people from different communities because caregivers draw on culturally based knowledge to guide their decision making (LeVine, 1977). Culture tailors the phylogenetically based aspects of caregiver investment strategies to the locally specific, relatively stable, social and physical features of the environment. Most important, culture helps define those features of the child's behavior and communication that require attention and response, as well as the culturally appropriate form of the response. Needless to say, culture is not the exclusive factor influencing investment strategies, but one of several factors (e.g., ecological, phylogenetic, demographic).

To put the strategic model in more mechanistic terms, the infant can be seen as a device for garnering resources from the environment to help accomplish its goals. Caregivers often provide the necessary resources because their goals overlap with the goals of their infant. Yet, while there is no question that children actively influence the care they receive, a child's ultimate dependence on caregivers effectively limits the extent to which he or she modifies their strategies; that is, the child has no choice but to make his or her acquisition strategies conform to the caregiver's strategies, including the cultural components making them up. Thus, the child's strategies take on a cultural form as does its central nervous system from the moment it begins to act. To quote Prechtl again, "Within limits, a new intact but biologically different brain may be formed, with a rather different functional repertoire" (Connelly & Prechtl, 1981, p. 212).

To illustrate this caregiver-child strategy model, consider some of our work on the Efe and their system of care. The Efe are a people of short stature who live in the Ituri rainforest of northeastern Zaïre. Efe women give birth to infants whose average weight is 2.4 kg. and average length, 43.4 cm (Winn, Morelli, & Tronick, 1989). U.S.-born infants born at this weight/length would be considered at risk for medical complications. While this also may be the case with Efe neonates, we believe that the caregiving strategy adopated by the Efe mitigates against threats to infant survival and, at the same time, communicates cultural messages to the infant and community members alike.

Efe childrearing practices must deal with immediate hazards to survival such as dehydration, and long-term hazards to social functioning such as anti-social behaviors. How is this accomplished? Nursing the infant by individuals in addition to the mother may increase the infant's fluid balance, reducing the small infant's vulnerability to dehydration. Multiple nursing may also foster the development of social capacities for relating to many different individuals, and the development of multiple secure bases for attachment. The competencies emerging from these social experiences serve infants well throughout their lifetime. Infants and toddlers are often left in the camp in the care of others while their mothers forage for forest foods (Morelli, 1987), a practice unlike that observed among foraging communities such as the !Kung (Draper, 1976). Further, mortality is high among the Efe, leaving many infants motherless or parentless. Thus, the ability to form trusting relationships with a variety of individuals is likely to be important for the Efe infant. In addition, the Efe—adults and children alike—are almost always in social and often physical contact with one another and are largely dependent on each other for their survival. The ability to get along with community members appears to be an essential part of Efe living, and the parental investment strategy of the Efe fosters this ability. Clearly, the form that Efe infant and caregiver strategies take will be different from that observed in other communities. And one can only speculate that the Prechtilian brain of these infants and their adult caregivers will differ as well.

The chapters in this volume provide many exemplars of the interplay of

caregiver and infant strategies. Each chapter documents infants' behavioral organization at birth using the BNBAS, and most authors relate this organization to
the infant's and mother's medical status during the perinatal period. Many of
the chapters examine the relation between caregiving strategies and infant behavioral organization, and how this relation changes in the first year of life. Finally,
some authors consider the role cultural institutions such as hospitals play in the
type of care the infant receives. Most important, however, each study examines
the relation between sociocultural features like caregiving practices and infant
development.

These studies have helped set the direction for future research, and we should
continue to conduct research that expands our knowledge of the diversity of
practices. However, we must also begin to select for study communities that
allow us to examine more systematically our assumptions about culture and
development. For example, we selected the Efe of Zaïre for study because their
system of care will help us understand the process by which infants develop
relationships with their caregivers.

The task we have identified is somewhat daunting, in that it requires detailed
specification of cultural belief systems, ecological factors, caregiver and infant
strategies, and the interplay amongst them. Nonetheless, the effort will be worth-
while. With carefully chosen research questions, and communities that best
allow these questions to be addressed, we will broaden our understanding of
the relation among culture, infant behavior and neurological organization, and
caregiving.

References

Connelly, K.J., & Prechtl, H.F.R. (Eds.) (1981). *Maturation and development: Biolog-
    ical and psychological perspectives* (Clinics in Developmental Medicine No.
    77/78, Spastics International Medical Publications). London: William Heinemann
    Medical Books; Philadelphia: J. B. Lippincott.
Draper, P. (1976). Social and economic constraints on child life among the !Kung. In
    R.B. Lee & I. DeVore (Eds.), *Kalahari hunter-gatherers: Studies of the !Kung San
    and their neighbors* (pp. 199–217). Cambridge, MA: Harvard University Press.
LeVine, R.A. (1977). Child rearing as cultural adaptation. In P.H. Leiderman, S.R.
    Tulkin, & A. Rosenfeld (Eds.), *Culture and infancy: Variations in the human
    experience* (pp. 15–27). New York: Academic Press.
Morelli, G.A. (1987). *A comparative study of Efe (Pygmy) and Lese one-, two-, and three-
    year-olds of the Iture Forest of northeastern Zaïre: The influence of subsistence-
    related variables, and children's age and gender on social-emotional development.*
    Doctoral dissertation, University of Massachusetts, 1987. (Dissertation Abstracts
    International, 48/02B, P. 582, (8710487).)
Winn, S., Morelli, G.A., & Tronick, E. (1989). The infant and the group: A look at Efe
    care-taking practices. In J.K. Nugent, B.M. Lester, & T.B. Brazelton (Eds.), *The
    cultural context of infancy* (Vol. 1, pp. 86–109). Norwood, NJ: Ablex Publishing.

PART I

NEWBORN BEHAVIOR AND
LATER DEVELOPMENT

CHAPTER 1

Newborn Behavior, The Quality of Early Parenting and Later Toddler–Parent Relationships in a Group of German Infants*

Karin Grossmann and Klaus E. Grossmann

Institut fuer Psychologie
Universitaet Regensburg
D - 8400 Regensburg
West Germany

In studies of parent–infant relationships, it is necessary to pay attention to the contribution of the infant to the developing relationship with his or her parents (Campos, Caplovitz Barrett, Lamb, Hill, Goldsmith, & Stenberg, 1983). Even in the area of parenting disorders (Kempe & Kempe, 1978), the following important question developed: Are there infants who make it especially easy or difficult for their parents to care for them, and to accomplish mutually satisfying interactions with them?

The Brazelton Neonatal Behavioral Assessment Scale (NBAS) was designed

* This research has been supported by a grant from Stiftung Volkswagenwerk under the title "Ontogenesis of Behavior of the Human Neonate" to Klaus E. Grossmann.

We were trained in the application of the NBAS by Dr. H. Als and gratefully received much support and encouragement from her during the early phases of our endeavor. The collection of the magnitude of data would have been impossible without the help of many students of the Paedagogische Hochschule Westfalen-Lippe in Bielefeld, and especially Jutta Ermshaus and Elisabeth Heimesaat. We are indebted to the late Dr. Phillip Lachenicht and the staff of the St. Franziskus Hospital for their friendly and generous support of this study. We also want to thank Gottfried Spangler and Karin Dorsch for their help with the data analyses.

Our German prejudice, that no one will let you know what is going on inside a family, was generously disproved by the families of this study. We are grateful for their openness toward us and their willingness to let us learn from them.

3

to document individual differences in behavioral and interactive style and tempo at birth (Brazelton, 1973). It allows for an evaluation of the infant's capabilities along dimensions that are thought to be relevant to the infant's developing social relationships (Brazelton, Nugent, & Lester, 1987).

It proved, however, to be difficult to establish a high day-to-day reliability for the NBAS: Many studies done in the U.S. with this scale (cf. Sameroff, 1978) have shown that the behavior of U.S. born infants changed significantly over the first 10 days of life. On the other hand, looking at NBAS assessments done in other countries such as Israel (Horowitz, Sullivan, & Linn, 1978), the day-to-day reliabilities within a 4-day period were more frequently significant in the Israeli sample than in a Kansas sample. Horowitz et al. (1978) suggested that the high doses of medication given to U.S. mothers during birth may account for some of the instability. And, more generally, since infants mature quickly, stability should not be expected. This argument, however, cannot be restricted to U.S. infants and is therefore not very plausible.

The results to be reported here suggest that environmental changes like early discharge from the hospital may effect the newborn's behavior. As Als once described U.S. mothers to us, they "jazz up" their babies once they are home. This could result in some of the changes or "instabilities" observed in U.S. samples.

Despite this stability problem, NBAS results have been successfully used as valuable predictors of later qualities of mother–child relationships (Brazelton et al., 1987). Egeland and Brunnquell (1979) showed that the infant's orienting ability as a newborn was an important variable in determining at-risk-for-abuse mothers. Crockenberg (1981) looked at the mitigating effects of environmental variables on the mother–child relationship of irritable infants: High irritability of the infant was associated with anxious attachment to the mother only if the mother felt that she had little social support from the father, from older children in the family, or from others. Als and Lewis (1975) presented some case examples to support the following hypothesis: NBAS scores may provide a basis for estimating the effort a mother has to invest in order to interact successfully and satisfyingly with a given infant.

It still remains to be shown, however, if and how the newborn's ease of social interchange and the parents' effort and quality of caretaking interact during the development of certain types of parent–child relationships. Also, it would be interesting to see whether this newborn characteristic could be detected at later ages, of course with proper consideration of the appropriate behavioral transformations.

Our longitudinal study in northern Germany of the development of parent–child relationship patterns was designed to discover such transactional processes. We concentrated on the following questions:

1.   Can we find stability across assessments over the first 9 to 10 days of the

newborn period, and are there stable individual differences in newborn characteristics indicative of the infant's interactive readiness?

2. Can we find, on the basis of the transactional model, influences of these newborn characteristics on parental quality of caretaking and/or the child's style of interacting with his or her parents or strangers?

3. When looking at the quality of children's attachment to their parents as one important developmental outcome of their interactions in the first year, can we identify the child's contribution to a more or less secure relationship with the parents?

Because of the longitudinal character of questions 2 and 3 above, attempts for finding answers required diverse methodological strategies. To insure the highest quality of the data during collection and at the same time independence of data analysis, one of the authors was always part of the data collection team, whereas the final data analyses were done by graduate students unfamiliar with any other but their own age- and situation-related data set. The various kinds of data required different methods of analysis which seemed most appropriate for the specific questions in a given situation at a specific age. Six different methods of data analysis will be presented here, which, for the reasons stated above, are closely linked to the results and their interpretations. Therefore, as well as for the purpose of clarity, we will report methods and results together for each situation.

Subjects

At the beginning of the study, 54 families participated. The mothers or both parents were asked for their consent prior to the birth of the target infant. The families came from all social classes but predominantly from the lower-middle class (53%). All except five mothers were full-time homemakers. One pair of parents shared their job and also the caretaking of their baby. In one family the father was the primary caretaker. (The sample has been described in K. Grossmann, Thane, & Grossmann, 1981; K. Grossmann, Grossmann, Spangler, Suess, & Unzner, 1985.) All mothers have had uncomplicated pregnancies and deliveries. The medication given to the mothers during labor and delivery was traditionally low (no spinal anesthesia) in the hospital selected. The mothers were awake and had an active role during birth. Also, most infants were, at least temporarily, awake after birth (Table 1).

Lying-in time for mothers and infants was 8 to 11 days, with a mean of 9.2 days. The postpartum conditions for mothers and infants were varied according to the experimental design presented in Figure 1.

1. Normal routine ($n=12$): after birth the infant is cared for, dressed, and put in a bassinet beside the mother's delivery bed.

2. Early contact ($n=12$): 0 to 10 minutes after birth, the nude infant is put into his or her mother's arms on the delivery bed for at least 30 minutes.

Table 1.   Data on the Infants, Mothers, Labors, and Deliveries

Sex of infant:	27 male, 27 female
Mother's age:	range 18 to 42 years, mean 25.9 years
Parity range:	first to fifth child, 52% or 28 firstborns
Length of Labor:	range 2–24 hours, mean 8.4 hours
Medication received by mothers:	no medication $n = 2$
	only 6 h prior to birth $n = 4$
	standard amount[1] $n = 39$
	more than standard amount $n = 9$
Birth weight:	range 2420 g–4470 g, mean 3490 g, SD 398 g
Apgar scores:	1–min: range 4–10, mean 9.59
	5–min: 10 for all infants
State 4 within 60 minutes after birth:	not at all, $n = 16$
	frequent phases, $n = 28$
	continuously more than 15 min., $n = 10$
Lying-in time of mothers:	range 8–11 days, mean 9.2 days

[1] Standard amount: 100 mg meperidine plus 10 mg diazepam

3.   Extended contact ($n=17$): after a routine birth, mother and infant experience rooming-in for 5 extra hours each day.
4.   Early plus extended contact ($n=13$).

Mothers and infants were assigned successively to the four groups, because the staff was willing to change permanently from normal routine to early plus extended contact along with this study.

The four groups did not differ significantly with respect to any of the background variables except for sex of infant: Group 1 had significantly more male infants than group 2, but this proved to be irrelevant for the dependent variables.

Administration of the Neonatal Behavioral Assessment Scale

The Neonatal Behavioral Assessment Scale was administered to each infant on day 2 or 3, 5 or 6, and 8 or 9. Two infants were tested only twice because one mother–infant pair was discharged on the seventh day, and for one infant, the pediatrician advised us not to do the NBAS during the first 3 days. The choice of the specific day was made according to the circumstances in the nursery: Days of major disturbances, of medical examinations and inoculations, were avoided. Four conditions had to be met before an infant was examined: The preceding rest period of the infant had not been disturbed; at least one and a half hours had passed since the last feeding; the infant had taken the normal amount of milk at the last feeding; and the infant's body temperature had been within the normal range in the morning.

Early contact

no   yes

Group 1 n=12 (11)	Group 2 n=12 (10)	n=24 (21)
Group 3 n=17 (14)	Group 4 n=13 (12)	n=30 (26)
n=29 (25)	n=25 (22)	n=54 (47)

Extended contact   no / yes

(n) = group sizes after two years

Figure 1.   Experimental variation of the hospital situation for the 54 mother–newborn pairs.

The examinations took place in a small, quiet, dimly lit, warm room, where the examiner was alone with the infant. The main examiner (first author), who did about 50% of the assessments, was trained to 90% reliability by Als. Two additional examiners were trained by the first author. Interrater reliability between the three examiners of this study was repeatedly checked and kept at 90% level during the 3 months of alternate testings.

The test results were factor analyzed with Varimax rotation. For each testing day two stable and three less stable factors emerged: ORIENTATION composed of the NBAS items 5 to 10, and IRRITABILITY composed of the variables 16 to 19, 24, and 25. The less stable factors were composed of different items on each assessment day. Therefore they were not included in any longitudinal analysis.

The two factors Orientation and Irritability accounted jointly for 33.5% of the variance on the first assessment day, for 36.2% on the second, and for 36.9% on the third assessment day.

Reliability and Stability of Individual Differences Between Newborns in Their NBAS Performance

In the hospital environment where mothers and infants stayed during the 9-day assessment period, the NBAS yielded reliable results. This contrasts with many U.S. studies (cf. Sameroff, 1978; Vaughn, Taraldson, Crichton, & Egeland, 1980). Table 2 presents the significant correlations between the 27 individual items for every combination of two assessments. Between the first and the

Table 2.   Significant Test-Retest Reliabilities (Spearman-Brown Coefficients) For the NBAS Items for 54 Healthy German Infants

Scale Item	Day 2/3 with Day 5/6	Day 2/3 with Day 8/9	Day 5/6 with Day 8/9
1. Habituation to light			
2. Habituation to rattle		.42	
3. Habituation to bell	.41		
4. Habituation to pinprick			.47
5. Orientation to ball			.33
6. Orientation to rattle			.25
7. Orientation to face	.23		.37
8. Orientation to voice	.35	.33	.42
9. Orientation to face + voice	.31		.35
10. Alertness	.33		.33
11. Muscle tone	.24	.35	.54
12. Motor maturity		.47	.48
13. Pull-to-sit	.35	.49	.52
14. Cuddliness		.30	.35
15. Defensive Movements			
16. Consolability			.30
17. Peak of excitement			.33
18. Rapidity of buildup		.28	.27
19. Irritability		.36	.50
20. Activity			.43
21. Tremulousness	.37	.53	.45
22. Startle			
23. Colour changes	.24		.39
24. Lability of states		.31	.33
25. Self quieting		.24	.25
26. Hand-to-mouth facility	.38	.36	.44
27. Smiles			

Significance levels ($n = 53$ for some comparisons, otherwise $n = 54$)
$.23 < r_s < .28 : p < .05$
$.30 < r_s < .38 : p < .01$
$.40 < r_s < .54 : p < .001$

Table 3. Means, Standard Deviations and Reliability Indices of the NBAS Orientation and Irritability Item Set Scores and the a priori Dimension Scores for 54 Healthy German Infants

Item Sets	Day 2 or 3			Day 5 or 6			Day 8 or 9	
	Mean	SD	Rel. Ind.	Mean	SD	Rel. Ind.	Mean	SD
Orientation (5, 6, 7, 8, 9, 10)	6.43	1.25	$r_{1/2} = .28$*	6.15	1.12	$r_{2/3} = .49$***	6.52	1.20
Irritability (16, 17, 18, 19, 24, 25[1])	3.45	1.56	$r_{1/2} = .31$**	4.61	1.56	$r_{2/3} = .43$***	4.59	1.62
Interactive Processes (Dim. 1)	1.9	0.7	34%	2.1	0.8	41%	1.9	0.7
Motoric Processes (Dim. 2)	2.0	0.3	77%	2.0	0.7	77%	1.9	0.5
State Organization (Dim. 3)	1.8	0.5	57%	2.0	0.5	72%	1.9	0.5
Response to Stress (Dim. 4)	1.2	0.6	83%	1.0	0.3	96%	1.0	0.0

*$p < .05$, **$p < .01$, ***$p < .001$

[1]Because the items 16 and 25 correlated negatively with the others in this set, the values $10 - x$ were entered

second assessment, 10 correlations (37%) were significant, 7 of these at the 1% level; between the second and the third assessment 21 correlations (78%) were significant, and 18 (66%) of these at the 1% level of significance. Even between the first assessment on day 2 or 3 and the third assessment on day 8 or 9, 12, or 44%, of the correlations were significant.

In Table 3, the mean sum scores of the two stable factors Orientation and Irritability, are shown, as well as the mean dimension scores according to the a priori cluster scheme suggested by Brazelton et al. (1979). Pearson correlations between the sum scores of two consecutive assessments are presented, as well as the percentage of infants having the same dimension score on two consecutive assessments. The greatest shift in individual cluster scores of the newborns occurred in the dimension "interactive processes"; the infants changed little with respect to the dimension "motoric processes" and "response to stress."

The significant and high correlations of the two NBAS item sets Orientation and Irritability, especially between the second and third assessment day, also attest to the stability of individual differences between the newborns during their first 9 days of life. This stability prompted us to define two newborn characteristics as assessed by the NBAS: (a) Orienting Ability as the mean sum of the 5 orienting items plus the item Alertness for all three assessments, and (b) Irritability as the corresponding mean sum of the items Peak of Excitement, Rapidity of Buildup, Irritability, Lability of States, Consolability, and Self-Quieting. For the latter two items we subtracted the received score from 10 to account for the negative correlation of these items with the rest of the irritability item set. All subsequent longitudinal comparisons with the two newborn characteristics Orienting Ability and Irritability are performed with these mean sums of all three assessments.

In addition to the demonstrated reliability of the NBAS, the newborn behavior as assessed by the NBAS during the 9 days in the hospital was strikingly stable. Figure 2 illustrates the frequencies of the dimensional scores for each of the four dimensions on the three assessment days. There was no significant increase in the mean dimension scores over the hospital period for any of the four dimensions. The dotted lines in Figure 2 represent the frequencies of the scores of the standardization sample as reported by Als (Als, 1978; Brazelton et al., 1979). Incidentally, Als's standardization sample also consisted of 54 healthy full-term white newborns delivered at the Boston Hospital for Women Lying-in-Division. The Boston sample was assessed daily, on days 5–10 at home. The dotted horizontal lines in Figure 2 indicate the marked increase in optimal scores in the Boston sample for the first three dimensions Interactive Processes, Motoric Processes, and State Organization over the first 10 days. This development could not be seen in our German sample.

On the other hand, the low occurrence of the scores evaluated as worrisome shows that the German sample is indeed a healthy group of newborns. There are two additional indices for the healthiness of this group: Aleksandrowicz and Alexandrowicz (1975) proposed eight criteria for the NBAS procedure to define

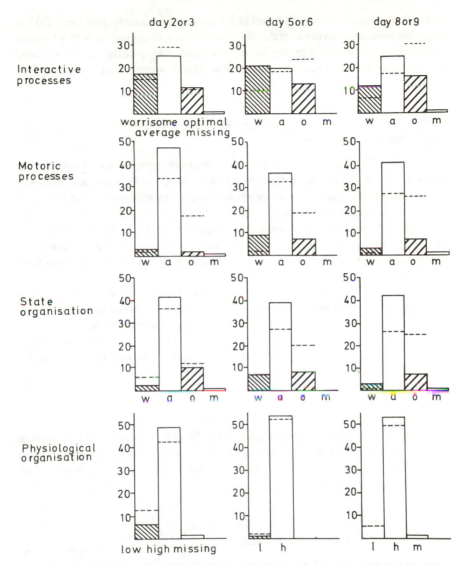

Figure 2.   Distribution of the NBAS a priori dimension scores of 54 healthy German infants on three assessments as compared to 54 healthy Boston infants. Dotted lines represent the frequencies of the Boston infants.

the "difficult infant syndrome." In our group, not one of the infants fulfilled the criteria for the "difficult infant syndrome" on any one assessment day. In addition, according to Als and Lewis's (1975) concept of the "well-modulated infant," about 75% of the German infants were well modulated on each assessment day.

For the group of 54 healthy German infants, we have shown that the NBAS is a reliable instrument to document individual differences during the 9-day lying-in period. The newborns' Orienting Ability and Irritability qualified for being called newborn characteristics. Furthermore, the infants were rather stable in their overall performance on the NBAS.

The Newborn's Characteristics as Related to Demographic and Independent Variables

During the hospital stay, all mothers were given extensive questionnaires asking about their pregnancy, their birth experience, their health care and smoking before and during pregnancy, their relationship to their spouses and family of origin and similar topics. None of these variables were significantly related to the newborns' orienting ability or irritability. Similarly, neither gender of child, birth order, age of mothers, amount of medication during birth, Apgar score, nor presence of father during birth could be related meaningfully to these two newborn characteristics.

Only two of the independent variables were related to the factor scores of Orienting Ability and Irritability. We found a positive relationship between birthweight and Irritability ($rs = 0.26$, $p < 0.03$). The amount of time the newborn was in state 4 within the first hour of birth—rated on a 5 - point scale—was positively and significantly related to the mean sum of the orienting item set for all three assessments ($rs = 0.30$, $p < 0.017$).

The variable "duration of state 4 after birth" was also positively and significantly related to the additional observation on the NBAS How the Infant Quiets Self: Infants who had been in state 4 after birth for a longer time showed "locking onto visual or auditory stimuli" significantly more often during the first exam (Chi Square (1) = 7,34, $p < 0.01$) and markedly more during all exams (Chi Square (1) = 4.89, $p < 0.05$) than infants who were in state 4 after birth only for short periods or not at all.

Experimental Variation of Postpartum Contact and Neonatal Assessment Performance

The experimental design allowed for increasing amounts of time mothers and newborns spent together. The four treatment groups did not differ with respect to any of the motoric items or in their response to stress, but they differed in two of the 5 irritability items and in 5 of the 6 orientation items. Figure 3 presents the mean scores of the NBAS orienting items and the mean scores of the orientation item set of the four experimental treatment groups.

The orienting ability of the newborns was better if they had experienced more than the standard amount of interaction time with their mothers. Early contact alone had a significant effect on the items Orientation to Ball, Orientation to Voice, Orientation to Face and Voice, and Alertness. Most striking group dif-

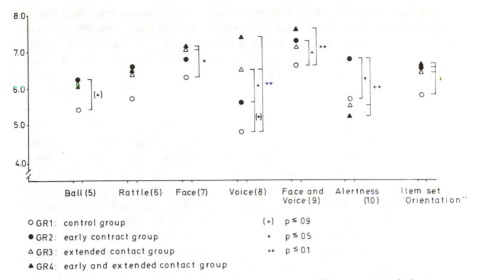

○ GR1: control group
● GR2: early contract group
△ GR3: extended contact group
▲ GR4: early and extended contact group

(+)   p ≤ 09
+   p ≤ 05
++   p ≤ 01

Figure 3. **Comparison of the four treatment groups with respect to their mean scores of the NBAS orientation items and their means of the orientation item set.**

ferences occurred on item Orientation to Voice: the control group had the lowest mean score, the early contact group scored significantly higher, extended contact infants again significantly higher, and the early and extended contact infants performed best. For most orientation items, however, the effect of early contact was not increased by extended contact.

An interesting additional finding was that the two nonextended contact groups were consistently more successful in self-quieting and hand-to-mouth contacts than the infants of the two extended contact groups: the mean differences for NBAS items 25 and 26 were highly significant ($p < 0.002$ and $p < 0.01$ respectively). It is already known that newborns cry more under nursery conditions than under rooming-in conditions (Sander & Julia, 1966). Our data may be taken as an indication that newborns also learn to quiet themselves more easily under nursery conditions. Irritability of the infants was only slightly related to the experimental treatment: the one consistent finding was with respect to the Group 2 (early contact group) only. These 12 infants were significantly less irritable on all three assessments ($p < 0.05$). But this finding is difficult to interpret, since group 4 had also experienced early contact together with extended contact, but the mean irritability scores of groups 1, 3, and 4 were not notably different.

Maternal Sensitivity and Related Variables During
the First Year and Newborn Characteristics

Parallel to the NBAS assessments, the mother–newborn interactions during feeding were videographed. The majority of the observations were made during the feeding period prior to the NBAS, but this was not always possible. Each feeding period lasted about 25 minutes, even under the extended contact conditions, because most mothers were bottle feeding and thus depended on the nurses' schedules for bringing and taking away the bottles. The details of the video-graphing, together with the results of the various postpartum contacts on maternal tenderness toward the newborn, have been reported in K. Grossmann et al. (1981).

From two of the three videotapes made of each mother–infant pair maternal sensitivity to the newborn's behavior was rated. We adapted Ainsworth's sensitivity scale (Ainsworth, Bell, & Stayton, 1974) for mother–newborn interactions in the hospital.

After the lying-in period, 49 families agreed to be visited at home. The infants' ages at the home visits were 2, 6, and 10 months. Each visit began with an extensive interview with one or both parents. For 2 hours, the observers took notes on the behavior of the mother, the infant, and other people present. In addition, an audiotape recorder recorded the vocal interactions. After the visit, a detailed narrative report was written by the two observers.

Maternal sensitivity to the infants' communications, maternal cooperation, acceptance of infant, and maternal judgment of easiness of infant were rated according to Ainsworth's scale on the basis of the narrative reports and interviews. (The home visit procedure and the data analyses of the narrative reports were described in detail in K. Grossmann et al., 1985.)

The newborns' *mean* orienting ability was not significantly correlated with any rating of maternal sensitivity, cooperation, or acceptance of the infant. But infant's orienting ability during the third assessment on day 8 or 9 was significantly related to maternal judgment of the baby's easiness vs. difficultness as rated from the interviews at 2 months ($r = .294, p \leq .026$) and at 6 months ($r = .224, p = .065$). The correlation with the mean rating of the first year was $r = .291, p = .023$.

The mean irritability of the newborn as assessed by the NBAS was found to be significantly and positively related to maternal sensitivity *only* during the newborn period.

The most parsimonious interpretation of this finding seems to be that, under the scrutiny of other mothers and nurses in the hospital, the mothers of irritable infants were especially sensitive to their infants' cues to prevent crying. This interpretation is supported by the subsequent result that the correspondence between newborn irritability and maternal sensitivity did not extend beyond the newborn period.

Although we found no relationship between newborn irritability as assessed in this study and the amount of infant crying during the home visits as measured from the audiotapes, the newborn's irritability was significantly related negatively to the overall maternal acceptance of her infant during the first year ($r = -.237, p = .051$) and her judgment of her baby's easiness ($r = -.273, p =$

.029). Thus, the two purely interactive ratings of maternal sensitivity and cooperation were unrelated to newborn irritability, but in the maternal descriptions of her infant we could trace early irritability as a negative influence.

Infant's Friendliness Toward the Home Visitors at 6 Months of Age and Newborn Orienting Ability

To the 6-month home visit, the observer brought a stuffed animal as a present for the infant. After greeting the mother, and as soon as the infant was sitting alone on the couch or in an infant seat, one of the visitors approached the infant in a friendly manner and presented the toy to the baby. The other observer, as part of the usual observation, took notes on the infant's reactions to the unfamiliar visitors, to the toy, and on all later approaches of the infant to the visitors. Because the infant's behavior was the designated focus of all observations, no special shift of focus was necessary for this specific situation.

From the written protocols the number of communicative initiations of an infant to at least one visitor within the first hour was counted: smiling at, vocalizing in a "talkative" cooing manner to the observer, or reaching out or touching the visitor; we termed this behavior *friendliness*. In addition, the warm-up time for the infant, i.e., the time that elapsed before the infant communicated with the visitor for the first time, was noted.

The total amount of friendly overtures within the first hour of the home visit ranged from 0 to 25, the warm-up time from less than 5 minutes (26 infants were friendly to the visitors within the first 5 minutes) to more than 60 minutes. Three infants never addressed a visitor during the whole 2-hour visit; two infants took longer than 60 minutes to do so.

The friendliness of the 6-month-old infants correlated with the newborn's mean score of the three social orienting items (to face, to voice, to face plus voice) $r = 0.26$, $p = 0.032$. The infants' warm-up time correlated correspondingly negatively with the newborn's orienting ability, but this coefficient was not significant ($r = -0.157$). The infants' friendliness scores were independent of maternal sensitivity during the 6-month visit, as well as of any other previous sensitivity ratings. Responses to the toy by the infants were unrelated to any newborn measure.

Maternal Conversational Style to Her Infant as Related to Newborns' Orienting Ability

From the audiotape recordings during all home visits the specific ways in which the mothers talked to their 2-, 6-, and 10-months-old infants was assessed (Grossmann & Grossmann, 1985). First, the mother's tone of voice for each of her utterances was coded in categories such as neutral/sober, tender/loving, playful/joyous, and inviting/luring. Second, her contingencies with the infant's vocalizations, in terms of promptness and being the initiator or respondent in a vocal interchange, were specified. Third, three different conversational styles emerged to which each mother was independently assigned for each home visit. The three styles were called: the *sober conversational style* (this turned out to be the most frequent style), the *tender style,* and the *lighthearted style.* The assignment of the mothers to the three groups was found to be very stable over the three visits during the first year of the infant's life (Grossmann & Grossmann, 1985). The main features of the conversational styles shall be described briefly.

The sober conversational style. This type of mother does not talk much to her infant. When she talks, her tone of voice is predominantly neutral, sober, as if she is talking to an adult. Her utterances are rather short, unsystematic, and not very rhythmical. More often she comments upon the infant's behavior to the visitor instead of talking to her infant directly. She is relatively unresponsive to the infant's vocalizations. She reacts to the infant's crying with comforting, but she is little persistent in soothing and may give up trying to calm her infant. Mother and infant give the general impression of being often out of synchrony with each other.

The tender conversational style. This type of mother talks frequently to her infant, usually in a soft, warm, tender tone of voice. She never seems to get irritated at the infant and appears patient most of the time. She seldom initiates conversations by calling or enticing the infant in an intense, stimulating way. On the other hand, she rarely misses an utterance of her child and answers promptly. Her responses to her child's distress are usually prompt, patient, and enduring, without signs of anger, resignation, or attempts to distract the infant.

The lighthearted conversational style. This type of mother addresses her infant very often, but rather in sudden bouts than in a steady flow of talking. She is very expressive, and she likes to surprise her infant. She usually has a playful tone of voice and often lures the infant into stimulating games. She usually reacts promptly to her infant's vocalizations, but she may also have phases where she does not seem to listen. When her infant cries, she tries to calm her or him, but not as patiently and enduringly as a tender mother. She often switches between intensive soothing bouts and attempts to quiet the child through diversions. Overall, more vocal interchanges are started by the mother than by her infant.

For each visit a few of mothers could not be assigned to any one style, but, if the mother had one specific style during the two other home visits, she was assigned to that group. In this way, 45 of the 49 mothers could be grouped: 22 were assigned to the sober group, 12 to the tender group, 11 to the lighthearted group, and 4 remained without a group assignment.

In terms of maternal sensitivity, as rated from the written reports, the three groups of mothers differed significantly. The tenderly communicating mothers scored more than two points higher on the sensitivity scale for each home visit (highly significant) than the soberly talking mothers, and the lighthearted mothers scored always in between (Grossmann & Grossmann, 1985).

Table 4.   Distribution of the Good Newborn Orienters (Above the Median on the Mean Sum of the Orienting Item Set) and the Poor Newborn Orienters Among the Four Groups of Maternal Conversational Styles

	Newborn Orientation	
Maternal Conversational Style	Good	Poor
Tender	6	6
Sober	14	8
Lighthearted	3	8
No Group	2	2

Comparison of the orienting ability of the newborns with their mothers' conversational styles revealed a disproportionate distribution of the infants among the groups (Table 4). Newborn irritability was also tested, but no relationship to conversational style emerged.

In the group of tenderly talking mothers there were as many "good" (above the mean) newborn orienters as "poor" orienters (6:6), in the group of soberly communicating mothers there were almost twice as many good orienters as poor orienters (14:8), and in the group of lightheartedly talking mothers there were less than half as many good orienters as poor orienters (3:8). (The Chi-Square Value with $df = 2$ barely missed significance, however.) Of the four mothers who could not be grouped, two had good orienters and two had poor orienters as newborns.

This finding could indicate that the newborn's readiness to attend to incoming stimuli may have influenced the mother's efforts to communicate with her infant, though not her sensitivity towards her baby, as the independence of newborn orienting ability and maternal sensitivity has shown. The soberly communicating mothers seemed to be least eager of all to get their infants to talk to them. They were reinforcing their infants' vocalizations only little through answering. But because most of them have had good orienters as babies, they may not have had to try so hard. The well orienting infants may make communication easy, because of their greater attentiveness.

The lighthearted mothers seemed to try so much harder by initiating and enticing the infant to respond to them, which may have been a reaction to the infants' previous reluctance to respond to social and sensory stimuli in the NBAS. The tender, sensitive mothers seem to accept their infants' characteristics, and their readiness to interact with the infant is seen in their great responsiveness to all infant behaviors.

But this is still speculation. Because we do not know the mother's conversational style before she had this infant, we cannot know whether her style was a reaction to her infant's readiness to interact, or whether both are linked through some other factors. The stability of the mothers' conversational style over the three home visits also points toward a personality trait of the mother. Nevertheless, the correspondence between the infants' initial readiness to interact and their mothers' conversational style is noteworthy. We will be presenting a similar correspondence at 2 years of age later in this report.

Parent–Child Attachment Qualities at 12 and 18 Months

All 49 infants and mothers who were visited at home were also seen in the Ainsworth's Strange Situation (Ainsworth, Blehar, Waters, & Wall, 1978) within 4 weeks of the infant's first birthday. Forty-six infants were also seen with their fathers at 18 months in this situation. The procedure consists of eight episodes involving the infant, the parent, and a stranger. The degree to which the infant seeks contact and interaction with the parent after stressful separations from him or her determines the classification of the quality of the infant's attachment to his or her mother or father as secure, insecure-avoidant, or insecure-ambivalent. Few infants cannot be classified.

In this sample, 16 of the 49 infants showed the secure attachment pattern, 24 the avoidant pattern, and 6 the ambivalent pattern toward their mothers. The corresponding figures for the child–father attachment classifications are: 19 secure, 25 avoidant, and 1 ambivalent pattern. Three children could not be classified with their mothers and one with her father (Grossmann, Grossmann, Huber, & Wartner, 1981).

We found a significant relationship between secure versus insecure attachment classification of the infant to *both* mother and father and the orienting ability of the newborn as assessed by the NBAS. Figure 4 illustrates the predominance of good orienters in secure attachment relationships with either parent, but also shows the independence of the toddler's attachment qualities to each parent. Of the 29 children who have at least one secure attachment relationship to a parent, 20 (69%) have been good orienters. This is true for only 5 (25%) of the 20 children who were insecurely attached to both parents. This difference is highly significant (Chi Square (1) = 9,42, $p < 0.01$).

The mean values of the three attachment groups on the individual NBAS orienting items show that the orienting responses of the infants later classified as securely attached to their mothers (group B, n = 16) was markedly higher on the second and third of the three assessments than the orienting responses of the later insecurely attached infants (group A, $n = 24$) ($p < 0,08$). The item Orienting to Face showed the greatest significant difference ($p < 0.03$) in favor of the securely mother-attached infants.

Irritability scores on the NBAS did not differentiate systematically between the attachment groups, except for the second assessment. At this time group A infants had been more irritable than group C infants. Figure 5 illustrates the

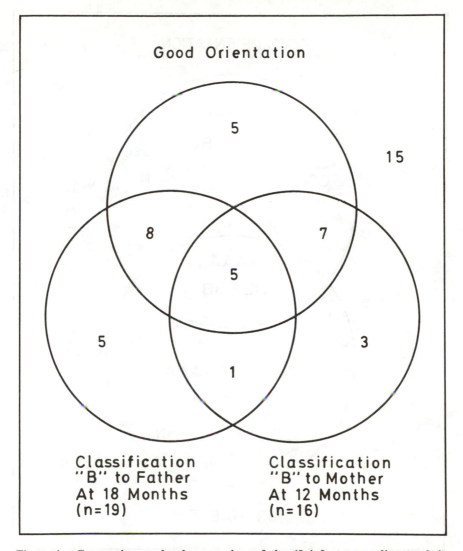

Figure 4. Group sizes and subgroup sizes of the 49 infants according to their classification as above the median in orientation, and their attachment quality to both parents.

predominant role of the newborns' orienting ability over their irritability in another Venn-Diagram: 12 of the 16 (75%) children classified as securely attached to their mothers had been good (above the median) orienters. This is true for only 9 of the 24 (37.5%) children classified as insecure-avoidantly attached (Chi Square (1) = 5.4, $p < 0.02$).

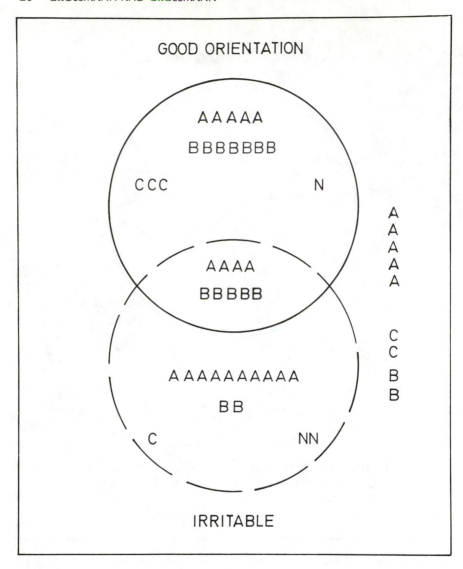

Figure 5. Distribution of the infants according to their attachment classification at 12 months to their mothers with respect to their orienting ability and irritability as newborns.

A: Infants with an insecure-avoidant attachment to mother ($n = 24$)

B: Infants with a secure attachment to mother ($n = 16$)

C: Infants with an insecure-ambivalent attachment to mother ($n = 6$)

N: Infants not classifyable in the Strange Situation ($n = 3$).

Fourteen (58%) of the group A children had been more irritable newborns but also 7 (44%) of the group B children. A larger percentage of the more irritable group B children, however, had also been good orienters. As a group the insecure-ambivalently attached infants (group C) were not conspicuously different from the other infants on the NBAS assessment. Half of them had been good orienters, and only one was irritable above average.

The Transactional Pathway to Secure Attachment: Good Orientation as a Newborn and a Responsive, Tender, Sensitive Mother

We have shown that 12 of the 16 securely mother-attached infants had been good orienters as newborns. In another report, we already showed that maternal sensitivity, especially during the first half year of the infant's life, was also a significant predictor of the infant's secure attachment to his or her mother (K. Grossmann et al., 1985). Thirdly, we found that the newborn's orienting ability was unrelated to maternal sensitivity, but it was related to maternal conversational style. Maternal sensitivity and her conversational style were, in turn, related to each other and both were related to the infant–mother attachment quality. Table 5 lists all 49 infants according to the following variables: NBAS orientation, maternal conversational style, maternal sensitivity, and the infants' attachment classifications. This listing shows the transactional pathway to a secure infant–mother attachment in our sample.

Starting from the infants' orienting ability as newborns, and keeping in mind that for the whole sample the percentage of securely mother-attached children was 33%, Table 5 shows the following associations:

1. All good orienters who had a tender talking, sensitive mother, developed secure attachment relationships (six out of six in this subgroup = 100%). Of the six poor orienters with a tender talking, sensitive mother, two (33%) established a secure attachment relationship to their mothers, a figure that equals that for the whole sample. Thus, if the mother is very sensitive, the infant is very likely to develop a secure attachment to her, even if, as a newborn, the infant was not too responsive and ready to interact during the NBAS.

2. If a good orienter had a soberly communicating mother, who usually showed less than average sensitivity, he or she still had a good chance to establish a secure attachment relationship to her (38%), as good as for the whole sample despite the fact that his or her mother was not very sensitive. For the poor orienter with a sober mother, the chances for a secure attachment were very low (1:8 = 12.5%).

    Thus, when a mother is not very sensitive, it makes a decisive difference whether the infant is attentive and eager to interact. These infants seem to succeed in finding a secure base even in a less sensitive mother.

Table 5.   Listing of the 49 Infants According to Their Orienting Class (good = above median, poor = below median), Their Mothers' Predominant Conversational Style, Their Attachment Quality to Their Mothers at 12 Months of Age, and the Mean Sensitivity Scores of Their Mothers (in Parentheses) During the First Year of the Infants' Lives

			Newborn Orientation				
		Good				Poor	
		Conversational Style of the Mothers					
Tender	Sober	Light-hearted	No Group	Tender	Sober	Light-hearted	No Group
B (8.0)	B (4.5)	A (5.0)	B (5.0)	B (7.6)	B (2.6)	B (6.3)	A (5.0)
B (7.6)	B (4.0)	C (5.3)	A (5.6)	B (5.3)	A (5.0)	A (7.3)	A (3.0)
B (7.3)	B (4.0)	ntc (6.3)		A (7.3)	A (4.3)	A (6.6)	
B (7.0)	B (4.0)			A (6.0)	A (4.0)	A (5.0)	
B (7.0)	B (3.3)			A (4.0)	A (4.0)	A (3.6)	
B (5.6)	A (4.6)			C (5.3)	A (3.0)	A (3.6)	
	A (4.0)				C (4.0)	ntc (3.3)	
	A (4.0)				C (1.6)	ntc (1.3)	
	A (3.6)						
	A (2.6)						
	A (1.5)						
	C (4.0)						
	C (1.6)						

Attachment qualities:
B—secure, A—insecure/avoidant, C—insecure/ambivalent, ntc—not classifiable
Frequencies of the maternal conversational styles:
Tender $n = 12$, Sober $n = 22$, Lighthearted $n = 11$, No Group $n = 4$

3. The lighthearted style of communicating with the baby seemed to be incompatible with the formation of a secure attachment relationship, although these mothers were, as Table 5 shows, more sensitive to their infants' communications than the soberly communicating mothers. Only one of the 11 lighthearted mothers was a secure attachment figure to her toddler in the Strange Situation. On the other hand, only three good orienters were in this group. Because of the small group size, it is difficult to say whether the original readiness to interact of these three good orienters was overridden by their very expressive, initiating mothers despite the fact that these three mothers were all above the mean in sensitivity.

It was a surprising finding that 27% of the infants of the soberly communicating mothers, none of whom had mean sensitivity ratings above 4.6, were securely attached as compared to only one of the 11 lighthearted, fairly sensitive mothers. We want to interpret this finding with respect to the rate of initiating versus responding in these mothers. Although the lighthearted mothers generally responded well, as reflected in their intermediate sensitivity scores, they also had sudden outbursts of vocalizations which may have been overstimulating or perhaps even anxiety producing to their infants. This could reduce the mother's predictability to the infant and thus make it more difficult for the infant to develop a sense of security with this mother. On the other hand, the group of soberly communicating mothers may have, in their way of talking little, given the infant more opportunities to try to start a conversation, even if they were often unsuccessful. A relatively passive, but available mother—the sensitivity scores of these mothers were not very low—may be sufficient for an infant who is actively seeking out interaction and responds easily. Such a mother may be even more appropriate for an eager baby than a very active mother. It seems to be optimal when a mother can hold herself back but reacts at the same time sensitively to the infant's signals, as is exemplified by the tenderly communicating mothers.

A relevant detailed finding of the analysis of the development of the infants' vocalizations was: The positive vocalizations of the infants of the group of lighthearted mothers *decreased* significantly between 6 and 10 months. In contrast, the number of positive vocalizations of the infants of the group of tenderly talking mothers, and even of the group of sober mothers, increased significantly during the same time period (Grossmann & Grossmann, 1985).

More support for the argument that parents' interactive style and the child's initiative are related will be presented in connection with the results of the characterizations of these parents and their 2-year-old toddlers at play. But first, some data on the development of the infant–father relationship will be presented.

Fathers' Interactive Quality, Their Involvement in Infant Care, and the Toddler–Father Attachment Quality

The focus of our longitudinal project was the development of the mother–child relationship. But it often happened that the father came home during an afternoon visit or that he took off from work to participate in the observations. In our sample, the age of the fathers ranged from 19 to 46. Three-quarters of them helped the mothers to take care of the infant, although only one-half was willing to change soiled diapers. At the 2-month home visit, already 53% (or 26) of the mothers said that the father could soothe the infant if she was not available.

The preferred activity of the fathers with their infants was playing. Only eight fathers did not play on a fairly regular basis. Very often, especially in the early months of a second child in the family, the fathers tended to the older sibling so that the mother could concentrate on feeding or bathing the infant. In West Germany, mothers get a 6-week paid maternity leave after the birth of an infant. About one-fourth of the fathers also took a few days off work, so that they could help their wives to adjust to the new baby.

Half of the fathers were present at the infant's birth. The general attitude in the years 1976–77 about the father's presence at birth was still somewhat reserved, but, if the parents wanted it, the father was allowed into the delivery room. The father's presence at birth was not correlated with the quality or quantity of his later involvement with the infant, but it was positively related to the number of home visits in which he was also present.

In another study of 100 German fathers, Grossmann and Volkmer (1984) found that not the actual presence of the father at birth but his wish to be present was related to his later involvement with his infant.

Almost 70% of the fathers of this sample participated during at least one home visit. Information on the amount of the father's involvement in daily infant care was obtained from the mother or the father, if present, at each home visit. The interactions between the father and his infant during the home visits at 2, 6, and 10 months were recorded in the same way as the infant–mother interactions. The infant–father encounters were rated for their interactive smootheness, the child's reaction to the father's approaches, and the father's empathy while playing with the infant (Wutz, 1985). But in almost all families, the mother took the primary responsibility for the infant's well being, especially when the infant was crying. Therefore we were unable to assess the father's sensitivity to the infant's distress signals.

In our sample of mostly homemaker mothers, the fathers were free to choose between the role of the provider for the family or the more interactive role of the infant's play partner or parttime caretaker. The mothers enjoyed the fathers' involvement, if they chose to participate, but they rarely requested it, because they themselves felt responsible for the child's care. We gained the impression that the fathers in our sample allowed themselves to be quite open about their attitude toward their involvement in child care. If a father felt incompetent or did not want to take responsibility for any part of the infant's care, the mother would usually accept his decision. Some of the fathers more or less openly resisted to be part of the study at all.

The infant's performance on the NBAS during the newborn period was not related to paternal involvement nor paternal interactive quality.

At 18 months, as reported, 19 of the 46 children (41%) seen in the Strange Situation were securely father attached, 25 insecurely avoidantly attached (54%), and one child showed ambivalence toward his father. One child could not be classified.

We found no relationship between paternal involvement in child care or paternal interactive quality during the first year and the quality of the child's attachment to him. An explanation may be that paternal interactive quality did not include paternal sensitivity to the infant's distress, which we could not observe. Maternal responsiveness to her infant's distress has been found to be an important aspect in the development of the child's attachment to her or his mother (Ainsworth et al., 1978). Nonetheless, as for the infant–mother attachment relationships, more good orienters were among the securely father–attached toddlers than among the insecurely father-attached toddlers (Chi Square $(1) = 4.39$, $p <$ 0.05; see Figure 4).

Ratings of the Child's Interactive Style in Three Play Situations at Age 24 Months and Their Relationship to the Newborn's Orienting Ability

Forty-seven of the families were visited again in their homes around the children's second birthday. Among other assessments, three 5- to 10-minute play sessions were videotaped: In the first, mother and child played with wooden, colored mosaic pieces; in the second, father and child played with Play-Doh; and in the third, the child was given a jack-in-the-box, a toy unknown to all of these families. the mother was asked to help the child with this toy.

Each videotaped play session was rated by 10 different judges (students of Psychology) on 23 aspects of the child's activity, mood, and interactive style with the parent, and 31 aspects of the parent's characteristics and their style of interaction. All aspects were rated on 7-point scales. The items were selected from various Q-sort assessment sets by J. Block and J. H. Block (Block, 1961, 1972; Block, Block, & Morrison, 1981; Block, Jennings, Harvey, & Simpson, 1964), rating scales devised by Matas, Arend, and Sroufe (1978), and issues of Ainsworth's sensitivity and cooperation scales (Ainsworth et al., 1978). Subsequently, factor analyses with varimax rotation were performed separately on the means of the 10 ratings for each item for each play situation. Each two factors emerged for the fathers and the mothers, and 3 factors for the children. Factor scores were obtained for each child and each parent on each factor by multiplying the factor loading of the item on a factor with the mean rating of the subject on that item (Grossmann, 1984).

Correlations of the descriptive items of the 2-year-olds with their NBAS results yielded a number of correspondences with the newborns' orienting responses but next to none with the newborn's irritability measures. Table 6 shows the parametric correlation coefficients between individual child and parent items, as well as the factor scores on one child and one parent factor with the mean newborn's orienting responses for all three play sessions.

The ratings on the items "Child Initiates the Interaction, versus Child Waits for Instructions or Suggestions From the Parent" and, correspondingly, "Parent is Controlling, versus Parent Surrenders Control to the Child," were significantly positively related to newborn orienting ability for each of the three play sessions. Because we used different judges for each of the three play sessions, this consistent finding is convincing.

Twenty-three items were used to describe a child's interactive style with her or his mother or father in the three play sessions. Seven, or almost a third, were related to newborn orienting ability in at least two play sessions, as was the child factor "Initiating, Expressive Child." Although the correspondences between

Table 6.   Relationships Between Ratings of Toddlers' and Their Parents' Interactive Characteristics in Three Different Play Situations at Age 24 Months and the Children's Newborn Orienting Ability as Assessed by the Neonatal Behavioral Assessment Scale

Descriptive Items	Jack Box Play[1]	Father–Child Play[2]	Mother–Child Play[2]
CHILD			
Initiates interaction vs. Waits for suggestions	.33**	.41**	.29*
Emotionally expressive vs. Inexpressive	.35**	.19(*)	.08
Proud of self vs. No positive self evaluation	.34**	.24*	.12
Active vs. Passive	.29*	.26*	.09
Cheerful vs. Grouchy	.21(*)	.23(*)	.08
Expresses anger openly vs. Suppresses anger	.27*	.06	.17
Extroverted vs. Introverted	.19(*)	.29*	.14
PARENT			
Controlling vs. Noncontrolling	−.26*	−.46**	−.29*
Quarrels with C. vs. Compliant	—	−.17	−.37**
Competes with C. vs. Does not excel C.	—	−.39**	−.36**
Likes to teach vs. Waits for C's ideas	—	−.40**	−.30*
Has high standards of excellence for C. vs. Not	—	−.30*	−.25*
Gets angry with C. vs. Accepts C's decisions	−.12	−.25*	−.23(*)
Strict vs. Lenient	−.09	−.26*	−.25*
Descriptive Factors			
CHILD			
Initiating, expressive child[3]	.34**	.32**	.09
PARENT			
Lenient, patient, accepting parent[3]	.22(*)	.36**	.25*

[1] Non-parametric correlations with the mean sum of all NBAS orienting items 5, 6, 7, 8, 9, 10.
[2] Non-parametric correlations with the mean sum of the NBAS social orienting items 7, 8, 9.
[3] Weighed factor scores were used
(*)$p < .10$, *$p < .05$, **$p < .01$
—These items were not in the rating lists for the jack-in-the-box play sessions

newborn orientation scores and the child's characterization in the mother–child play were not significant, all of them were in the same direction as for the father–child and the jack-in-the-box play sessions.

The reactions of the children to the jack-in-the-box deserve a special description. The most predominant impression of the children while playing with this toy was their degree of anxious behavior. The sudden opening of the lid, the jumping mechanism, and the squeaking sound of the appearing or vanishing doll was greeted and elicited great fun in some children, while other children showed varying degrees of apprehension, and a few children panicked and tried to run away from the toy. Some children decided to leave the box open after only very few openings in order to be able to explore the doll and the box but at the same time to avoid to operate the mechanism (Grossmann, 1984).

The descriptive infant factor called "Initiating, Expressive Child" in the jack-in-the-box session describes a child that engages actively in the surprise toy, even if he or she does not like it. In case of dislike they push the box actively away or demand its removal from their mothers instead of being just wary or passively afraid of it. The scores of the infants on this factor were positively and significantly related to the mean score of the set of all NBAS orientation variables ($r = 0.344$, $p < 0.009$).

Those parent items that correlated significantly with their newborns' orienting ability describe mothers and fathers whose characteristic interactive pattern is holding back in favor of the child's initiative.

For the mothers' and fathers' interactive style with their child, we found two comparable factors with independent factor analyses. We named the first factor "Cheerful, Cooperative, Expressive Parent," and the second factor the "Lenient, Patient, Accepting Parent." The factor scores of the second factor correlated significantly with the NBAS orienting variables, as Table 6 shows. Parents who scored high on this factor readily relinquished control to the child, accepted the child's play products instead of criticizing their often imperfect works, and let themselves be guided by the child's wishes and intentions in the play sessions.

As a corollary, it should be mentioned that mothers *and* fathers, who had been a secure attachment figure in the Strange Situation, scored very ($p < 0.01$) significantly higher on the "Lenient, Patient, Accepting Parent" factor, than those parents, to whom the toddler had shown an insecure attachment (Grossmann, 1984).

The description of the lenient, patient, accepting parent's interactive style is comparable to the tender maternal conversational style described earlier. Both styles have in common that the parent is noncontrolling, but reactive, and lets the child have the lead. Both parental interactive styles are related to the newborn's orienting ability, as well as to the quality of the child's attachment to each parent.

The association between the newborns' orienting ability and the ratings of 24-month-old children in a play session with mothers, with fathers, and during exploration of a toy with surprise effects are three convergent, independently assessed, findings.

Task-Oriented, Social, and Emotional Behaviors of the 2-Year-Olds During a Bayley Mental Exam as Related to Their NBAS Assessments

During the latter part of the 24-month home visit, the children were given the Bayley Scales of Mental Development by the home visitor. The first 20 minutes of the tests were videotaped and subsequently analyzed by students who were not familiar with the history of the children. The 20-minute observation time was divided into 30-second intervals, and the occurrence of the following eight major behavior categories were recorded at most once for each interval: (a) Eagerly waiting or reaching out for the material of the next item; (b) Problem-solving behaviors; (c) Reactions to solving or failing an item; (d) Non-task-related play with the material; (e) Distraction or resistance behaviors; (f) Vocal communications with the examiner independent of the verbal items; (g) Social behaviors toward the examiner; and (h) Affective expressions, i.e., interest, pleasure, anger, and distress as rated on 9-point scales. Each major category was made up of several subcategories. (Grossmann, Baierl, & Machl, 1983).

No NBAS item or item set was associated with the children's MDI. But the newborns' overall orienting responses, especially their social orienting ability, was significantly related to the following three major categories: Eagerness to go on with the test ($r = 0.37$, $p < 0.01$), Vocal communications with the examiner ($r = 0.41$, $p < 0.002$), and two of the four affective expression ratings. Newborn social orientation responses correlated $r = 0.26$, $p < 0.05$ with the children's interest ratings and $r = -0.21$, $p < 0.07$ with the children's anger ratings (Grossmann et al., 1983). One subcategory of the children's affective expressiveness, General Excitability, was significantly related to the newborns' irritablity ($r = 0.33$, $p < 0.01$).

Corresponding to the unrelatedness of NBAS variables to the children's MDI none of the children's behaviors pertaining to their attempts to solve or avoid the items on the Bayley exam correlated with the newborns' orienting ability or any other NBAS item set. The categories that were linked to the newborns' orienting responses were emotional and social behaviors; Eagerness to Go On With the Test is also an affective expression. Together with the children's general interest for the test and their readiness to communicate more often than necessary with the examiner, this set of behaviors appears very similar to the 6-month-olds' friendliness toward the unfamiliar home visitor who offered a toy.

At 6 months and at 24 months, infants who responded friendly and curious to unfamiliar visitors, who wanted to play with them, had more often than not been newborns who responded well to social stimuli during the NBAS assessment. It seems compelling to infer a special readiness of these well-orienting infants to enjoy social situations even with unfamiliar persons.

The Ecology of the Families of This Study and Some Observations on Their Child Rearing Practices and Attitudes

The city of Bielefeld, where the study was done, is in Northern Germany. It is a region where people are said to be fairly reserved and reluctant to relate to strangers (Grossmann & Grossmann, 1981). The city is of medium size (130,000 in the "old" city, 250,000 with the new counties), has mainly small industry and commerce, and has not had a large wave of new citizens within the last hundred years. Thus, many families have their roots here.

For 75% of the families in this study, grandparents were readily available as support for the mothers, and 14 families had at least one pair of grandparents living in the same house or next door. The maternal grandmother was most often named as the major support person for the young mother. She helped the mother to take care of the infant, often looked after the child or children when the parents wanted to go out, and to her many infants had an additional trusting and tender relationship. Even if the maternal grandmother was not available, most mothers looked for another woman in their family or neighborhood with whom they already had or established a friendly relationship so that they could leave the child in the care of that familiar person if they needed to. Eighty-six percent (42 out of 49) of the mothers in this sample said that somebody outside the nuclear family had at least occasionally looked after or cared for their infants during the first year of the infant's life (Ziemer, 1982).

This willingness of the mothers to let the child form additional friendly

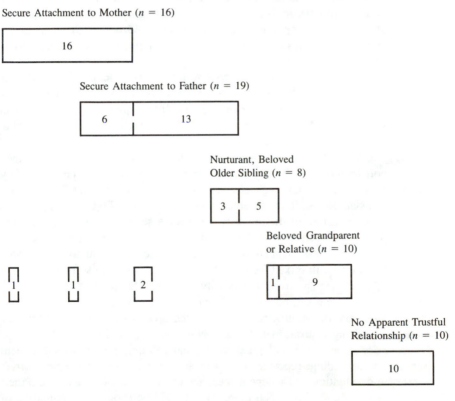

Trustful* Relationships of the 49 Bielefeld Infants
within their First Two Years of Life

Secure Attachment to Mother (*n* = 16)

16

Secure Attachment to Father (*n* = 19)

6 | 13

Nurturant, Beloved
Older Sibling (*n* = 8)

3 | 5

Beloved Grandparent
or Relative (*n* = 10)

1 | 9

No Apparent Trustful
Relationship (*n* = 10)

10

*Infant likes to cuddle that person and can be soothed by him/her

Figure 6.   Trustful relationships of the 49 infants to various people in their immediate environment. An infant can have more than one trustful relationship.

relationships to other people seems to ameliorate the fact that only one-third of the infants had formed a secure attachment to their mothers, if we accept the Strange Situation as a criterion for the quality for the child-parent relationship (see Grossmann et al., 1985 for a discussion of this point.)

Figure 6 illustrates that the majority of infants, who were not securely attached to their mothers, nevertheless developed trustful relationships to other persons. We have defined a trustful relationship as one in which the infant seeks comfort from and likes to be cuddled by that person.

The graph shows that an infant who does not have a secure attachment to either mother or father could have a trustful relationship to an older sibling (Grossmann, 1986), a grandparent, or another relative, or even to a friend of the family. However, for 10 (20%) of the 49 infants, we could not find an indication that they had any such trustful relationship.

An important feature of the ecology of our sample is the generally accepted practice by German parent to leave the infant alone at home in his or her bed for short periods of time particularly in the evenings. Eighty percent of the parents (39 out of 49) in our sample did so. This is considered part of the training for self-reliance, which seems to be important to the parents (Grossmann & Grossmann, 1981).

Another indication of the parents' wish to have self-reliant children was their answer to our question: "What kind of toys does your baby like?" The mothers never failed to comment upon their children's ability to play by themselves, and upon whether they were satisfied with the extent to which their babies were able to play alone. It was a reason for complaining, if their infants always needed company or wanted to be entertained. Many mothers were concerned that they would spoil their infants if they reacted to every cry of his or hers, but they usually made sure that nothing "serious" was the matter. Crying for company was not considered "serious" (Ziemer, 1982).

Still another feature of the mothers' wish for a self-assertive child were the many reports about their infants' "own will." Almost half of the mothers felt that their 2-month-old already had an own will. This piece of information was related to the interviewer with mixed feelings. Most mothers were, in some way, proud of the early signs of a strong personality in their infants. At the same time, however, they were also a bit annoyed because it made the infant less compliant, in their view. By 10 months, 63% or 30 of the infants were described by their mothers as having a strong will of their own (Ziemer, 1982).

These are some of the ecological factors and childrearing attitudes that seem to relate to our findings reported here. If most parents, as in our sample, cherish signs of individuation and independence, which, in their view, may make their child care less demanding, then these parents will be proud and supportive of infants who are attentive and easy to interact with. Furthermore, they will not interfere with their infants' initiative in social interactions. If, however, the infant is more passive and less eager to interact, her or his parents may feel that they have to push the infant toward more interactions.

One could speculate that, in a child-rearing environment which stresses individuation, early differences between infants may become more prominent and
thus may remain more stable. If, however, as may be in other cultures, most
parents believe that children have to be made into personalities by them, early
individual differences may not receive much attention.

Discussion

The Neonatal Behavioral Assessment Scale proved to be a useful tool in our
longitudinal study of the developing social relationships of healthy German
infants. It served well as a method to assess objectively the newborn's readiness
to interact with a social partner. The NBAS helped us to describe the transactional path from early infant characteristics, and from parental caretaking
qualities, to the qualities of their attachment relationships to both parents and
their interactive style in three different play situations at 2 years. The newborns'
orienting ability, as assessed by the NBAS, ran like a red thread through many of
our longitudinal findings.

For our sample of, originally, 54 healthy newborns who stayed with their
mothers in the hospital for 9 days, the Neonatal Behavioral Assessment Scale
was a reliable instrument to document individual stable differences in the newborn period. Although the absolute levels of the single correlations between the
assessment days were not very high, the pattern was nonetheless impressive.
Twenty-one of the 27 correlations (78%) between the last two of the three
assessments were statistically significant.

We also found a surprising stability of newborn behavior in the hospital
setting: There was no significant increase in the mean scores of the whole sample
with respect to the four a priori cluster dimension Interactive Processes, Motoric
Processes, State Organizations, and Physiological Organization. Part-time rooming-in did not affect this stability, perhaps because many German mothers still
believe and act as if newborn infants need a quiet surrounding and their sensory
perception is too immature to profit from social interaction. Mother–newborn
interaction is generally quiet but, nevertheless, tender and prompt (Grossmann,
1978). It may not be as intense and expressive as Als (1975) or Stern, Beebe,
Jaffe, and Bennett (1977) described it for U.S. mothers.

However, despite the general stability, the newborn's interactive responses on
the NBAS did in fact improve with increasing opportunity to interact with their
mothers. All of the following events enhanced the infants' ability to orient to
visual and auditory stimuli: being awake and alert after birth, early contact, when
most mothers were in a heightened state of readiness to interact with the newborn
infant, and part-time rooming-in of infant and mother.

The newborns' readiness to orient toward incoming sensory stimuli, especially to the social ones from the examiner, and independent of the variations
in postpartum contact, was longitudinally related to the mother's style of communicating with her infant and the infant's attachment quality to mother and fa-

ther. The transactional pathway to a secure child–mother attachment was inferred from the following findings:

1. Infants who had been good orienters as newborns were more likely to have a secure attachment relationship to their mothers.
2. Mothers were described, according to their conversational style and their sensitivity to the infant's signals, as talking and behaving tenderly, lightheartedly, or soberly to their babies. Any infant who had a tender, very sensitive mother, was very likely to develop a secure attachment to her.
3. If the infant had been a good orienter as a newborn *and* had a tender, sensitive mother during the first year of life, then the probability of developing a secure attachment relationship to the mother was 100%. If, however, a mother was behaving soberly and less sensitively to her infant, then it was important that the infant had been a good orienter as a newborn for a secure attachment to develop. It seems as if such infants were either able to tolerate less sensitivity in their mothers or made more use of her reluctant responsiveness to still develop a relationship based on emotional security.

In contrast, if a mother was described as lighthearted, initiating, and expressive, though still medium sensitive, the original interactive readiness of well-orienting newborns *never* resulted in a secure attachment relationship. Although the number of such infants is too small for any major or far-reaching implications, we still want to suggest the following conclusion: It seems as if these very active mothers may often be overwhelming to their young infants, who, thus, have difficulty in finding in their mothers a receptive, secure base. On the other hand, the rather passive sober mothers may have been more predictable to their infants and encouraged more active interaction seeking from their infants. The rationale behind our assumptions corresponds to ideas already investigated by Brazelton, Koslowski, and Main (1974) and Field (1983).

Once a certain type of relationship was formed, we found it to remain stable to the second birthday of the child. In three different play sessions, two with the mother and one with the father, the formerly good orienters were now described as being initiating and expressive in their interactions with both parents, and both parents of these toddlers were independently characterized as lenient, patient and noncontrolling. These were also the parents of the securely attached children (Grossmann, 1984).

There were closely corresponding findings for the fathers as well as for the mothers for the second year. It may well be that similar processes have been operating also during the first year in the development of the child–father attachment relationship. More good orienters had developed a secure attachment to their fathers, and their fathers as well as their mothers were described as being lenient, patient, and accepting in the play session with their 2-year-olds. We did not find any correlation between the observed interactive quality of the fathers with their babies in the first year of life or their involvement in infant care and the quality of the toddlers' attachment to them. However, there are good reasons to assume that this is due, in part, to the incompleteness of our observations. There are no data to suggest that the process of the development of the child–father attachment is different from the process of the developing child–mother attachment.

The pathway to a secure child–parent attachment relationship for both parents then looks as follows: A newborn who is attentive and ready to interact with social partners will develop a secure attachment to the parents, if they allow the infant to have sufficient control over the amount and kind of interactions the infant wants with them.

Stability of the newborns' interactive readiness was also found in their subsequent reactions to new and social events. Good newborn orienters were friendlier to the unfamiliar home visitors at 6 months. At 24 months they were described as more initiating and expressive when they were confronted with a strange and potentially frightening toy. Also at 24 months, they were more interested, eager and sociable during a Bayley exam. All three kinds of reactions of the children were independent of maternal sensitivity during the first year of the infants' lives.

Our findings add to the hypothesis that individual, emergenetic tendencies exist from birth on (Lykken, 1982). Orienting ability may be a rather profound and influential one, although parental behavior of the "lighthearted" variety may easily mask in the infant what is definitely there. Without getting into the controversial issue of infant temperament, it can be seen that infants' orienting readiness, as measured by a number of NBAS items, definitely influenced the effects of parental behavior patterns on the developing quality of the child–parent relationships.

Rutter (1978) argues that certain infant behavioral features such as easiness, adaptability, and attractiveness may make a child less vulnerable to stressful family circumstances or inadequate mothering. We believe that we are able to lend some support to Rutter's notion.

In our North German sample of healthy newborns, the Neonatal Behavioral Assessment Scale has proven its potential usefulness for the estimation of the infant's contribution to the development of different relationship patterns with her or his parents. These are believed to be fundamental for the becoming person's appropriate emotional functioning especially in moments of distress (Grossmann & Grossmann, in preparation).

On the one hand, this concept is in line with Ainsworth's notion that, "although the infant through his own idiosyncratic patterns of behavior certainly contributes to the interaction with his mother, the extent to which his mother goes along with, disregards, or opposes the implications to the baby's behavioral cues makes a great deal of difference to the quality of the interaction" (Ainsworth, 1979, p. 45).

We have, on the other hand, ventured to show that, especially with less than optimal parental sensitivity, there are differences in the resulting relationship patterns. Part of it, within the correct notions of attachment research, comes from the infants themselves. We are lucky to have worked with mothers many of whom had provided their infants with an opportunity to reveal their individual contributions within the normal range, and already very early in their young lives.

Most of these families are still being studied. New co-workers visited the families and did observations and interviews when the children were 3 years old (Lütkenhaus, Grossmann, & Grossmann, 1985), 6 years old and 10 years old (Grossmann & Grossmann, in preparation). Longitudinal relationships of early orienting ability become increasingly less conspicuous (Lütkenhaus et al., 1985), but this may need more sophisticated methods of analysis as the number of variables increased with every assessment.

Summary

A set of results of the first phase of an ongoing longitudinal study in northern Germany is presented. One major aim of the study was to describe the ontogeny of parent–child relationships in a sample of average German families by assessing the infant's characteristics at birth, the quality of the parental caretaking during the first year of the infant's life, and the cultural background of child rearing practices in Germany, against which these results must be interpreted.

At the outset of the study, the Brazelton Neonatal Behavioral Assessment Scale (NBAS) was administered to 54 healthy German infants three times during their mothers' nine day lying-in period. The infants' behaviors on this scale showed an unexpected stability during this period as compared to a sample of normal U. S. infants.

Experimental variation of the postpartum conditions in the hospital, in terms of "early" and "extended" mother–infant contact, indicated that increasing opportunities to interact socially improved the newborns' orienting abilities.

Maternal sensitivity to the infant's communications was rated from two half-hour videotapes made during the lying-in period in the hospital, and from narrative reports of three 2-hour-long home visits when the infants were 2, 6, and 10 months old. In addition, paternal empathic interactive quality with the infant was observed, and the fathers' participation in infant care was ascertained at each visit. None of the five maternal sensitivity ratings correlated in any systematic way with the newborns' orienting responses, nor did the father's interactive quality or his involvement in infant care.

Mothers of more irritable newborns were more sensitive during the newborn period, but not during the first year and they described their infants as less acceptable and less easy in the first year.

From the audiotapes of each visit, mother and infant vocalizations were categorized. Three maternal styles of conversation with infants were identified on the basis of the mothers' predominant tone of voice, the contingency of their vocalizations with the infants' vocalizations, and the length and quality of their bouts of vocalizations. The conversational styles were called the sober style, the tender style, and the lighthearted style. The newborn's orienting ability was associated with the sober and the lighthearted conversational styles.

To the 6-month home visit, the observer brought a toy for the infant and presented it to the infant at the beginning of the visit. The friendliness of the infant toward the visitors was positively correlated with their orientating ability as newborns.

At 12 and 18 months, the children's quality of their attachments to their mothers and fathers, respectively, were assessed from videotaped strange situations. Twelve of the 16 infants classified as securely attached to their mothers, and 13 of the 19 infants classified as securely attached to their fathers, had been better than average in their orienting ability as newborns. Of the toddlers securely attached to one and/or the other parent, 69% had been "good orienters."

At 2 years, the toddlers' interactive style in three videotaped play situations with the mother, the father, and a strange and potentially frightening toy was rated on 23 items by naive adults. The item "the child is the initiator in the interaction" was significantly related to newborn orientation scores in all three play situations. In the situation with the potentially frightening toy, the more active children have had significantly higher scores on the set of the NBAS orienting items. The kind of parent–child relationship at 2 years of age that was significantly associated with the newborns' orienting responses was a type called "initiating child and accepting parent".

The children were also given the Bayley Scales of Mental Development during the 24-month home visit, and their behavior during the test was videotaped and coded. Formerly "good orienters" showed more eagerness, interest, less anger, and were more communicative with the examiner than formerly "poor orienters."

We interpreted the results in such a way that "good newborn orienters" seem to tolerate less parental sensitivity and still develop a good relationship to them than "poor newborn orienters." Good newborn orienters also seem to be more ready to engage in social interactions and seek out new experiences, as is seen in the greater friendliness toward the unfamiliar home visitor at 6 months of age, the more active handling of the surprise toy at 24 months, and the greater eagerness and sociability during the Bayley exam, also at 24 months.

In addition, some observations on the child rearing attitudes of these families are added, and we offer some speculations as to why, in contrast to many U.S. studies, we found the newborn's orienting ability to have predictive value for some of the children's behavioral characteristics.

References

Ainsworth, M.D.S. (1979). Attachment as related to mother-infant interaction. In D.S. Lehrman & R.A. Hinde (Eds.), *Advances in the study of behavior, Vol. 9*. New York: Academic Press.

Ainsworth, M.D.S., Bell, S.M., & Stayton, D.J. (1974). Infant-mother attachment and social development: Socialization as a product of reciprocal responsiveness to signals. In M.P.M. Richards (Ed.), *The integration of a child into a social world*. Cambridge, England: Cambridge University Press.

Ainsworth, M.D.S., Blehar, M.C., Waters, E., & Wall, S. (1978). *Patterns of attachment*. Hillsdale, NJ: Erlbaum.

Aleksandrowicz, M.K., & Aleksandrowicz, D.R. (1975). The molding of personality; A newborn's innate characteristics in interaction with parents' personalities. *Child Psychiatry and Human Development, 5*, 4.

Als, H. (1975). *The human newborn and his mother: An ethological study of their interaction*. Unpublished doctoral dissertation, University of Pennsylvania.

Als, H. (1978). Assessing an assessment: Conceptual considerations, methodological issues and a perspective on the future of the Brazelton Neonatal Behavioral Assessment Scale (NBAS). In A. Sameroff (Ed.), *Organization and stability of newborn behavior: A commentary on the Brazelton Neonatal Behavioral Assessment Scale. Monographs of the Society for Research in Child Development, 43*, No. 5-6, Serial No. 177.

Als, H., & Lewis, M. (1975, April). *The contributions of the infant to the interaction with his mother*. Paper presented at the SRCD Conference, Denver, CO.

Block, J. (1961). *The Q-sort method in personality assessment and psychiatric research*. Springfield, IL: Thomas.

Block, J. (1972). *The California Q - set*. Palo Alto, CA: Consulting Psychologists Press.

Block, J.H., Block, J., & Morrison, A. (1981). Parental agreement-disagreement on child-rearing orientations and gender-related personality correlates in children. *Child Development, 52*, 965–974.

Block, J.H., Jennings, P.H., Harvey, E., & Simpson, E. (1964). Interaction between allergic potential and psychopathology in childhood asthma. *Psychosomatic Medicine, 26*, 307–320.

Brazelton, T.B. (1973). *Neonatal Behavioral Assessment Scale*. Spastics international medical publication. London: Heinemann Medical Books, Ltd.

Brazelton, T.B., Nugent, J.K., & Lester, B.M. (1987). Neonatal Behavioral Assessment Scale. In J.D. Osofsky (Ed.), *Handbook of infant development* (2nd ed.). New York: Wiley.

Brazelton, T.B., Koslowski, B., & Main, M. (1974). The origins of reciprocity: The early mother-infant interaction. In M. Lewis & L.A. Rosenblum (Eds.), *The effect of the infant on its caregiver*. New York: Wiley.

Campos, J.J., Caplovitz Barrett, K., Lamb, M.E., Hill Goldsmith, H., & Stenberg, C. (1983). Socioemotional development. In P.H. Mussen (Ed.), *Handbook of child psychology* (4th ed., Vol II). New York: Wiley.

Crockenberg, S.B. (1981). Infant irritability, mother responsiveness and social support influences on the security of infant–mother attachment. *Child Development, 52*, 857–865.

Egeland, B., & Brunnquell, D. (1979). An at-risk approach to the study of child abuse. *Journal of American Academy of Child Psychiatry, 18,* 219–235.

Grossmann, K. (1978). Die Wirkung des Augenoeffnens von Neugeborenen auf das Verhalten ihrer Muetter [The effect of the newborn's eye opening on the behavior of their mothers]. *Geburtshilfe und Frauenheilkunde, 38,* 629–635.

Grossmann, K. (1984). *Zweijaehrige Kinder im Zusammenspiel mit ihren Muettern, Vaetern, einer fremden Erwachsenen und in einer Ueberraschungssituation: Beobachtungen aus bindungs- und kompetenztheoretischer Sicht* [Two-year-olds in joint play with their mothers, fathers, a strange adult and in a surprise situation: Observations in view of attachment and competence theory], unpublished doctoral dissertation, Universitaet Regensburg, West Germany.

Grossmann, K., Baierl, A., & Machl, R. (1983, August). *Task-oriented, social and emotional behavior of two-year-olds during a Bayley mental exam.* Paper presented at the 7th Biennial Meeting of the International Society for the Study of Behavioral Development, Muenchen, West Germany.

Grossmann, K., Grossmann, K.E., Spangler, G., Suess, G., & Unzner, L. (1985). Maternal sensitivity and newborn's orientation responses as related to quality of attachment in northern Germany. In I. Bretherton & E. Waters (Eds.), *Growing points in attachment theory and research. Monographs of the Society for Research in Child Development, 50.*

Grossmann, K., Thane, K., & Grossmann, K.E. (1981). Maternal skin-touching behavior of her newborn after various post-partum conditions of mother-infant contact. *Developmental Psychology, 17,* 158–169.

Grossmann, K.E. (1986). From idiographic approaches to nomothetic hypotheses: Stern, Allport, and the biology of knowledge, exemplified by an exploration of sibling relationships. In J. Valsiner (Ed.), *The individual subject and scientific psychology* (pp. 37–69). New York: Plenum.

Grossmann, K.E., & Grossmann, K. (1981). Parent-infant attachment relationships in Bielefeld: A research note. In K. Immelmann, G.W. Barlow, L. Petrinovich, & M. Main (Eds.), *Behavioral development: The Bielefelder Interdisciplinary Project.* Cambridge, England: Cambridge University Press.

Grossmann, K.E., & Grossmann, K. (1985). *From attachment to dynamics of relationship patterns: A longitudinal approach.* Paper presented at the 8th biennial meeting of the International Society for the Study of Behavior, Tours, France, July 1985.

Grossmann, K.E., & Grossmann, K. (in preparation). Attachment quality as an organizer of emotional and behavioral responses. In P. Marris, J. Stevenson-Hinde, & C. Parkes (Eds.), *Attachment across the life cycle.* New York: Routledge.

Grossmann, K.E., Grossmann, K., Huber, F., & Wartner, U. (1981). German children's behavior towards their mothers at 12 months and their fathers at 18 months in Ainsworth's Strange Situation. *International Journal of Behavioral Development, 4,* 157–181.

Grossmann, K.E., & Volkmer, H.J. (1984). Fathers' presence during birth of their infants and paternal involvement. *International Journal of Behavioral Development, 7,* 157–165.

Horowitz, F.D., Sullivan, J.W., & Linn, P. (1978). Stability and instability in the newborn infant: The quest for elusive threads. In A.J. Sameroff (Ed.), *Organization and stability of newborn behavior: A commentary on the Brazelton Neonatal Be-havior Assessment Scale. Monographs of the Society for Research in Child Development, No. 177.*

Kempe, R., & Kempe, C.H. (1978). *Child abuse.* London: Fontana Open Books.

Lütkenhaus, P., Grossmann, K.E., & Grossmann, K. (1985). Transactional influences of infants' orienting ability and maternal cooperation on competition in three-year-old children. *International Journal of Behavioral Development, 8,* 257–272.

Lykken, D.T. (1982). Research with twins: The concept of emergenesis. *Psychophysiology, 19,* 361–373.

Matas, L., Arend, R.A., & Sroufe, L.A. (1978). Continuity of adaptation in the second year: The relationship between quality of attachment and later competence. *Child Development, 49,* 547–556.

Rutter, M. (1978). Early sources of security and competence. In J. Bruner & A. Garton (Eds.), *Human growth and development.* Oxford, England: Clarendon Press.

Sameroff, A. (1978). Organization and stability of newborn behavior: A commentary on the Brazelton Neonatal Behavioral Assessment Scale. *Monographs of the Society for Research in Child Development, 43,* No. 5-6, Serial No. 177.

Sander, L.W., & Julia, H.L. (1966). Continuous interactional monitoring in the neonate. *Psychosomatic Medicine, 28,* 822–835.

Stern, D.N., Beebe, B., Jaffe, J., & Bennett, S.L. (1977). The infant's stimulus world during social interaction: A study of caregiver behaviors with particular reference to repetition and timing. In H.R. Schaffer (Ed.), *Studies of interactions in infancy.* New York: Academic Press.

Vaughn, B.E., Taraldson, B., Crichton, L., & Egeland, B. (1980). Relationships between neonatal behavioral organization and infant behavior during the first year of life. *Infant Behavior and Development, 3,* 47–66.

Wutz, C. (1985). *Die Vater-Kind Beziehung im ersten Lebensjahr: Trost, Spiel, Pflege* [The father-child relationship in the first year of life: Comfort, play, care]. Diplom thesis. Universitaet Regensburg, West Germany.

Ziemer, J. (1982). *Das Zusammenleben mit 10 Monate alten Kindern aus der Sicht ihrer Muetter sowie ihre Einstellung zum Kind* [Life with 10-month old infants from the viewpoint of their mothers and their attitude toward the child]. Diplom thesis. Universitaet Regensburg, West Germany.

CHAPTER 2

Cultural Mediation Between Newborn Behavior and Later Development: Implications for Methodology in Cross-cultural Research*

Constance H. Keefer

Pediatrician, Harvard Community Health Plan, Boston, MA
Instructor in Pediatrics, Harvard Medical School, Boston, MA

Suzanne Dixon

Associate Professor of Pediatrics, UCSD School of Medicine, San Diego, CA

Edward Z. Tronick

Director, Child Development Unit, the Children's Hospital, Boston, MA and
Associate Professor of Pediatrics, and Education, Harvard Medical School, and Harvard Graduate School of Education, Cambridge, MA

T. Berry Brazelton

Clinical Professor of Pediatrics, Emeritus, Harvard Medical School, Boston, MA

* This research was carried out through the Child Development Unit of Children's Hospital Medical Center, Boston, MA, in conjunction with Robert LeVine, Ph.D., and the Child Research Project, Kisii, Kenya. The work was supported by grants from the National Science Foundation, Robert Wood Johnson Foundation, William T. Grant Foundation, and Carnegie Corporation.

The authors wish to thank Robert LeVine for inspiration, guidance, and support; the people of "Nyansongo" for their gracious acceptance of our presence in their community; Teresia Monari, Drucella Omboi, Anna Onchari, and Agnes Nyabete for their valuable assistance in the field; Amy Richman for statistical analyses; and Jane Arnold for patient retyping.

Introduction

In 1974, Robert LeVine, a psychological anthropologist, returned to "Nyansongo," the Gusii community of Kenya whose children he had observed for the Six Cultures Study conceived by John and Beatrice Whiting (LeVine & LeVine, 1966; Whiting & Whiting, 1975). That original work with the Gusii looked at the cultural variability of the behavior of children from 3 to 6 years of age. It was an attempt to look at the process by which a society prepares and shapes its young to become culturally appropriate adults. LeVine's new work with the Gusii would study the same process but would expand the age to be examined back to the newborn period.

Our contribution was to study the behavior of the newborns and young infants. Differences in behavioral profiles of newborns in other cultures had been described (Brazelton, Koslowski, & Tronick, 1976; Brazelton, Robey, & Collier, 1969; Freedman & Freedman, 1969; Goldberg, 1971), and we wanted to understand whether Gusii infants had a unique profile and, if they did, to what extent it influenced later development. Correlations had been found between some aspects of newborn behavior and later infant development in a study of American infants (Rosenblith, 1974).

In this paper we present the results of Brazelton Neonatal Behavioral Assessments (BNBAS) (Brazelton, 1973) of a group of Gusii newborns and the results of the Bayley Scales of Mental and Motor Development (Bayley, 1969) administered to those same infants later in the first year of life. The relationships between the newborn behavior and later developmental outcome are discussed in light of the culture's goals for, and beliefs about, infancy. The mediating roles of factors such as infant health and nutrition and infant care-giving practices are examined. We also raise questions about the use of BNBAS and Bayley Scales in cross-cultural research.

The Gusii People: The Cultural Setting

The Gusii are a Bantu-speaking agricultural group from the highlands (5000 feet above sea level) of southwestern Kenya (50 miles south of the equator and 40 miles east of Lake Victoria). The Gusii population was greater than 900,000 in 1975, and they had the highest fertility rate in the world at the 1979 census (Mosley, 1980). Hence, there was a tremendous pressure of population growth on the existing, limited tribal land. The study community of 2,000 lived around a small market place seven miles from the main tribal town of Kisii. In this community the population pressure translated into an average of two or three acres per family for both food and cash crops, compared to an average of 10–20 acres in 1957.

Traditionally, women did the agricultural work in this community, while men herded cattle, built houses, and carried on tribal business. The decrease in available grazing land, caused by the increased population density as well as the conversion of more land to cash crops, made animal husbandry nearly impossible. Traditional male roles were undermined. Labor migration, with fathers' absences, became the norm. In 1975, two-thirds of the men with children under the age of 3 worked outside the local area. Some went as far as Nairobi or Mombassa, hundreds of miles away, returning only once a year to their Kisii homesteads; others worked in nearby towns, returning weekly or monthly to this community.

In this patrilineal society, a woman moved to her husband's family land when she married. On two to three acres, she had a mud-walled house with thatch or aluminum roof and a garden. She tilled and planted her fields by hand, often alone, raising both food (maize, finger millet, vegetables, bananas) and cash crops (coffee, tea, pyrethrum). Some women had goats, cows, or chickens.

Most families suffered some nutritional deprivation in the preharvest time. The effect of this deprivation was observed in the children's growth records, which showed mild to moderate nutritional compromise in most children between 3 months and 3 years of age. However, the few children who developed severe malnutrition were already at risk because of other factors, e.g., alcoholic or absent mothers (Dixon, LeVine, & Brazelton, 1982). These malnourished children were similar in number and in types of risk factors to children who suffer failure to thrive and neglect in this country.

Figure 1.   A Gusii family outside their traditional house. (Source: Eliza Klein).

A Gusii woman's work consisted of not only the hard labor in the fields, but also of bearing and rearing children. Children have been extremely important and highly valued by the Gusii. The women said that they wanted as many children as they could have; and most in our sample had a child every 2 to 3 years until menopause. Interviews with postmenopausal women revealed an average live birth rate of 10, so these goals were realized by most women.

Children were important to secure a woman's place within her husband's family. A woman's position within her mother-in-law's territory was usually adversarial or isolated. She and her sisters-in-law, and her mother-in-law to a lesser extent, were in competition for limited land. A woman had to compete with her co-wives for her husband's attention and support. A woman secured a share of the lineage's resources (primarily land) only by the birth of sons who would be loyal to her and who would eventually bring wives to work the land and support the woman in her old age.

Children were also important as a source of household labor. Young children assumed duties of infant care and simple household tasks, such as fetching water and firewood, by the age of 4 years. Older preteen and teenage girls assisted their mothers in the fields or in heavier household tasks of laundry, cleaning, repairs, and going to market. In a comparative study, Gusii children were found to be among the hardest working in the world (Whiting & Whiting, 1975). In addition to being wanted, these children were loved and well cared for, as their lifelong strong attachments to their mothers attested. The one person an adult Gusii woman felt the most strong attachment to was her own mother, even though she rarely saw her after she married.

However, the interactions that could be seen between mothers and their infants did not show a high degree of intense affect as we had come to expect in attached mother–infant pairs in a Western population. Gusii mothers were rarely seen playing with their infants. The rare playful interactions which we observed were subdued, seldom leading to mutual laughing or affectionate hugging and kissing. The mothers rarely talked to their infants. We saw no attempts to stimulate the infants' development, or even to notice or praise developmental progress, although the mothers were keen observers of these processes.

The intensity of affect in these Gusii mother–infant interactions was held in check by two Gusii beliefs. First, Gusii mothers believed that infants just developed without specific input other than food and protection; they didn't recognize a direct role for themselves to stimulate or teach the infant. Why talk to the infant, one woman replied, when she obviously can't talk back? Second, the Gusii believed that getting ahead of one's neighbor or overachieving were to be avoided, because such attitudes incited jealousy in others, leading to witchcraft. Witchcraft was a serious matter among the Gusii. It was the presumed cause of death, fires, crop failures, and infertility. And good fortune, including the production of a healthy child, attracted the malevolence of witchcraft. Gusii women, therefore, did not announce their much-wanted pregnancies until they were undeniably obvious, for fear of witchcraft reprisals by jealous women. Neither did they express or demonstrate publicly their pleasure in their infants, nor any pride in the child's accomplishments. In fact, any extreme of affect, either positive or negative, was to be avoided. Anger or great joy, if openly expressed, might have aroused divisive feelings within the tightly interdependent community. Even with an infant, social interactions were highly structured, to avoid such threatening emotional displays, and would more likely calm or contain the infant than stimulate or excite him or her.

These beliefs and the interactions which they supported were consistent with the Gusii goal of a smoothly functioning society where cooperation and equality of achievement were more highly valued than competition and achievement beyond the norm. The Gusii mother's interactions supported her goals of ensuring both her infant's cultural as well as physical survival.

The Study: The Mothers and the Conditions of Pregnancy, Labor, Delivery, and the Postpartum Period

From February through August, 1975, we saw all pregnant women in the study community of 2,000 people during the third trimester of pregnancy, and in some instances as early as the second trimester. The pregnant women were examined periodically by two of the authors for weight gain, growth of the fundus, fetal heart tones, blood pressure, presence of edema, murmurs, anemia, and proteinuria. Height and head circumference were measured at the first prenatal contact.

Most of the women delivered at home, one third attended by another adult woman, one third alone, and one third attended only by a child. Delivery was recognized as a very vulnerable time, and women avoided any possible witchcraft threat, even at the expense of delivering alone. We observed one birth, a woman delivering her fourth child:

For several hours, the laboring woman roamed freely and squatted at will in and around her home. She drank a potion of ash and dirt from under her fire, mixed with water, and had her abdomen massaged by her mother-in-law, to assist contractions. Older women of her kinship group came in and out; her older children peeked in periodically. At the moment of delivery, she squatted on the floor, supporting herself by clinging to ropes hung from the ceiling beams, and was supported under her arms by her mother-in-law. The infant was delivered onto the dirt floor, falling a few inches after a rapid expulsion. The cord was cut with a nonsterile blade before delivery of the placenta. The infant was immediately bathed in cold water and then wrapped and passed to attendants or observers to be greeted. Only later was the infant given to his mother. Over the next hours and days relatives and neighbors came to greet the newborn, handling the baby vigorously and often admonishing, 'You have burned your first home behind you.' (*Mosamba mwaye*, the Gusii word for newborn, means just that (LeVine & LeVine, 1966).) Immediately after delivery, the mother was given a bottled soft drink for rehydration and she rested and warmed herself, paying little attention to her newborn for some hours.

When a newborn was seen as at risk (being small, premature, multiple birth, or born after previous child or fetal loss), the newborn and mother were not allowed to be seen until certain ceremonies could be performed, usually several weeks and occasionally some months later. This provided a period of seclusion for the mother and infant, and an avoidance of witchcraft's evil eye to which they were particularly vulnerable. Some protective power was attributed to the placenta, so that those present before it was discarded were considered to be "safe" for even the most vulnerable newborn. We missed a delivery of twins by a few hours, and the mother, who knew we were anxious to examine the babies, saved the placentas until we arrived, hence allowing us to visit her and the infants during the period of protective seclusion.

After a normal, full-term delivery the infants were given some water on a spoon or a few "practice" sucks at the breast in the first 24–48 hours. Colostrum was not believed to be of any special value to the newborn. Nursing didn't begin until the milk was in, which was usually by 48 hours in these multiparous women. Most women, in the few days after delivery, tried to eat a certain spinach-like vegetable, *chinsaga,* which they believed enhanced the production of milk; it did contain large amounts of calcium. Once nursing was initiated, the infant was put to breast at any movement or awakening, usually every hour during the first several weeks of life.

Most women stayed in their homes with the infant for 1 to 4 weeks. A few days' rest by a continuous fire prepared by someone else was all the help a woman could expect. While relatives came with gifts for the infant, there was no expectation that they would help with household or farm chores. An expectant mother had to plan for this time and most were caring for their families very soon after delivery and returning to a fairly full work load near the house by 1 month. It was usually only after 2 to 3 months that a woman resumed field work away from the house, because it entailed leaving the infant for several hours at a time in the care of a child. The timing of this return to heavy field work was determined, one woman told us, by a sense of the infant's weight and sturdiness: she gently tossed her 2-month-old in her hands, saying, "When she's a real bundle."

The Study: Infants

Thirty-one infants were born during the study period. We assessed the health of all of these infants within the first 3 days of life with a general pediatric physical exam and a gestational aging exam (Dubowitz, Dubowitz, & Goldberg, 1970), and we recorded length, head circumference, and weight. Weights were repeated at the time of each behavioral exam, and weights and lengths and head circumference were repeated periodically throughout the first year of life. The Brazelton Neonatal Behavioral Assessment Scale (BNBAS) (Brazelton, 1973) was chosen as a way to organize our observations of newborn behavior and to compare the results to other groups of newborns and to relate them to later development. We performed the BNBAS one to seven times on each of these infants during the first 2 weeks of life. Fifteen infants had three BNBAS exams available for grouping in the following ages: "early exam" (days 1, 2, or 3, mean 2.2), "middle exam" (days 4, 5, 6, or 7, mean 5.5), and "late exam" (days 9, 10, 11, or 12, mean 10); nine infants had two exams available, from the middle and late exam periods. Seven had only one exam and were omitted from the analyses.

The BNBAS assessments were carried out in the homes, with the exception of the "early" exam on two infants who were delivered in local hospitals. Because the homes were dimly lit and the infants' skin color relatively dark, we were unable to reliably score changes in skin color and dropped that item from our exams.

Infants nursed much more frequently than every 4 hours, so exams were not always done at the "2-hour postprandial" time designated in the scale manual. All of the BNBAS exams were carried out by one of the authors (Keefer or Dixon). Interscorer agreement between the two examiners was at least 85% for all scale items.

In the analyses reported, the data comparing the Gusii and American samples are based on the 15 Gusii infants with three exams and use the seven five-point cluster scores as described in Lester, Als, and Brazelton (1982).

Twelve newborns formed a longitudinal study sample; 10 of these were from the 15 with three BNBAS exams, and two were from the newborns with two BNBAS exams. The Bayley Scales of Mental and Motor Development (Bayley, 1969) were chosen for the longitudinal study as measures of developmental outcome which might have a relationship with newborn behavior as measured by the BNBAS. We administered Bayley Scales to these 12 infants two to five times between 3 and 13 months of age. For the correlational analyses with the BNBAS scores, two Bayley exams per child were chosen, one at 5 to 7 months, one at 8 to 10 months. These exam ages were chosen because there were more infants at each of these ages who had completed usable mental and motor exams. At 5 to 7 months, 11 infants had usable mental scale scores and 10 had usable motor scale scores. At 8 to 10 months, nine infants had usable scores for both mental and motor exams. One infant missed both exams at 5 to 7 months, and two infants missed both exams at 8 to 10 months.

We provided medical care to these infants and kept a record of their illnesses during the first year of life. To assess the relationship between illness and performance on the Bayley Scales, we derived a "severity of illness" score for each infant. Table 1 shows how the illnesses were scored for severity, with a 10 indicating the most severe illness. These ratings were made on an a priori basis

Table 1.   Illness Scores.

Illness	Score
Pneumonia or Diarrhea	10
Wheezing, bronchitis, or fever	9
Otitis media	7
Cough	6
Colic	5
Cold, constipation, conjunctivitis, or scabies	3
Range of total illness score for sample infants:	9–54

retrospectively by one of the investigators who is a pediatrician and who had provided care in the field.

Results

Prenatal assessment and newborn physical. The results of our prenatal assessments of the mothers, which are presented in Table 2, were reported by Dixon, Keefer, Tronick, and Brazelton (1982). They led us to worry about the outcomes of the pregnancies. Many mothers did not gain weight during the third trimester and many were grand-multiparas. Most were anemic, had intestinal parasites, and had episodes of fever, probably malaria. These conditions, and the conditions of delivery without septic precautions, were not considered optimal by Western standards (Aubry & Pennington, 1973; Prechtl, 1968). The infants proved our prenatal concerns to be inaccurate. As Table 2 shows, these infants' birth weights, lengths, ponderal indices, and postnatal weight gains were normal. By our pediatric judgements, based on examining them and observing the way they were handled by the Gusii adults, they were vigorous and healthy, responsive and robust.

BNBAS. The behavioral performances of the Gusii babies matched their physical well-being:

A typical Gusii newborn was a rather chubby but solid infant, with a·mop of soft, curly black hair. He would lie quietly on a blanket, even though he was undressed. All of his movements were particularly vigorous and smooth. When he was picked up and handled, his motor tone increased. He became a solid package with very little headlag; he responded with an alerting look, a quietly increasing interest in everything around him. He seemed to become more and more alert and vigorous as he was handled. Crying was rare, but a vigorous state six was available. Position change and sucking were the usual and effective self-consoling actions. If he did become fussy or cry, an elicited Moro would often calm him and return his motor control. This remarkable integration of alertness and motor control was observed in the early exam and usually persisted throughout the next month.

Table 2.   Maternal Characteristics

Parameter (reliability)	Number of Subjects	Mean	S.D.	Range
Age (years)	24	29.1	± 5.9	17–45
Parity	24	5.1	± 2.5	1–10
Number of living children	24	4.5	± 2.2	1–10
Prior birth interval (months)	22	34 mo.	±16 mo.	24–84
Presentation weight (Kgs., ±.2 Kg)	24	62.92	6.59	51.52–75.04
Height (cms, ±1.8 cm)	15	159.8	5.6	147–166
Head circum. (cms., ±0.5)	19	55.2	± 1.3	53.58
Weight gain (Kgs/wk)				
Late second	15	0.44	—	.2–.75
Early third	18	0.22	—	0–1.0
Late third	24	0.02	—	0–8.0

Infant Characteristics.

Parameter (Reliability)	Number of Subjects	Mean	S.D.	Range
Weight (±.2 Kg)				
"Birth" exam	15	3.49	± 0.42	3.0–4.4
Exam 2	24	3.68	± 0.58	2.9–4.4
Exam 3	24	3.79	± 0.41	3.1–4.9
Length (±1.5 cm)	22	50.0	± 2.17	46.9–54.6
Head circumference (±.5 cm)	23	35.1	± 1.56	33.0–39.4
Gestational age (weeks)	24	40.9	± 0.85	39.5–42.5
Percent weight for age	24	37%	± 24%	3–90%
Ponderal index	24	2.84	± 0.24	2.53–34.5

Note: From S. Dixon, C.H. Keefer, E. Tronick, & T.B. Brazelton, 1982, *Perinatal circumstances and newborn outcome among the Gusii of Kenya: Assessment of risk* (pp. 11–32). Norwood, NJ: Ablex Publishing Corporation. Copyright 1982 by Ablex. Reprinted by permission.

We compared the results of the Gusii BNBAS exams with those of a group of 15 healthy fullterm white American infants who had been chosen for study because of low-risk pregnancy, labor, and delivery characteristics (Keefer, Tronick, Dixon, & Brazelton, 1982). Table 3 shows the results of this comparison of BNBAS items and clusters. The Gusii infants performed extremely well. The most consistent and highly significant difference between Gusii and American infants was in motor maturity. The Gusii infants performed better at each age on this item (F_1, 26 = 18.75, $p < .001$).

Six other items showed significant differences. The Gusii infants had better hand-to-mouth behavior, were less irritable, had fewer startles, and were less tremulous. The American infants showed better habituation to light and had fewer state changes. With the exception of cuddliness, the Gusii infants' perfor-

Table 3.   BNBAS Scores of Gusii (G) and American (A) Infants.

	Early Exam		Middle Exam		Late Exam		ANOVA Effects	
	G	A	G	A	G	A	Group	Age × Group
Motor Performance Items								
Tonus	5.8	5.7	5.8	5.5	6.1	5.9	N.S.	N.S.
Maturity	6.6	4.3	6.8	5.2	6.9	5.3	.001	N.S.
Pull to sit	6.2	6.0	5.5	5.8	5.3	5.7	N.S.	N.S.
Defensive reaction	5.8	6.4	6.8	7.2	6.6	6.5	N.S.	N.S.
Activity level	5.0	4.8	4.8	4.6	4.8	4.6	N.S.	N.S.
Motor cluster	5.6	5.2	5.7	5.4	5.6	5.1	N.S.	N.S.
Reflex Cluster								
Reflex cluster	1.4	2.2	1.2	1.0	1.4	1.0	N.S.	N.S.
Orientation Items								
Inanimate visual (ball)	5.9	5.3	6.0	6.1	6.7	6.8	N.S.	N.S.
Inanimate auditory (rattle)	5.7	5.5	6.5	5.8	6.3	6.0	N.S.	N.S.
Animate visual (face)	5.7	6.5	5.9	6.6	6.0	7.2	N.S.	N.S.
Animate auditory (voice)	6.0	5.6	6.1	5.7	6.5	6.1	N.S.	N.S.
Animate visual & auditory (face and voice)	6.1	6.6	6.1	6.8	6.7	7.5	N.S.	N.S.
Alertness	5.0	5.4	5.6	6.0	6.2	6.2	N.S.	N.S.
Orientation cluster	5.6	5.6	6.0	6.0	6.3	6.2		
Habituation Items								
Repeated light flash	5.7	6.6	6.2	8.3	6.5	7.3	.06	N.S.
Repeated rattle	6.8	5.6	7.3	8.3	6.7	6.6	N.S.	N.S.
Repeated bell	7.4	6.0	7.0	9.0	7.4	6.0	N.S.	N.S.
Repeated pin prick	3.5	4.6	4.7	4.6	5.5	3.0	N.S.	N.S.
Habituation cluster	6.0	6.1	6.4	6.5	6.5	6.0	N.S.	N.S.
Regulation of State Items								
Cuddliness	4.8	6.0	6.1	5.6	6.0	6.7	N.S.	.02
Consolability	6.4	7.1	6.4	5.1	6.3	4.8	N.S.	N.S.
Self quieting	5.4	6.1	4.9	4.9	5.6	4.4	N.S.	N.S.
Hand to mouth	6.8	5.6	6.4	5.6	6.1	4.8	.08	N.S.
Regulation cluster	5.8	6.1	5.9	5.4	6.0	5.3	N.S.	N.S.

Table 3.   *(Continued)*

Range of State Items							
Peak of excitement	5.9	5.8	5.8	5.6	5.9	5.5	N.S.	N.S.
Rapidity of build-up	3.1	3.9	4.1	3.5	4.1	3.8	N.S.	N.S.
Irritability	5.2	4.5	5.7	4.3	4.7	4.2	.06	N.S.
Lability of state	3.3	2.9	3.4	2.4	3.4	3.0	.10	N.S.
Range cluster	3.7	3.9	3.9	3.6	3.8	3.6	N.S.	N.S.
Autonomic Regulation Items							
Tremors	3.1	5.1	3.4	3.7	2.7	3.7	.09	N.S.
Startles	3.0	4.7	3.5	3.7	3.0	3.2	.10	.04
Lability of skin color		4.2		2.9		4.1		

Note: From C.H. Keefer, E. Tronick, S. Dixon, & T.B. Brazelton, 1982, Specific differences in motor performance between Gusii and American newborns and a modification of the Neonatal Behavior Assessment Scale. *Child Development, 53,* 754–759. Copyright 1982 by The Society for Research in Child Development, Inc. Adapted by permission.

mance was strikingly stable over this period of examination; startles of American infants decreased with time. In general, Gusii infants' performances were better than expected, given the potential prenatal risks, and they compared very well in all areas to a low-risk American sample, surpassing them in motor performance.

The quality of motor performance was striking to us in observations both with and without the BNBAS framework. We observed mothers and other adults handling these babies with much more vigor than is tolerated with American infants, without gasps of "watch her head, you'll hurt her neck" from grandparents and other protective adults. Among the Gusii, a common practice after bathing an infant was to toss him or her lightly a few inches into the air in order to shake off water. The Moro reflex which this behavior elicits was labeled "the fright" by Gusii mothers. They observed that this tossing maneuver enabled the baby to get over the fright by 3 or 4 months of age. After handling only a few of these infants with our previously learned cautiousness, we found ourselves becoming much more vigorous. These infants invited such handling. We were drawn in by their vigor and sturdiness and adapted our own behavior to it. The BNBAS was particularly useful in capturing these unique Gusii characteristics because it is not a rigid instrument into which the babies' behaviors were forced to fit. Rather, it is a framework of articulated descriptors through which one can see more highly detailed behavior. For example, within motor maturity, we were able to use the scale points to describe what we saw in the Gusii babies and to capture the fact that they differed significantly from their American counterparts on this item.

However, with the general tone scale, which categorizes amounts of resting

Table 4. Expanded General Tone Scale.

Score	Resting	Amount of Tone	% Time in Most Tone	Timing of Tone Response	Modulation or Control of Tone Response
6	variable tone in resting	good tone	75% time handled		
6A	variable tone in resting as in 6	tone increased slightly over 6	75%	slight delay	usually matches applied tone, some breaks
6B	less variable—more resting tone than 6 or 6A	tone moderately increased over 6	75%	variable delay	always matches tone, few breaks
6C	resting tone as in 6B	amount of tone as in 7	75%	no delay	always matches applied tone, no break
7		hypertonic	50%		

Note: From Keefer et al. (1982). Copyright 1982 by the Society for Research in Child Development, Inc. Reprinted by permission.

and elicited tone, we failed to describe what we were seeing while handling the Gusii infants. We had to change the scale to accurately describe these babies. Because the scale is so highly articulated, we were able to identify the spot where the Gusii infants' unique motor tone fit best. We elaborated the scale at that spot (between scores six and seven), adding three points with graded characteristics of the amount of tone and the degree of control of tone. The new scale points and their descriptors are found in Table 4. This change in scale was described by Keefer et al. (1982).

In the analysis of relationships using the BNBAS general tone item and the motor cluster (to which the general tone score contributes), the new general tone scale points were not used. Any new scale score of 6A, 6B, or 6C was coded as a 6, which seemed the optimal scale point for the comparison sample. For this reason, the unique difference in Gusii babies' motor tone did not show up in the statistical analysis. However, the highly articulated, flexible nature of the BNBAS did allow us to recognize and capture this unique quality of motor tone and extremely mature motor behavior of these infants. It also made clear that the motor performance in other areas (pull-to-sit, etc.), and neurological reflexes, were not advanced or unique. No American sample has required these changes to be made. Ten of the Gusii infants required the use of a new tone score at least once. The distribution of the expanded tone scores in the three exam periods is shown in Table 5.

Bayley Exams. Results of Bayley Scales of Mental and Motor Development at 5 to 7 and 8 to 10 months on the 12 infants of the longitudinal sample are presented in Table 6. The average score on the mental scale was 103 at 5 to 7

Table 5. Distribution of General Tone and Expanded Tone Scores.

		Exam Period		
General Tone Score		**1 ($N = 10$)**	**2 ($N = 12$)**	**3 ($N = 12$)**
4		1		
5		1	3	2
6			1	2
E x p a n d e d	T o n e			
	6A	1	2	1
	6B	1	3	5
	6C	4	3	1
7		2		1
8				
9				

Table 6.   Bayley Scale Scores.

	5–7 Months		8–10 Months	
Subject	MDI	PDI	MDI	PDI
1	115	113		
2	102	120	92	
3			140	106
4	96	106	120	98
5	98	120	143	119
6	103	139	114	134
7	108		105	97
8	99	111	101	125
9	94	96	95	100
10	108	106		
11	103	124		100
12	107	113	99	110
Mean	103	115	112	109
Range	94–115	96–139	92–143	97–134

months and 112 at 8 to 10 months. The average score on the motor scale was 115 at 5 to 7 months and 109 at 8 to 10 months.

Correlations between BNBAS cluster scores and Bayley Scale scores. Correlations were obtained between BNBAS cluster scores at all three exam periods and the two sets of Bayley scores. Only data on the 12 longitudinal sample infants were used in this correlation. There were four statistically significant correlations. The range of state cluster score on the late BNBAS exam correlated negatively with Bayley Mental Scale performance at 8 to 10 months ($r = .73$, $p = .028$).

Three BNBAS cluster scores correlated with Bayley Motor Scale scores (PDI): the interactive cluster of the early BNBAS exam with the PDI at 8 to 10 months ($r = .77$, $p = .044$), the range of state cluster of the early exams with the PDI at 5 to 7 months ($r = .70$, $p = .037$), and the habituation cluster of the late exam with the PDI at 8 to 10 months ($r = .79$, $p = .034$). Neither the BNBAS motor cluster score nor any motor item score correlated significantly with the Bayley Motor Scale.

Since the expanded tone score had not gone into the BNBAS motor cluster score, we thought its absence might explain the lack of significant correlation with later motor performance on the Bayley exam. In order to look for the influences of newborn tone on Bayley Motor scores, we derived a "composite newborn tone" score. The three possible expanded tone scores, and the adjacent scores of five, six, and seven, were each assigned ascending numerical value. No

Table 7. Illness and Bayley Motor Scores.

Illness Score	Change in Bayley Motor Score
48	−5
37	−24
36	−8
27	+4
22	−3
10	−1
10	+14

$Z = -2.14, p < .05$

significant correlations between this composite tone score and the Bayley Motor scores were found.

We wondered if illness had an influence on Bayley performance. We computed the difference in motor scores between 8 to 10 and 5 to 7 months on the seven infants who had motor scores at both ages. It appears that illness significantly affected motor performance. As can be seen in Table 7, those infants with high illness scores tended to lose more points in the Bayley Motor scores than those with low illness scores ($z = 2.14, p < .05$).

We computed the change in weight percentiles for each infant during the first 10 months of life. The correlation between change in weight percentile and change in Bayley scores, mental and motor, was not significant.

Discussion

The Gusii mothers produced vigorous, healthy, apparently well-nourished newborns whose behavior on the BNBAS was comparable to that of a group of very low-risk American infants. In fact, the motor performance of this group of Gusii newborns was superior in motor maturity. The tone of these infants was uniquely strong and controlled. We had predicted that this tone and motor maturity would correlate with later motor achievements, because it would elicit more vigorous handling. As described above, the infants were often tossed in the air in the early months of life in a greeting or playful exercise. By 3 months of age they were able to be lifted by one arm, without loss of head or trunk control, to be swung on the mother's back. Clearly, the unique characteristics of these infants' tone influenced the handling and expectations of their caregivers, which, in turn, provided further opportunity for improving tone and control in the developing infant.

Other investigators have found significant correlations between newborn motor performance and later Bayley Motor scores (Field, Hallock, Ting,

Figure 2.   Young Gusii child caregiver (*omoreri*) with infant in conventional back wrap. (Source: Eliza Klein).

Dempsey, Dabiri, & Shuman, 1978; Fish & Crockenberg, 1981; Rosenblith, 1974), though not consistently (Sostek & Anders, 1977; Vaughn, Taraldson, Crichton, & Egeland, 1980). Rosenblith's and Fish and Crockenberg's samples were comparable to the Gusii, being full-term and having the later motor testing at 8 to 10 months of age. The samples studied by Field et al. were either premature or dysmature, so their findings may not be generalizable to a full-term sample. Vaughn et al. did not find any motor–motor correlation in their full-term sample when studied at 9 months of age, nor did Sostek and Anders, although their Bayley motor exams were done at 10 weeks of age. Despite the inconsistencies in the literature, we had expected to find some correlation between the newborn's striking motor performance and later motor development.

Our expectation, however, was not confirmed. Five to ten months later this same group of Gusii infants performed in an above-average way on the Bayley Scales of Motor Development, but there was no significant correlation between BNBAS motor performance and the Bayley Motor scores.

Based on our experience with the Gusii, we can advance a few explanations for this lack of correlation. First, these infants experienced frequent and often severe illnesses in the first year of life. We saw a correlation between their degree of illness and decrement in motor scores from the first period of testing (5 to 7 months) to the second period (8 to 10 months). It is possible that the physical effects of illness interfere with the development of these infants and with their capacity to benefit from the handling they receive; or caregivers may be inhibited from vigorous handling of the ill child. Second, there may not have been enough variation in this sample to provide a wide enough range for meaningful correlation. This sample was quite uniform in their development.

Third, additional observations were made of these Gusii infants in naturally occurring interaction with their care-givers over the first year of life. The infants' performances on the BNBAS were correlated with these observations. We know from Caron's analysis of these data (Caron, 1986) that the newborns who had better motor performance were held significantly less by all caregivers during the first 6 months of life than were those infants with poor newborn motor performance. While we had observed that the handling of all infants was vigorous, this finding means that those infants with superior newborn motor behavior were getting less holding, and, therefore, perhaps less stimulation and maintenance of that superior tone and movement. The effect could be a leveling of motor performance, an avoidance of pushing the already more advanced and bringing the poorest performers up to a minimal level. This would make these child caretaking activities highly consistent with the Gusii values and effective in achieving the cultural goals.

We now turn to the task of explaining the significant correlations we did find between the newborn and Bayley data. Only four BNBAS cluster scores correlated significantly with later Bayley scores: orientation on the early exam with Bayley Motor at 8 to 10 months, range of state on the early exam with Bayley Motor at 5 to 7 months, range of state on the late exam negatively with Bayley Mental at 8 to 10 months, and habituation on the late exam with Bayley Motor at 8 to 10 months.

The negative correlation between range of state and Bayley Mental is the most interesting. It has not been reported previously. Vaugh et al. (1980) found a positive correlation between newborn state scores and Bayley Mental scores at nine months of age; Sostek and Anders (1977) found the same between newborn state organization and mental Bayley at 10 weeks of age. Fish and Crockenberg (1981) did not do Bayley exams, but found a strong positive correlation between irritability in the newborn and social behavior at 9 months of age. It appears that the fullterm newborn's state of alertness and irritability is related to later mental development. Why is the direction of the relationship changed for the Gusii as compared to these American infants? If it is a result of caregiving, a clarifying question might be what aspect of the low range of state cluster scores could be salient for caregivers differentially across cultures? Caron's (1986) analysis of caretaking in relation to newborn behaviors is helpful in answering this question. The three lowest scoring infants on the late exam range of state cluster all received that rank by virtue of being quieter with less irritability, lability of state, and rapidity of build up. In the first six months, these newborns who performed poorly on the range of state cluster (i.e., the quieter infants) were held more by all caregivers than were the less quiet but well modulated infants. Mother was more available to the quieter infants. The quieter infant was viewed as more at risk and hence got more attention from mother and more holding by all. We assume that this increased attention and holding contributes in some way to the better Bayley Mental Scales performance at 8 to 10 months.

An example from the Efé of Zaire provides a contrast and a demonstration of how various aspects of caretaking behavior and values converge to form such different developmental ecological niches for infants. Winn, Morelli & Tronick found that the Efé infants who were held more by their mothers were the fussier infants (E. Tronick, personal communication, October 10, 1987). The quieter infants were held and cared for more by the many adult caretakers available; these quieter infants were favored by adults. By contrast, among the Gusii, multiple adult caretaking was not valued and rarely practiced. So when the Gusii mother turned her attention to the infant who was seen as more needy, i.e., the quieter infant in this instance, the better modulated infants were left with only a child caretaker to provide attention beyond nursing. Therefore, among the Gusii, the better modulated infants did not get the more enhancing interaction and stimulation from adults which the better modulated Efé received. We may be seeing the effect of this interaction of caretaking with newborn behavioral style in the later developmental outcome as captured on the Bayley Mental Scales.

The finding of positive correlations between state and orientation clusters and later motor development is also not consistent with the literature. Only Field et al. (1978), on their sample of high risk and premature infants, found positive correlation between neonatal orientation and later motor development. Once again we can turn to Caron's (1986) analysis for a possible explanation. Gusii newborns who performed well on state and orientation clusters were cared for more in the first 3 months by a child care-giver; the poorly performing were seen as more vulnerable and therefore cared for by mother. When cared for by a child care-giver, a Gusii newborn got more physical contact and movement than when in the mother's care. This selection of greater physical stimulation in caretaking by virtue of state and orientation skills may then lead to enhanced motor development.

Hence our unexpected results are made more comprehensible when considered in light of Gusii cultural goals for infants and their actual child care prac-

Figure 3.   Gusii children in typical child-care mixed-age group. (Source: Eliza Klein).

tices. Gusii infant care-givers bring culturally approved techniques to interactions which are designed to support the most vulnerable for survival, not to enhance the development of the most advanced. Too much unique advancement is a threat to group solidarity and would invite jealousy and all its attendant hazards.

While Caron's (1986) analysis provides a basis for making sense of the few significant correlations in our data, it may be that these correlations do not demonstrate a meaningful relationship between newborn and later infant behavior as we have measured them. We do have to note that, given the large number of correlations run on the data (3 sets of BNBAS × 7 clusters in each set × 2 sets of Bayley exams × 2 types of Bayley exams in a set), the finding of four significant correlations at the $p < .05$ level is no more than expected by chance.

The lack of more highly significant correlations may result from our use of inappropriate instruments for measuring infant behavior in another culture. We have accepted our instruments as objective and as grounded in a biological reality, separate from ourselves, universal, and inevitable. But, in fact, to a large extent these instruments are linguistic products of us and our culture-bound state. The exams we used were developed by American researchers and clinicians whose conceptualization of behavior and choices about which infant behaviors are important enough to be recorded are partly culturally shaped. In addition, both the BNBAS and Bayley are developed from observations of American infants. Our own and others' research indicates that infants' behaviors are shaped by their cultures from the earliest days of life. So these exams are constituted by descriptors of American babies (and not of a "generic" human infant), and by a culturally based selection of descriptors formed in culturally shaped language.

Both the BNBAS and the Bayley suffer from these cultural biases, the BNBAS less so. The great strength of the BNBAS is in the high degree of detail provided around any one behavioral concept. Rather than a simple score of pass or fail for the performance of a discrete behavior, a continuum of possible performances is provided with which the infant behaviors can be compared. As we demonstrated on the general tone scale, we were able to discover a type of behavior which was not included in the BNBAS, but it was the high degree of detail of the BNBAS which allowed us to detect and describe the new aspects of the continuum as seen in the Gusii babies. It remains to be seen what other types of behaviors may be discovered in cross-cultural research on newborn behavior which the BNBAS has not denoted on American infants.

The BNBAS is affected more by cultural biases in the conceptualization and scoring of the a priori clusters. In creating the a priori clusters, we are moving from the use of more objective behavioral descriptors of the scale items to the more abstract or "experience-distant" (Geertz, 1974) terms of the cluster categories. We risk the loss of the meaning of the behavior in its context by this shift to cluster terminology. And certainly our cultural bias shows in the definitions of "optimal" areas of performance on these cluster items. Take, for example, the folding of the state scores for computing the range of state cluster score. This maneuver groups both fussy and quiet infants at the poorer performing end of the scale, leaving the average modulated babies at the better performing end of the scale. This fits well our American babies and our ideas of who's more fit or more at risk, but, as noted above, the Efé don't value the average baby as much as the quiet, and the Gusii see the quiet baby as more at risk than the fussy.

Our knowledge of newborn behavior in other cultures, and especially of the meaning of that behavior, is not ready yet for the application of such culturally biased abstractions. Much more work remains to be done with data which can be derived from the BNBAS scale items themselves. The BNBAS as now constituted may suffer from omissions and distortions, but it is as close as we have to a usable instrument for beginning cross-cultural observations. The work with the BNBAS should proceed not with the assumption that we are comparing infants to an absolute standard, but with the assumption that we are using a partly culturally biased set of behavioral descriptors to discover the range and form of possible newborn behaviors. The ways in which infants of other cultures go beyond or do not conform to the BNBAS should be as much the object of our study as the scores on the scorable items themselves. The areas of nonconformity should be as completely and carefully recorded as were the American infant behaviors in the original scale development. And our observations and descriptions of these infants should be guided by "experience-near" (Geertz, 1974) descriptors from the culture in question.

Like the BNBAS, the Bayley is based on an American sample and American theories and beliefs about development. As such, it often emphasizes items that we think of as biological and universal, but which, in fact, are as much reflective of our cultural values and ecology. For example, the emphasis on the scoring of reaching for objects and handling of objects may be uniquely Western, with our value on curiosity and manipulation of objects. Moreover, we give our infants a lot of object-mediated experience, whereas the Gusii do not. The Gusii emphasize obedience and sharing among their children. The Bayley exam does not include items to capture those emerging behaviors which reflect sharing, such as the late-in-the-first-year-of-life behavior of offering to feed another and handing a toy back with a vocalization and visual contact. These are only two of many possible infant behaviors not contained in the Bayley which may be as biologically based as reach but have more meaning in this other culture.

The Bayley score system leaves even less room than the BNBAS for adaptation in another culture. The Bayley scores are simple pass or fail, not allowing for assessment or acknowledgement of a continuum of behavior around a particular response. Our observations of the Gusii infants' responses to the toy doll are a case in point. The vast majority of infants we tested, starting from around 9 months of age, reacted to the toy doll with fear or wariness or withdrawal. We were usually unable to score the specific doll item because of these responses. In fact, Gusii adults reacted to the doll in a similar but more modulated way. They told us that the inert form (of the doll) was too much like a dead baby. The range of Gusii infant behaviors to the doll was limited and predictable; scored, it could be a meaningful measure of infant development in the Gusii culture. But as the Bayley is constituted, none of the Gusii infants' responses could be captured and used in the assessment.

Our study of infant behavior is directed by a belief in the biological grounding of behavior and by a desire to understand the relative roles of biology and culture in the behavioral outcome. In fact, in many ways the behaviors of newborns and young infants of all cultures look compellingly similar and evocative to an adult of any culture. The argument in this chapter is not that there are not biological bases for behavior nor universal behaviors, but that the biological may be better thought of as a mechanism for mapping environment and culture on behavior, and not as a fixed set of constraints or capacities. Also, great care must be taken in making assumptions about the universal applicability of our methods of measurement and the results they yield, because of the strong cultural influences on what we can see in our own infants' behaviors and on the ways we can conceptualize their behaviors.

In summary, we identified uniquely strong and controlled motor tone and a significantly high degree of motor maturity in the Gusii newborns on the BNBAS exam. While the Gusii infants also performed well on the Bayley Scales of Motor

Development, we were unable to trace the newborn profiles directly to their later motor development. In addition, contrary to findings on other samples, Gusii newborn orientation did not predict to later mental development and Gusii newborn state organization predicted negatively to later mental development. These results are explained somewhat when considered in light of Gusii beliefs and goals for infants, and in light of observations of Gusii care-giver–infant interaction, demonstrating the cultural mediation of the relationship between newborn and later infant development. In addition, these results lead us to argue strongly for more recognition of the cultural biases in our methods of infant assessment and for the adaptation of these instruments for more accurate and meaningful recording of infant behavior in all cultures.

References

Aubry, R.H., & Pennington, J.C. (1973). Identification and evaluation of the high-risk pregnancy: The perinatal concept. *Clinical Obstetrics and Gynecology, 16,* 1–27.

Bayley, N. (1969). *Manual for the Bayley Scales of Infant Development.* New York: Psychological Corporation.

Brazelton, T.B. (1973). *Neonatal Behavioral Assessment Scale.* London: William Heinemann Medical Books Ltd., Spastics International Medical Publications.

Brazelton, T.B., Koslowski, B., & Tronick, E. (1976). Neonatal behavior among urban Zambians and Americans. *Journal of the American Academy of Child Psychiatry, 15,* 97–107.

Brazelton, T.B., Robey, J.S., & Collier, G.A. (1969). Infant development in the Zinacanteco Indians of Southern Mexico. *Pediatrics, 44,* 274–290.

Caron, J.W. (1986). Infant effects on caretaker responsiveness: Influences of infant characteristics on the infant care environment among the Gusii of Kenya. Unpublished doctoral dissertation, Harvard University. *Dissertation Abstracts International, 46,* 12832B.

Dixon, S., Keefer, C.H., Tronick, E., & Brazelton, T.B. (1982). Perinatal circumstances and newborn outcome among the Gusii of Kenya: Assessment of risk. *Infant Behavior and Development, 5,* 11–32.

Dixon, S., LeVine, R.A., & Brazelton, T.B. (1982). Malnutrition: a closer look at the problem in an East African village. *Developmental Medicine and Child Neurology, 24,* 670–685.

Dubowitz, L.M.S., Dubowitz, V., & Goldberg, C. (1970). Clinical assessment of gestational age in the newborn infant. *Journal of Pediatrics, 77,* 1–10.

Field, T., Hallock, N., Ting, G., Dempsey, J., Dabiri, C., & Shuman, H.H. (1978). A first-year follow up of high-risk infants: Formulating a cumulative risk index. *Child Development, 49,* 119–131.

Fish, M., & Crockenberg, S. (1981). Correlates and antecedents of nine-month infant behavior and mother-infant interaction. *Infant Behavior and Development, 4,* 69–81.

Freedman, D.G., & Freedman, N. (1969). Behavioral differences between Chinese-American and American newborns. *Nature, 224,* 1227.

Geertz, C. (1984). "From the native's point of view": On the nature of anthropological understanding. In R.A. Shweder & R.A. LeVine (Eds.), *Culture theory: Essays on mind, self and emotion*. Cambridge, Cambridge University Press.

Goldberg, S.A. (1971, April). *Infant care and growth in urban Zambia*. Presented at meetings of Society for Research on Child Development, Minneapolis, MN.

Keefer, C.H., Tronick, E., Dixon, S., & Brazelton, T.B. (1982). Specific differences in motor performance between Gusii and American newborns and a modification of the Neonatal Behavioral Assessment Scale. *Child Development, 53,* 754–759.

Lester, B.M., Als, H., & Brazelton, T.B. (1982). Regional obstetric anesthesia and newborn behavior: a reanalysis toward synergistic effects. *Child Development, 53,* 687–692.

LeVine, R.A., & LeVine, B.B. (1966). *Nyansongo: A Gusii community in Kenya*. New York: Wiley.

Mosley, W.H. (1980). *Population growth, family size expectations and the level of contraceptive practice among married couples. Implications for strategy and planning of the National Family Planning Program in Kenya*. Unpublished manuscript, Population Studies and Research Institute, University of Nairobi.

Prechtl, H.F.R. (1968). Neurological findings in newborn infants after pre- and paranatal complications. In J.H.P. Jonxis, H.K.A. Vissen, & J.A. Troelstra (Eds.), *Aspects of praematurity and dysmaturity*. Springfield, IL: Charles C. Thomas.

Rosenblith, J. (1974). Relations between neonatal behaviors and those at eight months. *Developmental Psychology, 10,* 779–792.

Sostek, A.M., & Anders, T.F. (1977). Relationships among the Brazelton Neonatal Scale, Bayley Infant Scales and early temperament. *Child Development, 48,* 320–328.

Vaughn, B.E., Taraldson, B., Crichton, L., & Egeland, B. (1980). Relationships between neonatal behavioral organization and infant behavior during the first year of life. *Infant Behavior and Development, 3,* 47–66.

Whiting, B.B., & Whiting, J.W.M. (1975). *Children of six cultures: A psychocultural analysis*. Cambridge, MA: Harvard University Press.

CHAPTER 3

The Influence of Infant Irritability on the Development of the Mother–Infant Relationship in the First 6 Months of Life*

Dymphna C. van den Boom

University of Leiden

Recent perspectives on the development of interaction in infancy stress the reciprocal nature of the parent–infant relationship. However, in general, in empirical research the reciprocal nature of interactions has been its most neglected aspect, and it is, in fact, also the most difficult to analyze and specify. Studies focused on infant attachment, for instance, concentrated more or less exclusively on the caregiver's role, attributing the quality of attachment to the quality of caregiving provided to the infant. This focus is certainly not inappropriate, given the large body of research indicating that caregiver behavior is related to the quality of an infant's attachment relationship to the caregiver at the age of 1 year. In particular these studies suggest that the development of a secure attachment relationship seems to be most dependent on the sensitivity of the caregiver to the infant's signals (Ainsworth, Blehar, Waters, & Wall, 1978).

This analysis does not, however, address the antecedents of caregiver sensitivity, and leaves open the possibility that there may be attributes of the infant or of the environment that may contribute to the quality of caregiving provided (Sameroff & Chandler, 1975). Some infants may be less effective in eliciting responses from their caregivers, and some environmental factors may preclude

---

* This research was supported by the Netherlands Organization for the Advancement of Pure Scientific Research. The author gratefully acknowledges Gera Kofman, Yvonne Mathijsen, and Daniëlle Mol for assistance in collecting the data, and André Nierop for his help in analyzing the data. The author's address: Department of Developmental and Educational Psychology, University of Leiden, Wassenaarseweg 52, 2300 RB Leiden.

caregiver sensitivity to infant cues. In such cases one would indeed find a relation between attachment security and caregiver sensitivity, but it would be inappropriate to implicate the caregiver as the single causal agent (Holmes, Ruble, Kowalski, & Lauesen, 1984).

In the specific context of parent–child relationships, the idea that the child is an active participant has been most vigorously propounded by Bell (1968, 1977). If this fact is accepted it follows that characteristics of the infant should be taken into account when studying mother–infant interaction.

In this study we investigated the influence of infant irritability (assessed shortly after birth) on the development of the mother–infant relationship during the first 6 months of life. To detect possible differences in patterns of interaction in dyads with irritable and nonirritable infants, naturalistic observations were made at home. Observed behavior in the home is likely to be closer to "normal parent–child interaction" than is behavior arranged and observed in the laboratory (Lytton, 1980). During the first year of life infant behavior changes quickly due to maturational and environmental forces impinging on the child. Therefore, developmental changes in social interaction can only be described accurately if one observes regularly and if the time lapse between observations is short.

The remainder of this chapter describes first the culture from which the data were gathered. Then, the general plan of the study is set out and data are reported on the developmental change in social interactions in dyads with irritable and nonirritable infants in Dutch lower-class families.

The Setting

The Netherlands lie in the Northwestern part of Europe. On the north and the west the country is bounded by the North Sea, on the east by Germany, and on the south by Belgium. For the most part the landscape is flat; only the very south is hilly.

The Netherlands is a small country (36.842 km^2) with a very good railway and road system. Therefore, traveling is easy and does not take much time. Because of the small distances to each other there is a lot of social contact between close relatives.

The families whom we studied lived in a thickly populated area in the west of the country. As in most studies we used a social class categorization to select lower-class families, which constitute the sample for this study. Although in different countries the same labels are used for the subdivision in social classes, this is no guarantee that what is meant by a particular class in one country is the same in other countries; e.g., lower-class families according to Dutch standards would be considered upper-lower or lower-middle class according to American standards. One of the reasons for this is the very good social security system in the Netherlands with consequently little poverty. This system consists of a number of employee and national insurances which replace, supplement, or guarantee income. One aspect of this social security system is the system of health insurance. By government regulation everyone below a certain income level is compulsorily insured. Seventy percent of the Dutch population falls below this income level. The majority of the other 30% is privately insured. The insured services include general practitioner services, inpatient and outpatient care, and postnatal care.

Demographic Description of the Netherlands

Since the beginning of this century the population has grown rapidly. In 1900 it was 5.1 million, and now it is almost 14 million. Few parts of the world have such a high population density as the Netherlands. Statistical data show that, at present, the average number of inhabitants per square kilometre is 384. The density of population shows considerable diversity. Economic factors are held especially accountable for density variation. A noteworthy feature of Dutch demography is that nearly one third of the total population is concentrated in the low-lying polder region of the Western Netherlands, where the large cities are situated, e.g., Amsterdam, the capital, Rotterdam, and The Hague, the seat of the government. This polder region, spreading over three of the twelve provinces, namely North Holland, South Holland, and Utrecht, and constituting only two-ninths of the country's area, is referred to as the "Randstad Holland" or "Edgetown Holland," because of the number and closeness of big cities.

The sample for this study was drawn from Leiden, a smaller town in the "Randstad Holland" and famous for its university, as well as from the rural population of eight villages lying in the Leiden area. In the following section we shall more specifically characterize a feature which makes the Netherlands unique among Western industrialized countries, namely the high proportion of home deliveries and a low infant mortality rate.

Dutch Perinatal Care

The Netherlands stands out from other western countries in the high proportion of deliveries occuring at home. This is possible because few people live more than 9 miles from a hospital. However, this situation of home deliveries is changing. In 1960 about 70% of deliveries took place at home. In less than 20 years this is reduced to 40% (van Arkel, Ament, & Bell, 1980). The Netherlands has a strong and long tradition of supervision of pregnancy and delivery by midwives. Despite the changes in location of delivery, the proportion of deliveries supervised by midwives has remained the same. The midwife has lost less ground in home deliveries and has actually increased the proportion of deliveries supervised by her which take place in the hospital. The category of hospital deliveries includes what are known as *outpatient deliveries*. In these cases the hospital stay is restricted to 1 or 2 days. Approximately 10% of hospital deliveries are outpatient deliveries.

Theoretically, the obstetrician attends all hospital deliveries upon referral from the general practitioner or the midwife. In comparison to their North American colleagues Dutch obstetricians appear to be conservative in the use of techniques such as instrumental deliveries and Cesarean sections. In 1975 instrumental deliveries were eight times as high, and Cesarean sections were three times as high, in the United States than the Netherlands (van Arkel et al., 1981). The incidence of drug use among mothers before, during, and after their deliveries seems to be different, too. Although the United States maintains no registry on drugs released by the FDA for clinical use, all available statistics indicate that, for drugs as a class, drug administration for obstetrical purposes is on the increase (Brackbill, 1979). The use of obstetrical medication seems to be much lower in the Netherlands. Midwives, for instance, are not allowed to prescribe or administer drugs, so every delivery done by a midwife is done without the use of any medication. In the hospitals one seems to be conservative too in the use of obstetric medication. The changes that have occurred in the last 20 years in the Netherlands can be summarized as follows: the specialist has gained an increasing role in deliveries and practices in the hospital setting; the midwife has maintained her share of deliveries and has partly moved into the hospital setting; and the general practitioner has lost ground, particularly in home deliveries (van Arkel et al., 1981).

Postnatal care services are an important element in the whole of perinatal care in the Netherlands. For both home and outpatient deliveries, postnatal nursing is an essential element of the service pattern. This care is provided by maternity aides in the home after both types of deliveries. There is a well organized system of postnatal care aides. Besides that, every mother visits a health center for infants and toddlers when her child is 1, 2, 3, 6, 9, 12, 14, and 30 months of age. Nearly every mother uses this service system. During the visits the child is examined by a physician, and the mother is given advice concerning changes in feeding schedule—the kind of food to give to her child and whatever questions she might have about raising it.

Family Life

The population type within the "Randstad"—from which the sample for this study was drawn—is regarded as the result of a complex process of industrialism and urbanism through which institutions and the people are showing adaptability in response to conditions of rapid social change. The nuclear family is the dominant and universal family form in this region and has reached a high level of individualization. Since the influence of urbanization is universal throughout the Netherlands, the rural–urban differences are greatly minimized. Practically every Dutch village is within half an hour's drive of a town of 20,000 or more inhabitants. In fact the modern urban family has evolved out of the rural one and, indeed, seems to be but a few steps ahead of its rural counterpart in its adaptation to modern conditions of life. One difference that can still be observed between rural and urban people is that the former are more home and family minded. Although this difference was much stronger before the process of urbanization and industrialization, it still exists.

What will be said about family life in this section will be restricted to lower-class families, since these constituted this study's sample. In the Netherlands mothers are permitted 6 weeks paid maternity leave. Once this was expended, however, most mothers in our sample did not return to work. One of the reasons for this is the preference for full-time motherhood. The ideology that "a woman's place is in the home" is still rooted in the cultural traditions of these families. Another reason might be that most of these women do not have much school training and thus not very interesting jobs. So quite a few were glad that they were having a baby, so that they could quit their uninteresting jobs.

Nearly all of the families live in small apartments or small houses. All apartments and houses have at least three rooms, in addition to a kitchen. Most of the babies have their own bedroom. Only a few share the bedroom of the parents. Home furnishings remain generally simple, with only necessities present.

A routine weekday varies, depending on the kind of job the father has. In some professions (e.g., building workers) fathers work on the shift system. They leave for work very early in the morning (around 6 a.m.) and return around 4:00 in the afternoon. In other professions (e.g., drivers, fishermen) the father stays away for a week or several weeks and has leave after that. In still other jobs (e.g., clerks) the father leaves for work around 8:30 a.m. and returns at 5 p.m. The daily schedule is determined by the father's working hours.

Household chores are done in the morning and daily food shopping in the afternoon. When the husband returns from work, the family eats the main meal, then customarily rests for an hour afterward. Dutch fathers returning from work spend relatively little time observing or interacting with their young babies. Evening is spent in relaxing at home while watching t.v. or rented videotapes, going to local cafes, or entertaining family or friends.

The foregoing is a description of the ecological context in which our study took place. Knowledge about the context in which the behavior under study occurs is necessary to avoid serious errors in interpretation. It is important to have sufficient knowledge of the group under study to understand properly how the observed behaviors are embedded in the culture or subculture. We set out to provide an account of the developmental changes in social interactions during the first year of life in the Leiden area in the Netherlands. In doing so we were working in our own community. This has the advantage of being able to fully understand both the ecological context in which the behavior occurs and the cultural meaning of a particular behavior.

Infant Irritability and Social Interaction

Both parent and child constitute important elements in one another's interpersonal environment. Because influence flows in both directions, neither person nor environment stands still, and this is true whether one is taking the parent or the child as the focus of analysis. For either party, both person and environment have been influenced to some degree by prior interactions between the pair (Maccoby & Jacklin, 1983). In describing developmental changes in patterns of interaction it is therefore important to take into account both the initial constitution of the infant and the social environment. Especially in the first year of life the rate of development is high and is influenced by maturational and environmental factors. In studying the contribution of the infant to the interactional process, it is thus desirable to assess individual differences shortly after birth, and also to do the assessment independent of caretaker behavior. The Neonatal Behavioral Assessment Scale (Brazelton, 1973) offers this possibility. We were especially interested in the role of infant irritability in the regulation of social interactions, because, despite many years of research and numerous published articles on infant crying, surprisingly little is known about the topic (Lester, 1985).

Developmental changes in patterns of interaction in dyads with infants, selected on irritability, have not been studied very often. Only Crockenberg and her colleagues followed such a group during the first few years of life. A first study showed that a combination of infant irritability and lack of social support negatively influenced the quality of mother–infant attachment (Crockenberg, 1981). The results of a second study, however, indicate that mothers with an initially irritable infant engaged in a lot of social interaction when the infants were 9 months of age (Fish & Crockenberg, 1981). The results are interpreted as follows: Crying of the infant elicits interaction from the caretaker, which in turn stimulates positive social behavior of the infant. This results in increased stimulating behavior by the mother. Fish and Crockenberg (1981) point out the possibility that this pattern of responsive behavior of the caretaker in initially irritable infants might be a function of certain characteristics of their sample. Firstly, all of their mothers had high school training. Secondly, they got a lot of social support in raising their children. That these variables might have influenced the results seems to be supported by a study of Vaughn, Egeland, and

Sroufe (1979), who found that lower-class mothers experience more stress and less support from their environment than middle-class mothers. The results of these studies indicate that a combination of infant irritability and low social support is a risk factor in the development of the quality of the mother–infant relationship.

The purpose of our study was to describe in detail the developmental changes in patterns of interaction in a group of mothers with irritable and nonirritable infants during the first 6 months of life. Despite the dearth of information about early mother–infant interactions, and widespread beliefs about the long-term importance of the initial formation of the relationship, very little is known about how the process occurs and what variations are related to maternal or infant influences.

Assessment of Infant Irritability

The Neonatal Behavioral Assessment Scale (NBAS) offers the possibility to assess individual differences shortly after birth and to do the assessment independent of caretaker behavior. The primary aim of the NBAS is the detection of individual differences in full-term infants. We chose the NBAS instead of other scales for newborns, e.g., the neurological examination technique developed by Prechtl and Beintema (1964), because their method is intended to be sufficiently insensitive so as not to reveal individual differences between normal infants. The instrument is designed to differentiate between normal and specific abnormalities (Prechtl, 1982). Other formalized behavioral examination techniques which are specifically designed for the newborn full-term infant the Graham Behavioral Test for Neonates (Graham, Matarazzo, & Caldwell, 1956) and its modified version the Graham/Rosenblith scale (Rosenblith, 1961) are both designed to identify groups of infants "at risk."

The NBAS consists of 27 behavior items scored on a nine-point scale and 18 reflex items, which are usually combined into seven a priori clusters (Lester, Als, & Brazelton, 1982). One of these clusters, "range of state," relates to infant irritability. In our study we used the items "peak of excitement," "rapidity of buildup," and "irritability" to divide our sample of infants into an irritable and a nonirritable group. We did not use the item "lability of state" to determine the degree of infant irritability. In a pilot study we observed that infants who are extremely irritable can only be soothed for very short periods of time. These periods are too short to be counted as a state change. So, extremely irritable infants scored low on the item "lability of state." Other researchers interested in irritability in infants also determine the degree of irritability by means of the scoring on the items "peak of excitement," "rapidity of buildup," and "irritability" (Kaye, 1978; Crockenberg, 1981). To assess degree of irritability, we used the same criterion Crockenberg (1981) used. Infants with a mean score of six or higher on three items of the cluster "range of state" on two administrations of the NBAS were considered irritable.

Procedures

The subjects in this report were 30 firstborn infants (16 females and 14 males), and their mothers, who were recruited through the obstetrics department of the University Hospital and through midwives in the Leiden area. Approximately 67% of the women approached agreed to participate in the study, and only two of them did not complete the project through the first half of the first year. All the families were lower class, as indicated by the social group division of the Central Bureau of Statistics.

When they joined the study 29 families were intact, with only one father unemployed. One mother was single. In all instances the mother was the primary caretaker. The age range of the mothers at the time of birth was 19–33 years (mean: 24.7 years).

All infants were carried to term (between 38 and 42 weeks) and had birth-weights of at least 2,500 grams. The sample contained no dysmature infants. No complications occured during labor. Apgar scores were at least seven and eight at 1 and 5 minutes, respectively.

All mothers and infants were in good physical condition after delivery and were not considered at risk.

The Neonatal Behavioral Assessment Scale

Instructions for administering and scoring the NBAS were followed exactly as described in Brazelton (1973). The assessments were made in the infant's homes on the tenth day of life, and all infants for whom data are presented in this report had been examined for the first time by the thirteenth day of life. The second exam was scheduled for 5 days after the first. The most common reason for delaying either of the two exams was the examination of the infant's hips, which is done in the Leiden area during the second week after birth, and the blood test to check for signs of phenylketonuria. The principal investigator administered the NBAS during the course of the study.*

Scores from the "peak of excitement," "rapidity of buildup," and "irritability" items were combined in an irritability cluster and averaged across the two administrations. Infants whose irritability scores were six or higher were

---

* The principal investigator was trained to administer the NBAS at the Child Development Unit of The Children's Hospital Medical Center in Boston by Dr. Brazelton and his group.

considered irritable; those with scores below six were considered nonirritable. The NBAS had to be administered in 89 cases to find the predetermined number of 15 irritable infants (17%). Besides these 15 irritable infants, the sample consisted of 15 nonirritable infants. The average irritability scores of the irritable and the nonirritable group were 6.42 and 2.78, respectively.

Mother–Infant Observations

During the first 6 months of life, mother–infant interaction was observed at home every month on two occasions lasting 40 minutes each. One visit was scheduled in the morning, the other one in the afternoon. So, every month we collected 80 minutes of observational data per dyad.

The most important problem in studies of this kind is choosing what to record. Choosing direct observations as a methodology does not in itself determine the categories of behavior to be recorded. We produced our list of behavioral categories out of a long series of pilot observations using intuitive usefulness and reliability as the main criteria of selection. The observational system consisted of 14 categories for infant behavior and 23 categories for the mother. For the infant the behavioral codes were concentrated around positive and negative social behaviors. In case of the mother, stimulating and soothing behaviors were registered. The observational system included ten categories for soothing behavior, since we were interested in the kind of strategies mothers use to calm their infants.

The observational procedure was based on a combination of the time-and-event sampling technique in which the behavior of both mother and child was registered every 6 seconds (indicated by high-pitched beeps from a timer which only the observer could hear by way of an earphone). The form of behavior record chosen was a code that served as a kind of shorthand. The observational data were collected using a sheet of paper consisting of 10 lines. Each line was divided into 10 6-second parts. Mother behaviors were listed above the line, while infant behaviors were listed below the line. In using this method, we did not simply collect frequency data, but our measure was truly interactive and the sequence of behavior was preserved. We wanted to obtain as dynamic a picture of the infant–mother relationship as possible, and not merely a frequency count of behavior.

Every month one visit was paid by one observer, while the other visit was done by two observers. Only the principal investigator knew whether an infant was irritable or not. The other observers did not. In order to obtain 80 minutes of observational data, more than two visits to the home were sometimes required. When an infant fell asleep, observation was stopped, and, if the infant did not awaken within a reasonable time, another visit was scheduled. The first observer (always the same person) explained the course of things to the mother during the visits. The mothers were instructed that the observer was interested in studying the infant's behavior. The observer remained out of the infant's sight as much as possible. Moreover, the mother was to try to forget the presence of the observer and not engage her in conversation. Prior to observation, the observer spent time with the mother with the aim of putting her at ease. Although every attempt was made to make the observation session as natural as possible, the presence of the observer is bound to have an effect. However, this is the only procedure available for collecting this kind of data.

We computed interobserver agreement by having two observers observe the same interaction and code it independently. When both observers coded the same categories within a 6-second interval, it was counted as an agreement (A). When they coded the same behavior by different codes, it was counted as a disagreement (D). Agreement was then calculated by the formula $A/(A + D)$. The reliability coefficients for the mother codes ranged from .42, for one code with a very low frequency, to .92. The reliability coefficients for the infant codes ranged from .36 for one code, with a very low frequency, to .94. These results are comparable to the results obtained in other research in this area. In fact, to achieve agreement on recording precisely the same action at the same time in a free-flowing situation with a multitude of activities going on is extremely difficult (Lytton, 1980), and the criterion employed was therefore quite a severe one.

Through these monthly observations we tried to gain a detailed insight into the developing relationship between mother and child.

Infant Evaluation

Infant irritability was determined by means of three items of the cluster "range of state" from the Neonatal Behavioral Assessment Scale (Brazelton, 1973). In order to be able to score these particular items, the NBAS had to be administered totally. One of the problems in analyzing the items of the NBAS is that many of the scale items are metrically or distributionally inimical to common statistical manipulations. All items are not constructed alike as an equal interval scale that goes from poor to excellent. For some items a mid-range score is considered optimal, with different behavioral implications at either extreme. Nor are the items independent (Brazelton, 1978). Because of the lack of uniformity in the statistical properties of the subscales, many different kinds of analysis have been attempted. In deciding to use the computerprogram PRINCALS (Gifi, 1983), we add another technique to the list. Since this technique is pretty new and, to our knowledge, has never been used on the NBAS, we will first give a description of this type of analysis.

PRINCALS is an acronym for *PRIN*cipal *C*omponents *A*nalysis by means of *A*lternating *L*east *S*quares. PRINCALS is an extension of *principal components analysis* (PCA) in that it can not only handle numerical variables but ordinal and nominal variables as well. As in factor analyses, in PRINCALS the number of dimensions is determined in advance. The *eigenvalue* of a dimension is the amount of variance explained by that dimension. The *sum* of the eigenvalues of the dimensions is the total amount of variance explained (*total fit*). The contribution of a variable to the dimensions is expressed in *component loadings*. These component loadings could be compared to factor scores in factor analyses. The component loadings are represented graphically on the first two dimensions as points in a multidimensional space. The horizontal axis represents the first dimension, the vertical axis the second one. The representation of the variables can be elucidated by drawing vectors between the component loadings and the origin (Gifi, 1983). The length of the vector indicates the amount of variance explained by a variable (single fit). Variables with long vectors of about equal length, which are placed close together, are highly correlated and form a cluster. Orthogonal vectors of about equal length are independent. A dimension is named after the variable with the highest component loading on the longest vector (related to that particular dimension). Short vectors explain less of the variance, but they can also contribute to naming a dimension.

The scores of the subjects (object scores) are represented in the same multidimensional space. By placing both representations (of items and subjects) on top of each other, the relative importance of particular items for particular subjects is determined. In this way the projection of object scores onto the vectors of the items become visible. The placement of subjects provides information about their mutual relationships: Object scores of subjects with the same item pattern are placed close to each other in a cluster, while object scores of subjects with a different item pattern are placed more peripheral.

The advantage of PRINCALS is that data can be treated on a lower measurement level (e.g., ordinal or nominal) than is usually required for statistical techniques like factor analysis, regression analysis, etc. We preferred to use a statistical technique to discover the structure of the NBAS-data in our sample, since we were working with an atypical group (irritable and nonirritable infants). Both examinations of the total sample were analyzed by means of PRINCALS. One variable was omitted from the analyses of the scale. This was "smiles," because of the absence of any variance on this item. A two-dimensional solution was retained for reasons of interpretability. Two dimensions accounted for 52% of the variance. This is on the order of the amount accounted for in typical factor analyses of these kinds of data. The geometrical display of the items is shown in Figure 1.

The first dimension, which accounts for 40% of the variance, is associated with degree of irritability. The second dimension, accounting for 12% of the variance, is associated with habituation. Six clusters can be identified. In labeling the clusters, we used the same set of names as Lester et al. (1982), for reasons of consensus. The first cluster is *habituation*. It contains the response-decrement items except for the pinprick. This cluster should be viewed carefully,

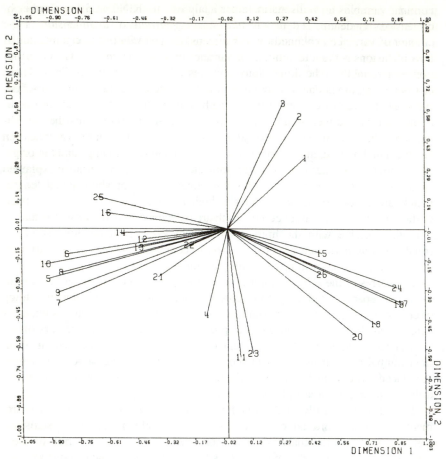

Figure 1.   PRINCALS of the NBAS-items (first and second exam), two dimensions. Eigenvalues .40, .12; total fit .52.

however, since it has some missing data, especially in the pinprick. The second cluster seems to be best identified as *orientation,* since it contains all the orientation items on the scale, which measure responsivity during quiet alert periods. The third cluster with the items motor maturity and pull-to-sit has been labeled *motor maturity.* All the scores of the items in the fourth cluster reflect an early reached continuous state of arousal. This cluster is called *range of state.* The fifth cluster is somewhat more related to state-control processes. It is defined by cuddliness, consolability, and self-quieting. This cluster is called *regulation of state.* Our last cluster, consisting of tremors and startles, is related to *autonomic stability.* Of the remaining items—tonus, skin color, defensive movement, and hand-to-mouth—the last two seem to be related to the cluster *range of state,* while the first two form a separate cluster opposite to the *habituation* cluster on the second dimension. It seems to be somewhat related to *range of state,* too.

The majority of investigators who have used the NBAS attempted to use some form of factor analysis to reduce the number of scores in the scale. When we compare our PRINCALS solution to the factor solutions summarized by Sameroff (1978), many similarities are found. The two large clusters *orientation* and *range of state* are nearly identical with the factor solutions, except that our *range of state* cluster includes activity. The same holds for *habituation,* except for the pinprick, which, however, had a lot of missing data, and in factor analysis the pinprick is loosely related to the other three items, too. The next three clusters are not completely identical to the factors found in factor analyses, but they all contain some items, which are in accordance with the items loading on the factors labeled *tonus* and *quieting* by Sameroff (1978).

How do our PRINCALS clusters compare with the a priori clusters identified by Lester et al. (1982)? The *habituation* cluster differs, in that the pinprick is not included in our case. The *orientation* cluster is the same. We did not find a clear *motor* cluster. The only items from that cluster that seem to be related are motor maturity and pull-to-sit. Our *range of state* cluster includes activity. On the other hand, our cluster *regulation of state* does not include hand-to-mouth, which seems to be more related to the *range of state* cluster in our sample. Our *autonomic stability* cluster contains the items tremors and startles and not skin color.

The conclusion from this comparison of clusters and factors is that, while there is substantial overlap, there are several instances where inconsistencies occur which might be related to the specific characteristics of the population under study (half of the sample are irritable babies). Since our sample differs on certain characteristics of research interest, it seems reasonable to suppose that these differences are at least partly determining differences in the resulting solution.

The corresponding representation of infants consists of 58 points in this two-dimensional space (29 infants × 2 administration). We had to remove one infant from the analysis. This infant (who was extremely irritable) had such extreme scores that, if he was included in the analysis, all the other infants clustered together. This representation of infants must be placed on top of the representation of the items. The intersections of the dimensions coincide, because the points lie in the same space. In this way one can determine which items are relatively important for which infants. By connecting the points of both administrations for every infant, one gets information about the stability of the two exams. The larger the distance between two points, the less stable; the closer two points are represented in the two-dimensional space, the more stable both exams are.

As can be seen in Figure 2, the irritable infants are placed in the right hand side of the two-dimensional space, meaning that the items of the cluster *range of*

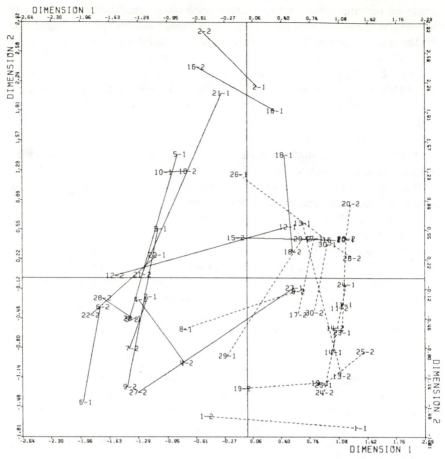

Figure 2. PRINCALS of the subjects (first and second exam), two dimensions. Eigenvalues .40, .12; total fit .52. ———— nonirritable infants. --------- irritable infants.

state are relatively important in these infants, as would be expected, since they were selected on this cluster. The nonirritable infants are placed on the left hand side of the origin, where the cluster *orientation* dominates primarily. Figure 2 also shows that two nonirritable infants (15, 18) seem to belong more to the irritable group, whereas infant 8 (an irritable infant) is placed in the nonirritable group on the first exam. But on the whole, the division between irritable and nonirritable infants is very clear. As for stability, it can be seen that in some infants the results of both exams are more stable (e.g., 2 and 16) than in others (e.g., 12 and 21). Although, in general, there is some distance between the two exams of one infant, most of the infants remain on the same side of the origin on both exams. This indicates that infants do not change in classification (irritable or nonirritable), and that on both exams the same cluster of items dominates infant functioning.

The PRINCALS solution allows us to draw some general conclusions about the NBAS data in our sample. The first dimension shows that infants scoring high on *range of state* score low on *orientation,* and vice versa. They also score low on the *regulation of state* and the *motor* cluster. So, generally speaking, in our sample irritable infants are bad orienters, are not good at state regulation, score low on motor maturity, and are of course irritable and active (since activity is included in our *range of state* cluster).

Using PRINCALS to discover the structure of the NBAS data has several advantages. In the first place, it allowed us to treat the data on an ordinal measurement level (instead of an interval level), which is more in accord with how the items actually behave and should be treated. Secondly, the items and subjects are visualized, so that it is easy to identify, e.g., extreme scoring subjects, which can then be removed from further analyses in order to avoid distortion of the solutions. Thirdly, it shows the mutual relationships between items by placing them graphically on the dimensions.

Observational Data

To detect developmental changes in patterns of interaction of the mother–infant dyads during the first 6 months of life, the observational data were analyzed by means of correspondence analysis. This statistical technique was selected, because it treats the observational data on a nominal measurement level. In contrast with tests for statistical significance, correspondence analysis is a more exploratory technique. Confirmation of the results must be gained from replication studies.

Correspondence analysis has been the most important data analysis technique in France for many years (Van der Heijden, 1985). Interest in this technique is growing rapidly in the English speaking countries, too. This recent popularity of correspondence analysis is probably due to the appealing geometrical aspect of the method. Correspondence analysis allows one to construct a multidimensional representation of the dependence between the row and column variables of a two-way contingency table. The rows and columns are represented as points in a multidimensional space. Rows with corresponding profiles are represented close to each other. These profiles are calculated by converting row frequencies to row probabilities that add up to one. The same applies to the columns. In case of a unique relationship between a row and a column, these are not only represented close to each other, but also more peripheral. For more details we refer to

Greenacre (1981), who wrote a practical introduction to correspondence analysis, and to Gifi (1981), who discusses relations between correspondence analysis and other techniques for exploratory, multivariate data analysis.

The observational data are summarized as follows, in a two-way matrix (see Figure 3).

The columns of the matrix contain the observational categories for both mother and infant (a total of 37). The rows represent the 30 mother–infant dyads, and the data are arranged per month. So the first row consists of data from the first dyad in the first month. The second row contains data from the first dyad in the second month, etc. Since every dyad was observed during 6 months, the total number of rows is 180. The cells of the matrix contain the frequencies of the observational categories for the dyads.

The matrix was subjected to correspondence analysis with a program called ANACOR (Gifi, 1982). A three-dimensional solution "explains" 64% of the value of χ^2. The first two dimensions are shown in Figure 4.

The observational categories placed near the pole of a dimension, furthest away from the intersection of the two dimensions, are decisive in naming the poles of that dimension. Compared to the other observational categories, these categories must have a reasonably high total frequency and not be unique for one

	OBSERVATIONAL CATEGORIES MOTHER								OBSERVATIONAL CATEGORIES INFANT							
	L	A	P	V+	V	S	SE	PS	L	LA	V+	V	SM	F	C	P
Dyad 1 Month 1																
Dyad 1 Month 2																
Dyad 1 Month 3																
Dyad 1 Month 4																
Dyad 1 Month 5																
Dyad 1 Month 6																
Dyad 2 Month 1																
Dyad 2 Month 2																

Figure 3.   Contingency table of the observational data.

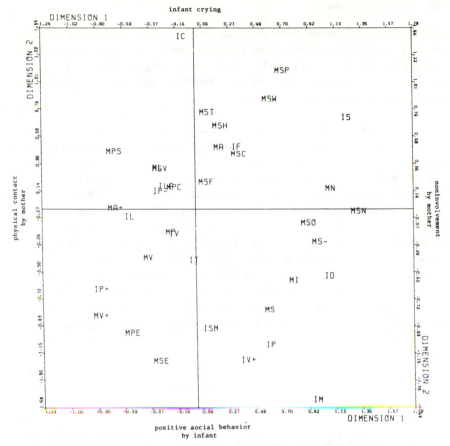

Figure 4. Correspondence analysis of the observational categories, first two dimensions. Singular values and percentage of information explained: $\lambda_1 = .33$ (.27); $\lambda_2 = .28$ (.20).

EXPLANATION OF THE ABBREVIATIONS USED FOR THE OBSERVATIONAL CATEGORIES:

MOTHER CATEGORIES:

ML = look; MA = attention; MP = positive expression; MV+ = positive vocalization; MV = other vocalizations; MS = stimulation; MSE = effective stimulation; MPS = physical stimulation; MPE = effective physical stimulation; MA+ = affective contact; MPC = physical contact; MSW = soothe by walking; MSC = soothe by picking up; MSH = soothe by holding; MSV = soothe by vocalizing; MSF = soothe by feeding; MST = soothe by touching; MSP = soothe by giving pacifier; MSO = soothe by offering object; MSN = soothe by ending a negative situation; MS = negative soothing behavior; MI = inability to soothe; MN = noninvolvement.

INFANT CATEGORIES:

IL = look; ILA = look at; IV+ = positive vocalization; IV = other vocalizations; ISM = smile; IF = fuss; IC = cry; IP = take object; IM = manipulate; ID = drop object; IP+ = positive physical expression; IP− = negative physical expression; IT = threatening situation; IS = suck.

dyad. As Figure 4 shows, the first dimension (27% of the total inertia is decomposed in this dimension) goes from affective contact by mother to mother behavior not directed at the infant. The observational category "sooth by ending a negative situation for the infant" is less important for naming the second pole of this dimension, because this category has a very low frequency. The first dimension then represents the amount of physical contact between mother and infant. The second dimension goes from infant crying to smiling. This second dimension (representing 20% of the information) represents the kind of social behavior shown by the infant. The third dimension (not depicted in Figure 4), finally, goes from looking by the mother to soothing. This dimension is a representation of the mother's activity in soothing her crying infant.

The corresponding representation of mother–infant dyads consists of 180 points in this two-dimensional space (30 dyads × 6 months). By placing this representation on top of the representation of the observational categories, it can be determined which behaviors occur relatively often in which dyads. By then connecting the points for 6 months for every dyad, a picture of the developmental changes in the interactions emerges. The geometrical representation of the dyads demonstrates that the course of the interactional pattern in particular dyads is very similar. For reasons of clarity the data of dyads having the same developmental pattern are averaged. Thus, the points in Figure 5 are means of dyads showing the same developmental pattern.

In Figure 5 it can be seen that, in both groups—irritable and nonirritable—three types of developmental patterns can be identified. The description of these patterns ought to be done on the basis of the place of the dyads with regard to the behaviors (Figure 4) and changes that occur during the course of development. Before passing on to such a description of the patterns, two kinds of stimulating behavior distinguished in the observational system will be defined. This is important in understanding the pattern characteristic of the subgroups. Just offering objects without engaging the infant in playful interaction (category MS in Figure 4) will be called *stimulation* in the sequel. Verbal and physical stimulation with or without objects leading to playful interaction with the infant (categories MPE and MSE in Figure 4) will be called *effective stimulation*.

First we discuss the types of developmental patterns identified in the *irritable group*.

In subgroup I (Figure 5), consisting of six dyads, infants cry a lot at the age of 1 month. In this subgroup the mother gradually retreats from interaction in the course of development. In the first months the interaction is characterized by lack of physical contact. Crying behavior of these infants decreases, but this seems to be no reason for the mother to get involved in social interaction. The mother stimulates relatively little, and the infant shows proportionally few positive social behaviors. The infants of subgroup II (4 dyads) show a decrease in crying and fussing during the first 6 months. In the first months there is physical contact between mother and infant which is replaced by stimulating behavior as the

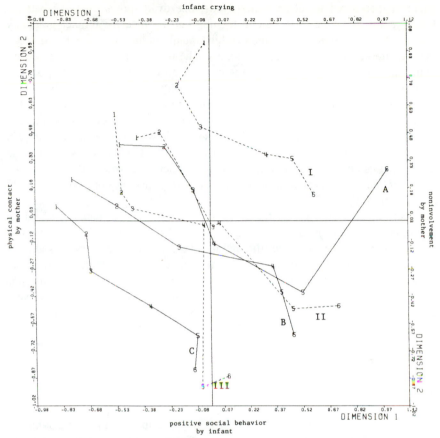

Figure 5.   Correspondence analysis of the dyads, first two dimensions. Singular values and percentage of information explained: $\lambda_1 = .33\ (.27)$; $\lambda_2 = .28\ (.20)$. ——— **nonirritable subgroups. --- irritable subgroups.**

infant gets older. This stimulating behavior does not lead to playful interaction, however. This subgroup falls midway between the other two irritable subgroups as far as decrease in infant crying and stimulating behavior by the mother is concerned. A remarkable decrease in crying is shown by the infants of subgroup III (3 dyads). This decrease is highest between the fourth and the fifth month after birth. This is related to effective stimulation by the mother during development. Infant crying decreases gradually and is replaced by positive social behaviors. Although these infants cry a lot, especially during the first 4 months of life, from the beginning on the mother engages her infant in social interaction, at first through physical stimulation, and later through effective stimulating behavior. Two dyads belonging to the irritable group could not be placed in the identified patterns. Compared to all the other dyads, one dyad shows a unique pattern. Initially, this dyad seems to belong to subgroup I, since the mother gradually retreats from interaction. But from the third month on the mother starts stimulating the infant, and infant crying decreases. The reason for this particular developmental pattern is not clear. This seems to be an irritable infant who does not need much attention from the mother to stop crying and who seems to be able to amuse himself. This is an exception compared to the rest of the group. Another irritable dyad shows pattern B (a pattern of the nonirritable group), despite the fact that the infant was initially classified as irritable with the NBAS. However in this case the classification was based on only one NBAS administration. The infant responded very different in both exams. Therefore, the mother was asked for her infant's normal way of responding. Possibly this did not lead to the right classification.

In the *nonirritable group* three types of developmental patterns could be identified, too. Crying and fussing of infants in subgroup A (5 dyads) decreases at first. However, between the fifth and the sixth month, infant crying suddenly increases substantially. Initially, the mother stimulates her infant, but then, between the fifth and the sixth month, she retreats from interaction. Moreover, it is striking that, during the first 5 months, the pattern of development looks very similar to that of subgroup II. None of the other subgroups shows a pattern in which the increase in amount of crying in the sixth month is so high and in which the mother suddenly retreats from interaction during that same period. In subgroup B (5 dyads) infants don't cry very much, and there is a slow decrease in fussing and crying. The mother gradually starts stimulating the infant as it gets older. Finally, in subgroup C (4 dyads), infant crying decreases, which is related to effective stimulating behavior of the mother leading to playful interaction. Together with subgroup III this is the only subgroup in which mothers stimulate effectively. In every other subgroup in which the mother stimulates, she uses mainly the other type of stimulating behavior (just offering objects). One nonirritable dyad shows the developmental pattern of subgroup II (an irritable subgroup). This infant fell ill during the course of the study and had to be treated in the hospital. The baby cried a lot, so it is no surprise that this dyad showed a pattern of the irritable group.

The above results can be summarized as follows. The subgroup of very irritable babies at 1 month (I) have mothers who retreat from interaction from the beginning on. There is neither much physical contact during the first months nor much stimulating involvement later on. In subgroups A, B, and II infant crying decreases, while the mother stimulates as the infant gets older. The sudden increase in amount of crying between the fifth and the sixth month in subgroup A, and the mother retreating from interaction during the same period, is striking. In subgroup III and C the mother stimulates effectively in the course of development. Infant crying decreases, while positive social behaviors increase. In subgroup III the sudden decrease in crying behavior between the fourth and the fifth month is remarkable.

As was shown, correspondence analysis provides a picture of the types of developmental changes in patterns of interaction in irritable and nonirritable mother–infant dyads. It also shows the variables in the mother's and in the infant's behavior that are related to and contribute to the origin of a particular type of developmental pattern.

Infant Fussing and Crying

Of particular interest for this study, of course, is fuss/cry behavior of the infant and the corresponding response of the mother. We divided our observational data into 6-second units, which involve the number of 6-second intervals for which both child and mother behaviors occur simultaneously. In interactional data it is often difficult to determine exactly which of the pair initiates a behavior sequence. Infant fuss/cry behavior, and the corresponding response of the mother, however, are a particular interesting context in which to observe behavior of the dyad. Unlike many other behaviors, this relationship is asymmetrical, in that there is no reason for studying the responses of the infant to the mother's cry. We realize that restricting the analysis to 6-second time units as an arbitrarily selected unit is a more conservative approach. However this measure may be useful as an overall interaction measure (Lewis & Ban, 1977). We were particularly interested in the behavior of the mother in those 6-second intervals in which the infant fussed or cried. Did the mother soothe the infant? Did she ignore the infant, or did she exhibit some other behavior? We calculated the percentage of intervals in which infant fuss or cry behavior occured to which the mother did not respond with soothing behavior. So, all behaviors other than soothing or ignoring the fussing and crying were considered nonsoothe behaviors. First of all, we calculated the overall amount of fussing and crying in both the irritable an the nonirritable group. This is shown in Table 1. The frequencies are calculated for the developmental patterns identified through correspondence analysis.

Overall, the irritable group—diagnosed as such shortly after birth—cried twice as much during the 6-month period of observations than the nonirritable group. In the irritable group it is interesting to note that the subgroup crying the most on the average shows such a great decline in fussing and crying after the fourth month of life. The differences between the patterns in the nonirritable group are not that large, except for the sudden increase in fuss/cry behavior by the infants in pattern A during the last month of observations.

Besides the overall amount of fussing and crying, we were particularly interested in corresponding mother behavior in the same time unit. Table 2 shows the amount of fussing and crying ignored by the mother, for the developmental patterns identified in both groups.

Table 1.   Mean number of 6-second units of infant fuss/cry behavior per developmental pattern

Month	Irritable Group			Nonirritable Group		
	Pattern I	Pattern II	Pattern III	Pattern A	Pattern B	Pattern C
1	151	119	170	55	38	35
2	81	129	163	75	45	70
3	79	69	157	55	32	49
4	91	108	186	38	37	38
5	122	85	52	77	59	82
6	65	101	88	171	44	40
Mean	98.2	101.8	136	78.5	42.5	52.3

Let us first take a look at mother behavior in the *irritable group*. Mothers in pattern I ignore infant fuss/cry behavior on the average in 66% of the intervals in which it occurs over the 6-month period of observations. Ignoring remains about the same during the first 6 months after birth, with a slight increase after the fourth month. In pattern II, infant crying is ignored in 44% of fuss/cry instances on the average. Here too, there is an increase in ignoring of infant crying after month 4. During the first 3 months, these mothers ignore crying considerably less than mothers in pattern I. In pattern III the same picture emerges: an increase in ignoring infant fussing and crying in the fifth and the sixth month. Overall, crying is ignored in 36% on the average, which means that these mothers ignore least in the irritable group. Thus, in pattern III, where infants cried most, mothers ignored their crying least. The high percentage of crying bouts ignored, on the other hand, by mothers in pattern I is striking. In general, there is an increase of ignoring after the fourth month of life.

Mothers in the *nonirritable group* show the following tendencies. Crying is ignored in 49% on the average by the mothers in pattern A. Ignoring remains

Table 2.   Percentage of 6-second units of infant fuss/cry behavior not accompanied by maternal soothing behavior.

Month	Irritable Group			Nonirritable Group		
	Pattern I	Pattern II	Pattern III	Pattern A	Pattern B	Pattern C
1	67	37	30	43	42	23
2	65	37	26	46	36	23
3	65	29	41	37	28	22
4	62	43	28	44	41	41
5	67	64	45	65	50	15
6	72	52	45	56	51	46
Mean	66.3	43.7	36	48.5	41.3	28.3

about the same during the first 4 months and then increases. In pattern B crying is ignored in 41% of crying instances on the average. Here too, an increase again appears after month four. A mean percentage of 28% of ignoring is shown by pattern C mothers. These mothers are very uniform in the first 3 months after birth; then, ignoring increases with a dip in the fifth month. Contrary to what we found in the irritable group, in the nonirritable group the mothers of infants that cry most (pattern A) ignore most. Ignoring of fussing and crying increases from the third month onwards, with month five in pattern C being the only exception to this rule.

Discussion

What emerges from this detailed description of the interaction in dyads with irritable and nonirritable infants? The developmental changes over the first half year in patterns of interaction in dyads with irritable infants differ markedly from the kinds of developmental courses shown by dyads with a nonirritable baby. In both groups three types of developmental patterns can be identified. These patterns show more variability in the irritable group.

In almost all instances where infants cry less as they grow older, this decrease in crying is accompanied by stimulating behavior of the mother. Mothers retreating from interaction do so from the beginning on. They do not physically stimulate their babies during the first months and remain noninvolved when their infants grow older. It is important to distinguish between two forms of stimulating behavior by the mother: (a) a form in which the infant is only offered objects, and the mother is not engaging the infant in playful interaction; and (b) a more effective form of stimulation leading to playful interaction with the child. Only in those cases where the mother stimulates effectively does the infant show relatively more positive social behavior around the age of 6 months. This is most clear in subgroup III (irritable). Other research also shows the important mediating effect of effective stimulation on an initially irritable infant. Thoman, Dreyer, Acebo, Becker, and Freese (1979) give an example of this mediating effect in their description of an initially irritable baby whose caretaker interacted very often and effectively with the infant, even if he fussed. At the age of 1 year this infant cried less than any other infant in the sample, and mother and infant were very responsive towards each other.

Most remarkable is the developmental pattern of subgroup A (nonirritable). This is the only subgroup in which the developmental curve shows a sudden upward shift (see Figure 5). This means that the mother retreats from interaction, while, at the same time, infant crying increases. As yet it is too difficult to interpret this trend unequivocally on the basis of the observational data alone. This sudden change in both mother and infant behavior might be interpreted in several ways. With additional information and follow-up data still to be analyzed we hope to gain more insight into the variables contributing to this developmental pattern.

The analysis of the percentage of fuss/cry units ignored in each developmental pattern indicates that the least stimulating mothers ignore most. This finding is in accord with a study by Donovan, Leavitt, and Balling (1978). One of the consequences of being confronted with an irritable baby may be that response to positive signals is reduced. Reduced sensitivity generalizes to signals other than negative ones such as fussiness and crying (Donovan & Leavitt, 1985). It seems as if both mother and infant fail to benefit from the mutual interchange of positive behaviors.

In comparing the results of our study with those of Crockenberg's (1981), we discovered interesting differences. Although in both studies the same criterion was used to determine the degree of irritability, the number of infants who met this criterion differed markedly. In Crockenberg's study 50% of all infants observed with the NBAS were classified as irritable, while in our study this was only 17%. This difference might be due to differences in sample characteristics. Crockenberg's sample was very heterogeneous with regard to parent education and circumstances during delivery. Some babies were delivered by Cesarean section, which might have affected infant behavior on the NBAS. Research aimed at studying the effects of obstetric medication both before and during labor indicates a disturbing effect on infant functioning (Brackbill, 1979). Whether the mothers who delivered their babies vaginally also received medication is not reported. However, this cannot be ruled out, since the use of obstetric medication is very common in the United States. This might have influenced infant behavior, since certain medicines seem to affect infant irritability. In our study we carefully controlled for the use of obstetric medication both before and during delivery. This might explain why so many more infants in Crockenberg's study were classified as being irritable. The difference in use of medication might also explain some differences in findings in the mother–infant interaction system. Fish and Crockenberg (1981) performed a follow-up study using the subjects of Crockenberg's (1981) first study. They found that much infant crying shortly after birth correlated highly with much interaction with the mother at the age of 9 months. In our study mothers with irritable infants, who stimulated effectively later on, were exceptions. The majority of mothers with irritable infants retreat from interaction or stimulate by offering objects without engaging the infant in playful interaction. If our assumption, that infants in Fish and Crockenberg's (1981) study were irritable due to obstetric medication administered to the mother before or during labor, is correct, it is not unthinkable that the decrease in irritability was caused by a decrease in the effects of medication on infant functioning. This might explain why the mothers with highly irritable infants were the ones who interacted a lot later on in development. Moreover, our assumption might explain why the crying of these infants was already replaced by positive social behaviors at the age of 3 months.

Our study shows that development is a highly complex interactive process and that it is too simplistic to talk of either infant or parent effects. One is always dealing with both. We started out with two groups of infants (irritable and nonirritable), and, in both groups, several developmental pathways could be depicted. We want to emphasize the contribution of variations between both mothers and infants to the process, as these seem to be very important in determining later differences seen in children.

Conclusion

In this chapter we have tried to describe a study that was designed to gain insight into the developmental process in mother–infant interaction early in life. Similarities to, and differences from, comparable psychological studies were discussed. Such studies are valuable to those who study a single community, because they help to define the salient ecology of the particular community under study (Richards, 1977). In our study we found striking differences in the number of irritable infants identified, using the same irritability criterion as in a comparable study conducted in the United States. Besides that, we found differences in the developmental process occuring from the period immediately after birth up to 6 months of age. We assume that these differences are partly determined by differences in the specific conditions surrounding childbirth in both countries. Taking these differences in mind, our conclusion is that one should be very careful in generalizing the results of studies done in one subculture to the same phenomena in other subcultures.

References

Ainsworth, M.D., Blehar, M.C., Waters, E., & Wall, S. (1978). *Patterns of attachment*. Hillsdale, NJ: Erlbaum.

van Arkel, W.G., Ament, A.J., & Bell, N. (1980). The politics of home delivery in the Netherlands. *Birth and the Family Journal, 7*, 101–112.

Bell, R.Q. (1968). A reinterpretation of the direction of effects in studies of socialization. *Psychological Review, 75*, 81–95.

Bell, R.Q. (1977). Socialization findings reexamined. In R.Q. Bell & L.V. Harper (Eds.), *Child effects on adults*. Hillsdale, NJ: Erlbaum.

Bell, R.Q. (1979). Parent, child, and reciprocal influences. *American Psychologist, 34*, 821–826.

Brackbill, Y. (1979). Obstetrical medication and infant behavior. In J.D. Osofsky (Ed.), *Handbook of infant development*. New York: Wiley.

Brazelton, T.B. (1973). *Neonatal behavioral assessment scale*. Philadelphia, PA: Lippincott.

Brazelton, T.B. (1978). Introduction. In A. Sameroff (Ed.), *Organization and stability of newborn behavior. Monographs of the Society for Research in Child Development,* *43* (5–6, serial no. 177), 1–13.

Crockenberg, S.B. (1981). Infant irritability, mother responsiveness, and social support influences on the security of attachment. *Child Development, 52,* 857–865.

Donovan, W.L., & Leavitt, L.A. (1985). Physiology and behavior: Parents' response to the infant cry. In B.M. Lester & C.F.Z. Boukydis (Eds.), *Infant crying: Theoretical and research perspectives.* New York: Plenum Press.

Donovan, W.L., & Leavitt, L.A., & Balling, J.D. (1978). Maternal physiologic response to infant signals. *Psychophysiology, 15,* 68–74.

Fish, M., & Crockenberg, S.B. (1981). Correlates and antecedents of nine-month infant behavior and mother–infant interaction. *Infant Behavior and Development, 4,* 69–81.

Gifi, A. (1981). *Non-linear multivariate analysis* (Tech. Rep.). Department of Datatheory, University of Leiden.

Gifi, A. (1982). *ANACOR user's guide* (Tech. Rep.). Department of Datatheory, University of Leiden.

Gifi, A. (1983). *PRINCALS user's guide* (Tech. Rep.). Department of Datatheory, University of Leiden.

Graham, F., Matarazzo, R., & Caldwell, B. (1956). Behavioral differences between normal and traumatized newborns, II: Standardization, reliability, and validity. *Psychological Monographs, 70* (21, whole no. 428).

Greenacre, M.J. (1981). Practical correspondence analysis. In V. Barnett (Ed.), *Interpreting multivariate data.* Chichester, England: Wiley.

Holmes, D.L., Ruble, N., Kowalski, J., & Lauesen, B. (1984, April). *Predicting quality of attachment at one year from neonatal characteristics.* Paper presented at the International Conference on Infant Studies, New York.

Kaye, K. (1978). Discriminating among normal infants by multivariate analysis of Brazelton-scores: Lumping and smoothing. In A. Sameroff (Ed.), *Organization and stability of newborn behavior. Monographs of the Society for Research in Child Development, 43* (5–6, serial no. 177).

Lester, B.M. (1985). Introduction. In B.M. Lester & C.F.Z. Boukydis (Eds.), *Infant crying: Theoretical and research perspectives.* New York: Plenum Press.

Lester, B.M., Als, H., & Brazelton, T.B. (1982). Regional obstetric anesthesia and newborn behavior: A reanalysis toward synergistic effects. *Child Development, 53,* 687–692.

Lewis, M., & Ban, P. (1977). Variance and invariance in the mother-infant interaction: A cross-cultural study. In P.H. Leiderman, S.R. Tulkin, & A. Rosenfeld (Eds.), *Culture and infancy: Variations in the human experience.* New York: Academic Press.

Lytton, H. (1980). *Parent-child interaction: The socialization process observed in twin and singleton families.* New York: Plenum Press.

Maccoby, E.E., & Jacklin, C.N. (1983). The "person" characteristics of children and the family as environment. In D. Magnussen & V.L. Allen (Eds.), *Human development: An interactional perspective.* New York: Academic Press.

Prechtl, H.F.R. (1982). Assessment methods for the newborn infant, a critical evaluation.

In P. Stratton (Ed.), *Psychobiology of the human newborn*. New York: Wiley & Sons.

Prechtl, H.F.R., & Beintema, D.J. (1964). *The neurological examination of the full-term newborn infant* (Clinics in developmental medicine, no. 12). London: Heinmann.

Richards, M.P.M. (1977). An ecological study of infant development in an urban setting in Britain. In P.M. Leiderman, S.R. Tulkin, & A. Rosenfeld (Eds.), *Culture and infancy: Variations in the human experience*. New York: Academic Press.

Rosenblith, J.F. (1961). The modified Graham behavior test for neonates: Test-retest reliability, normative data and hypotheses for future work. *Biologia Neonatorium, 3*, 174–192.

Sameroff, A.J. (1978). Summary and conclusions: The future of newborn assessment. In A. Sameroff (Ed.), *Organization and stability of newborn behavior. Monographs of the Society for Research in Child Development, 43* (5–6, serial no. 177), 102–117.

Sameroff, A.J., & Chandler, M. (1975). Reproductive risk and the continuum of caretaking casualty. In F. Horowitz, E.M. Hetherington, S. Scarr-Salapatek, & G. Siegel (Eds.), *Review of child development research* (Vol. 4). Chicago, IL: University of Chicago Press.

Thoman, E., Dryer, C., Acebo, C., Becker, P., & Freese, M. (1979). Individuality in the interactive process. In E. Thoman (Ed.), *Origins of the infant's social responsiveness*. Hillsdale, NJ: Erlbaum.

van der Heijden, P.G.M. (1985). Transition matrices, model fitting and correspondence analysis. In E. Diday (Ed.), *Data analysis and informatics* (Vol. IV). Amsterdam: North Holland.

Vaughn, B., Egeland, B., & Sroufe, L. A. (1979). Individual differences in infant-mother attachment at twelve and eighteen months: Stability and change in families under stress. *Child Development, 50*, 971–975.

PART II

MOTHER–INFANT
INTERACTION IN CONTEXT

CHAPTER 4

Facilitating Early Motor Development: An Intracultural Study of West Indian Mothers and Their Infants Living in Britain*

Brian Hopkins

Department of Educational Sciences
Faculty of Human Movement Sciences
Free University, The Netherlands

In the past, various individuals have attempted to identify the objectives of cross-cultural research in human behavior. One of the most concise attempts was made by Biesheuvel (1958), who identified three fundamental objectives (see also Tatje, 1973; Rohner, 1977):

1. To test the universality of theories and concepts.
2. To study the modifiability of behavior in two respects: (a) to establish which environmental factors have a significant influence on behavior, and (b) to measure the magnitude of these effects.
3. To understand the behavior of people from another culture.

The first two objectives stress that cross-cultural research is a testing ground for theories, concepts, and notions about human behavior. Along with the major

---

* Grateful thanks are expressed to Dr. T.B. Brazelton for instruction in the use of his neonatal assessment scale; to Dr. M. Parkin for instruction in assessing gestational age; to Drs. S. Oldham, P. Manfield, and J. Moore for help and advice in carrying out the study; to Mrs. J. Smith, Personal and Child Services, Birmingham, and her Health Visitors, for help in maintaining continuity with subjects; to Drs. S. Crawford and W. Fothergill for advice in constructing the neonatal screening procedure; to Dr. M. Smrkovsky for help with the LPA2 program; and finally to Drs. G. Kraaijenbrink for taking considerable care in drawing Figures 3 to 14. This study was financially supported in part by the Leverhulme Trust.

conceptual changes that have taken place in the last two decades in the study of ontogenetic development, the interpretation and application of these two objectives by students of infant behavior have changed also. As they stand, these objectives emphasize descriptive and proximate analyses.

However, instead of trying to identify the universals of infant behavior, a quite different (but equally legitimate concern) would be based on the question: What is the survival value of this behavior? As some sociobiologists have pointed out (e.g., Barash, 1977), the cross-cultural study of behavioral development is well suited to functional analyses. When Ainsworth (1967) submitted Bowlby's theory of infantile attachment to the first of Biesheuvel's objectives, it brought to light the potential of cross-cultural research for such analyses. More recently, this potential has been used by the physical anthropologist Konner (1972, 1977a) in his ethnologically oriented research on the behavioral development of the !Kung San infants in northwestern Botswana. But a concern for proximate explanations, rather than ultimate ones, still tends to dominate the thinking of those concerned with unraveling the relationships between infancy and culture.

The second objective has undergone change since Biesheuvel's original presentation. Earlier studies and speculations on the developing human infant were unidirectional in nature, emphasizing either the impact of the environment on the infant (e.g., Bing, 1963) or the converse (e.g., Bell, 1968). More recent approaches have highlighted the reciprocal relationship between the young organism and its external environment, particularly with regard to cognitive and social development (e.g., Sameroff, 1975a, 1975b). These changing views have been reflected in cross-cultural studies of infant behavior (e.g., Brazelton, Robey & Collier, 1969; Konner, 1977b). Nevertheless, a concern for Biesheuvel's original second objective still continues to reveal important information about the channelling effects of environmental influences on early development, particularly for motor (Super, 1976) and perceptual (Streeter, 1976) behaviors.

It is the third objective which has suffered the most neglect, particularly at the hands of psychologists. In practice, cross-cultural research should begin with this objective, so that relevant sociocultural information is gathered, not only from literature reviews, but also from fieldwork carried out before actual data collection. And even more profitably, "anthropological data should attend the research in all its phases" (LeVine, 1970, p. 570). Failure to do so may result in the reputed environmental influences having little substance in reality or in the irretrievable loss of opportunities for extending the scope of the research. The importance of the third objective is stressed in an approach to the study of culture and cognition termed *ethnographic psychology* (e.g., Cole & Scribner, 1974; Scribner, 1976).

It is against the background of these objectives and their subsequent modifications that the particular type of comparative research on infant behavior outlined in this paper was carried out. It was largely concerned with motor development during the first 6 months of postnatal life and, as such, was concerned with the second of Biesheuvel's objectives. The subjects were caucasian infants of English parentage and black infants of West Indian (Jamaican) parentage. After the period of hospitalization following birth, all of them were living in the same general environment formed by the inner ring of a large industrial British city.

The study also paid particular attention to the methodological problems involved in cross-cultural and cross-ethnic studies of infant behavior. Until recently, many such studies concerned with motor behavior have been replete with methodological inadequacies, a point which formed the basis of Warren's (1972) critical article on African infant precocity. This contribution focuses largely on some intracultural findings in the study that pertain to the West Indian infants. It is, therefore, more concerned with Biesheuvel's third objective than with the other two.

Some Comments on Methodology

One of the major problems of cross-cultural research is the limited amount of control that the researcher can exert on unwanted or confounding variables. Consequently, the validity of any findings is threatened by alternative explanations or plausible rival hypotheses which stem directly from this lack of direct control over extraneous factors. Major sources of confounding variables in studies of infant behavior may include the prenatal and perinatal histories of the subjects involved. In addition, marked differences among cultures in the provision of maternal and child health facilities during early postnatal development can constitute a wealth of confounding variables.[1] Such threats to internal validity have been discussed in detail by Campbell and Stanley (1963) and Cook and Campbell (1975). In the present study both direct and statistical controls were used to combat the incursion of possible confounding variables into the interpretation of the findings. However, given the controversy surrounding the use of covariance statistics (e.g., Evans & Anastasio, 1968; Sprott, 1970; Maxwell & Cramer, 1975), it was decided to give more emphasis to direct control. Accordingly, a rigorous screening procedure was designed so that only newborns free from most pre-, peri-, and immediate postnatal adversities were included in the study. Another criterion for selection was that the parents lived in the same inner ring area of a large industrial city and therefore had access to the same maternal and child health care facilities.

West Indian subjects included only those parents who had immigrated to Britain from the rural areas of Jamaica. After the hospitalization period, checks were made via health visitors and general practitioners for any interval complica-

---

[1] On the other hand, variations in such histories and facilities can constitute the rationale for carrying out cross-cultural, cross-ethnic, and intracultural research on infant behavior (e.g., see Coll et al., 1981; Dixon et al., 1982). Obviously whether or not they are considered to be confounding variables depends on the particular question being asked.

tions that may have happened to the infants, as well as to the general health of the mothers.

Any attempt to improve the internal validity of a study can increase the problems associated with external validity, that is, with the generalizing of findings to other populations, setting, treatment, and measurement variables (Campbell & Stanley, 1963). Thus, if considerable control is exerted, for example, in the selection of subjects as a means of improving internal validity, then the potential for generalizing of findings can be concomitantly reduced. Cross-cultural psychology, with its commitment to the "psychic unity of mankind" has presumably more than just a passing interest in the external validity of its findings.

Paradoxically, however, few cross-cultural research psychologists pay attention to it, particularly those concerned with infant behavior. Such neglect is perhaps due to the fact that much of their research is field based in approach, an approach that is incorrectly assumed to have built-in external validity. According to Tunnell (1977), external validity is troublesome for all research, including the field approach. This is also pointed out by Campbell and Stanley (1963): External validity, like inductive inference, can never be satisfactorily defended.

Cross-cultural studies of infant behavior have had until recently a poor record in dealing with the problems associated with internal validity. A decision was made to concentrate, therefore, on these problems in the present study, with the understanding that, unless internal validity is adequately controlled for, there will be little or nothing from which to generalize.

A concern for combating possible confounding variables is ultimately a concern for counteracting the number of plausible rival hypotheses that can assail the interpretation of results. In the few cross-cultural studies that have dealt with such hypotheses (e.g., Segall, Campbell, & Herskovits, 1966; Cole, Gay, Glick, & Sharp, 1977), the strategy adopted has been the interpretation of cultural differences in terms of patterns of performance rather than levels of performance on individual items (e.g., by comparing correlation matrices or profiles). This study adopted a similar strategy in data analysis for both between- and within-group comparisons. This is important in multivariate comparative research, since it provides a means of assessing the psychometric comparability of measures between groups (Poortinga, 1971, 1975; Hopkins, 1977a). A lack of such comparability between groups makes a comparison by levels statistically invalid. Little or no attention has been given to this problem in cross-cultural research on infant behavior (Hopkins, 1977a).

Frijda and Jahoda (1966) recommended that cross-cultural research psychologists supplement their research with intracultural comparisons. In the case of a two-cultural comparative study, the systematic use of intracultural variation has been strongly recommended to overcome the possibilities for misinterpretation inherent in such studies (Holtzman, Diaz-Guerrero, Swartz, & Tapia, 1969). The typical approach to this is to follow the cross-cultural comparison with intracultural explorations on socioeconomic levels (e.g., Geber & Dean, 1958; Leiderman, Baber, Kagia, Kraemer, & Leiderman, 1973). The approach is weak, because within-culture distinctions by social and/or economic factors neglect psychologically meaningful variables. Furthermore, the cross-cultural equivalence of such factors is open to question.

The incorporation of intracultural comparisons into cross-cultural research is the essence of Roberts and Sutton-Smith's (1962) methodological innovation termed *subsystem validation*. Here, particular hypotheses or questions are examined both cross-culturally and intraculturally so that general explanatory variables and their relationship may be tested at two levels (Berry & Dasen, 1974). Differences in results between the two levels may make the behavioral comparisons between cultures invalid.

A strategy similar to subsystem validation was incorporated into the design of this study. After comparing infant motor and other behaviors between ethnic groups in terms of both levels and patterns, the same behaviors were studied further within the West Indian sample. This intracultural research differed from the usual approach in that subsamples were distinguished in terms of response patterns which were then related to possible determinants that had been identified during a pilot study.

These two broad methodological topics have been treated in more depth elsewhere (Hopkins, 1976a), as well as other topics central to the enterprise of cultural comparisons of infant behaviors. These included the importance of choice of statistical tests appropriate to multivariate comparative research, the selection of research instruments, the issue of comparability involving an examination of the reified emic–etic distinction, and the meaning of the term *culture*.

Background to the Study

The general aims of the study were as follows: (a) to indicate the specific differences in early development between selected samples of West Indian (black) and English (white) infants starting in the newborn period; (b) to examine further the purported universality of negro infant precocity by a method of direct comparison involving a group of phenotypical black infants who have been used infrequently as subjects in previous research on this topic; (c) to identify environmental factors, both social and inanimate, that may account, in part, for any observed differences in behavior between the West Indian and English infants; and (d) to provide information that would be of assistance to those health authorities who have to plan for child care in areas inhabited by families of West Indian origin. The main concern, however, was with the third aim, and more specifically with the question of specific environmental influences that can help to explain behavioral variability within the West Indian sample of infants.

The study was initiated in November 1970 and finished in October 1973. The period from November 1972 until October 1973 was taken up with final data collection. The previous period was concerned with preliminary preparations, selection and construction of assessment procedures, training in the use of particular assessment techniques, reliability testing, and two pilot studies involving West Indian and English infants at 3 days and 6 months of age.

During the preliminary preparations, contact was made with the appropriate hospital and health services personnel as well as with a West Indian community leader. The latter proved to be an invaluable contact. He arranged for a number of informal meetings with West Indian mothers of young infants in their homes (N = 5). These meetings, and further discussions with the community leader and some of his associates, directed attention to relevant West Indian childrearing practices. All the West Indian mothers interviewed carried out a routine, composed of a series of exercises and messages with their infants, from the first few days of life onwards. This routine was demonstrated, and contrasts in use noted. With the help of mothers and the community leader, a complete inventory of the routine was made and converted into a questionnaire to be used in the final data collection. It was noted that the mothers were initially hesitant to talk about the routine. It was also observed that all the mothers put their infants to sleep in the prone position. They all considered it to be a common West Indian practice that not only stopped the baby from swallowing any vomit but also strengthened muscles. To facilitate what the study required in the way of assessment procedures, a simple schema was devised to reflect the different levels of organization involved and their interrelationships (see Figure 1).

Ecology is depicted in Figure 1 as two interdependent forces: the geodynamic influences (Level A) and the anthropo-dynamic influences (Level B). The former refers to the physical environment (terrain and climate or meteorological conditions), and the latter to the man-made environment made up of social and inanimate components. Level C refers to the level of the individual organism, which at birth is a product of the species' phylogenetic history and any prenatal and perinatal adversity factors. The interpretation of the different components within each level depends on the nature of the study: for example, whether the subjects are children or adults, and whether the man-made environment is examined through detailed observations of the home situation or by global statements of stimulus conditions such as enriched versus impoverished and social class.

It should be noted that the experimenter (E) or observer is included in the scheme of things. Too little attention has been paid to E effects in cross-cultural studies of infant behavior, despite warnings from field-based research in Western settings (e.g., Pederson, 1980). In the present context, there was the troublesome situation of a male E questioning the mothers. For the West Indian mothers, E's ascribed status included sex and ethnic category. For all mothers in the sample there was the more subtle, but no less important factor of acquired status (e.g., a research worker from a hospital). Both ascribed and acquired status may lead to distortions in both maternal behavior and responses.

For the posthospital follow-up assessment, therefore, a strategy was adopted

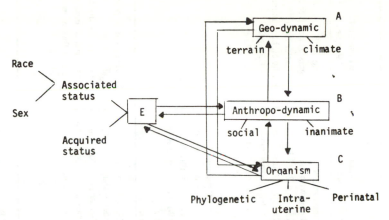

Figure 1.   Schematic summary of the general entities and their interrelationships involved in the study.

in which female family health visitors were employed. During unannounced home visits the health visitors carried out some of the same assessments as E. In this way a comparison could be made between the two sets of assessments as a means of checking the possible influence of E on maternal behavior and responses.

In general the selection of assessment procedures was based on the following questions: (a) Had the same or similar procedure been used in black–white infant studies before? (b) How suitable was the procedure for use in a one-man research project where data was to be collected on a broad basis? (c) How well had the procedure been evaluated by other researchers? The selection of appropriate assessment procedures was mainly concerned with Levels C and B. There appears to be little research on examining Level A relationships with measures of infant behavior in the literature (however, see Piaget, 1952, for some anecdotal evidence on his children, and also Faust, Weidman, & Wehner, 1974). In this study, Level C influences were assessed only very indirectly through measures of household temperatures and humidity. The construction and selection of assessment procedures at Level C consisted of two major aspects: a screening instrument for the selection of healthy newborns and instruments for assessing relevant aspects of infant behavior. The selection criteria for healthy infants, consisting of 23 items, are given in Table 1.

Two other criteria were also included: no evidence of sickle-cell anemia in the case of West Indian newborns, and no circumcision in the case of all male subjects. Selection is based on inclusive and excusive criteria (See Table 1). The former are items containing either a range within which subjects must fall (e.g., II A1) or that require the presence of a discrete variable (e.g., IV A1) or state (e.g., IVA4). Exclusive criteria are formed by items requiring the absence of a state (e.g., IIB1).

Table 1. Selection criteria for newborns.

	I Parental characteristics	II Maternal characteristics	III History of Pregnancy	IV Perinatal Factors	V Postnatal Factors
A (Inclusive)		1. Age range 18–40 years	1. Length of gestation in range 259–287 days (confirmed by objective assessment)	1. Spontaneous maternal labor with 1st 2 stages in range 2–13 hrs. 2. Drugs > 4 hrs. prior to delivery not more than 100 mg narcotics & 50 mg of other drugs. 3. Vertex presentation 4. Spontaneous vaginal delivery or thru low (Wrigley's) forceps delivery.	1. Single birth 2. Apgars 7-8 at 1 & 5 min. after birth * 3. Birthweight in range 2.5–4.3 kgs.
B (Exclusive)	1. No family histories of any abnormalities such as severe metabolic neurological disease or mental retardation. 2. No statement of previously suspected infertility	1. No Rh negative with antibodies 2. No previous miscarriages or abortions 3. No mother < 5 ft in height.	1. No severe preeclampsia 2. No ante-partum haemorrhage 3. No hydramnios	1. No intra-partum haemorrhage 2. No suspicion of fetal anoxia 3. No cord loops	1. No suspicion of post-natal anoxia 2. No haemolytic disease 3. No referral to intensive care unit for any period of time

*Including a rating of least 1 for respiratory effort and heart rate 1 min. after birth and ratings 2 for 5 mins.

The selection of items for the construction of the screening procedure was guided by Butler and Alberman (1969), Crawford (1972), Montagu (1962), Bonica (1967), and Korner (1971). One of the most important items was the estimation of gestational age as mothers from non-Western societies are often unaware of their last menstrual period (e.g., Singer et al., 1973). With the help of Caesar and Akiyama's (1970) comprehensive survey of the methods available for estimating gestational age, it was decided to use an examination based on external physical characteristics (Farr, Mitchell, Neligan, & Parkin, 1966). The examination had the advantage of having been subjected to a cross-cultural comparison involving British and Ugandan babies (Parkin, 1971).

On the basis of the pilot study, a decision was made to make assessments and observations at the ages of 3 days, 1 month, and 6 months. The selection of further Level A assessment procedures suitable for these ages was aided by Cronbach's (1960) 26-item system for evaluating a test. This comparative evaluation resulted in the Brazelton newborn behavioral examination (NBAS) being used at 3 days and 1 month and the Griffiths (1970) mental development scale at 6 months. In addition to the Griffiths scale, which essentially assesses gross and fine motor abilities and underlying postural control during the first 6 months of life, another instrument was used. An evaluation of suitable instruments resulted in the selection of the Object Permanence and Space scales from the Albert Einstein series of Sensorimotor Development scales (Escalona & Corman, n.d.) for use as Level C instruments at 6 months of age. Both scales had shown adequate evidence of ordinality at 6 months (Corman & Escalona, 1969).

The choice of Level B instruments will be restricted to the follow-up made at 6 months. At this age a decision was made to assess the social and inanimate components of the home environment by means of direct observation and interviewing. To this end, Caldwell's (1970) HOME inventory, consisting of six sections, was incorporated into the study.[2] It is an instrument which has been carefully evaluated for both reliability and validity and, in addition, had been used in cross-cultural research (Goldberg, 1972; Cravioto & De Licardie, 1972) which has included West Indian subjects (Richardson, 1972), In order to provide an extensive assessment of the inanimate component of the home environment at 6 months, Yarrow, Rubenstein, Pedersen, and Jankowski's (1972) three dimensions of inanimate stimulation (responsiveness, complexity, and variety of play materials) were employed in addition to the HOME inventory.

The evaluation, construction, and selection of assessment procedures was a protracted process of which only a broad outline has been given here (see Hopkins, 1976a, for further details). The ultimate goal of the process was to ensure the inclusion of assessment procedures which were most appropriate to

---

[2] The six sections are: emotional and verbal responsivity of the mother, avoidance of restriction and punishment, organization of physical and temporal environment, provision of appropriate play materials, maternal involvement with child, and opportunities for variety in daily stimulation.

the aims of the study. For Level C instruments this process was relatively straightforward, but for Level B the situation was more complicated. The major complication was developing an understanding of the West Indian culture, particularly as it relates to childrearing practices and attitudes to young children in general. Surprisingly little has been written on these two topics in the last few years. The next section considers some of the published literature and supplements it with some of the observations made during the author's pilot and final studies. It is this supplementary information that helped to form the basis of the intracultural study.

The West Indian Subjects: Historical and Contemporary Perspectives

Childhood in Jamaica

Early childhood in Jamaica has been described, among others, by Henriques (1953). According to this source, Jamaican children are often fed by surrogate mothers or 'nans' until the age of 18 months, contrary to medical advice that weaning should begin between 8 to 9 months. More recently, the incidence of bottle feeding has increased in the capital, Kingston (Grantham-McGregor & Back, 1970). This increase in bottle feeding, combined with poor, unsanitary home environments, has undoubtedly helped to promote kwashiokor and maramus, both frequently reported for young infants in Jamaica (Miall, Desai, & Standard, 1970; Richardson, 1975).

Evans (1965) presented one of the most comprehensive descriptions of childhood environments in rural Jamaica, but he did not deal specifically with the first year of life. He reported that, from his own observations, 45.1% of rural Jamaican children grew up under the sole influence of women, and termed it a "self-sustaining cultural trait" for the low socioeconomic groupings. His findings confirmed Clarke's (1959) report that 60% of rural Jamaican children grow up in unstable family backgrounds. While many working-class families are typified by aspects of instability (e.g., father's absence), the general trend in Jamaica is to show young infants great permissiveness and to feed on demand, according to Fitzherbert (1967).

Fitzherbert also gave some details on the inanimate environment of rural Jamaican infants. They spend most of time out-of-doors wearing unrestrictive clothing but are given few toys or play materials to stimulate their imagination or to exercise finger muscles and develop a sense of precision. The notion that children need to play, or that it is in any way beneficial for development, is unfamiliar to most mothers. Playing, according to Fitzherbert, is the nearest thing to being naughty. Children are seen in an adultomorphic framework and are referred to as the "little people" who cannot quite achieve what adults can. Such childrearing attitudes are the polar opposites of those that pertain in Britain (Newsom & Newsom, 1963) and America (Rebelsky, 1967).

The question can be asked to what extent African influences still operate in Jamaican culture, especially on child-rearing practices. Doob (1960) considered that the only resemblance between African societies and Jamaican society was a strong British influence from colonial times. But from the viewpoint of modern culture, the African heritage of most Jamaicans is almost completely irrelevant. This interpretation was in agreement with that of Patterson (1966), who challenged the Herskovits Afro-American school of ethnohistorical anthropology which argued for strong West African influences on Caribbean cultures. Herskovits (1966) considered that many Caribbean child-rearing practices still reflected salient aspects of the West African scene, although his ethnological evidence in this respect was not very extensive in comparison with other areas (e.g., religion).

West Indian Childhood in Britain

During the early 1960s, large-scale immigration of people from the Caribbean to Britain began in response to the British government's campaign in the islands to recruit labor, chiefly for British public services. Britain at that time was in a period of rapid social change and increasing individual wealth. It seemed a land of promise to potential Commonwealth immigrants, and especially for those living under poverty in the Caribbean Islands.

Most of the West Indian immigrants settled in London or in major industrial cities of the Midlands and the Northwest. This social and cultural upheaval had potential consequences for the early childhood environment of the developing West Indian infant. However, from the study's observations, and those of others, it appears the child-rearing practices and attitudes were highly resistant to this upheaval. It seems almost that the parents made an effort to maintain a state of "being" in the face of "becoming." Some factors related to the early childhood environment of the West Indian infants in Britain have been discussed by Fitzherbert (1967). The vast majority of West Indian immigrants to Britain came from lower social-class backgrounds, where there is considerable deviation from accepted Western standards in family affairs. Fitzherbert stated that there are four types of marriage based on paternal attitudes and behavior. In what is termed the *middle-class marriage,* the father provides everything and has the status of breadwinner, disciplinarian, and family protector. Fitzherbert contended that the father in the *working-class marriage* does his best to support the family, but that circumstances may be economically adverse and the mother may have to work. Like the middle-class marriage, the family structure is authoritarian, with the children being strictly disciplined and kept away from supposedly evil influences. Fitzherbert termed the third type of marriage *faithful concubinage.* Here, the father supports the family as best he can, but the mother may have to help.

Parents tend to have an egalitarian relationship and share authority in the family. The relationship is always a more or less temporary or transitional arrangement which can develop into a middle-class marriage or break up, leaving the father in the situation of the fourth type of marriage, which Fitzherbert referred to as *extraresidential affairs* or *broken common-law marriage*. The father pleases himself whether he should support his children or leave it entirely to the mother. His behavior can range from regular support, and great personal interest and affection, to complete neglect. Some men vacillate from one extreme to another.

According to Fitzherbert, illegitimacy is very high among the lower social class West Indians. There are no moral regrets, merely social ones, because illegitimacy identifies them with the working class. No moral stigma is attached to the illegitimate child provided its paternity is known, which is nearly always the case. The West Indian family system is so adaptive and elastic that there are few rules to be broken. The system can stand situations that might permanently damage the social fabric in a more stringent society like Britain. One interesting piece of information provided by Fitzherbert was that West Indians consider physical appearance at all ages to be very important. From an early age, children have their skin oiled to keep it in good condition.

Moody and Stroud (1967) give a short descriptive comment on home conditions during infancy in a sample of 98 West Indian immigrant families living in Britain. The major impression was of the cramped, overcrowded, and inconvenient housing conditions. In a more objective study, Rutter, Yule, Morton, and Bagley (1975) stated that, in a sample of 51 London-based West Indian families, half the families were living in circumstances in which there were at least 1.5 persons (adults or children) per room usable for living, eating, or sleeping (i.e., excluding bathroom and toilet). Moody and Stroud also stated that half their sample of infants (61) were child-minded or fostered while the mother worked. In all, 48 infants were looked after by an illegal child-minder, and a quarter of the total sample were put in the care of more than one of these unofficial agencies. According to Jackson (1971) unofficial child-minding among West Indian immigrants has reached a "national emergency." She estimated on rather subjective information that half of the preschool West Indian children in Britain are being illegally minded, often in overcrowded and unstimulating conditions which "must seriously damage their future educative chances."

Rutter et al. (1975) reported that two-fifths of the children in their West Indian sample had received unofficial child-minding compared with only one in 20 of the children from the nonimmigrant sample.

Information on social conditions of West Indian immigrant families outside London is rather scant. Halliday (1971) reported that, in Birmingham, the majority of West Indians were confined to specific areas in the inner ring of the city where housing was in a state of deterioration and the worst in the city.

Relevant comparisons between social conditions in Britain and the West Indies suggests that the immigrant infant is at a developmental disadvantage compared to his Caribbean Island counterpart. A Community Relations Commission (1971) report put the situation as follows:

> West Indian children are not expected or encouraged to play with toys and the educational value of this sort of activity is often not recognized by the West Indian mother. In the Caribbean islands there are many alternative opportunities for play in the area around the house and the communal yard. In Britain the child often spends the day cooped up in a room, continually restrained from making a noise or engaging in energetic activity. In the West Indies mothers often work, but the children are then left with a childminder in very unstimulating conditions and their essential pre-school experience is limited and stunting. Motor skills are also undeveloped in the pre-school years and both the child born here and then placed with a childminder and the child from the Caribbean who has not had to conquer the hazard of urban living—crossing busy roads for instance—suffer from great difficulties when they reach the infant schools.

A major change in social conditions for the West Indian immigrant family living in Britain appears to be the break-up of the extended family system. In Rutter et al.'s (1975) West Indian sample, only 12% of wives' parents and 6.5% of husbands' parents live in this country. Only 13.7% of the West Indian families had help and assistance from relatives and friends in looking after the children, compared to 30.7% in the nonimmigrant families ($p < .05$). An important consideration raised by Rutter et al. was that it would be misleading to consider West Indian immigrants as homogeneous. There was a considerable heterogeneity in their sample due both to island of origin and other reasons.

Behavioral Research Involving West Indian Infants

Only a few studies have been carried out on the early development of West Indian children living in the Caribbean or in Britain. The earliest investigation was conducted by Curti, Marshall, and Steggarda (1935) in the Kingston City Day Nursery. Eighteen selected items from the Gesell schedules were administered at 12 months. At this age, Jamaican infants performed at the same level or higher on 39% of the items, when compared with the norms from Gesell's white American subjects. In particular, they were better at standing, walking, and accepting an additional cube.

Curti et al. were particularly struck by the irregular and inconsistent performances of the Jamaican infants. The observation was considered to be a result of using a white examiner. Taking into consideration such factors as the poor home conditions and nutritional standards of the infants, the researchers concluded that the fact the Jamaican children scored as high as they did was impressive. With 'fairer' tests, the Jamaican infants would probably have made a better comparative showing. Such conclusions were not in keeping with the thinking on black–white differences at that time.[3]

It was not until almost 40 years later that further relevant research appeared in the literature. A longitudinal study in Kingston suggested developmental precocity for Jamaican infants that was maintained during the first year of life, most clearly for gross motor behaviors such as head control, sitting, and walking alone (see Grantham-McGregor & Back, 1971; Grantham-McGregor & Hawke, 1971). However, as with Curti et al., a comparison was only made with the Gesell test norms.

There are only four relevant British based studies prior to the present research (Brett, 1965; Hood, Oppe, Pless, & Apte, 1970; Pollack & Mitchell, 1974; Scott, 1975). The last two studies were truly comparative in nature, and their findings provided interesting contrasts with the earlier Jamaican research. Furthermore, Scott's study included a comparison of newborns.

The Pollack and Mitchell findings revealed West Indian infant advancement over English and Cypriot coevals in antigravity responses requiring control of head, neck, and back muscles at 1 month. This initial advance in responses along the corporeal axis was not maintained at later ages in activities such as sitting. Scott's results showed clear evidence for West Indian maturity in motor and sensory responses during the newborn period. These advancements were less obvious by 6 weeks and had disappeared by 26 weeks. Once again the strongest evidence for West Indian infant precocity was restricted to antigravity responses reflecting head control, but this precocity was lost by 6 months. In this respect, Scott's findings were similar to those of Pollack and Mitchell. Scott considered that the newborn results reflected genetic influences, and the decline in West Indian performance to be due to poor environmental conditions.

The differences between the Jamaican- and British-based studies are difficult to interpret clearly given the methodological contrasts. However, all the studies point to West Indian precocity early in development, regardless of environmental differences, which appears to be an aspect of the neuromuscular control of gross motor behavior involving antigravity responses along the vertical axis of the body.[4] This conclusion proved relevant in the interpretation of some of the findings from the intracultural study concerned with the ways in which West

---

[3] In McGraw's (1931) Florida-based study, black American infants scored lower on Gesell-type items than white babies. Garrett (1960), among others, interpreted this finding as demonstrating a genetic inferiority of blacks. Since McGraw, most of the relevant studies in Africa and the U.S. have given the reverse result, thus requiring a different interpretation of genetic inferiority (e.g., Jensen, 1973). Such interpretations have been based on a misunderstanding of the neoteny hypothesis which is concerned with species differences and not with racial ones (see Gould, 1977).

[4] In fact, contrary to Warren (1972), this conclusion seems a small pillar of support for the notion of universal negro infant precocity based on a review made by the author of nearly 50 published studies (Hopkins, 1977b). This review is obtainable on request.

Indian mothers attempted to stimulate the motor development of their infants (see Hopkins, 1977a).

Subjects in the Present Study

The breakdown in the final study of the West Indian sample by social class and sex is given in Table 2. A similar breakdown was obtained for the English sample with overall N = 46.

The subjects were born in the same hospital as used during the pilot studies. All mothers were multiparae. All parents approached agreed to participate in the study, which was explained to them as being concerned with the general development of healthy infants during the first 6 months of life.

Thirty-two mothers were married (18 boys, 14 girls); 8 had formed common law unions (4 boys, 4 girls). All came from rural Jamaica. The educational level of the mothers varied considerably, with about half receiving only an elementary education. Only four mothers received an examination-based secondary education, and the remaining 20 had non-examination secondary schooling. Twenty-six infants were seen until 6 months of age. Another 22 were followed up until the end of the first month of life (i.e., until 30 days of age). The babies were screened for "optimality" on 25 pre- and perinatal variables (see Table 1).

Table 3 gives data for three basic body measurements—birthweight, head circumstance, and crown–heel length—as well as for birth order and gestational age (assessed according to Farr et al., 1966). Head circumference and crown–heel length were measured with appropriate instruments to the nearest .50 cm within 24 hours of delivery, while birthweight was taken from the infant's hospital record.

Previous assessments of full-term newborn West Indian birthweight (Barron & Vessey, 1966) and head circumference (Grantham-McGregor & Desai, 1973) are quite similar to those in the present sample. Appropriate data for crown–heel length measures were not found. By European standards birth order indicates a high parity, with a range of 2 to 12 live births. The gestational age assessment confirms that the sample as a whole can be considered full-term.

Mothers and infants were discharged from hospital on the third or fourth day

Table 2.   Breakdown of WI sample by sex and social class.

Social Class	Sex		Total
	Male	Female	
III	12	13	25
IV & V	11	12	23
Total	23	25	48

Table 3.   Means and standard deviations for three newborn anthropometric measures, birth order and gestational age.

Variable	Mean	S.D.
Birthweight (Kgs.)	3.31	0.40
Head circumference (cms.)	33.81	1.31
Crown-heel length (cms.)	49.26	2.39
Birth order	4.65	2.77
Gestational age (days)	276.56	6.12

after delivery. They returned with their infants to what can best be described as a slum area consisting of dilapidated Victorian terraced houses. Most of the family accomodation consisted of two to three rented rooms within such houses. In general, the state of upkeep of the West Indian housing was inferior to that of the English families as indicated by the significant differences in humidity measures between the two samples at the 1 month and 6 month follow-ups ($p < .001$). Inadequate heating during the winter months meant that the babies slept in rooms that were generally colder than those for the English infants ($p < .01$). Thus, most infants were confined to cots, heavily swaddled in blankets, for longer periods of time than their English counterparts during the colder months of the year ($p < .01$).

Assessments of the home environment at 6 months gave results in keeping with previous reports on the child-care environment in Britain. After demonstrating metric equivalence between the two samples for the home measures according to Poortinga's (1971) method, mean differences on these variables were subjected to multivariate analysis. Using Hotelling's T2, the result was highly significant ($F = 5.58$, $df = 9.44$, $p < .0001$). In short, the inanimate dimensions of the home environment provided the greatest discrimination between samples. The lack of play materials for the West Indian infants, rather any other aspect of the home environment, represented the most striking differences between the samples ($p < .0001$).

It is interesting to note that when the nine measures of the home environment were correlated with social class none of the West Indian coefficients were significant.[5] The pattern of relationships within the English sample was strikingly different. Here, social class was significantly related to the HOME subscales "provision of appropriate play materials" ($r\,pb = .512$; $p < .015$) and to "variety of play objects" ($r\,pb = .435$; $p < .05$). These sample differences argue against the wisdom of using only social class as a means of representing varia-

---

[5] Six subscales of HOMEinventory and 3 dimensions of inanimate stimulation from Yarrow et al. (1972).

tions in major environmental dimensions for studies concerned with infants from non-Western settings.

When the infants were 6 months old, 23 health visitors attempted HOME inventory assessments during unannounced home visits within 1 week after the author's follow-up. Between them, they managed to complete 17 assessments out of a possible total of 26 in the sixth-month West Indian sample. Agreements between E and the health visitors on the items of the HOME inventory ranged from 65% to 100%. For all those items based on direct observation rather than questioning, agreement was from 82% to 100%. The results suggest that a reasonable degree of confidence can be invested in the study's findings using the HOME inventory, despite the fact that the researcher's sex and ethnicity, as well as acquired status, had the potential for producing distortions in both maternal behavior and responses.

Further details on some West Indian child-rearing practices and attitudes concern breast feeding, use made of postnatal clinics, and infant sleeping position. During interviews many of the West Indian mothers stressed the importance of breast feeding for the general health of their infants. Its importance was shown by the fact that 79.3% of the West Indian mothers began with breast feeding, and 58.3% were still breast feeding at 1 month. In contrast, only 28.3% of the English mothers started by breast feeding ($p < .001$), with 17.4% still maintaining the practice until the end of the first month. In the remaining West Indian sample, only one mother was still breast feeding at least once a day at 6 months, with a similar picture obtaining for the English sample (N = 2).

As far as taking the infant to the health clinic for a check-up during the first month was concerned, there was no significant difference between the samples, although there were more West Indian mothers (70.8%) than English mothers (54.3%) who did not make use of this facility. A similar picture pertained to the remaining samples at 6 months (67.4% West Indian versus 50.7% English).

For infant sleeping position, as expected from the pilot study, there was a notable difference. At 1 month, most West Indian infants (66.7%) were always placed in the prone position for sleeping, while only 6.5% of the English had this experience ($p < .001$). A similar difference was found for those infants seen again at 6 months ($p < .001$). All West Indian mothers who put their infant in a prone position for sleeping mentioned that the infant rested on a pillow. They felt that lying prone on a pillow would help to strengthen the infant's neck and back muscles and thereby facilitate the acquisition of sitting alone, an important developmental milestone for most West Indian mothers (see Figure 2).

Not only did the West Indian mothers demonstrate a marked involvement with their infants' gross motor behaviors but also with their physical appearances. All mothers interviewed in the pilot study stressed the importance of their babies having a healthy skin and regular facial features as well as long and supple limbs. In the final study, this figure stood at 75%.

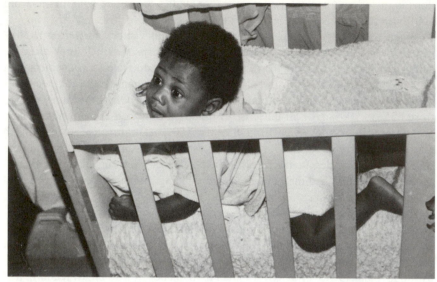

Figure 2.   A 6-month-old infant just after wakening from a period of sleep. Prior to sleep, he had been placed in the typical West Indian position of prone lying with the head lying on a pillow.

During the pilot and final studies, an attempt was made to identify beliefs and practices about childrearing that were particular to the West Indian parents. A selection is given in an Appendix. It reveals a use of folk medicines and desire to counteract the "evil eye" influence.

The selective review of findings reported here can be summarized as follows. The West Indian infants lived in more impoverished circumstances than their English coevals. The impoverishment was particularly striking with regard to the provision of inanimate stimulation that is generally assumed to be important for the development of fine motor abilities. However, set against this were marked concerns shown by the West Indian mothers for stimulating gross motor development and improving the physical appearance of their infants. It is these concerns that manifest themselves in a formalized system of infant handling carried out by West Indian mothers. Before dealing with this topic, we must first define what is meant by handling.

Handling the Human Infant

Handling is defined here as proximal sensory manipulation of an infant's physical features and postural and motor behaviors, through the juxtaposition of the infant's body and the caregiver's hands. This definition has been somewhat pedantically formulated to restrict its application to the act of handling per se. Handling thus defined means that the infant can move (actively) or be moved (passively). Passive movement consists of movements that are effected by the caregiver's, and not the infant's action, such as massaging. Active movement is caregiver action that facilitates the infant's own movements, such as encouraging voluntary walking by supporting the infant in an upright position.

Based on a cross-cultural review (Hopkins, 1976b), infant handling procedures can be considered as consisting of two types: formal and informal. Both types are learned by the caregiver within a social or institutional context. *Informal handling* is the manner in which a caregiver incidentally handles a child in completing routine daily activities associated with childcare such as bathing, feeding, dressing, and soothing. *Formal handling* as a method of handling that is prescribed in its operation and can be an end itself rather than incidental to some other purpose.

The major distinction to be made between formal and informal handling is that the former encompasses functions that can be seen as being educational in the broadest sense of the word. The function of informal handling is concerned with immediate effects such as the relief of somatic discomfort, while that for formal handling is somewhat more long-term and less concerned with the here-and-now. Formal handling routines seem to be a feature of childcare practices in many non-Western countries but particularly in West Africa (e.g., Uka, 1966) and India, where it is termed *shantala* (Leboyer, 1974).

In recent years, field-based researchers have paid increasing attention to formal handling routines as means of demonstrating empirical relationships between aspects of infant behavior and culturally determined forms of childrearing practices. For example, Super (1976) carried out a study of infant development in a western Kipsigi Kenyan farming community. By American standards his results indicated that these infants were advanced in those gross motor behaviors (i.e., sitting and walking alone) that were subjected to formal instruction and could be practiced during daily activities. Furthermore, preliminary results from other Kenyan societies suggest that formal handling routines are widespread and that the content of such routines is directly related to the average age of attainment of particular gross motor behaviors. The degree of advancement in an infantile gross motor behavior may be therefore predictable from environmental measures.

In the pilot study for this research, interviews about formal handling routines were carried out with mothers and nurses from Nigeria, Uganda, Sierra Leone, India (Gujaret), and Pakistan. The general conclusion was that formal handling routines in West Africa and the Indian subcontinent were more extensive than those reported for East African cultures, including those investigated by Super. In particular, the description of the Nigerian routine was very similar to that observed in the West Indian sample.

The specific aims of the intracultural aspect of this study were threefold: (a) to provide descriptive data on the use of formal handling in the sample; (b) to assess if certain newborn characteristics prior to the imposition of formal handling are related to the contents of the routine, if any, used by the mothers; and (c) to evaluate the influence of formal handling on sensorimotor development during the first 6 months.

In the between-culture comparison part of the study, highly significant differences had appeared between the West Indian and English samples both in terms of the level and patterning of behavior (Hopkins, 1976a). These differences could be related to contrasts in the home environments between the two samples, particularly at 6 months. The general aim of the intracultural study was, therefore, to see if the nature of the empirical relations found between samples could be replicated intraculturally.

Formal Handling Used by West Indian Mothers Living in Britain

To recapitulate, the West Indian sample consists of 48 mothers and their healthy offspring who were seen 3 to 4 days after birth and then followed up in their homes when the infants were 1 month old. A further follow-up in the home was made of 26 of the infants from the original sample when they were 6 months old. At 1 and 6 months it was noted that the West Indian subjects lived in more impoverished conditions than their English counterparts who were also residents in the same general housing area. By 6 months it was clear there were striking differences in home environments between the two samples such that the West Indian parents provided little in the way of appropriate play materials for their infants. However, the West Indian parents put greater store on the gross motor development of their infants than did the English ones, one element of which was the formal handling routine. Information on the West Indian formal handling routine was obtained through semistructured interviews and direct observation. Video recordings were made of 5 of the West Indian mothers performing the routine.

Data Collection, Statistical Treatment and Other Considerations

Data was collected in the following areas: behavioral and paramedical characteristics of the newborns prior to formal handling (antecedent characteristics), behavioral development after formal handling had begun (subsequent development), and certain background variables assumed to have some bearing on the results.

In addition to birthweight, head circumference, crown–heel length and birth order, the *paramedical variables* included 10 of the items assessing physical appearance in the Farr et al. (1966) procedure (skin color excluded). *Behavioral assessment* was carried out at 3 days, 30 days, and 6 months of age. The first assessment was made in a quiet room in the hospital, while the other two were completed in the home. The day 3 and day 30 examinations were in accordance with Brazelton's (1973) protocol, and at 6 months the complete Griffiths infant test (Griffiths, 1970), along with measures of object permanence and spatial ability (Escalona & Corman, n.d.), were used. The raw scores for the last two measures were the number of items passed, an approach used previously by King and Seegmiller (1973) and Matheny (1975), with similar data (cf. Gottfried & Brody, 1975). Only three of the Griffiths test subscales were retained for analysis as the personal-social and hearing-and-speech ones relied heavily on maternal reports. Those retained were locomotor (AQ), eye–hand (DQ), and performance (EQ) subscales (see Schaffer & Emerson, 1968).

In addition, five items were abstracted from the locomotor subscale which were considered to reflect postural control. These were: "sits with slight support (16)," "sits alone for a short time (20)," "can be left-sitting alone on the floor (23)," "stands when held up (25)," and "sits well in a chair (26)." The number of items as listed in the inventory of items for the locomotor subscale are given in brackets (see Griffiths, 1970, her Appendix II). They will be referred to as *static responses.* Measurements of ambient room temperature and humidity were taken at all assessments.

Background variables were certain parental behavioral and nonbehavioral characteristics (e.g. personality, age of mother arriving in U.K.) and assessment of home conditions through a combination of direct observation and questioning (Caldwell, 1970; Yarrow et al., 1972).

This study is essentially a single population study in which an attempt is made to demonstrate that variations in maternal handling are related to variations in infant behavior. Subjects could be grouped on some a priori basis (e.g., handled versus no handling), and then difference testing could be carried out (e.g., with Hotelling's T^2) using infant behavioral assessments as the dependent measures. Such an approach, however, suggests unwarranted confidence in the validity of the mother's interview responses on their use of formal handling.

An alternative approach more in keeping with the exploratory nature of this research would be to use the different sets of measures as a basis for evaluating a typology of respondents as in, for example, the factor analytic Q technique. A suitable taxonomic procedure for this approach is latent profile analysis (LPA). This classification model was developed by Gibson (1959) within the overall system of relations between latent and manifest variables previously concerned with dichotomous items (Lazarfeld & Henry, 1968). The aim of LPA is to classify *p*-dimensional score vectors into homogeneous clusters which can then be interpreted in terms of individuals or materials they characterize.

One distinct advantage of LPA over the factor analytic model is that it is not restricted to the same extent by considerations of multivariate normality. Not only does LPA use second-order moments (variances, covariances, and correlations), but also third and higher-order moments. A suitable clustering program (LPA2) has been written by Mardberg (1974) in Fortran IV based on Green's (1951) solution of latent class analysis (LCA) for dichotomous variables. The program permits the user to derive a number of solutions of different profiles from which the "best" one may be selected. Each cluster of individuals is described by standard score means ($\times 100$) of manifest variable which form the profile of the cluster. The program can be used with LPA and LCA. The criteria for selecting the 'best' solution, and further details on LPA, can be found in Hopkins (1976b).

The main data analysis is carried out in three steps. Firstly, it takes place within the framework of LPA, which leads to the separation of the sample into different profiles. The West Indian mothers did not use the handling routine in the same ways (another group did not use it at all); therefore, the content of these profiles will be checked to see if the distinctions made in the use of the routine are reflected in the profiles. Secondly, the n profiles are incorporated into a profile $\times$ group frequency table to test whether, for example, they significantly distinguished from each other in terms of a preponderance of one or other group of infants.

Finally, as an additional source of analysis and verification, the different groups of infants are compared on the same behavioral and environmental items used in the LPA analysis, but this time relative to the median scores on those items for the sample. Here, frequency data will be cast in group $\times$ 2 (above and below median) contingency tables. An LCA analysis is carried out on the five dichotomous variables taken from the Griffiths test. Following this, the n classes are used in a class $\times$ group contingency table. Statistical tests for the contingency tables will be either χ^2 (for independent samples) or Fisher's exact probability test. The level will be set at .05, two-tailed.

A final consideration is that of item reduction. The full protocol of the NBAS was administered and scored for every infant in the sample.[6] However, there were too many behavioral items in the scale relative to the number of subjects for a multivariate analysis such as LPA. A system of item reduction was therefore devised which resulted in the retention for analysis of 12 items out of the original 26 scored. Briefly, the system considered the direct relevance of a particular item for a study chiefly concerned with sensorimotor development. In addition, it assessed reliabilities of item clusters using coefficient alpha (Nunally, 1967) in a way suggested by McKennell (1970), and then went on to check characteristics of item distributions and other criteria. Overall, an attempt was made to maintain the original integrity of the protocol while at the same time removing items that could have a distorting influence on the results.

The following items were retained for the day 3 and 1 month assessment occasions: orientation inanimate visual, orientation inanimate auditory, orienta-

---

[6] Complete results can be obtained on request.

tion animate visual, orientation animate auditory, alertness, general tonus, pull-to-sit, activity, peak of excitement, irritability, lability of states, and hand-to-mouth facility.[7]

Description of the West Indian Handling Routine

Formal handling of the West Indian infants by their mothers consists of passive stretching movements and massaging during the early months and the addition of other interventions from about the third month to provoke active movements (e.g., stepping). The stretching exercises and massaging are carried out at the end of bath time, usually when the baby is still wet. At the beginning, the infant is suspended by both arms and gently shaken up and down (Figure 3). Each arm is stretched separately in suspension (Figure 4), and then the baby is turned upside down and held by the ankles (Figure 5). The mother holds the baby's head on both sides and lifts upwards, thus stretching the neck (Figure 6).

The baby is placed on the mother's lap or on a bed, and then the arms and legs are partly rotated at the joints, with accompanying stretching movements (Figure 7). Most large joints and the small of the back are tapped with the open hand with the infant either lying downward on the mother's lap or, at later age, held in the standing position (Figure 8). The infant is placed face downward, and the mother then strokes his back three times on each side of the vertebral column with downward movements (Figure 9). The baby is thrown into the air and caught (Figure 10). Some mothers stated that it was important to hear the joints "crack" during the stretching exercises. After the baby is dry, the body is massaged vigourously with some form of oil, usually olive oil. The oil is applied to all parts of the body with combined rubbing and stretching movements, so that even the fingers are stretched. Finally, different parts of the body are subjected to cosmetic "shaping." The mother attempts to mold her baby's head (Figure 11), nose (Figure 12), small of the back (Figure 13), and the buttocks. In a few instances, after exercising, the baby was swaddled in a large, specially warmed towel which helped to induce sleep.

At later months infants are given direct encouragement to sit and walk. When a girl reaches 3 months of age she is propped up with a cushion or pillow which is gradually removed as she shows increased ability to sit upright. The process is called *catching up*. Boys are not caught up until 4 months of age, and the most common reason given for this sex difference was that boys have longer (and therefore weaker) backs than girls (Figure 14). Stepping responses are elicited by standing the baby up in the caregiver's lap. Once stepping has begun, the baby is

---

[7] To the uninitiated, the orientation items involve visual and auditory location and fixation of social (examiner's face, voice) and nonsocial stimuli (red ball, rattle). Peak of excitement involves the ability to maintain a quiet state in the face of aversive stimuli. The names of the remaining items should be self-explanatory.

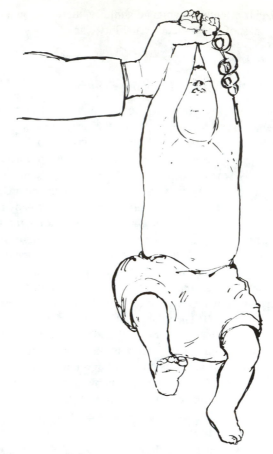

Figures 3 to 13.   Aspects of the West Indian formal handling routine. Drawn by Geert Kraaijenbrink from photographs taken by the author.

'walked' up the caregiver's body (Figure 15). When the infant can support his own weight, he is placed on the floor, held up by the hands, and coaxed to make steps (Figure 16). In the interviews with West Indian mothers, it was obvious they attributed considerable importance to the attainment of basic motor abilities and that these were facilitated by the passive and active components of the formal handling routine.

It was noted that the formal and informal handling of infants by mothers were not discrete caregiver–infant interactions. Certain aspects of formal handling tended to be incorporated into informal handling on some of the occasions when a West Indian mother was involved in the playful activity with her infant. The two types of handling interacted to produce a general style of mother–child

Figure 4.

Figure 5.

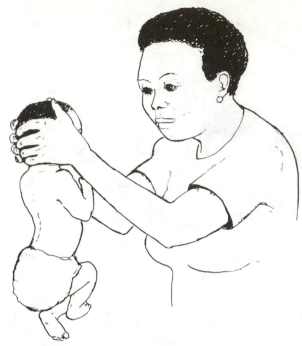

Figure 6.

interaction that was distinctively non-European in morphology (cf. Goldberg, 1970).

The routine started on returning home from the hospital. In Jamaica formal handling begins shortly after birth, and the delay in onset with immigrant West Indian mothers is possibly due to their fear of being reprimanded by the nurses and doctors. (In fact, some mothers stated that they thought the routine was illegal in Britain.) Most mothers reported that they endeavored to keep up the

Figure 7.

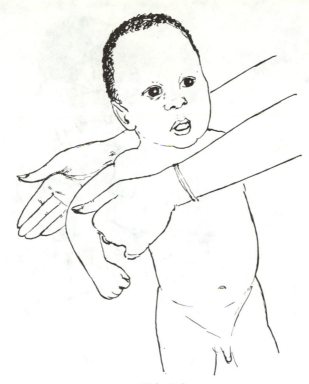

Figure 8.

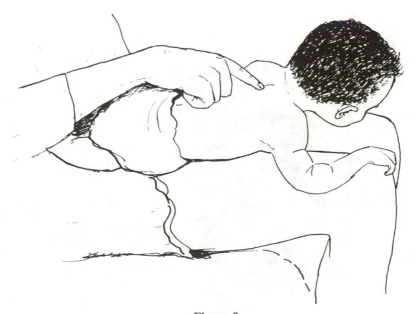

Figure 9.

Figure 10.

Figure 11.

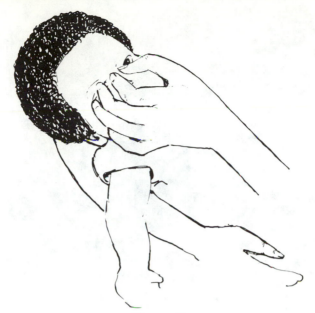

Figure 12.

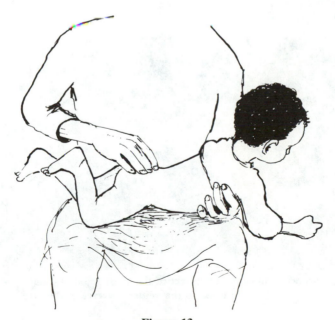

Figure 13.

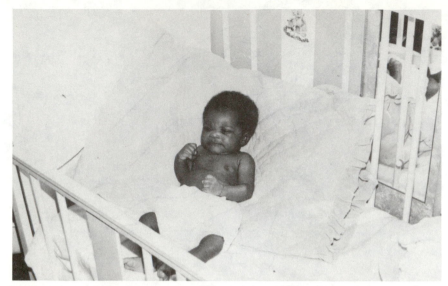

Figure 14. Another aspect of the West Indian formal handling routine termed "catching up."

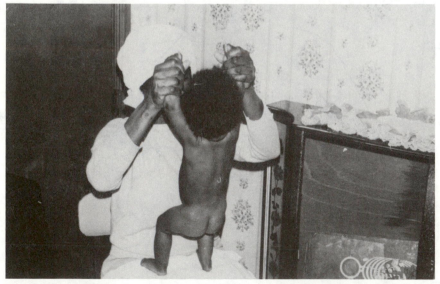

Figure 15. An active intervention aspect of the West Indian formal handling routine: Encouraging the baby to walk up the ventral surface of the caregiver.

Figure 16.   Another active intervention aspect of the West Indian formal handling routine: Encouraging the baby to take steps on the floor while supported. This infant is 5 months old.

passive exercises until the infant was too heavy to handle, which usually coincided with expected time of sitting. There was a gradual reduction in the number of exercises, with neck stretching (Figure 6) the first one to be discontinued. Massaging was maintained for about the first year of life, although one mother claimed she was still rubbing down her 2-year-old son with olive oil. In practice, the stretching exercises, massaging, and the active movement interventions tended to be greatly reduced if and when the mother had to return to work.

Breakdown of Formal Handling in the Sample

Table 4 shows that the majority of mothers (60.4%) used both exercising and massaging in their formal handling, while 20.8% did not use it at all. Where only

Table 4. Frequency data on formal handling.

Formal Handling	Absolute Frequency	Relative Frequency (per cent)
1. Exercises only	2	4.2
2. Massage only	7	14.6
3. Exer. & mass.	29	60.4
4. None	10	20.8
Total	48	100.0

part of the routine was used, more mothers (14.6%) dispensed with exercises than with massaging (4.2%).

To facilitate discussion of the data, categories 1, 2, and 4 were collapsed to derive a new catagory, "part or none" (PN), and category 3 was left as "exercise and massaging" (EM). (See Table 5 for summary.) A breakdown of two categories by sex is given in Table 6. More girls (27.1%) than boys (12.5%) were subjected to part or none of the routine. Information on the frequency with which mothers used all or part of the routine ($N = 38$) is given in relation to the sex of the infant in Table 7.

The category "less than every day" results from a pooling of two categories [i.e., "every other day" ($N = 7$) and "once a week" ($n = 8$)]. A fourth category, "less than once a week," contained no subjects.

The frequency data on the inclusion or exclusion of the neck stretching exercise is given according to sex in Table 8 ($N = 31$). Subjects who either received no formal handling or were massaged but not exercised were excluded from the evaluation of this item.

Mothers who used all or part of the routine ($N = 38$) were asked why they carried it out, with the following responses: (a) Because their mothers had carried out the routine: All mothers gave this response; (b) To help the baby grow up strong and healthy: given by 33 mothers; (c) To find out if the baby had injured himself: as babies cannot talk it is necessary to have an alternative method of finding out if there are any injuries: given by 18 mothers; (d) To help babies grow up into supple children and adults: if a child has a fall (e.g., when learning to walk), he or she will incur little or no injury because of this suppleness. Adults who are "stiff" in their movements have not been exercised and massaged sufficiently as young children: given by seven mothers; (e) It is a playful thing to do with babies: given by two mothers.

Table 5. Reorganized frequency data on formal handling.

Formal Handling	Absolute Frequency	Relative Frequency (per cent)
1. Exer. & mass.	29	60.4
2. Part or none	19	39.6
Total	48	100.0

Table 6.   Frequency data on formal handling by sex.

Formal Handling	Sex		Total
	Male	Female	
Exer. & mass.	17	12	29
Part or none	6	13	19
Total	23	25	48

The mothers who reported that they employed no part of the routine ($N = 10$) said without exception that it was old-fashioned. In three of these cases, the mothers also reported that they were frightened of using the routine because it seemed to be too vigorous to use with young babies. Those mothers using only part of the routine ($N = 9$) tended to be unclear about why they did not use all aspects. The impression given was that the complete routine was too time consuming. Figure 17 provides a schematic summary of the West Indian formal handling routine as reported which indicated three aspects (I, II, III) that are increasingly specific in content. Aspect I shows that the sample can be divided into three groups on the basis of all, part or none of the routine being used. Those mothers using part of the routine are differentiated on the basis of whether or not they incorporate the neck-stretching item into their routine. Table 9 indicates how each aspect will be evaluated as well as the sample size involved. (The Ns are somewhat less for the parental personality measures in all aspects.) Thus, in Aspect Ib, two sets of criterion measures will be evaluated. Aspects I and II are concerned with the second and third aims of the study, while Aspect III is restricted to the second aim.

LPA and Median Comparison Results

The results of the LPA of the behavior-antecedent characteristics of *Aspect Ia* are presented in Figure 18 (i.e., cluster analysis of the twelve day 3 NBAS items).

For each profile, the first five items along the horizontal axis can be treated as "general alertness" and "peak of excitement" to lability of states as something akin to "temperament." The last item, hand-to-mouth facility, can be regarded as one or other type of latent variable.

Table 7.   Frequency data on how often formal handling used.

Frequency	Sex		Total
	Male	Female	
Every day	11	12	23
Less than every day	8	7	15
Total	19	19	38

Table 8.   Frequency data on neck stretching excercise by sex.

Neck stretching	Male	Female	Total
		Sex	
Yes	10	7	17
No	7	7	14
Total	17	14	31

There are two profiles typifying two clusters of West Indian infants. Profile 1 consists of 21 subjects (Ss) and can be described in terms of a lower level of responding than Profile 2, except for a slightly greater amount of state changes. Profile 2 has 27 Ss who are generally more alert and "tonic" during the examination, and slightly more "temperamental" than those in Profile 1. It can be seen that the two profiles show a mirror-image relationship.

The membership of each profile relative to the use of formal handling can be described as follows. Neither profile contains a predominant grouping of either

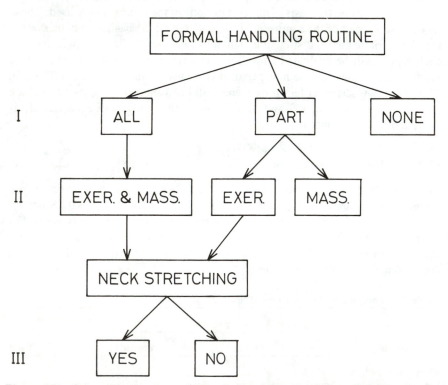

Figure 17.   Schematic summary of West Indian formal handling routine indicating 3 aspects (I, II, & III) for evaluation.

Table 9. Procedure for evaluating 3 aspects of WI formal handling routine.

Aspect	Predictor variable(s)	Criterion variable(s)	Day 3/ 1 month	6 months
Ia	x, z	Use made of formal handling	48	26
Ib	Use made of formal handling	y	48	26
IIa	x, z	Frequency of application of formal handling	38	18
IIb	Frequency of application of formal handling	y	38	18
III	x	Use made of neck stretching	31	

Key: x = antecedent characteristics
       y = subsequent development
       z = background variables.

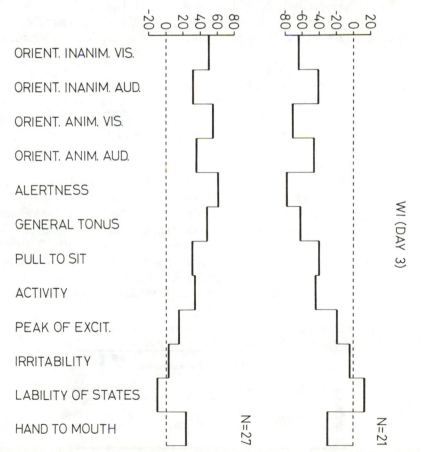

Figure 18. Behavioral profiles of the 12-day 3 NBAS items for Aspect Ia. Right-hand scale is Profile 1.

Table 10.   Frequency data on profile membership (Aspect Ia) in terms of formal handling and sex.

Formal handling	Sex				Sex		
	M	F	Total		M	F	Total
Exer. & mass.	8	4	12		9	8	17
Part or none	3	6	9		3	7	10
Total	11	10	21		12	15	27
		Profile 1				Profile 2	

formal handling category. Profile 1 has 12 EM and 9 PN infants, while Profile 2 has 17 and 10, respectively ($\chi^2 = 1.01$, $df = 1$, n.s.). The membership of each profile, relative to the use made of formal handling and sex, is given in Table 10.

In contrast, the median comparisons on each item reveal identical significant differences ($\chi^2 = 8.44$, $df = 1$, $p < .01$) for general tonus and head control in the pull-to-sit-maneuver (Table 11).

Those infants who received the complete handling routine (EM), later have proportionally more subjects above the overall sample median for these two items than those who do not (PN). However, for both items there were more PN girls (7) than boys (4), which suggests that the combined affects of sex and how strong a newborn "feels" when handled might determine the extent of formal handling subsequently received.

The paramedical characteristics of the newborn prior to formal handling consist of two sets of data: firstly, the 10 gestational age items based on physical appearance, and secondly, head circumference, crown–heel length, birthweight, and birth order, taken together. The gestational age item LPA produces two profiles, one indicating greater physical maturity than the other. Profile 1 ($N = 23$) is typified by newborns with more mature physical characteristics. Profile 2 ($N = 25$) contains 15 out of 19 Ss in the PN category, while for Profile 1 it is 19 out of 29 EM Ss ($\chi^2 = 7.40$, $df = 1$, $p < .01$). Median comparisons of the 10

Table 11.   Median comparison result (Aspect Ia) for general tonus and pull-to-sit maneuver.

Median	Formal handling		
	EM	PN	Total
Above	25	8	33
Below	4	11	15
Total	29	19	48

$\chi^2 = 8.44$, $df = 1$, $p < .01$

items results in significant differences ($p < .01$) between the two profiles for skin texture and skull hardness such that more EM infants ($N = 20$) score above the median values for these two items than their PN counterparts ($N = 17$). The more physically mature newborns have, therefore, a greater likelihood of receiving the complete formal handling routine at a later age.

The other paramedical LPA results in a major and minor profile but is less conclusive than the first LPA. In Profile 1 ($N = 12$) there are larger babies with a higher birth order, and six of the newborns are from the PN category. The remaining 13 PN newborns are in Profile 2 ($N = 36$), a nonsignificant result. The same inconclusive result applies to all the median comparisons. In both LPAs sex does not exert any marked influence in relation to the extent of formal handling, unlike the newborn behavioral LPA.

The LPA of subsequent development on the twelve NBAS items at 1 month (Aspect Ib) results in three profiles ($Ns = 17, 18$, and 13). None of the profiles differentiate between the EM and PN infants. The median comparisons of individual items do not provide any additional information to that given by LPA. Nor is a sex effect apparent in the analysis.

At 6 months, the LPA of the three Griffiths test subscales (locomotor, eye–hand coordination, and performance), and the measures of object permanence and spatial abilities (Escalona & Corman, n.d.), results in two profiles for the "best" solution ($N1 = 9$; $N2 = 17$). Neither profile can be satisfactorily explained in terms of formal handling. The median comparisons for the individual measures leads to the same conclusion, since none of the five comparisons are significant.

For the LCA analysis of the static responses at 6 months taken from the locomotor subscale of the Griffiths test, the number of items was reduced from five to four, as no infant failed "sits with slight support" (16). On this basis, two classes of Ss are identifiable (see Table 12).

In the first class ($N = 11$) there are a greater number of failures on all four items. On two of the items "can be left sitting on the floor" (23) and "sits well in chair" (26), there are no passes. In the second class, all subjects pass item 23,

Table 12.   Latent class analysis result
(Aspect Ib) for 4 "static response" items
taken from Griffiths test locomotor subscale.

Formal handling	Class 1	Class 2	Total
EM	3	12	15
PN	7	4	11
Total	11	15	26

$p = .028$ (Fisher's exact probability test)

and 80% pass item 26. The first class contains 7 out of 11 subjects in the PN category of formal handling at 6 months, while there are proportionally more EM subjects in the second class ($N = 12$), a significant difference ($p = .028$). Infants who receive the complete formal handling during the first few months of life are more likely to have better muscular power and postural control than the PN ones.

The final predictor measures examined in *Aspect Ia* are the background variables which are grouped into these data sets. The first are parental demographic characteristics consisting of number of preschool children, maternal and paternal ages, maternal and paternal lengths of stay in U.K., ages of parents on arrival in Britain, and number of children born in the West Indies. The second consist of paternal personality based on extroversion, introversion, and lie scale scores from the Eysenck Personality Inventory. The final set is made up of the home environment assessment made at 6 months.

The first two data sets lead to results that are not interpretable in terms of formal handling. The same result obtains for the LPA of the home environment assessments. However, the median comparisons of the individual assessments lead to one significant result. Here, the two handling groups differ significantly in the number of infants scoring above or below the overall sample median for 'provision of appropriate play materials' ($p = .043$), as shown in Table 13.

Those infants receiving the whole formal handling routine are more likely to come, therefore, from homes providing more suitable play materials at 6 months than the PN infants.

Overall, the results of *Aspect II* on the frequency of formal handling are not clear cut for the LPAs and the LCAs, and for the median comparisons of individual items. The only result to lend itself to anything like a tentative interpretation is the LPA of parental demographic characteristics for *Aspect IIa*. Here the "best" solution contains two profiles ($N1 = 18$; $N2 = 20$) in which, out of 15 parents in the "less than everyday" category, 10 are placed in Profile 2. This profile contains the younger parents who had arrived at an earlier age in Britain

Table 13.   Median comparison result (Aspect Ib) for "provision of appropriate play materials."

Median	Formal handling		
	EM	PN	Total
Above	10	1	11
Below	5	10	15
Total	15	11	26

$p = .043$ (Fisher's exact probability test)

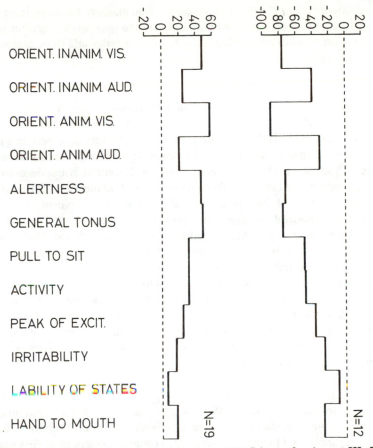

ORIENT. INANIM. VIS.

ORIENT. INANIM. AUD.

ORIENT. ANIM. VIS.

ORIENT. ANIM. AUD.

ALERTNESS

GENERAL TONUS

PULL TO SIT

ACTIVITY

PEAK OF EXCIT.

IRRITABILITY

LABILITY OF STATES

HAND TO MOUTH

Figure 19.   Behavioral profiles of the 12-day 3 NBAS items for Aspect III. Right-hand scale is Profile 1.

than those in Profile 2. However, the χ^2 analysis and median comparison results are not significant.

The LPA results in *Aspect III* on the relationship between antecedent behavioral characteristics and neck-stretching exercise of the formal handling routine are the final consideration in this section. The LPA of the three 12-day NBAS items is shown in Figure 19.

Profile 1 (N = 12) contains 10 out of 14 subjects who were subsequently reported as not receiving the neck-stretching exercise. The profile is characterized by lower levels of performance, particularly for the general alertness and motor items. From the 12 median comparisons, two are worth mentioning. For general tonus, proportionally more infants not receiving neck stretching fall below the median sample value, a result which just fails to reach significance

($\chi^2 = 3.70$, $df = 1$, $p < .10$). In both cases, though, there are more female than male subjects who were not eventually subjected to neck stretching. For general tonus, it is six females and three males, and five females and three males in the case of pull-to-sit.

Discussion and Conclusions

This study was exploratory in nature. Within the context of a between-groups comparative design, it was designed to provide descriptive information on a routine of formal handling and its relations with certain antecedent newborn characteristics, as well as with subsequent development measures during the first 6 months of postnatal life, in a "normal" but select sample of obstetrically healthy infants born of working-class West Indian parents resident in a major industrial British city. In addition, other so-called background variables were considered in order to supplement, and possibly clarify, the heuristic value of the infant physical and behavioral characteristics used.

The results of this small-scale study tended to show intracultural validation for those results found in the comparison between West Indian and English infants in that a similar pattern of findings was found at these two levels (see Hopkins, 1976a, for further details). The incorporation of a means for intracultural validation was one of the major concerns of the research project. However, such concerns apart, the present study has revealed hitherto unreported details about the early childrearing environment of West Indian infants living in Britain, while at the same time confirming with greater objectivity details reported by others.

Some of these details may be of interest to infancy researchers, but others are of such a depressing nature they are deserving of closer attention from the appropriate social and health care services. Having experienced at first hand the impoverished and stressful conditions of immigrant West Indian families during the early '70s, the so-called racial riots of the early 1980s in Britain came as no great surprise to this author. The only surprising thing was that this social and economic protest had not taken place earlier.

The main implication of the findings reported in the previous section is that certain paramedical and behavioral characteristics of the West Indian newborn prior to the onset of formal handling are related to the extent of the routine eventually employed by the mother. In particular, this tentative evidence bearing on the second aim of this study suggests that the West Indian newborn may affect his or her mother's judgment on the use she makes of a traditional handling routine through his or her physical appearance (gestational age variables), general "feel" or motor maturity (general tonus and head control), and degree of alertness.

This evidence was relatively clear in Aspect Ia of the study, when infants who were administered the full routine were compared to those who received only received only part or none of it. Aspect III provided some corroborative evidence when subjects who either received no part of the routine or only the massaging component were excluded, and the presence or absence of the neck-stretching exercise was used as a basis for discriminating between groupings of subjects. However, in most cases, the possible influence of the newborn antecedent characteristics was made less distinct when consideration was given to the sex of the infant. Females seemed to be overrepresented in those mother–infant dyads where either the formal handling was used in part (or not at all) or where the neck-stretching exercise was omitted.

It is possible that sex is a more important factor than the behavioral abilities of the newborns, as defined by 12 NBAS items, in terms of influencing how the West Indian mother will use the formal handling routine. There is some evidence that American mothers respond differently to male and female infants, with the former receiving more proximal stimulation in the early weeks of life (Moss, 1967). The most likely explanation, however, could be in terms of an interaction effect between newborn behavioral organization and sex of the infant.

The 1-month results for Aspect Ib and Aspect IIb produced little evidence of any formal handling influences on subsequent development up to that age. Two speculations could account for this general finding. One is that some of the NBAS items might be redundant for this select group of black infants (i.e., there was a ceiling effect operating). The other speculation is that, by the age of the 1-month assessment, the mothers had been home for only 3 weeks or so, which may not have been long enough for the routine to have a systematic effect.

By 6 months, the routine appeared to be related to specific, rather than to general, behavioral outcomes, that is, the so-called static responses. More specifically, those infants who received the full routine tended to do better on items that assessed the ability to sit alone at this age. This finding can be seen as lending some support to that of Super's (1976) derived from a different black culture. It was quite clear from the present study that many of the West Indian mothers placed considerable emphasis in their childrearing on infants achieving the major gross motor milestones, especially sitting alone, as soon as possible.

Some implications of this emphasis can be brought out with reference to LeVine's (1977) functional model on the role of childrearing values in a cross-cultural perspective. Here such values are treated as basic goals parents set for themselves in relation to their offspring, so that it is not a question of what they want *from* the child but rather what they desire *for* him or her. LeVine speculates that parental goals are hierarchically organized, from short-term ones concerned with survival and health, through a concern for economic self-maintenance in maturity, to the long-term goal of maximizing cognitive capacities throughout the lifespan. He hypothesizes that, in Third World countries with high mortality rates, the main parental concern will be with the first goal, while in cultures with low rates and adequate economic resources, the third goal would be most conspicuous.

Given the obvious survival value of early motor behavior, as demonstrated by Konner (1972), it might be expected that parents in Third World countries with infant health hazards would attribute more importance to adaptive motor development than to cognitive development and consequently adopt appropriate forms of stimulation. The widespread use of formal handling routines in sub-Saharan Africa and the Indian subcontinent would seem to suggest, in the context of LeVine's model, that they are one of the instruments for achieving a culturally appropriate parental goal which is short-term in nature (viz., offspring survival during one of the most vulnerable periods of postnatal development).

In the case of West Indian parents who have immigrated to Britain, a change in parental goals, with improved pre- and postnatal care of mothers and their infants, might be expected. As a result the more acculturated parents might have a lower level of involvement with the handling routine. The Aspect IIa results gave some evidence in this respect, as the infants who were administered the routine less than every day tended to have younger parents who had arrived in Britain at a relatively earlier age. Given the tentative nature of this result, it should be borne in mind that, with similar immigrant populations, the reverse could take place in certain aspects of the acculturation process.

Logan (1973), for example, states that acculturation in medical beliefs has often not kept up other facets of folk society; that is, traditional health practices are maintained and modern medicine operates as an additional system to traditional forms of folk medicine. This line of thought is compatible with a multidimensional concept of modernization as put forward by Schainberg (1970) and Wober (1971) in which an individual can be "modern" on one dimension and "traditional" on others. The possibility cannot be excluded that West Indian parents living in Britain may consolidate rather than diminish aspects of their culturally determined childrearing practice such as formal handling, as part of a general movement to strengthen ethnic identity. Such practices may have become the case for parents of West Indian origin living in Britain at the present time.

Other background variables were generally uninformative except in the case of the home environment results in Aspect Ia. Here the median comparisons led to the conclusion that mothers who used only part or part or none of the routine (PN) tended to provide less stimulating home environments for their children at 6 months than mothers employing all of it (EM). In particular, the PN mothers provided less appropriate play materials. This finding implies that the more child-centered a mother, the more likely she is to make use of all the handling routine. The findings of Solkoff, Yaffe, Weintraub, and Blasse (1969) are of interest here. They report that preterm infants experimentally handled in the hospital lived in more stimulating home environments at 7 to 8 months uncorrected postnatal age (e.g., more toys were available to them) than the nonhandled group. They go on to state:

It is tantalising to speculate whether the handling procedures may have more positively affected the infant's behavior, thereby resulting in a more positive attitude on the part of the mother toward her infant. (p. 767)

The present study can be improved methodologically. It had the drawback of a small sample size (brought about, in part, by a strict method of screening) which necessitated collapsing categories for the purpose of data analysis. This study was subservient to a larger one in which it was thought necessary to control directly for obstetrical histories between black and white babies. Such an optimal group of black newborns could have lessened the impact of formal handling on subsequent developmental outcomes, in that it may have reduced behavioral variation. It is possible that complications of pregnancy and delivery have important influences on how a mother uses formal handling. It would be of interest to study clinically abnormal newborns in a society that practices formal handling to see whether mothers use the routine in a manner analogous to that described by Solkoff et al. (1969) (i.e., as a remedial medium as well as a prophylactic one).

During the course of the study, the author was put in contact with a West Indian mother, 41 years old, who had given birth to a Down's syndrome baby (Trisomy 21), her fourth child. The delivery was normal and uncomplicated. The infant was assessed at 6 days and then in the home at 1, 2 and 3 months, using the NBAS on each occasion. Even by 3 months the infant was still scoreable on all NBAS items except those assessing temperament, because at this age the infant never became upset. The only items to show consistent improvements were pull-to-sit and general tonus. On leaving the hospital, the mother was determined to use the complete handling routine in the hope of helping him overcome his deficient motor behavior.

Once she started using the routine, "everything felt wrong," according to her. She then drastically modified the routine both in extent and frequency of application, the baby mainly receiving massaging every other day. By 3 months, the mother had almost completely discarded the routine. It was quite obvious that the child's poor motor abilities severely disrupted the process of interaction involved in the formal handling routine, which requires active cooperation from the baby for its successful application. Figure 20 shows this lack of active cooperation for one aspect of the routine when the infant was 3 months old.

The mother tried to adjust the routine to suit her infant's motor abilities, but with little success. This case study demonstrates that young infants can, by their patterns of behavior, influence well-established practices of traditional childcare. In other words, feedback from Level C can bring about striking alterations in Level B (see Figure 1).

Another improvement that can be made to the present research is to study the interrelationships between formal and informal handling. Numerous questions arise in this respect. For example, are there any differences in informal handling between mothers who use the formal routine and those who do not? Do the two

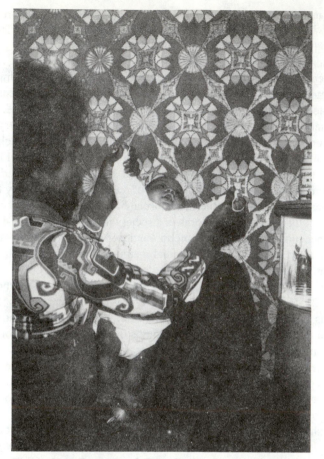

**Figure 20.   Example of West Indian Down's syndrome
infant being subjected to part of formal handling routine
at 3 months of age. Notice general "floppy" appearance of
baby during this particular maneuver.**

groups of mothers develop a different style of interacting with their infants, for
example, in the sense of maternal style as outlined by Hess and Shipman (1965)?

Perhaps the main value of this study has been in pointing out the potential
value of formal handling routines for research carried out on the topic of African
infant precocity. Warren (1972) recommended that future research should aim to
isolate more clearly relevant independent variables so that an "exit may be made
from the cross-cultural cycle, and further testing may proceed in an intra-cultur-
al, even experimental fashion" (p. 365). Formal handling seems to have some
potential for meeting this recommendation.

At a general level, the concern of cross-cultural behavioral research is to provide a reply to the question "What is the nature of human nature?" Many of the Piagetian-based cross-cultural studies on infant development are implicitly concerned with this question. Outside these studies, there are many more infant studies which are involved with a different question: "What is the nature of human nurture?" Answers to that question can only emerge from a careful compilation and integration of a broad range of intracultural studies. Hopefully the present study has provided one small piece in the vast jig-saw puzzle formed by human nurture of the young.

References

Ainsworth, M.D.S. (1967). *Infancy in Uganda*. Baltimore: Johns Hopkins Press.

Barash, D.P. (1977). *Sociobiology and behavior*. New York: Elsevier North Holland.

Barron, S.L., & Vessey, M.P. (1966). Birth-weight of infants born to immigrant women. *British Journal of Preventive and Social Medicine, 20*, 127–134.

Bell, R.Q. (1968). A reinterpretation of the direction of effects in studies of socialization. *Psychological Review, 75*, 63–72.

Berry, J.W., & Dasen, P. (1974). Introduction: History and method in the cross-cultural study of cognition. In J.W. Berry & P. Dasen (Eds.), *Culture and cognition: Readings in cross-cultural psychology*. London: Methuen.

Biesheuvel, S. (1958). Objectives and methods of African psychological research. *Journal of Social Psychology, 47*, 161–168.

Bing, E. (1963). Effect of child rearing practices on development of differential cognitive abilities. *Child Development, 34*, 631–648.

Bonica, J.J. (1967). *Principles and practice of obstetric analgesia and anesthesia. Volume 1: Fundamental considerations*. Philadelphia: Davis.

Brazelton, T.B. (1973). *Neonatal behavioral assessment scale*. London: Heinemann Medical Books.

Brazelton, T.B., Robey, J.S., & Collier, G.A. (1969). Infant development in the Zincanteco Indians of Southern Mexico. *Pediatrics, 44*, 274–293.

Brett, E.M. (1965). The estimation of foetal maturity by the neurological examination of the neonate. In M. Dawkins & B. Macgregor (Eds.), *Gestational age, size and maturity. Clinics in Developmental Medicine, 19*. London: Heinemann Medical Books.

Butler, N.R., & Alberman, E.D. (1969). *Perinatal problems*. Edinburgh: Livingstone.

Caesar, P., & Akiyama, Y. (1970). The estimation of the post menstrual age: a comprehensive review. *Developmental Medicine & Child Neurology, 12*, 697–729.

Caldwell, B.M. (1970). *Home inventory for infants*. Little Rock: Center for Early Development and Education, University of Arkansas.

Campbell, D.T., & Stanley, J.C. (1963). *Experimental and quasi-experimental designs for research*. Chicago: Rand Macnally.

Clarke, E. (1959). *My mother who fathered me*. London: Allen & Unwin.

Cole, M., Gay, J., Glick, J.A., & Sharp, D.W. (1971). *The cultural context of learning and thinking*. London: Methuen.

Cole, M., & Scribner, S. (1974). *Culture and thought*. New York: Wiley.

Coll, C.G., Sepkoski, C., & Lester, B.M. (1981). Cultural and biomedical correlates of neonatal behavior. *Developmental Psychobiology, 14,* 147–154.

Community Relations Commission Publication (1971). *The background to the educational difficulties of West Indian children in Britain.* Russell Square, London W.C.1.

Cook, T.D., & Campbell, D.T. (1975). The design and conduct of quasi-experiments and true experiments in field settings. In M.D. Dunnette (Ed.), *Handbook of industrial and organizational research,* Chicago: Rand McNally.

Corman, H.H., & Escalona, S.K. (1969). Stages of sensorimotor development: a replication study. *Merrill-Palmer Quarterly, 15,* 351–361.

Cravioto, J., & Delicardie, E.R. (1972). *Nutrition, the nervous system and behavior* (No. 251). Pan American Health Organization (World Health Organization) Scientific Publication.

Crawford, J.S. (1972). *Principles and practice of obstetrical anaesthesia* (3rd Ed.). Oxford: Blackwell.

Cronbach, L.J. (1960). *Essentials of psychological testing.* New York: Harper.

Curti, M., Marshall, F.B., & Steggerda, M. (1935). The Gesell schedules applied to one, two and three year old Negro children of Jamaica. *Journal of Comparative Psychology, 20,* 125–156.

Dixon, S., Tronick, E., Keefer, C., & Brazelton, T.B. (1982). Perinatal circumstances and newborn outcome among the Gusii of Kenya: measurement of risk. *Infant Behavior & Development, 5,* 11–32.

Doob, L.W. (1960). *Becoming more civilized.* New Haven, CT: Yale University Press.

Escalona, S.K., & Corman, H.H. (n.d.). *Albert Einstein scales of sensorimotor development.* New York: Albert Einstein College of Medicine, Yeshiva University.

Evans, P.C.C. (1965). *School and society in rural Jamaica.* Unpublished PhD, University of London.

Evans, S.H., & Anastasio, E.J. (1968). Misuse of analysis of covariance when treatment effect and covariate are confounded. *Psychological Bulletin, 69,* 225–234.

Farr, V., Mitchell, R.G., Neligan, G.A., & Parkin, J.M. (1966). The definition of some external characteristics used in the assessment of gestational age in the newborn infant. *Developmental Medicine and Child Neurology, 8,* 507–511.

Faust, V., Weidmann, M., & Wehner, W. (1974). The influence of metereological factors on children and youths. *Acta Paedo-psychiatrica, 40,* 150–156.

Fitzherbert, K. (1967). *West Indian children in London.* London: Bell.

Frijda, N., & Jahoda, G. (1966). On the scope and methods of cross-cultural research. *International Journal of Psychology, 1,* 109–127.

Garrett, H.E. (1960). A review: Klineberg's chapter on Race and Psychology, *Mankind Quarterly, 1,* 1–7.

Geber, M., & Dean, R.F.A. (1958). Psychomotor development in African children: The effects of social class and the need for improved tests. *World Health Organization Bulletin, 18,* 471–476.

Gibson, W.A. (1959). Three multivariate models: factor analysis, latent structure analysis, and latent profile analysis. *Psychometrika, 24,* 229–252.

Goldberg, S. (1972). Infant care and growth in Zambia. *Human Development, 15,* 77–89.

Gottfried, A.N., & Brody, N. (1975). Interrelationships between and correlates of psychometric and Piagetian scales of sensorimotor intelligence. *Developmental Psychology, 11,* 379–357.

Gould, S.J. (1977). *Ontogeny and phylogeny.* Cambridge, MA: Harvard University Press.

Grantham-McGregor, S.M., & Back, E.H. (1970). Breast feeding in Kingston, Jamaica. *Archives of Disease in Childhood, 45,* 404–409.

Grantham-McGregor, S.M., & Back, E.H. (1971). Gross motor development in Jamaican infants. *Developmental Medicine and Child Neurology, 13,* 79–87.

Grantham-McGregor, S.M., & Desai, P. (1973). Head circumference of Jamaican infants. *Developmental Medicine and Child Neurology, 15,* 441–446.

Grantham-McGregor, S.M., & Hawke, W.A. (1971). Developmental assessments of Jamaican infants. *Developmental Medicine and Child Neurology, 13,* 582–589.

Green, B.F. (1951). A general solution of the latent class model of latent structure analysis. *Psychometrika, 16,* 151–166.

Griffiths, R. (1970). *The Abilities of babies.* London: University Press.

Halliday, A. (1971, March 7, 14, 21). Immigrants: fallacies and facts. Parts 1, 11 & 111. *Sunday Telegraph.*

Henriques, F. (1953). *Family and colour in Jamaica.* London: Eyre & Spottiswood.

Herskovits, M.J. (1966). *The New World negro.* Bloomington, IN: Indiana University Press.

Hess, R.D., & Shipman, V.C. (1965). Early experience and the socialization of cognitive modes in children. *Child Development 36,* 869–886.

Holtzman, W.H., Diaz-Guerrero, R., Swartz, J.D., & Tapia, L.L. (1969). Cross-cultural longitudinal research on child development: studies of American and Mexican schoolchildren. In Hill, J.P. (Ed.), *Minnesota Symposia on Child Psychology* (Vol. 2). Minneapolis: University of Minnesota Press.

Hood, C., Oppe, T.E., Pless, I.B., & Apte, E. (1970). *Children of West Indian immigrants.* London: Institute of Race Relations.

Hopkins, B. (1976a). *A comparative study of sensorimotor development during the first six months of life.* Unpublished PhD, University of Leeds.

Hopkins, B. (1976b). Culturally determined patterns of handling the human infant. *Journal of Human Movement Studies, 2,* 1–27.

Hopkins, B. (1977a). Considerations of comparability of measures in cross-cultural studies of early infancy. In Poortinga, Y.H. (Ed.), *Basic problems in cross-cultural psychology.* Amsterdam: Swets & Zeitlinger.

Hopkins, B. (1977b). *Tabulated summary of comparative studies of psychomotor development involving black and white infants.* Unpublished manuscript, University Hospital, Groningen.

Jackson, S. (1971). *The illegal child-minders.* Cambridge: Cambridge Educational Development Trust.

Jensen, A.R. (1973). *Educability and group differences.* London: Methuen.

King, W.L., & Seegmiller, B. (1973). Performance of 14- to 22-month-old black first born male infants on 2 tests of cognitive development. *Developmental Psychology, 8,* 317–326.

Konner, M.J. (1972). Aspects of the developmental ethology of a foraging people. In N.G. Blurton-Jones (Ed.), *Ethological studies of child behaviour.* London: Cambridge University Press.

Konner, M. (1977a). Evolution of human behavior development. In P.H. Leiderman, S.R. Tulkin, & A. Rosenfeld (Eds.), *Culture and infancy*. New York: Academic Press.

Konner, M. (1977b). Infancy among the Kalahari Desert San. In P.H. Leiderman, S.R. Tulkin, & A. Rosenfeld (Eds.), *Culture and infancy*. New York: Academic Press.

Korner, A.F. (1971). Individual differences at birth: implications for early experience and later development. *American Journal of Orthopsychiatry, 41*, 608–619.

Lazarfeld, P.F., & Henry, N.W. (1968). *Latent structure analysis*. New York: Houghton Mifflin.

Leboyer, F. (1974). *Shantala*. Paris: Seuil.

Leiderman, P.H., Babu, B., Kagia, J., Kraemer, H.C., & Leiderman, G.F. (1973). African infant precocity and some social influences during the first year. *Nature, 242*, 247–249.

LeVine, R.A. (1970). Cross-cultural study in child psychology. In P.H. Mussen (Ed.), *Carmichael's manual of child psychology*. London: Wiley.

LeVine, R.A. (1977). Child rearing as cultural adaptation. In P.H. Leiderman, S.R. Tulkin & A. Rosenfeld (Eds.), *Culture and infancy*. New York: Academic Press.

Logan, M.H. (1973). Humeral medicine in Guatemala and peasant acceptance of modern medicine. *Human Organisation, 32*, 385–395.

Mardberg, B. (1974). LPA2: a computer program for Green's solution of latent class analysis applied to latent profile analysis. *Research from the Psychological Institute of Bergen, 5*(2).

Matheny, A.P. (1975). Twins: concordance for Pieagetian equivalent items derived from the Bayley mental test. *Developmental Psychology, 11*, 224–227.

Maxwell, S., & Cramer, E.M. (1975). A note on analysis of co-variance. *Psychological Bulletin, 2*, 187–190.

McKennell, A. (1970). Attitude measurement: Use of coefficient alpha with cluster or factor analysis. *Sociology, 4*, 227–245.

McGraw, M.B. (1931). A comparative study of a group of Southern white and negro infants. *Genetic Psychology Monographs, 10*, 1–105.

Miall, W.E., Desai, P., & Standard, K.L. (1970). Malnutrition, infection and child growth in Jamaica. *Journal of Biosocial Science, 2*, 31–36.

Moody, V., & Stroud, C.E. (1967). One hundred mothers. *The Nursery Journal, 57*, 4–8.

Montagu, M.F.A. (1962). *Prenatal influences*. Springfield, IL: Thomas.

Moss, H. (1967). Sex, age and state as determinants of mother-infant interaction. *Merrill-Palmer Quarterly, 13*, 19–36.

Newsom, J., & Newsom, E. (1963). *Infant care in an urban community*. London: Allen & Urwin.

Nunally, J. (1967). *Psychometric theory*. London: McGraw-Hill.

Parkin, J.M. (1971). The assessment of gestational age in Ugandan and British newborn babies. *Developmental Medicine and Child Neurology, 13*, 784–788.

Patterson, H.O.L. (1966). Slavery, acculturation and social change. *British Journal of Sociology, 17*, 151–164.

Pedersen, F.A. (1980). *The father-infant relationship: observational studies in the family setting*. New York: Praeger.

Piaget, J. (1952). *The origins of intelligence in children*. New York: Columbia University Press.

Pollak, M., & Mitchell, S. (1974). Early development of negro and white babies. *Archives of Disease in Childhood, 49,* 40–45.

Poortinga, Y.H. (1971). Cross-cultural comparison of maximum performance tests: Some methodological aspects and some experiments with simple auditory and visual stimuli. *Psychologica Africana, 14,* 1–100.

Poortinga, Y.H. (1975). Limitations on intercultural comparisons of psychological data. *Nederlands Tijdschrift voor de Psychologie, 30,* 23–39.

Rebelsky, F. (1967). Infancy in two cultures. *Nederlands Tijdschrift voor de Psychologie, 22,* 379–385.

Richardson, S.A. (1972). In *Nutrition, the nervous system and behavior,* Pan American Health Organization (World Health Organization) Scientific Publication, no. 251.

Richardson, S.A. (1975). Physical growth of Jamaican school children who were severely malnourished before 2 years of age. *Journal of Biosocial Science, 7,* 445–462.

Roberts, J., & Sutton-Smith, B. (1962). Child training and game involvement. *Ethnology, 1,* 166–185.

Rohner, R.P. (1977). Why cross-cultural research? *Annals of the New York Academy of Sciences, 285,* 3–12.

Rutter, M., Yule, B., Morton, J. & Bagley, C. (1975). Children of West Indian immigrants. III. Home circumstances and family patterns. *Journal of Child Psychology and Psychiatry, 16,* 105–123.

Sameroff, A.J. (1975a). Early influences on development: fact or fancy? *Merrill-Palmer Quarterly, 21,* 267–294.

Sameroff, A.J. (1975b). Transactional models in early social relations. *Human Development, 18,* 65–79.

Schaffer, H.R., & Emerson, P.E. (1968). The effects of experimentally administered stimulation on developmental quotients of infants. *British Journal of Social and Clinical Psychology, 7,* 61–67.

Schnaiberg, A. (1970). Measuring modernism: Theoretical and empirical explorations. *American Journal of Sociology, 76,* 399–425.

Scott, J.P. (1972). *Animal behavior* (2nd ed.). London: University of Chicago Press.

Scott, S. (1975). White and West Indian infants in London: development from birth to 44 weeks of age. *Child: care, health and development, 1,* 203–215.

Scribner, S. (1976). Situating the experiment in critical research. In K.F. Riegel & J.A. Meacham (Eds.), *The developing individual in a changing world.* Chicago: Aldine.

Segall, M.H., Campbell, D.T., & Herskovits, M.J. (1966). *The influence of culture on visual perception.* New York: Bobbs-Merrill.

Singer, B., Blake, L., & Wolfsdorf, J. (1973). Estimation of gestational age of African newborn infants by a scoring system. *South African Medical Journal, 47,* 2074–2077.

Solkoff, N., Yaffe, S., Weintraub, D., & Blase, B. (1969). Effects of handling on subsequent development of premature infants. *Developmental Psychology, 1,* 765–768.

Sprott, D.A. (1970). Note on Evans and Anastasio on the analysis of covariance. *Psychological Bulletin, 73,* 303–306.

Streeter, L.S. (1976). Language perception of 2 month old infants shows effects of both innate mechanisms and experience. *Nature, 259,* 39–41.

Super, C.M. (1976). Environmental effects on motor development: the case of "African precocity". *Developmental Medicine & Child Neurology, 18,* 561–567.

Tatje, T.A. (1973). Problems of concept definition for comparative studies. In R. Naroll & R. Cohen (Eds.), *A handbook of method in cultural anthropology.* New York: Columbia University Press.

Tunnell, G.B. (1977). Three dimensions of naturalness: an expanded definition of field research. *Psychological Bulletin, 84,* 426–437.

Uka, N. (1966). *Growing up in Nigerian culture* (Occasional Publication No. 6). Nigeria: Institute of Education, University of Ibadan.

Warren, N. (1972). African infant precocity. *Psychological Bulletin, 78,* 353–367.

Wober, M. (1971). Adapting Dawson's traditional versus western attitudes scale and presenting some new information from Africa. *British Journal of Social and Clinical Psychology, 10,* 101–113.

Yarrow, L.J., Rubenstein, J.L., Pedersen, F.A., & Jankowski, J.J. (1972). Dimensions of early stimulation and their differential effects on infant development. *Merrill-Palmer Quarterly. 18,* 205–218.

Appendix
Some West Indian Child-Rearing Practices and Associated Superstitions

The information presented here was gathered in informal discussions with West Indian parents, mostly mothers. In almost every case, both parents came from Jamaica. It is not known, therefore, to what extent these practices and superstitions can be generalized to other Caribbean islands. The information was given without the apparent use of any coherent framework, and is presented as such here.

1. In the infant's sleeping quarters, mirrors were often covered by a sheet. Mothers said that children must not look into a mirror until they are more than 1 year old. If they see their own reflection before this age, they will have bad startles in their sleep which will upset them and possibly make them ill.

2. Lying beside many of the infants in the cot was a tape measure. Some mothers became extremely embarassed when asked about its presence, and questioning was not pushed any further. Finally, one mother reported that the tape measure was to keep out evil spirits who might want to take the child away (i.e., induce death). If they saw the tape measure, they would assume they were going to be measured up for a coffin and would leave in haste without returning.

3. Herbal medicines were administered by many of the mothers to their children. They bought them from a local shop that imported the herbs from Jamaica. To get rid of a head cold, coconut oil was mixed with crushed garlic and rubbed into the anterior fontanelle.

4. If the baby was vomiting, a gizzard of a fowl was boiled and the juice given to the child to drink.

5. To keep the infant's tongue clean, an important consideration, it was wiped with glycerine. Some mothers said that the only way to keep a baby's tongue clean was to wipe it with a urine-soaked diaper.

6. Some of the infants were bathed in water dosed with Reckitt's blue dye. One reason given for this practice was that it kept away evil spirits. It was alright to make eye-to-eye contact with the baby when he or she was immersed in this blue water.

7. After bathing, babies were given a drop of the bathwater to drink, as it was supposed "to put their strength back into them."

8. Babies should never be lifted by one arm, as it will cause very bad earaches with discharge. However, it was for some reason acceptable to do so during the formal handling routine.

9. If the baby starts hiccoughing, the mother should make a sign of the cross with spittle on the baby's forehead. Alternatively, she can put a piece of cotton on his or her forehead or a matchstick in the hair. Any one of these methods was guarenteed to stop the hiccups.

10. A boy's hair should not be cut in the first year, or he will lose his strength.

11. The soles of a baby's feet should not be tickled, or speech development will be retarded, possibly leading to stuttering.

12. One should not say a baby is pretty unless it is really meant, as he or she will turn out to be ugly.

13. If a young child looks up the mother's skirt, it means she is going to have another baby.

14. A mother from Nevis mentioned that, if a child had reached one year of age and was not walking, he or she would be taken down to the beach and buried up to the knees in sand. The sight of the incoming waves would soon develop the urge to walk.

CHAPTER 5

The Mature Primipara and Her Infant in Sweden: A Life Course Study*

Barbara L. Welles-Nyström

*Behavioral Sciences Research Department
Stockholm College of Nursing
Stockholm, Sweden*

In recent years the phenomenon of the mature primipara has become more common in contemporary industrial societies. Many women who have postponed parenthood until after age 30 have questions about the ramifications of childbirth at this point in the life cycle, especially regarding the health of the infant. Unfortunately, there are few prospective studies that investigate the medical, social, and/or psychological effects of the late timing of first birth for the woman or her child.

---

* Support for this study, which was a doctoral dissertation at the Graduate School of Education, Harvard University came from the American Scandinavian Foundation, Stockholms Socialförvaltning, Första Majblomman, and the Pediatric Clinic at the Karolinska Hospital. Special thanks go to Associate Professor Peter deChateau for advice during the data collection, suggestions during analyses, and comments on the paper. Dr. Berit Hagekull provided statistical advice on the BBQ analyses and gave comments on the paper, and is gratefully acknowledged. Dr. Christina Wood's critical comments on the paper were especially appreciated, and I thank her for the suggestions. Thanks, too, go to Dr. Barry Lester for providing statistical advice on the BNBAS scores. Requests for reprints may be sent to Barbara Welles-Nyström, Head of Behavioral Sciences Research Department, Stockholm College of Nursing, Jägargatan 20, S-116 69 Stockholm, Sweden.

This manuscript was submitted for publication in 1983. The term "mature primipara" was chosen to differentiate, in a positive manner, women who were of a "mature age" when having their first child (rather than using the more medically accepted label of "elderly primipara"). As this volume has been several years in preparation, several researchers have published articles about older first-time mothers, referring to them, also, as "mature". I mean no disrespect in not citing these studies, but rather would submit this article as it was originally prepared. However, I have taken the liberty to include, in the bibliography, those studies I have published during this period.

The aim of this cross-cultural research was to examine, in Sweden, the effect of timing on the transition to motherhood by comparing two cohorts of Swedish primipara at two different stages in the life course: women in their 20s and women in their 30s. The study was organized to investigate women's adjustment to the new role of mother and adaptation to their new infant in respect to some biomedical, behavioral, and social variables at three periods in the transition. The general research questions addressed were: How does timing affect the transition to motherhood of Swedish primiparas entering their reproductive careers at different stages of the life course? What are the effects of maternal age on infant biomedical and behavioral variables?

Culturally specific beliefs and practices concerning patterns of reproduction exist in all societies (Mead & Newton, 1967). For example, the ethnographic literature includes, not only descriptions of initiation rites for pregnant and parturient women (Brown, 1981) and the varied positions for labor in human populations (Engelman, 1883), but also reports of taboos for pre- and postnatal nutrition and sexual behavior (Mead & Newton, 1967).

Across cultures, the phenomenon of the first birth is universally recognized as a significant marker of a female rite de passage into adult status, the time when a woman's new position as mother is established in society (Van Gennep, 1960). However, the cultural implications of giving birth to the first child differ. In traditional societies the birth of a first child is perceived as fundamental to the process of attaining adult status. The biological events of pregnancy and birth serve as social markers in the transition from pubescent girl, through marriage and motherhood, to woman. The status of adulthood is achieved through reproduction.

In complex industrial societies, where schooling is compulsory and child labor prohibited, public recognition of adulthood is based on chronological age (e.g., age 21), educational markers (such as graduations), and/or entry into the work force. Marriage and reproduction are often postponed until after these other insignia of adult status have been awarded in the third or even fourth decade of life. In such a society, childbearing tends to be the last in a series of rites or acts of transition into adulthood. Full adult status is finally granted with the birth of a first child, after other cultural prerequisites, such as the establishment of an economic career, have been fulfilled. Thus, adulthood is not attained, but rather is confirmed through reproduction.

As in the previous example of the variations in the timing of first birth (industrial versus nonindustrial), so, too, is the issue of timing culture dependent even among industrial societies. For instance, Erikson (1950), who considered "generativity" the "critical issue" to be resolved in attaining adult status, saw the age of women's reproduction beginning in their early 20s. At the time, the theory reflected a cultural and historical norm, but it now proves to be inapplicable to many contemporary societies. In Sweden, Erikson's stage theory has since been revised by Cullberg (1975) to fit Swedish culture, so that generativity is shown to occur in the young middle ages of the 30s and 40s. However, regardless of when it occurs, the transition into the parental role or "career" is one of the most important events of adulthood (LeVine, 1979).

Culture affects the milieu in which a woman becomes attached to her child and assumes parental responsibilities (Bowlby, 1969; Brazelton, 1972). Far from being a passive recipient of a maternally structured relationship, the infant actively influences his or her mother's response by responsive and elicitory behaviors (Lewis & Rosenblum, 1974). Such methods of behavioral assessments as the Brazelton Neonatal Behavioral Assessment Scale (BNBAS) (Brazelton, 1973) help measure these interactive capacities; they have also been used cross-culturally to document group differences among neonates (Freedman & Freedman, 1969; DeVries & Super, 1979; Lester & Brazelton, 1982). Horowitz believes that these neonatal behaviors may be one element in the perpetuation of cross-cultural differences of parental behaviors (Brazelton, 1973).

Yet another such impact of the neonate's influence may be on the mother's role transition. For example, is the ease or difficulty with which she perceives her transition to motherhood dependent on perceptions of her infant's behavior, so that an "easy baby" correlates with an "easy" transition? Questions such as this deserve to be explored, for the complex behaviors involved in the interplay between mother and infant have both universal and culture-specific implications.

There is a lack of empirical research on how modern, industrial societies organize the major social and personal transitions of adult women, even for an event as "common" as the first birth. Little is actually known about the constitution of the rites and rituals of passage for the modern woman as she becomes a first-time mother. In most of the industrial societies the management of the transition to motherhood is handled by the medical profession (rather than by the older generation of female kin, as in many third world countries), which has an interest in both the reproductive status and age of the woman about to become mother. Women entering their reproductive career for the first time are labeled either primigravida (first pregnancy) or primipara (first birth) and are considered to be in a risk status because of reproductive inexperience. This is especially true when primiparity is confounded by age, be it the younger or older first-time mother. If a woman is older than age 35 when having a first child, she is considered "elderly" (Morrison, 1975), and both she and her child are carefully watched for problems, some of the most common being genetic, such as Down's Syndrome (Hook & Lindsjö, 1978; Holmes, 1978).

Regarding the timing of the birth of her first child, "modern" woman has begun to postpone the event so that the phenomenon of the elderly or mature first-time mother has become common in recent years. Since motherhood now begins for many women in middle adulthood (early 30s) rather than early adulthood, questions have emerged about the risks and consequences for such decision making. What does the literature say about the situation, experience, and outcome for these "new" mothers and their babies?

The empirical research on late motherhood has generally been partitioned into two fields: medical and psychosocial. The classic medical literature on the subject of the older primipara has tended to be pessimistic in its prognoses. However, due to methodological weaknesses (e.g., retrospective investigation, the confounding of age and parity, not controlling for other aspects of aging, such as diabetes), no clear conclusions can be drawn about the negative affects of age, per se, of first birth. A recent review of this medical literature even suggests that the effects of maternal age have been overstated (Mansfield, 1983). It remains that the actual relationship between age and first birth has yet to be carefully documented for its medical and psychological ramifications for healthy women who are becoming mothers after age 30.

The psychological impact of the late transition to motherhood has been given minimal scientific attention, although in recent years there has emerged a popular literature on various aspects of the subject (Fabe, 1979; Daniels & Weingarten, 1979, 1982). That literature which attempts to deal with some of the unique aspects of the psychological transition of the older first-time mother generally concerns the category of genetic counselling (Holmes, 1978).

Otherwise, the empirical data concerning primiparas is contained within the psychological and sociological literature of the "regular" or on-time transition to motherhood (Deutsch, 1944; Benedek, 1952; Bibring, Dwyer, Huntington, & Valenstein, 1961; Shereshefsky & Yarrow, 1973; Oakley, 1980a, 1980b). This vast body of research can perhaps elucidate certain aspects of first-time motherhood, such as the "crisis" element of a first pregnancy (Deutsch, 1944) or the "maturational" aspects of becoming a mother (Bibring et al., 1961), but it does not take into account the experience of the mature mother. This body of literature also makes the mistake of overgeneralizing patterns of maternal behavior and presupposing that all Western societies have organized the transition in similar ways (e.g., through hospitalized birth). The ethnocentricity reflected in the psychological research concerning the first birth must be explicated, particularly in regard to the issue of timing, if the complex reproductive patterns of women in modern industrial societies are to be compared across cultures. One theoretical paradigm for conceptualizing the maternal role transitions over time and culture is the *timing events model*, a developmental model used in this study, described briefly below.

"Age is a major dimension of social organization" from which the dynamics of social and psychological meaning can be charted for the individual as he or she progresses through the life course (Neugarten & Hagestad, 1976). Individuals develop a mental map of the life cycle, they anticipate that certain events will occur at certain times, and they internalize a social clock that tells them whether they are on- or off-time. They also internalize other cultural norms that tell them if their behavior in various areas of life is age appropriate (Neugarten & Hagestad, 1976).

Individuals typically make these transitions as members of a named group (graduates, primigravidas), creating a collective shifting of people from one life stage to another whereby each *cohort* (people born in the same time interval or entering a social system at the same time) faces given transitional periods in a unique way within a unique historical context. How the individual perceives this change and adapts to it, which is part of the aging process, depends, not only on the physiological and psychological changes that occur as a result of the transition, but also on the social constructs provided by the culture and which mediate the process. That is, life course transitions are more than an individual matter; they involve an interplay between the individual and what he or she confronts as society and the social structure. They are not a simple result of developmental processes, but instead reflect specific kinds of institutional structures where age and aging have significance, not only as properties of the individual, but also as essential components of social structure and change (Foner & Kertzer, 1978).

Researchers studying the phenomenon of first birth in industrial societies often make the mistake of assuming that their own cultural pattern is representative of all Western societies. In fact, Western reproductive customs vary across national cultures. Giving birth in England differs from giving birth in the United States; becoming a Swedish mother is different from becoming a mother in Holland (Jordan, 1978). Therefore, a Western researcher studying other Western societies should first document these cultural patterns so that antecedents of behavior can be better studied.

In 1981, this short-term, longitudinal study was carried out in the Obstetrical and Neonatal Units at the Karolinska Hospital in Stockholm (Welles, 1982). Basic ethnographic techniques and precoded questionnaires were used to elicit information about women's adjustment to motherhood from two cohorts of primiparas; a younger sample of first-time mothers aged 21–29 years which comprised Cohort 1, and an older sample of first-time mothers aged 30–40 years which comprised Cohort 2. These methods were used at three key points of the transition period: Contact 1, *Prenatal* (8 months pregnancy); Contact 2, *Perinatal* (at the hospital); and Contact 3, *Postnatal* (4 months postpartum). Infant behavior was assessed during the Perinatal and Postnatal contact periods. The methods used are discussed in more detail below.

Sweden, a country of approximately 8.5 million people, was chosen as the field site for this study because of its unique medical, demographic, and social characteristics. First, it has the world's lowest infant mortality rate (Karlberg & Ericson, 1979) and one of the oldest populations of first-time mothers, whose average age is 26.4 years. Second, as in most other industrialized Western societies, the birth rate in Sweden is declining. Contraceptive technology has made parenthood an option, not a necessity. Third, the cultural norm for women is to establish their occupational careers before beginning to bear children. Fourth, a cultural pattern of "postponed" parenthood has been maintained for over 40 years, therefore providing an excellent natural research site for an investigation of first-time parenting at different stages of the life course in one industrial, medically advanced society.

Research questions regarding the study infants and their mothers included the following:

1. Do infants of older mothers behave differently in the perinatal period than do the infants of younger mothers as assessed by the Brazelton Neonatal Behavioral Assessment Scale (BNBAS)?
2. Are the two cohorts of mothers similar in their expectations and perceptions of the "average" infant versus their own infant, as assessed by the Neonatal Perception Inventory (NPI)? (Broussard, 1971).
3. Is neonatal behavior related to later infant temperament as assessed by the Baby Behavior Questionnaire (BBQ)? (Hagekull & Bohlin, 1981). Are there cohort differences in diagnostic ratings of difficult babies?

Research hypotheses concerning maternal biomedical variables were that Cohort 2 mothers would have longer and more complicated deliveries, because of advanced maternal age (Lundh, 1925–1926, 1926; Morrison, 1975). Regarding maternal adjustment to motherhood, it was hypothesized that cohort-specific attitudes and behaviors would be exhibited, due to differences in life experiences (Daniels & Weingarten, 1982).

Research hypotheses concerning infant biomedical and behavioral variables reflected the issue of increased medical risks for the Cohort 2 infants (Morrison, 1975; Holmes, 1978). Therefore the following hypotheses were made:

1. That Cohort 2 infants would be less healthy especially those born to the "at risk for age" cohort of women over 35 years of age.
2. That, due to constitutional differences, Cohort 2 neonates would "look" different as assessed by the Brazelton Exam.
3. That cohort differences would appear in later infancy in respect to behavior and temperament as assessed by maternal questionnaires.
4. That there would be a relationship between early neonatal behavior and later infant temperament.

Methods

Sample

A list of 58 prospective sample mothers was compiled from the rosters of the five maternal health clinics which use the Karolinska Hospital for delivery. From

January through April, 1981, midwives solicited the 8-months-pregnant women for inclusion in the study during their regular prenatal visits if they met the following criteria: 20–40 years of age; no previous full-term pregnancy, or second or third trimester spontaneous abortion or termination; normal, uncomplicated pregnancy; no known fertility problems, defined for the purpose of this study as not waiting more than 1.5 years to conceive; single birth. Only Swedish women were included in the study, since the focus was on the cultural patterning of reproduction, (although their mates could be of foreign birth). The sample was selected to include chronological progression of ages.

Because there were fewer women over age 30 who met the research criteria, they were recruited first. When one of the "older" mothers agreed to participate in the study, a younger woman was selected from the same maternal health clinic to match expected date of delivery.

Fifty-three women participated: 27 primiparas aged 21–29 years comprised the younger Cohort 1; 26 older primiparas aged 30–40 years comprised Cohort 2. Five women did not participate, because they did not want to have a later home visit.

As in other Western industrial societies, the Swedish primipara older than age 35 is considered to be at biological and medical risk. However, the social timetable for procreation in Sweden is not like that of any other society. In Sweden the average age of first birth is around 26–27 years of age (compared to 24 years in the United States). Since the timing of first birth is perceived to be most optimal around that time, the social marker of late entry into the reproductive career occurs around age 30. Therefore, this study was organized to include women who spanned that age by a decade in each direction.

The sample size fell from 53 to 51 women at the Perinatal Contact period after delivery, and from 51 to 48 women who were interviewed at the Postnatal Contact period, the 4-month home visit. This attrition had been allowed for, since the original design had called for 40 families. Because the focus of the research was on the "usual" transition to motherhood, two women who had given birth to sick babies were not reinterviewed. Three families moved out of the area before the home visit was completed. The final sample of women who returned questionnaires from the Postnatal Contact contained 26 women in Cohort 1 and 24 in Cohort 2.

Procedures

As mentioned, semistructured interviews, precoded questionnaires and infant assessments were used at three key points in the transition: Contact 1, *Prenatal* (8 months pregnancy); Contact 2, *Perinatal* (at the hospital after birth); and Contact 3, *Postnatal* (4 months postpartum).

The following analyses were performed on the data after each contact period:
Prenatal. (a) Maternal biomedical data were collected from individual medi-

cal journals and analyzed using Student's *t* test. (b) Chi-square analyses were performed on the interview and questionnaire items.

Perinatal. (a) Maternal and infant biomedical data collected from obstetric records were analyzed using Student's *t* test. (b) Chi-square analyses were performed on interview and questionnaire items. (c) Infant behavior was assessed with the Brazelton Neonatal Behavioral Assessment Scale, (BNBAS), a critical method for assessing infant behavior based on neurological as well as interactional responses to a set series of stimuli. The scale includes 27 behavioral items, each of which is scored on a nine-point scale (e.g., alertness, activity, tonus) and 20 elicited responses which are based on a three-point scale (e.g., Moro-reflex, sucking). The scale differs from many other assessments in that the infant's optimal responses are recorded. The exam was designed for normal infants of 37–42 weeks gestational age and is applicable for infants up to 1 month of age (Brazelton, 1973).

The sample infants were examined by the investigator using the BNBAS in a test situation where at least half of the infants were examined blind to maternal age. The first BNBAS exam was performed when the infant was about 20 hours old (range 7–60 hours). The second exam followed 2 days later (mean time lag for the second exam was 22 hours). After completion of the second exam, each infant was taken to the mother's room, and a simplified version of the BNBAS was performed to acquaint her with the research method. Items demonstrated included orientation and motor behaviors. (See Table 6 for a brief description of BNBAS items and clusters.)

The neonatal behavioral exams were coded and analyzed by a 2 (group) by 2 (day) repeated measures analysis of variance cluster schema developed by Lester, Als, and Brazelton (1982). These scores were interpreted in four ways: *group scores,* which compare infants by cohort; *day scores,* which assess changes in scores over time, often referred to as "recovery"; *day and group scores,* which compare the "interaction" effect of the recovery scores by cohort; and *behavioral item analyses,* which show single-item differences. (d) Maternal expectations and perception of infant behavior were assessed with the Neonatal Perception Inventory (NPI), a self-administered questionnaire (Broussard, 1971). This inventory is based on the cultural premise that American first-time mothers want their infants to be better than average. That is, in comparison to their own expectations of an average baby, mothers have a more positive perception of their own infants. The six behavioral items that mothers rate are crying, spitting, feeding, elimination, sleeping, and predictability, totaling 12 responses. The NPI was administered to mothers on day 5 postpartum, after having completed a delivery interview. Posthoc analyses were performed on maternal attitudinal inventories. These included *t* test analyses to compare posthoc cohort differences on expected and perceived values, a median test was made to compare the cohorts on each of the 12 individual items, and median scores for inventories were dichotomized into high and low maternal attitude values and compared.

Postnatal. (a) Interview and questionnaire items were compared by cohort using chi-square analyses. (b) Infant temperament was assessed by the Baby Behavior Questionnaire (BBQ), a Swedish revision of the Carey Infant Tempera-ment Questionnaire (Hagekull & Bohlin, 1981; Carey, 1973). This is a self-administered, standardized questionnaire which assesses dimensions of behav-ioral individuality in 3- to 10-month-old infants. The BBQ contains 37 of the original Carey items and an additional 17 items constructed from interviewing Swedish parents, so that most infant behaviors in everyday situations are cov-ered. The parent responds to each item on a five-step response scale. Thus, through the use of the BBQ parental ratings, six dimensions of infant behavior can be delineated (see Table 6) and measured with adequate reliability and validity (Hagekull & Bolin, 1981; Hagekull, 1982). The BBQ was left with parents at the 4-month postpartum home visit to be filled in and returned within a few weeks. The questionnaire was returned by 50 families.

The baby behavior/temperament scores were analyzed in three ways: a *t* test was made to compare infant behaviors by cohort, a correlation matrix was performed with the neonatal BNBAS scores, and a score was computed for the clinical dimensions of "difficult, intermediate and easy" babies (Carey, 1970, 1973) and compared posthoc with American sample scores (Carey, 1970; Vaughn, Taraldson, Crichton, & Egeland, 1981).

Pictures were taken of all sample babies and their families. Copies of pictures taken during the second and third contact points were sent to the sample families (see Photo 1 and Photo 2).

Results

Prenatal. The majority of the demographic dimensions, including the marital and reproductive status of the two cohorts, were similar. Almost all of the women were married to, or lived with, the father of their babies. Cohort 2 women tended to have had fewer previous pregnancies than did Cohort 1 women. Most of the women from Cohort 1 were from the Stockholm area; the majority of women in Cohort 2 were not. However, there was a significant difference be-tween cohorts ($\chi^2 = 4.8, p < .05$) regarding whether the pregnancy was planned or not. The vast majority of women in Cohort 2 had planned the pregnancy, while only half of the sample of younger women had done so.

Education and income are closely related to social class, so, for the classifica-tion of women in this study, those dimensions were simplified to include high, middle, and low status. Because so many women work in Sweden, their own social class is always considered independent from that of their mate. There was a significant cohort difference between high- and low-class inclusion ($\chi^2 = 6.97, p < .01$), which was expected because of the age dependent aspect of the variable. That is, Cohort 2 mothers had a higher social class due to their ad-vanced position in the life cycle, which in Sweden translates to mean either higher education, seniority on the job, and/or increased income. However, if

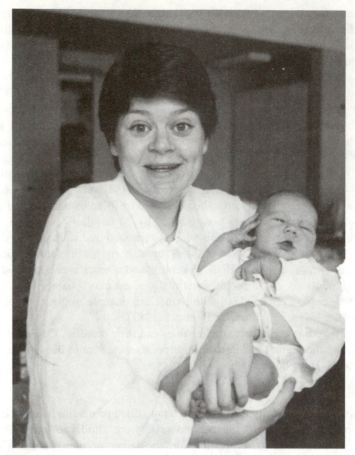

Photograph 1.   4-day-old infant and her mother.

middle and high class are combined, which is how Swedes themselves prefer to think of social class, there were no significant differences between cohorts (70% of Cohort 1, and 85% of Cohort 2, were in the higher class).

Regarding the fathers of the study infants, Cohort 2 mothers mated with a different sample of men than did the Cohort 1 mothers. These men were often younger and/or of foreign birth, while Cohort 1 mothers mated with Swedish men who were the same age or older. The demographic dimensions of sample fathers were the following: paternal age ranged from 22 years to 52 years of age; the mean paternal age of Cohort 1 was 28 years, and 35 years of age for Cohort 2. Seventy-four percent of Cohort 1 fathers were in the high/middle class, compared with 85% of Cohort 2. Less than 20% of the fathers had children from a previous relationship.

Perinatal. The infants did not vary on most of the biomedical dimensions

Photograph 2.   4-month-old infant and her mother.

such as length, gestational age, or sex, nor were their obstetric histories different. Most babies were born "normally" with "routine" administrations of pudendal or paracervical blocks and minimal dosages of the painkiller pethidine. However, a statistically significant difference in infant birth weight was found between the two cohorts. Infants born to mothers in Cohort 1 weighed significantly more ($p < .05$) than the infants born to mothers in Cohort 2 (see Table 1). All Cohort 1 infants were healthy, while in Cohort 2 one child was born with a cleft lip and palate, and one infant was stillborn with no genetic or other physical anomalies at 42 weeks gestational age. Both infants were born to mothers 37 years of age.

Minimal cohort differences in neonatal behavior were found using the BNBAS. Of the 53 infants whose mothers were subjects in the study, 45 infants had complete Brazelton exams: 25 in Cohort 1, and 20 in Cohort 2. Infants in the older cohort who did not have two complete exams included the malformed and stillborn infants. Other excluded infants were those who were located so late as to have only one exam each. (The original study design had called for a blind examination by maternal age of the babies. However, this was very difficult to arrange, and several infants were "lost" to the tracking system.) Blind exams were performed on only 25 infants, 11 in Cohort 1 and 14 in Cohort 2.

Table 1.   Infant Biomedical Variables.

Infant Variables	Cohort 1	Cohort 2
Status	27 healthy	24 healthy
		1 stillborn
		1 birth defect
Sex	13 males	12 males
	14 females	14 females
Gestational age	40 weeks	40 weeks
Length	51 cm	50 cm
Weight	3769 g*	3487 g*
Obstetric history		
normal[a]	17	18
normal epidural[a]	7	4
C-section elective	0	1
C-section acute	3	3
Vacuum extraction[b]	4	7

*$p < .05$
[a] includes pudendal and paracervical blocks, and/or Pethidine and/or nitrous oxide.
[b] these infants were included in the "normal" birth methods listed above

There were no group differences between cohorts on any of the seven BNBAS cluster items. There were two significant *day,* or "recovery," score differences. Infants in both cohorts improved behaviors significantly in the motor cluster ($p < .001$) and the reflex cluster ($p < .001$). These scores indicated that, as a group, infants had better motor control and fewer worrisome reflexes on day 3 than on day 1 (see Table 2). No significant *group,* or *day and group,* interaction effects were found between cohorts.

In an *item analysis,* within the motor score cluster, one behavioral item score—tonus—showed a significant day by group interaction ($p < .04$) as well as a day effect ($p < .03$). Tonus, which assesses the resistance of the body to passive movement, increased significantly for the infants in Cohort 2 over time, while in Cohort 1, infants scores remained constant over time. (Note: This is not a cluster score; hence, the result is not included in Table 2.)

Maternal biomedical variables of the cohorts were compared as one outcome measure of the effect of maternal age. There were few discrepancies between the cohorts when comparing the women's physical factors such as maternal height or weight; or in the medical management of labor and delivery, such as delivery time, frequence of amniotomy, and incidence of Cesarean section. Fewer women in Cohort 1 had vacuum-extractioned births than did Cohort 2 women, although it was not a significant difference (see Table 1 for obstetric histories). Nor were there differences in maternal report of the ease of delivery or amount of pain; few women reported it as matching their expectations. The vast majority thought labor much worse, or much easier, than they'd anticipated.

All sample mothers breastfed their infants while at the hospital. Cohort 2

Table 2.   Analyses of Brazelton Scores on Days 1 and 3.

	Cohort 1		Cohort 2	
Cluster Scores[a]	mean	s.d.	mean	s.d.
1. Habituation				
1st exam	7.03	1.47	6.60	1.70
2nd exam	6.95	2.13	7.34	1.50
2. Orientation				
1st exam	7.16	1.40	7.46	.91
2nd exam	7.18	.93	7.26	.77
3. Motor				
1st exam	5.98	0.70*	6.00	.87*
2nd exam	6.33	.51*	6.44	.68*
4. Range State				
1st exam	3.95	.62	3.83	.90
2nd exam	4.00	.51	4.20	.39
5. Regulation State				
1st exam	6.58	1.40	7.00	1.10
2nd exam	6.46	1.41	7.05	1.55
6. Autonomic				
1st exam	6.51	.83	6.84	.66
2nd exam	6.48	.54	6.52	.73
7. Reflexes				
1st exam	3.84	2.44*	3.80	2.84*
2nd exam	2.20	1.91*	2.30	2.08*

*$p < .001$
[a]2(group) × 2(day) repeated measures analysis of variance.

mothers reported having more difficult in establishing breastfeeding ($\chi^2 = 4.2$, $p < .05$), and they were more likely to describe the hospital routines as stressful ($\chi^2 = 4.4$, $p < .05$). A significant number of older mothers stayed longer than the usual 7 days at the hospital ($\chi^2 = 4.4$, $p < .05$), while the younger mothers returned home after the customary 1 week stay or prior to that time.

Maternal expectation of the average infant and perception of her own infant's behavior as assessed by the NPI varied significantly only on the item "ease of feeding." Cohort 2 mothers had lower expectations of the "average baby's" nursing ability ($\chi^2 = 4.2$, $p < .05$). Unlike the Cohort 1 mothers, they also perceived their own infants as having more trouble than the "average" baby establishing breastfeeding ($\chi^2 = 4.96$, $p < .05$) (see Table 3).

Postnatal. At the 4-month home visit most sample infants were still breast-feeding and most were sleeping the night. There was no cohort difference in

Table 3. Maternal Attitude (NPI)

	Cohort 1	Cohort 2
Expectation of "average baby's" nursing ability:		
High	17	8*
Low	7	14*
Perception of "own baby's" nursing ability:		
High	23	16*
Low	1	6*

*p < .05
Note. Only 46 mothers returned this questionnaire.

incidence of colic as defined by the parents: approximately one-third of the babies in each cohort had colic.

No cohort differences on the infant temperament dimensions were found at 4 months of age, nor were there cohort differences exhibited in the diagnostic scores of difficult and easy babies. The Swedish sample had ratings similar to American samples from both Carey (1973) and Vaughn et al. (1981) (see Table 4).

There were significant relationships between four baby temperament scores and two of the neonatal behavioral cluster scores. The BBQ dimensions approach ($-.35$, $p < .05$) and sensory/sensitivity ($+.26$, $p < .05$) were correlated with the BNBAS orientation cluster, which meant that neonates who were high on the orientation scores were infants who later exhibited more initial approach behaviors and were also likely to have a low sensitivity to adverse stimuli at 4 months of age.

Two other BBQ dimensions, approach ($-.27$, $p < .05$) and manageability ($-.35$, $p < .05$), were related to the BNBAS state regulation cluster. These scores indicated that newborns with a high control of state were those babies at 4 months who were more adaptable in new situations and were rated by their parents as being more manageable (see Tables 5 and 6).

Table 4. Comparative Diagnostic Ratings of infant Temperament.

Diagnostic Ratings	Swedish BBQ (1981 study)	ITQ (Carey, 1970)	ITQ (Vaughn, 1981)
Easy	38 %	40 %	34 %
Intermediate Low	32 %	34 %	36 %
Intermediate High	18 %	15 %	18 %
Low/Difficult	12 %	11 %	12 %

Table 5.   Correlations Between BNBAS and BBQ.

	BBQ Scales[a]					
BNBAS Clusters	A	B	C	D	E	F
Habituation	.11	.02	.22	−.09	.11	.20
Orientation	.10	−.10	−.35*	.26*	.06	−.19
Motor Performance	.16	.10	−.24	.10	.07	−.25
Range of State	.08	−.02	−.03	−.13	.14	.07
State Regulation	.14	−.03	−.27*	.08	−.18	−.35*
Autonomic Regulation	−.12	−.12	−.25	.00	−.11	.04
Reflexes	−.08	−.01	.19	.12	.02	.18

*p < .05
[a]A = Intensity/Activity
  B = Regularity
  C = Approach/Withdrawal
  D = Sensory/Sensitivity
  E = Attentiveness
  F = Manageability
Note: Brazelton clusters listed vertically.

Table 6.   Relations Between Neonatal Behavior and Infant Temperament

BNBAS	BBQ
1 *Habituation:* Light, rattle, ball, pinprick	A *Intensity/Activity:* Intensity of reactions to familiar people, new food; diaper change
2 *Orientation:* inanimate visual & auditory, animate visual & auditory, visual auditory, alertness	B *Regularity:* regularity in sleep, feeding, bowel movements
3 *Motor:* tonus, maturity, pull to sit, defense, activity	C *Approach/Withdrawal:* adaptability in new situations; mood when meeting strangers
4 *Range of State:* peak of excitement, rapidity of buildup, irritability, lability of state	D *Sensory Sensitivity:* intensity of reaction to rapid movement, strong sound, bright light
5 *Regulation of State:* cuddliness, consolability, self quiet, hand to mouth	E *Attentiveness:* differential reaction to adults & children; new voices, physical differences in people, new toys and foods
6 *Autonomic:* tremors, startles, skin (temperature)	F *Manageability:* mood and activity during diaper change, bath, etc,; persistance in self-amusement, playing with a new toy, and adaptability in new situations
7 *Reflexes:* 2 = normal score; all else scored as abnormal	

Note. High scores = better behaviors
low scores *in reflexes* = better behavior

Note. Low scores = positive behaviors

Discussion

One question addressed in this study was how the timing of first birth (or age of mother) affected infant outcome. Even though the Cohort 2 mothers had had normal pregnancies, the original hypothesis based on the literature was that there would be cohort differences in infant outcome.

The infant biomedical research hypothesis was accepted due to the following findings regarding infant weight and infant health. Cohort 1 infants were significantly heavier than infants born to the older mothers (3769 grams versus 3487 grams). Evidence from an early study done in 1925–1926 in Sweden by Lundh had indicated that infant weight was not dependent on maternal age, although a later study indicated that the incidence of small-for-date babies increased with maternal age (Kajanoja & Widholm, 1977). Since there were no cohort differences in number of small-for-date infants, other biomedical factors were considered post hoc to see if they were related to the finding. The factors considered were: maternal weight at conception, maternal weight gain during pregnancy, maternal weight at delivery, and infant length. Only maternal age proved to be significantly related.

This finding, of interest to the Statistics Department of the Social Welfare Department, was checked against the entire 1981 Swedish population of first-born infants (38–42 weeks gestational age) to mothers aged 20–40. When the larger sample was compared for infant weight, there were no cohort differences. As the average weight of first-borns is about 3400 grams, it became apparent that the older sample of mothers gave birth to infants of normal weight, while the younger sample of mothers had unusually heavy babies. This finding, which could not be explained by any of the sampling procedures, is best considered a chance occurence (A. Ericsson, personal communication, November 12, 1983).

There was an increased morbidity and mortality rate among the Cohort 2 infants; as mentioned above, one female child was born with a cleft lip and palate and another was stillborn. Both of these infants were born to mothers 37 years of age. This was one of the first prospective, controlled studies of older primiparas, so there was little data in the literature on which to make predictions in respect to infant morbidity and mortality. (Most studies having anything to do with maternal age are retrospective and include comparisons over large samples of women, with no control for the health of the mother during pregnancy.) A post hoc consideration of the findings was made to make those cases from Cohort 2 more comprehensive.

The baby who was malformed was also small-for-date. Her mother smoked, which has been shown to have a relationship to both infant size and cleft palate (Ericsson, Kallen, & Westerholm, 1979). Increased incidence of malformation in infants born to older mothers is also documented in the literature (Morrison, 1975; Holmes, 1978).

The stillborn was more difficult to explain, given the high degree of medical involvement, the overall good health of the mother, and the fact that the infant, who had no other medical problems and weighed 3400 grams, was carried to term. Primiparous women who are over age 35 to 40 often have increased fetal risks, but most are due to complications caused by prematurity or small-for-date infants, (Morrison, 1975) or congenital abnormalities (Holmes, 1978).

When the findings from this study were again compared with the total population of Swedish first-time mothers, a stillbirth rate of 0.4% was found for the entire sample. This incidence increased slightly to 0.6% for the older cohort of mothers aged 30–40 years. According to the experts at the Social Welfare Department (A. Ericsson, personal communication, November 12, 1983), this figure meant that the expected stillbirth rate for my total sample would have been 0 or 1 stillborn infant, most predictably in the older cohort. Thus, having one mother in the oldest cohort giving birth to a stillborn baby was considered statistically likely.

The results of the BNBAS cluster analyses could not strongly confirm the research hypothesis that infant behavior would appear different as a result of maternal age. There was only a single item finding, on day 1 regarding the behavior "tonus," which indicated that babies born to the older cohorts of mothers had "less" resistance of the body to passive movement than did the Cohort 1 infants. This single difference was not considered to be a strong index of behavioral discrepancy.

The research hypothesis regarding the relationship of infant temperament to neonatal behavior was confirmed. The BBQ revealed no cohort differences in infant temperament at 4 months of age, nor were post hoc diagnostic ratings of the babies different by cohort. However, stability in infant behavior was indicated. There was a significant relation of four of the BBQ items to two of the BNBAS cluster scores. The BBQ items "approach" and "sensory/sensitivity" were correlated to the BNBAS cluster "orientation," and the BBQ items "approach" and "manageability" to the BNBAS cluster "regulation of state." This latter finding supports previous research results linking state control with distractability (Sosteck & Anders, 1977) suggesting that some early neonatal behaviors and later temperament are related.

Therefore, it appeared that there was a continuity exhibited along some social dimensions of behavior. Babies who were socially active and in control of state during their early days of life (i.e., were alert and interested in animate and inanimate visual and auditory stimuli) were those babies who at 4 months continued to react to social situations in a positive way (i.e., were not afraid of strangers and adjusted easily in new situations), and were minimally affected by strong stimuli. Those newborns who had a high regulation of state score were also rated as more manageable and adaptable by their parents at the 4-month period.

Several of the maternal demographic variables presented significant differences between cohorts, namely, the planning of the pregnancy and the choice of mates. More of Cohort 2 women planned their pregnancies than did the Cohort 1 mothers. This difference was interpreted as an indication that the aging process affected Swedish women in predictable ways, i.e., that older women generally had higher levels of education, familiarity with birth control measures, and body functioning.

Also, the theme of control is important to the average Swedish adult; one wants to control the direction of one's life; one likes things to be orderly and function properly. In Sweden, the issue of fertility control is a major theme, where to plan is considered the ideal; to not plan, irresponsible (Welles-Nyström, 1988). Since ideal reproductive behavior includes the planning of a first child after other adult agenda (such as occupational and economic stability) have been established, the women most likely to plan for their child's birth and time it accordingly were those women who had mastered those cultural ideals of behavior—women who were older.

The repercussions of late timing for the first birth were made evident in the choice of mates for the Cohort 2 women. Because they were older and "late" in respect to the social clock for reproductive entry, the pool of available mates was limited, since the same-aged men were subject to similar social reproductive timetables. This translated into a social reality of reduced availability for the Cohort 2 women of men their own age or nationality (as most of those men were already engaged in relationships or parenthood). Thus, the fathers of Cohort 2 babies were often of non-Swedish origin and/or younger than the mothers in this cohort. The phenomenon of women in their 30s marrying younger men has also been found in the United States (Daniels & Weingarten, 1982).

Regarding the maternal biomedical variables, the research hypothesis was rejected, since the older cohort did not have more complicated deliveries. There were no cohort differences in respect to length of labor, incidence of medical intervention, such as vacuum extractions, or frequencies of Cesarean-sectioned births. This finding was interpreted as an indication of the kind of involvement and management of the Swedish medical system, and corroborated Kajonoja and Widholm's findings (1977). Differences that might have occured naturally, such as longer labors for the older primiparas (Lundh, 1925–1926) are no longer allowed to do so, (since there is such a high degree of induced or chemically stimulated labor in contemporary deliveries).

The intent of the questionnaires and interviews was to elicit attitudinal and behavioral aspects of the pregnancy, delivery, and early postpartum periods. It was predicted that some attitudinal differences would occur between cohorts due to their different histories or position in the life course and the hypothesis was confirmed. Cohort 2 mothers had significantly lower expectations of average infant's ability to breastfeed, and perceived their own infants as having "more trouble" breastfeeding than did Cohort 1 mothers. Additionally, in the delivery interview, the Cohort 2 mothers reported more problems with breastfeeding in the first 5 days postpartum as well. This could be interpreted as a case of self-fulfilling prophecy where "what mother expects of her baby is what mother gets" (Snyder, Eyres, & Barnard, 1979), but it seemed likely that the process was more complex. This finding was therefore considered in three other ways.

First, it is possible that the more problematic nursing experiences of the older mothers were caused by physiological processes, such as latent milk production. This was not measured in the study. Further medical studies should be conducted to ascertain the physiological properties of breastfeeding in the older mother, and document whether there really is a behavioral difference or only a perceptual difference.

Second, the finding was considered historically, since current Swedish philosophies regarding infant care are subject to change as recent research continues to show what babies are capable of doing. It was considered likely that the older mothers would have a more "dated" and less appreciative set of expectations about infant behaviors, which included nursing.

Or that, because they were "older" and had more experience hearing about baby behavior from friends or family, it was considered possible of the Cohort 2 mothers that their set of expectations was more "realistic" compared to the younger, more "idealistic" Cohort 1 mothers. That is, that the more mature mother was aware of some of the difficulties of establishing breastfeeding and appreciative of the fact that it often takes several months of "practice" before nursing goes smoothly, and did not "mind" reporting it as such. Neither of these considerations can be validated at present, but offer interesting future research questions regarding parental goals and their formation.

The third way in which the data could be interpreted was as evidence for the prevalent attitude of the Cohort 2 mothers in general—that they were more cautious about expecting things to go well. This cautious attitude emerged as salient during the pregnancy interviews, when Cohort 2 women rated themselves as somewhat more anxious during the first trimester of pregnancy than did the Cohort 1 women. They were also somewhat more reserved talking about the baby they were carrying and their positive anticipation for the future (Welles-Nyström & DeChateau, 1987).

However, this cautious attitude in fact represents a cultural norm in Sweden, for one of the most common themes of Swedish pregnancy is that of anxiety. Little preparation is made for the infant prior to delivery, because of long-living superstitions that to do so would or could result in some misfortune. In this study, women, when asked whether they had prepared anything for their new baby, usually replied negatively, although they would admit that they knew friends and relatives would give them presents after the child was (safely) born. They said that, if anything were to happen (and here they meant if their infant were to die), they would not want to look at baby things or have to return them to the store. The material reminders of the expected infant would be too painful to endure. Even the purchase of the baby carriage, one of the most costly and important pieces of equipment that new parents desire, is usually bought on the installment plan, "just in case anything goes wrong." Therefore, in order not to tempt fate by being too optimistic, Swedish expectant mothers often couch their anxiety over the future birth and infant outcome with this "cautious attitude," which was more strongly articulted in the older mothers.

That the Cohort 2 mothers seemed more cautious reflected an awareness of increased risks which the older primipara faces—risks which were even corroborated in this study. The caution was interpreted as a defense mechanism for the Cohort 2 mother, just in case something happened. I believe that it continued as a "modus operandi" throughout the entire period (from pregnancy through the early postpartum period), where it was exhibited in other ways, such as the prolonged hospital stay.

The Cohort 2 mothers remained in the hospital for a longer period of time than did Cohort 1 mothers. At the time of this study, the general policy about the length of the hospital stay was that the mother and baby remained until breast-feeding was firmly established, and the infant had begun to gain weight. For first-time mothers, the average hospital stay was 1 week. Mothers who had delivered by Cesarean section normally stayed 10 days. Mothers of second or third babies usually returned home after 5 days (although new mothers had the right to decide when they would go home).

Although it is likely that the mothers in Cohort 2 needed to stay in the hospital for physical reasons such as fatigue, which were not ascertained in this study, or because they were anxious about how to manage the transition taking a new baby home, they nevertheless, regardless of the reason, used the hospital in a different way than did the Cohort 1 mothers. This prolonged stay was interpreted as an index of maternal strategy whereby the Cohort 2 women used their prerogative in deciding when they wanted to go home. Rather than leave at the usual time (or earlier, as did the youngest mothers), they remained in the hospital so as to optimize support and learning opportunities provided by hospital personel. Cohort 2 mothers often explained their wanting to remain in the hospital longer so that they could "really make sure breastfeeding was going well" or so that, "if anything should happen, I can ask a nurse what to do." It seemed as if the longer stay was used as a training period for motherhood.

Swedish women will not usually admit to asking their own mothers for advice in the early postpartum period, but the possibility of their doing so may have been precluded for the older sample because of the distance between their natal families, or because their own mothers no longer were living or were "too old to help out." The majority of Cohort 2 women's natal families lived outside the Stockholm area, while the vast majority of the Cohort 1 women's natal families lived in the same city. It is possible that this demographic fact also influenced the longer stay of the Cohort 2 mothers.

The lack of differences between the group of infants in either neonatal behaviors or temperament contrasted with the significant difference between cohorts in some of the maternal perceptions and expectations of the infants, suggesting that the two cohorts of mothers did differ in attitude. Especially after interviewing them at home, I felt that the differences were best explained as evidence of the "off-time phenomenon" for the Cohort 2 women. According to Neugarten and Hagestad (1978) awareness of age norms in respect to being off-time for a major life transition, such as a first birth, often means that the actual transition varies from the "normal" on-time experience. Thus, the off-time mother's experience, in its deviance from the norm, can be used to illustrate how the on-time event is organized culturally. "Like other realities which are so much taken for granted that their significance becomes apparent only in the breach, the fact that social timetables are significant in the lives of individuals can better be seen by study-ing persons who have been off-time rather than those who have been on-time" (Neugarten & Hagestad, 1976, p. 51).

Looking a bit more closely at the Cohort 2 experience may better illustrate the on-time transition. One variable that struck me as being important in their own evaluation of the ease in which motherhood had been "mastered" (if indeed it ever is) was the effect of employment. All of the sample women had worked during pregnancy, with the older sample having been involved in the labor market for a longer period of time.

Prior to the birth of their children, Cohort 2 mothers "worried" more about their transition, mentioning concern not only over how they were going to handle the adjustment of motherhood in respect to meeting the demands of a new baby, but also in respect to the change from the work environment.

After the child was born, and they were home taking care of the baby, another common complaint of both samples, although more prevalent in Cohort 2, was the fact that they "never got anything done." These women were used to being efficient at their job, and, now that their job at home included taking care of the baby, they were surprised to find that they were not as efficient with other household tasks that they had managed routinely before the birth. The new job of "mothering" preceded all else, leaving little free time.

The qualitative interpretation of the psychological interview material allowed the data to be considered in another way, which also used the off-time experience to describe the on-time. I believe, not only that these older first time mothers had different expectations for themselves prior to—and after—the birth of their child, but that they were also able to predict just what some of their problems would be. This aspect of mature motherhood impressed me time and time again, as the Cohort 2 mothers presented more realistic—or "cautious," if compared to the responses of Cohort 1 mothers—perceptions of their babies and evaluations of their own transition. The older mother, although perhaps hindered physiologi-cally in some aspects of becoming a mother (this has yet to be proved em-pirically), socially may have some advantages.

Some of the advantages mentioned by the Cohort 2 women, with respect to how they saw themselves at age 20, were the following: that they were now more mature, could handle problems and disappointments better, were more settled so that they did not feel so restricted by the baby, and were more patient and tolerant. In contrast, the younger mothers often mentioned these very aspects as being difficult for them. (Several of the youngest mothers in this study even planned on taking separate "swinging" type vacations from spouse and child, as the normal 20-year-old Swedish young person might do.)

Another psychological aspect which differed between the cohorts had to do with female identity. All of the Cohort 2 mothers perceived themselves as adults prior to becoming mothers, not only because of age, but because of life experiences. In contrast, some of the Cohort 1 mothers, especially those younger than 25 years, felt that their *adult identity* had finally been achieved by having a baby. These younger women also felt that their identity as adult females had been attained by being pregnant and giving birth (i.e., that they felt they had become women). For Cohort 2 women, feminine identity was enhanced by motherhood, not created by it.

Thus, the meaning of the birth of the first child was perceived differently by each cohort of women. The issue was, and is, not to judge which age is better for motherhood, but rather to describe how each cohort organizes and responds to the situation. It is also an individual matter, for each woman brings to her transition a unique set of life experiences, perceptions, and expectations.

References

Benedek, T. (1952). *Psychosexual functions in women.* New York: Ronald Press.

Bibring, G.C., Dwyer, T.F., Huntington, D.C., & Valenstein, A.F. (1961). A study of the psychological processes in pregnancy and of the earliest mother-child relationship. In *Psychoanalytic study of the child, XVI* (pp. 9–72). New York: International Universities Press.

Bowlby, J. (1969). *Attachment and loss* (Vol. 1). New York: Basic Books.

Brazelton, T.B. (1972). The early mother-infant adjustment. *Pediatrics, 32,* 931–935.

Brazelton, T.B. (1973). *Neonatal Behavioral Assessment Scale* (Clinics in Developmental Medicine, no. 50). Philadelphia, PA: Lippencott.

Broussard, E.R. (1971). Further considerations regarding maternal perception of the first-born. In J. Hellmuth (Ed.), *Exceptional infant studies in abnormalities* (Vol. 2). New York: Brunner/Mazel.

Brown, J. (1981). Cross-cultural perspectives on the female life cycle. In R. Munroe, R. Munroe, & B. Whiting (Eds.), *Handbook of cross-cultural human development* (pp. 581–610). New York: Garland STPM Press.

Carey, W.B. (1970). A simplified method for measuring infant temperament. *Journal of Pediatrics, 77*(2), 188–194.

Carey, W.B. (1973). Measurement of infant temperament in pediatric practice. In J.D. Westman (Ed.), *Individual differences in children.* New York: John Wiley and Sons.

Cullberg, J. (1975). *Kris och Utveckling* [Crisis and development]. Stockholm, Sweden: Wahlström och Widstrand.

Daniels, P., & Weingarten, K. (1979). A new look at the medical risks in late childbearing. *Women and Health, 4*(1), 5–36.

Daniels, P., & Weingarten, K. (1982). *Sooner or later*. New York: W.W. Norton.

Deutsch, H. (1944). *The psychology of women. Volume 2: Motherhood*. New York: Grune and Stratton.

DeVries, M., & Super, C. (1979). Contextual influences on the neonatal behavior assessment scale and implications for its cross-cultural use. In A. Sameroff (Ed.), *Organization and stability of the newborn behavior: A commentary of the Brazelton Neonatal Assessment Scale. Monograph SRCD, Serial No. 177, 43*(5–6), 1979.

Engelman, G.J. (1883). *Labor among primitive peoples showing the obstetric science of today from the natural and instincitive customs of all races, civilized and savage, past and present*. St. Louis, MO: J.H. Chambers and Co.

Ericson, A., Kallen, B., & Westerholm, P. (1979). Cigarette smoking as an aetiological factor in cleft lip and palate. *American Journal of Obstetrics and Gynecology, 135*(3), 348–51.

Erikson, E. (1950). *Childhood and society*. New York: W.W. Norton.

Fabe, M. (1979). *Up against the clock*. New York: Random House.

Foner, A., & Kertzer, D. (1978). Transitions over the life course: Lessons from age set societies. *American Journal of Sociology, 83*(5), 1081–1104.

Freedman, D.G., & Freedman, N. (1969). Behavior differences between Chinese-American and European-American newborns. *Nature, 224*, 1227.

Hagekull, B. (1982). Measurement of behavioral differences in infancy. *Acta University of Uppsala Abstracts of Dissertations from the Faculty of Social Sciences, 26*.

Hagekull, B., & Bohlin, G. (1981). Individual stability in dimensions of infant behavior. *Infant Behavior and Development, 4*, 97–108.

Holmes, L.B. (1978). Genetic counseling for the older woman: New data and questions. *New England Journal of Medicine, 298*(25), 1419–2122.

Hook, E.B., & Lindsjö, A. (1978). Down Syndrome in live births by single year maternal age interval in a Swedish Study: Comparison with results from a New York State study. *American Journal of Human Genetics, 30*, 19–27.

Jordan, B. (1978). *Birth in four cultures: A cross cultural investigation of childbirth in Yucatan, Holland, Sweden and the United States*. Montreal: Eden Press Women's Publication.

Karlberg, P., & Ericson, A. (1979). Perinatal mortality in Sweden. *Acta Paediatrica Scandinavica*, Suppl. 275.

Kajanoja, P., & Widholm, O. (1977). Pregnancy and delivery in women aged 40 and over. *Obstetrics and Gynecology, 51*(1), 47–51.

Lester, B., Als, H., & Brazelton, T.B. (1982). Regional obstetric anesthetic and newborn behavior: A reanalysis towards synergistic effects. *Child Development, 53*, 687–692.

Lester, B., & Brazelton, T. (1982). Cross-cultural assessment of neonatal behaviors. In H. Stevenson & D. Wagner (Eds.), *Cultural perspectives on child development*. San Francisco, CA: Freeman.

Lester, B., Als, H., & Brazelton, T.B. (1982). Regional obstetric anesthetic and newborn behavior: A reanalysis towards synergistic effects. *Child Development, 53,* 687–692.

LeVine, R.A. (1979). Adulthood among the Gusii of Kenya. In E. Erikson (Ed.), *Themes of love and work.* Cambridge, MA: Harvard University Press.

Lewis, M., & Rosenblum, L. (1974). *The effect of the infant on its caregiver.* New York: John Wiley and Sons.

Lundh, G. (1925–1926). On the problem of age and primiparity. *Acta Obstetrica et Gynecologica Scandinavica, 4,* 3–4.

Mansfield, P.K. (1983). *Advanced maternal age and pregnancy outcome; A critical review of scientific literature.* Unpublished doctoral dissertation, Pennsylvania State University.

Mead, M., & Newton, N. (1967). Cultural patterning of prenatal behavior. In S.A. Richardson & A.F. Guttmacher (Eds.), *Childbearing—Its social and psychological aspects.* Baltimore, MD: Williams and Wilkins.

Morrison, I. (1975). The elderly primigravida. *American Journal of Obstetrics and Gynecology, 121*(4), 465–70.

Neugarten, B., & Hagestad, G. (1976). Age and the life course. In R. Binstock & E. Shanas (Eds.), *Handbook of aging and the social sciences.* New York: Van Nostrand Reinhold.

Oakley, A. (1980a). *Becoming a mother.* New York: Schoken books.

Oakley, A. (1980b). *Women confined: Towards a sociology of childbirth.* New York: Schoken Books.

Sheresefsky, P.M., & Yarrow, C.J. (1973). *Psychological aspects of a first pregnancy.* New York: Raven Press.

Snyder, C., Eyres, S., & Barnard, K. (1979). New findings about mothers' antenatal expectations and their relationship to infant development. *American Journal of Maternal Child Nursing, 4*(6), 354–357.

Sostek, A.M., & Anders, T. (1977). Relationships among the Brazelton Neonatal Scale, Bayley Infant Scales, and early temperament. *Child Development, 48,* 320–323.

Van Gennep, A. (1960). *The rites of passage.* Chicago, IL: Chicago University Press.

Vaughn, B., Taraldson, B., Crichton, L., & Egeland, B. (1981). The assessment of infant temperament: A critique of the Carey Infant Temperament Questionnaire. *Infant Behavior and Development, 4,* 1–17.

Welles, B. (1987). *Maternal age and first birth in Sweden: A life course study.* Unpublished doctoral thesis. Harvard University Graduate School of Education, Cambridge, MA.

Welles-Nyström, B. (1988, Summer). Parenthood and infancy in Sweden. In R.A. LeVine, P.M. Miller, & M.M. West (Eds.), *Parental behavior in diverse societies. New Directions for Child Development, 40,* 75–80. San Francisco: Jossey Bass.

Welles-Nyström, B., & DeChateau, P. (1987). Maternal age and transition to motherhood: Prenatal and perinatal assessments. *Acta psychiatrica scandinavica, 76,* 719–725.

CHAPTER 6

Mother–Infant Interaction
in Denmark*

Hanne Munck, Gretty M. Mirdal, and Lotte Marner

Institute of Clinical Psychology
University of Copenhagen

Denmark is a small country with 5 million inhabitants, a homogeneous population, and a rather flat geographical and social structure which facilitates communication between different groups. This applies also to communication between
researchers and society at large. The dialectical relationship, where problems
taken up for research are inspired by the societal issues at a given period, and
where research in turn affects public opinion, has been especially intense in the
area of early parent–infant relationships.

The dialogue in society, and the public discussion about social and psychological conditions, are further facilitated in Denmark by political tradition, the
inhabitants' generally high degree of education, and, at the same time, an academic tradition of qualitative and phenomenological methods which values the
individual's subjective experiences.

In keeping with this tradition, it is natural to describe research, including our
study on the newborn period, in its cultural and social context. Accordingly, we
shall mention some relevant issues at the time of our work, and in the last section
of the chapter we shall give more information on the living conditions of the
Danish family around the birth of a child.

In the early 1970s there was an awakening interest in research regarding the
psychological conditions in connection with the birth of a child. One of the main
reasons for this was a rapid institutionalization of births, but the interest was due

* Writing of this chapter was supported in part by the Danish Humanistic, Medical, and Social
Science Research Councils.

to a multiplicity of factors. The traditional relatively high status of women in this country, an openness regarding sexuality, sensuality, and reproductive functions, as well as a growing consciousness of women's rights and reevaluation of feminine value, were also influencing factors. The parents' association called "Foraeldre og Fodsel" (Parents and Birth), which is still active and influences the public and official attitudes, was also established at that time. Until then, most changes around child births had been based on medical and practical considerations. The purpose of the association was to improve these aspects in terms of the psychological circumstances, to work for an increased influence of the parents on the birth of their children.

Knowledge and research about newborn babies as individualized human beings with a right to respect was not widespread at that time, and our work was therefore welcome. Almost at the same time, the French obstetrician Frederick Leboyer advocated a calm, homelike birth experience promoting a nonviolent delivery. Klaus and Kennell's work on the "nonseparating" policy had also an impact. All these trends were woven into a special pattern, a corner of which we would like to show in this chapter.

The Study

Background and Purposes. The project originated from a seminar on the psychology of infancy at the University of Copenhagen in 1974 (Mirdal, 1976). The purpose of the seminar was to review the literature on newborn infants and early mother–infant interaction and to observe infants at the maternity ward at the same time, thus combining theory and practice. It was at the end of the two-semester seminar that we came across the Brazelton Neonatal Behavioral Assessment Scale (Brazelton, 1973). Recognizing that this scale encompassed the whole range of behaviors and at the same time was systematized in a convincing way, we included it in the final plans for the project and invited Heidelise Als to direct a 4-day workshop in Copenhagen in the spring of 1975 in order to obtain the necessary reliability in the BNBAS.

Our research team started with different backgrounds of interest: in the infant with special reference to prediction, the psychodynamic processes in motherhood, and in minimal brain damage. These differences in orientation have resulted in inspiring interchanges of ideas and methods in the course of the study. The fact that we each have two children of our own should also be mentioned as part of our background; not only did we learn from them, but they indirectly played a role in the project, because most of the mothers asked us at some point whether we had children ourselves.

The theoretical background to the project was heterogeneous and eclectic. With respect to the mothers we found a psychoanalytically derived view on the dynamics of motherhood (as developed by Bibring, Benedikk, and Deutsch) to be the most useful and appropriate. One of us later wrote a thesis on this theme (Munck, 1978). In the understanding of the dynamics between mother and child we were influenced by the works of Winnicott, Ballint, and Brody as well as Bowlby and Ainsworth and the growing empirical literature on the subject. With regard to methods we were especially inspired by Richards and Bernal's studies (1972).

We took great care not to disturb the beginning mother–infant relationships, not to interfere with the mothers and their feelings, and not to place ourselves "in between" the mother and the baby. If we had the feeling that we evoked reactions (e.g., attention) from the infant that the mother had not yet experienced, we were careful to let her discover the infant's reaction first. In other words, we tried not to act as experts and to avoid any competition with the mother. This was dictated by a belief that seemingly insignificant events can have an impact on the mother in her sensitive and vulnerable state after delivery. This assumption played a role in what we did as well as in what we did not do.

The project had several purposes. One was to study the newborn infant's individual characteristics, with the expectation that this would in turn lead to more refined descriptions—a richer language concerning newborn infants and their activities. Another purpose was to compare the BNBAS observations with the parents' experience and descriptions of the infant. We also wanted to look for variations in the infant's early interaction with the mother in relation to sex, birth rank, and mode of delivery. Finally, we hoped that our focus on the newborn infant as an individual would legitimate a more "respectful" attitude towards the child in a period when institutionalization of deliveries has resulted in hospital routines which ignore the infant's individual needs.

The Ward and its Routines. The study was carried out at the maternity ward of the Copenhagen Municipal Hospital Gentofte, which at that time had 1200–1300 admissions per year. There were two one-bed rooms, five three-bed rooms, and one six-bed room. The period of admission was normally 5 days. The nursing staff was divided into teams, each consisting of one nurse, one assistant nurse, and one apprentice nurse. In this way, the ward aimed at having each mother and her baby, during their admission, taken care of by the same staff throughout the day.

From 5:30 a.m. until 10:00 p.m., the mothers had their babies next to their beds, in cribs where the one long side could be removed, making it possible for the mother to be in contact with her baby while she was lying in bed. This setting was especially valuable for women who had given birth by Caesarian section. The babies wore long, loose cotton gowns as well as diapers and trousers and were covered with an eiderdown. During night hours the babies were in separate rooms, looked after and nursed by the staff.

The mothers could, if they so wished, spend their time in a sitting room with a television set. Adult visitors were admitted without restrictions; children were only admitted to the sitting room. All mothers received written information on the routines of the ward soon after admission.

During the period of the study, the routine regarding feeding of the infants was as follows: fixed feeding hours at 5:30 a.m., 8:30 a.m., 12:30 p.m., 4:30 p.m., and 8:30 p.m. The babies were also given a bottle by the staff at 30 minutes after midnight while they were lying in their cribs. Very often a supplement to breast-milk was given; sugar water the first 2 days, and then ordinary milk formula. According to the head nurse, it was the rule rather than the exception that, at some time or other, the mothers would feed their infants with a bottle after the ordinary breastfeeding hours. In most cases, the weight of the infants was con-trolled immediately before and after feeding, starting from the fourth day.

Selection of Infants and Mothers. From January through June we examined 28 mothers and their babies, selected according to the following criteria: normal pregnancy; birth weight above 2500 gr; and delivery normal or with breech presentation, use of forceps, or vacuum extraction. Infants with perinatal com-plications necessitating admission to the infants ward and thus separation of mother and baby immediately after birth were excluded from the sample. (In-cluded in the sample, however, were infants transferred later in the period for treatment due to high percentage of bilirubin.)

All the mothers who were asked were interested in participating. The subjects had the following characteristics: 17 women were primiparae, 11 women were multiparae (of which 7 had their second and 4 their third baby). Twelve of the infants were girls; 16 were boys. Twenty-three mothers were married; five were not married but lived together with the father of the infant.

Method of Data Collection. In the ward, the BNBAS scale was administered on the third and fifth day. Observations of the interaction took place on the third and fifth day. A 24-hour diary-diagram was filled in by the mothers on the fourth day. Information from the mothers and from hospital records was also in-cluded.

At the 6-week home visit the investigators interviewed the mother, and the 24-hour diary-diagram was filled in by the mother before the home visit.

Observation of the Mother–Infant Interaction. In our study, the feeding situation was chosen for the observation of the mother–infant interaction. In the neonatal period an important part of the contact between the mother and the infant takes place around this activity, and it is therefore reasonable to choose the feeding situation to observe the interaction under natural circumstances and not in an experimental setting. Also the focusing of the entire study on the infant led to the natural choice of situation which involved the activity of the baby. Finally, feeding was of special interest to one of the researchers.

The routine of the ward as to fixed time schedules for breast feeding could be presumed to influence the quantity as well as the quality of the stimulation. The fixed hours could mean that the mothers started feeding infants in accordance with the clock and not as a result of the infant's expressed signs of hunger. Furthermore, since the mothers were aware that there were 3 hours until next feeding, a single feeding situation might involve considerably more and possibly also other kinds of stimulation, meant to induce the baby to suck as much as possible, than would have been the case under other circumstances.

The observations were made in the mothers' rooms and were carried out simultaneously by two persons. This meant that, if the mother spoke during the observation, one of us could answer and the other continue to observe. The observation began with assessing the state of the infant, before feeding was started. We then noted continuously the mother's and infant's behavior, using code signs. The behavior was registered in periods of 10 seconds during 20 minutes.

The variables included in the registration consisted of external, observable behavior. As regards the infant, 26 code signs for state, position, visual behavior, facial expressions, motoric behavior, sounds, and sucking were used. Regarding the mother's behavior, abbreviations and signs for 20 of the most common behaviors were used. Furthermore, we had signs to note whether we judged a certain behavior as functional, goal-directed, (i.e., essential for including the baby to suck, wake up, burp, or the like), or aimed at contact and expression of feelings.

Diary-Diagrams. We constructed a very simple diagram where the mother noted the periods during which the infant was sleeping or awake, crying or not crying, for at least 5 minutes. Activities such as feeding and bathing were also registered. This information gives an estimate of the amount of time spent in the different activities, as well as a rough picture of the infant's diurnal rhythm. The mother completed one diagram on the fourth day after delivery and another on the day before our home visit at 6 weeks.

NBAS. All the infants were examined with the NBAS on the third and fifth day after delivery. We were trained to reliability by Heidelise Als. Two of us were always present at all of the examinations, but there were rarely other participants. Since we have used the NBAS data qualitatively, we shall later present an example of a case study where the mother's information on her infant is compared with our NBAS observations.

Interview With the Mother at 6 Weeks. In the hospital we made an appointment with the mothers for a visit in their homes about 6 weeks after the birth of the baby. A semistructured interview with open questions was used to clarify a series of the mother's and infant's activities. Much of the interview intended to assess the mother's experiences with the baby in respect to some of the dimensions also described by the Brazelton scale, for example, the infant's consolability, irritability, and attention.

A second intention of the interview was to give an estimate of the mother's behavior, for example, what she did when the infant was crying and to what

Photo 1.   (Source: Åse Rosing).

extent her actions were guided by the infant's activities and reactions. Some of the questions specifically concerned the feeding situation, and information was collected regarding practice and attitudes towards breast-feeding. We also collected some retrospective information on the postpartum period at the hospital. The interviews, which were audiotaped, lasted about 1 hour.

Photo 2.   (Source: Åse Rosing).

Informal Results

Before presenting the formal results, we would like to emphasize that conducting research in an area of growing general interest can have implications beyond the formal results that are obtained from the collected data. The project elicited much interest and helped us to establish considerable interdisciplinary contacts. We regard these side effects of our study as our most important results.

For example, our presence at the ward and the focus on the newborn baby turned out to be indirect support for the growing forces desiring changes within the hospital system. While the study was still being conducted, self-demand feeding was initiated at the ward. Soon after our data collection a cooperation with the child psychiatry department was established. Hanne Munck, as a member of our research team, participated in the initiation of the cooperation and the work that followed the next 2 years, where weekly conferences were held.

Our study was primarily a "working project" in the sense that, on the one hand, we tried to integrate our knowledge of the theoretical and empirical literature with the information we were getting from the mothers and the ward personnel, and on the other hand gave this information back to the professionals working in the field, in a way that could be imply practical changes. We conducted several workshops, gave lectures, were invited to different hospitals and maternity wards that were interested in changing routines and in obtaining a better understanding of the dynamics of the mother–infant relationship.

In teaching we have always found it valuable to deal with the topic in an integrated way; that is, the infant's potential to learn, experience, and communicate is presented together with the mothers' special state of sensitivity and vulnerability and related to hospital practices and routines as factors affecting either positively or negatively the establishment of a sensitive interaction between mother and infant (Mirdal & Munck, 1985).

Although researchers are interested in the practical consequences of their work, this last phase of research is the most neglected in academic life. In the case of our study, however, the public interest in our topic was so intense and the need for information so pronounced that we were invited to formulate the results of our work in a form that could be used by the general public and official authorities. Apart from academic articles and lectures, therefore, we wrote information booklets on breast-feeding and on prematurity, and we were asked to prepare reports to be used by governmental committees in legislative work.

Results

The results are grouped in the following manner: analyses of the mother–infant observations, a qualitative case study based on the NBAS, and an analysis of the interviews with the mothers at 6 weeks.

Analyses of the Mother–Infant Observations

The analyses of the observation data will be limited to the infants' sucking activities at the breast (i.e., those activities that take place while the mother is

Table 1.   Number of 10-second periods the infants spend sucking and looking (i.e., open eyes) during feeding (Munck, 1977).

	Sucking	Looking
Sex: girls	53.53	17.17
boys	55.55	26.30
Birth order: first-born	44.14*	24.52
later-born	72.51	18.01
Delivery: normal	45.40	18.92
complicated	59.27	28.29

*$t = 2, 91; N = 25; p < 0.01$

holding the infant in a horizontal position at her breast). The infants' and mothers' activities will be presented in relation to sex of the infant, birth order, and delivery complications (forceps, vacuum extraction, and breech delivery).

The Activities of the Infants. In relation to the infants' activities we analyzed sucking (i.e., time spent with active sucking) and visual activities defined as time spent with eyes open. As can be seen from Table 1, the only significant difference was found in relation to parity, where later-born infants spent significantly longer time with active sucking than the first-born infants.

The Activities of the Mothers. As to the activities of the mothers, we analyzed the amount of tactile and auditory stimulation while the infants were placed in the feeding position. As can be seen from Table 2, first-born infants received significantly more stimulation than later-born infants. There was no difference in the amount of tactile stimulation between boys and girls. However, the mothers of girls talked and made sounds to them more often than mothers did to boys. This difference became even more pronounced when we considered primiparae. The average number of 10-sec periods that primiparae mothers spent with auditive stimulation of girls was 33.88 and of boys 11.32. This difference is highly significant ($t = 4, 36; N = 15; p < 0.001$).

Table 2.   Number of 10-second periods where the mothers stimulated the infants during feeding (Munck, 1977).

	tactile stimulation	auditive stimulation
Sex: girls	39.05	21.33**
boys	41.58	10.18
Birth order: first-born	46.87*	20.38**
later-born	30.60	9.18
Delivery: normal	44.84	13.43
complicated	38.26	17.06

*$t = 2.67, N = 25, p < 0.02$
**$t = 2.33, N = 25, p < 0.05$
***$t = 2.21, N = 25, p < 0.05$

The possible relationship between the infants' and the mothers' activities as described by Table 1 and Table 2 were analyzed. A significant negative correlation was found between the active sucking of the infant and the amount of tactile stimulation of the mother ($r = -0.68$; $N = 25$; $p < 0.01$). No other correlations reached statistical significance.

The Relationship Between Mother–Infant Interaction in the Neonatal Period and Breast Feeding at 6 Weeks. The data that were collected during our observations on the third and fifth day regarding mother–infant interaction with respect to time spent at breast, sucking activity, open eyes, and maternal tactile and auditive stimulation were related to breast-feeding versus discontinuation of breast-feeding at 6 weeks (16 mothers were still breast-feeding at 6 weeks, while 12 had discontinued). The only variable which was significantly different in these two groups was the infant's sucking activity during the observations at the maternity ward.

The average sucking activity, that is, number of 10-second periods in relation to percentage of time at the breast, was 38.29 for the group who had discontinued breast-feeding ($n = 12$) and 65.89 ($N = 16$) for the group who was still breast-feeding ($t = 2.88$; $p < 0.01$). In terms of frequency it is seen that, of the eight infants who had a sucking activity of below 50% of the time in which they were at the breast, only two were being breast-fed at 6 weeks of age (25%). Of the 19 infants with a sucking activity of over 50% of the time at the breast, 14 (75%) were still being breast-fed at 6 weeks of age.

Summary and Discussion of the Observation Analyses. In summary, the following results were found in the analyses of the mother–infant interaction during breast-feeding:

1. First-born infants sucked less than later-born.
2. Primiparae mothers stimulated their infants more often than did multiparae mothers.
3. Primiparae mothers talked more to their infants.
4. Mothers talked more to girls than to boys.
5. This last difference was especially obvious in the case of primiparae mothers.

These differences are in accordance with earlier studies which have found that parity and sex of infant are factors which affect mother–infant interaction. Thoman, Turner, Leiderman, and Olson (1972) studied the interaction between mother and infant with respect to feeding behavior and found that primiparae mothers stimulated their infants more while at the breast, and that their infants sucked less. They regarded these results as signs of inappropriate maternal stimulation, which was actually inhibiting the infants' sucking. This is also in accordance with Kay's (1975) results, where the length and frequency of pauses were reported to correlate with the mothers' stimulation. This negative correlation between the infant's sucking and the mother's stimulation could also be interpreted as the mother's effort to get an infant with low sucking activity to suck more.

In addition to the difference in experience, there are physiological differences between primiparae and multiparae mothers such as hormonal production and lactation, duration of labor, and sensitivity of nipples. These factors could affect both the primiparae mother and the first-born infant and, therefore, their interaction during breast-feeding.

There is also evidence in the literature that boys and girls are treated differently by their mothers in the first months of life. The mother's vocal and tactile behavior especially has been studied in relation to the sex of the infant. Moss (1967), Moss and Robson (1968), Thoman et al. (1972), and Lewis and Freedle (1973) have reported results which are in accordance with our findings, namely, that mothers talk more to girls than to boys. Hwang (1978) found that mothers of girls engaged in more talking, smiling, and "en face," and in more skin-to-skin contact, than mothers of boys.

According to de Chateau and Wiberg (1977a), the difference in maternal behavior found between primiparae and multiparae mothers is eliminated when primiparae have "extra contact" with their newborn (i.e., naked skin-to-skin and sucking contact immediately following delivery). Primiparae mothers with "extra contact" behaved like the more experienced multiparous mothers, and this effect of extra contact was greater on the behavior of mothers to boys than of mothers to girls, as seen both at 36 hours and at 3 months. These results reflect the extremely delicate and complex pattern of mutual accomodation and regulation that exists between mother and child. This is further illustrated when qualitative methods are used, as in the following case.

Qualitative Use of the NBAS: A Case Study

One of the purposes of the project was to compare our description of the infant based on the NBAS with the mother's description and to investigate whether our perceptions and "language" were usable in clinical practice. The following case description illustrates an attempt to compare our NBAS test and description of the infants on the third and fifth day with the mothers' replies and statements in the interview 6 weeks after birth, as well as their information according to the 24-hour diary-diagram, filled in the day before our home visit (Marner, 1980).

Description of the Behavior During First Week of Life. Infant P.M. was a first-born red-haired boy with a birthweight of 3300 gr., looking healthy and charming. In neither of the two observations was he in an awake, attentive state (alertness 1). He was the only infant in the study who showed so little attention. He cried a lot (peak of excitement 8). During the first observation, he was generally bothered by the entire procedure. After the Habituation trial with light, he woke up and cried (irritability 9). He cried and was restless, unless he was consoled, which could in most cases be done by putting a hand on his stomach, while he was lying in his crib (Consolability 6). With great effort it was possible to elicit some cuddliness (Cuddliness 4). Despite his almost constant motoric restlessness he reacted to auditive stimulation, after having been calmed (he turned his head to voice as well as rattle, even if he did not have open eyes).

In the first observation, where he cried very much, it was difficult to judge his motor maturity. In the second observation, he was a little hypertonic (General Tone 7), and he resisted attempts to establish body contact. Yet he had smooth movements (Motor Maturity 5) and normal reflexes. Clearly, he was a healthy and robust infant who was disturbed by the observation procedure, but who relatively easily calmed down again. He was rather uninterested in body contact and was in no state to permit visual contact, but he did react to auditory stimulation. His states were clear and relatively stable (Lability of State 3). He expressed clearly that the observation procedure disturbed him, and one had the distinct feeling that it was better for him to be left alone.

Mother's Description 6 Weeks Later. When visiting the mother and the infant at home 6 weeks later, we had the impression of a relaxed mother who had a quiet and harmonious daily life with her baby. He was exclusively breast-fed, which caused no difficulties, as he had relatively clear changes of state during the day (which corresponds to the evaluation of states in the observations). This may be illustrated by the following extracts from the interview:

> (Is he breast-fed?) "Yes."
> (Never bottle?) "Nope."
> (Is it at fixed hours?) "Just about when he wakes up, it is a pity to wake him, but on the whole he wakes up about the same time."
> (Are there no days when he gets a little extra?) "No."
> (Do you sometimes wake him in order to feed him?) "No, I did so a few times, when I went to bed around midnight. But sometimes he slept through anyway, so I don't know if I should wake him or not."
> (Is it easy to see if he is hungry?) "Yes, he screams and searches."
> (How many meals a day does he get now?) "Five, normally."
> (When he is hungry, does he accept waiting?) "Sometimes he may do that."
> (The feeding hours at the hospital, did they suit you?) "No, not quite, I think. And that was six times a day, and when we came home—I don't know—then it became five times."

The mother informed us that he has been sleeping through the night right from the beginning. He sleeps a lot in the daytime, but now and then requires a little support to keep a calm state. It is feasible and easy for the mother to make him calm down each time he gets restless.

> (Does he sleep much?) "He wakes up sometimes in between, maybe colic or . . . ."

(Does he go back to sleep by himself?) "No, then I will give him his comforter. I have a small music box, which I use now and then, and then he falls asleep, and then he wakes up a little later."

(What do you mean by 'a little later'?) "Well, half an hour, 1 hour, sometimes a little later."

(Does he sleep in the house or outside in the daytime?) "Outside."

(For how long periods does he sleep each time?) "I think 4 hours."

(Within these hours, does he wake up regularly?) "Then he sleeps, I think, 3 hours."

(When is it that he wakes up and you give him the comforter?) "That is when he has been sleeping 1 hour or 1 hour and a half."

(Is it each time?) "No, it is here (points to the 24-hour diary scheme), it is in the afternoon. He can sometimes also be awake without crying."

(Where is he lying then?) "Then he is lying in his bed, looking."

(Does he have anything to look at in the bed?) "Yes, in the afternoon, when he has been fed, about 4:00 or 5:00, then he will lying awake and he will lie and play and look . . . that is, play and play, but he is looking, you see."

We can now state that the baby has started to be awake and alert and takes pleasure in visual stimulation. The mother informs us, however, that, sometimes when he is tired, she has to turn him away from the toys in his crib, in order to enable him to fall asleep. Considering that so far he is, on the whole, content to be in his crib when he is awake, this might imply that there are still rather narrow limits for the amount of stimulation that he can make use of without getting irritated.

During the Brazelton observation he struggled and had difficulties in making use of body contact.

(Is he often being carried?) "How carried?"

(Do you walk around with him on your arm?) "No, that is seldom."

Until now it looks as if the infant's need of stimulation has been rather small, limited to the few breast meals, the daily bath, and the few times that the mother stimulated him with the comforter and auditorily, and he has long sleeping periods. All this is about to change, and new needs are emerging, which is revealed by the following:

(Is there anything he especially likes?) "Likes?"

(Yes, to be bathed or something to look at or . . . ?) "He likes being bathed; he also likes sitting with us a little, you see, especially if he is sitting like this." (As he is now sitting on his mother's lap.)

(Do you often let him do that?) "Yes, once in a while."

(Do you often sit in here (drawing room) with the baby in your lap?) "It is very seldom."

(Do you feel you have problems with him?) "Only that he cries now and then. Yes, sometimes in the evening he can be difficult."

(How?) "Well, sometimes—yes, it only was a couple of times—he has been really hysterical, but just as soon as one enters the room, puts one's hand under here, then he gets quiet, then we take him up a little, or just so a little bit, then I lay him down again, then he screams, then I give him the comforter, try everything possible, then just as soon as one touches him here, and he thinks he is going to be taken up, then he gets quiet."

(But do you intend to take him up?) "No, one should be careful about that, I think, or they may quickly get spoilt—it shouldn't be so that they just have to scream, and one comes and takes them up. I think you have to be careful about that. . . . So I think that, if you take them up too much, then they end up wanting to sit on your lap rather than lie in the bed. Of course I'll take him up once in a while, he doesn't lie in his bed all day long, I am not that strict."

The interview with the mother pointed up some features of the observation situation. The amount of stimulation that the infant could take without getting tired and crying was limited. An important part of the mother's actions was to calm him down. As in the observation situation, this was rather easy and could be done without taking him up. As in the observation situation, it was the auditory stimulation that he made use of (and therefore received?). Recently he had, however, started to take an interest in the visual aspects of his surroundings. He was not especially responsive to physical contact, nor was this a frequently used form of contact. He had relatively few and easily interpretable changes of state during the day, also as in the course of the test. Therefore, his mother was able to nurse him well and enter the interaction with him each time he so required, without his becoming a burden for her. However, this balance was now about to be disturbed, as the baby claimed more stimulation.

According to the NBAS description of the infant, the mother would have a little trouble with him. He was very irritable, cried a lot, and did not reach the alert and quiet state, which is rewarding for the mother and thus plays a role in establishing the mother's attachment to the infant. In contrast to this expectation, however, the relationship turned out to be harmonious and satisfying for the mother. Here is a discrepancy between an observation situation and everyday life, insofar as an NBAS examination interferes with the infant's spontaneous rhythm and thereby gives an inaccurate impression.

When this boy was given the opportunity to follow his own rhythm with his mother, he was less irritable and better organized. It is also important to consider other modes of contact and communication which the mother and the infant have been able to establish. In this case, the child had a good auditory responsivity, which the mother had been able to make use of, and he was easy to console. It was a very strong and rewarding feeling for the mother, not only that the infant was easy to console, but that this consolation could almost always put him in a stable quiet state, which gave her both time and energy for other activities. Another important element was that the baby slept throughout the night.

A mother might not be satisfied with this contact with the baby and would be frustrated by the lack of responsivity to visual stimulation and body contact, but apparently that was not the case with this mother. As a matter of fact, when the baby started to claim contact in these areas, the mother was reluctant to follow the baby's development and enter the relationship on those premises.

Analysis of the Interviews

Breast-Feeding at 6 Weeks. At 6 weeks after birth (57.1%), 16 mothers were still breast-feeding their children while 12 mothers had discontinued breast-feeding (42.8%). Of these 12 mothers, one had stopped breast-feeding at the hospital, three during the first week, two after 2 weeks, four after 4 weeks, and one after 5 weeks. Three of the mothers, who were still breast-feeding at 6 weeks, used supplementary bottle feeding.

Of the 12 mothers who had discontinued breast-feeding at 6 weeks, 10 referred to the quality and quantity of the breastmilk in relation to discontinuation. One of the remaining mothers had been hospitalized, and in one case the infant had never learned to suck at the breast. Only two of these mothers had not expected to breast-feed. The remaining 10 had expected to breast-feed for a longer period (i.e., about 3–4 months).

The mothers who were still breast-feeding 6 weeks after delivery were asked how long they thought they would go on breast-feeding, and gave answers which reflected differences both with respect to expectations regarding duration of the breast-feeding period and to the subjective experience of being in control of the duration.

With respect to their own capacity to breast-feed (the quantity of the milk, its quality, and so on) eight mothers expressed insecurity, while five other mothers were concerned with the possibility of continuing breast-feeding after they started working again. For most of the mothers, breast-feeding up to 5–6 months was desirable. As far as resuming work, 15 mothers had no plans to do so before the child was 1 year old, and 12 were to start working outside home again within the first 6 months after delivery. Leaves of absence stretched from 2½ months to 6 months. Of these 12 mothers, nine breast-fed their infants, and five of the nine wished to continue after they returned to work, but were uncertain about the possibility of doing so.

Only two mothers thought that it was difficult and unpleasant to breast-feed and refused to do so, while the rest of them said that it was a positive, delightful, pleasant experience; four mothers said that they were anxious as to whether the infant was getting enough, and that this anxiety reduced their pleasure at breast-feeding. Only eight mothers had known women who had breast-fed their infants for more than a few weeks, and four of these were breast-feeding at 6 weeks. The remaining 20 mothers did not know any woman who had breast-fed her infant or they said that they knew women who had started breast-feeding but who had given up after a few weeks.

It was our impression that breast-feeding according to a rigid time schedule had prevented a harmonious breast-feeding for many mothers, one-third openly expressing their dissatisfaction. A fixed schedule for breast-feeding was not considered desirable by the maternity ward either. It was not instituted in order to improve the chances of breast-feeding, but because it was considered a necessary evil in the daily life routine of the ward. The mothers were instructed that they could breast-feed at other periods, and more flexibly, after leaving the hospital. Despite this information many mothers, at 6 weeks, were still sticking to the same time schedule they had at the hospital, even though the breast-feeding hours did not suit them, neither while they were at the hospital nor after they had come home. This illustrates that deeds carry more weight than words, that actions performed have more effect than conflicting verbal directions and become norms for the patients.

Psychological Well-being in the Postpartum Period. At the time when we were conducting our study, there was no research in this country focusing on the mother's psychological condition around the time of delivery. We have ourselves tried to deal with this area with care and touched upon it only at our 6-week visit to the mother. It was our impression that many mothers were insecure and vulnerable in the postpartum period, and we decided to omit a detailed study of their psychological condition in view of the fact that we at that time had neither the capacity for offering them professional support nor possibilities of referring cases to other psychological or psychiatric facilities.

On the termination of the study, and as a result of our initiative, a close cooperation was established between the child psychiatry department of the hospital and the maternity ward, which by now felt the need to offer support to the mothers. In relation to the mothers' psychological well-being, it might be informative for English-speaking readers to be introduced to the Danish word *trivsel* (thriving). Thriving is a word that is seldom used in English in connection with mothers and infants, except in the case of infants' failure to thrive. In Danish, however, the word, which means development, growth, property, and being in harmony, is a very common expression used primarily in relation to psychological well-being. We have therefore used it in our study, not only in connection with the infants' weight increase, growth, and development, but also with respect to the mothers' feelings and adjustment to her delivery and the new baby.

Among the questions we discussed with the mothers at our 6-week interview was how they felt, when they were at the maternity ward. Of the 28 mothers, 12 answered that they had felt well and been fine during their stay at the hospital. While five of these mothers had expected to be low or depressed, their responses were rather formal and contained relatively little information. Very often their answers gave the impression that there was nothing to complain about and no special problems, rather than expressing a real deep-seated satisfaction.

Information which was mostly positive, but with reservations, was given by eight mothers, and in complaints which were more or less explicit: "I was more or less fine, somewhat moody, but generally ok"; "I missed home, but other than that it was nice, the staff was very fine, except that they did not help very much with breast-feeding, but otherwise . . . ." Negative experiences were expressed by seven mothers. Even so, they often began by saying: "It was really all right." One of them had considerable problems with the scheduled breast-feeding, but did not dare to protest, because she knew from a previous delivery that she cried very easily. Another mother, who delivered at night, mentioned that her child was taken from her and placed in a separate nursery, as it was customary to do at that time if the birth took place in the night hours. She said: "It is terrible to be separated, I think it was very wrong. I think I would have slept, if I had had him by my side." Again another told us: "I was quite fine, really, I was, almost all the time, that is except when I was really deeply depressed. . . . When [the baby] was control-weighed, I was so nervous each time as to whether she had gotten what she should, it was such a problem, and it seemed so huge." The same mother said with respect to scheduled breast-feeding: "I felt I was in some way being ignored, I mean it was my child, I thought, and I should have a say about my child and decide if my own child wanted to eat or not at that point, and they shouldn't really keep me from it, should they?"

It was our clear impression that the neonatal care routines at that time had a negative effect on both the mothers' "thriving" and the establishment of breast-feeding, especially concerning the rigid scheduled breast-feeding, the extra bottle feedings, and the control-weighing after each feeding. We were therefore surprised that the mothers were so cautious and careful, moderate in their criticism of the maternity ward, although they expressed at the same time that their stay had also been emotionally taxing for them. It may be difficult to take a comprehensive view and be critical towards rules and systems, especially when the interpersonal relations seem to be satisfactory, as was the case for most of the mothers, when their relationship to the ward personnel was reflected in the interviews.

In an American study, the same experience was seen (Sullivan & Beeman, 1981). The researchers had expected a high degree of dissatisfaction among a group of mothers on account of the early dismissal from hospital, often within 48 hours after delivery, and the lack of traditional care and instruction. Instead, less than one of every 10 women expressed dissatisfaction in their answer to the question about postpartum care. It was found that, in the absence of extraordinary circumstances, women are reluctant to criticize maternity care.

This may be due to the fact that women tend to be passive maternity patients with low expectations. Social norms dictate that they should be grateful for their healthy babies and not complain about care. An example showing the mothers' passive adaptation to unreasonable routines is that, at the time of our study, mothers rarely asked to attend our observation of their infants. However, now that the conditions are most reasonable, we find that mothers prefer to be present and take it for granted that they can follow all examinations of the infant.

Within the last years a series of studies have been conducted in Scandinavia regarding the families' psychic "thriving" after a child's birth. The results have supported the critical experience that psychological difficulties in this period of life are frequent, especially among primiparae.

In a comprehensive Swedish study (Uddenberg, 1974), 20% of the primiparae showed a severe psychological handicap with painful psychological symptoms within 4 months after delivery. They also showed considerable difficulties in their work, within as well as outside the house. Another 27% primiparae had psychological difficulties of more moderate character which, however painful, did not lead to a deterioration of their social or interpersonal functions.

In a follow-up study almost 5 years later (Uddenberg & Englesson, 1978), almost half of the women who had had a severe psychological handicap within the first 4 months were found to be still unable to solve their emotional problems, and had frequent and invalidating periods with severe psychological difficulties, both in relation to themselves, their spouse, or their child. These mothers were characterized by lack of self-confidence, and many felt that they were unsuccessful mothers. The children were often described by them with negative expressions, and the mothers considered that they had difficulty in bringing them up. Anxiety for the child's health was high, and these mothers visited the general practitioner frequently, without real illness in the child.

The children's view of the mothers was studied through the Family Relation Test. This showed that positive expressions on the child's part were often found in mother–child pairs where the mother had not been psychologically handicapped after the birth. In the case where the mothers had had severe psychological problems, the children, when they were almost 5 years of age, regarded them as being very restrictive and not very supportive.

In two later studies of 33 Swedish (Lagercrantz, 1975) and 29 Norweigian (Brudal, 1979) primiparae, a high frequency of psychological problems was also found for the period after birth: 33% of the mothers at 6 months, according to Lagercrantz, and 24% at a follow-up 1 year later. The main problems were an overwhelming feeling of responsibility, feelings of insufficiency, general worry, depression, anxiety at being alone with the child, anxiety at losing self-control, and a general ambivalence. In the Norwegian study, where both parents were interviewed, it is necessary to note that 14% of the fathers had psychological problems in relation to the birth of their first child.

Elisabeth Lagercrantz (1975) carried out a qualitative study in which 33 primiparae and their children were followed from birth up to 18 months. The mothers and infants were observed at the maternity ward, and the mothers were interviewed at 2, 4, 6, and 18 months. The degree of the mother's psychological problems, her resources in problem solving, and degree of acceptance of the child was apparent early in the interaction and was clearly reflected in the children's development from birth to 18 months, as assessed by intensive observations and Griffith's test. The children of the 33% mothers who described subjective psychological problems had contact difficulties, and were insecure and unhappy, at 6 as well as at 18 months. They did not try to establish contact with the mother and did not seek help or consolation. They seemed uninterested in the environment, had poor mimic, and were easily frustrated. They performed poorly in the Griffith test and they had the lowest average developmental scores of all groups.

The high degree of anxiousness and insecurity among mothers has, as mentioned already, been noticed by clinicians from different disciplines. The late pediatrician John Lind said in 1975: "If I should sort out an impression from my 25 years as a pediatric consultant at the maternity ward, an impression which is stronger and more persistent than any other, it would without the slightest doubt be the mothers' insecurity, anxiety, and incompetence on the day they were dismissed from the ward and went home with their first child" (Lind, 1975, p. 1545).

We do not believe that the results that have been presented in this section are due to a higher rate of psychopathology among young mothers in Scandinavia. Neither do we think that others here have poorer living conditions, which result in the psychological problems. On the contrary, it seems that the environment and society in which they live give them the possibility to deal more openly with the psychological problems. It could also be seen as valuable that research deals with how people feel and their level of psychological well-being, even when it is not a question of psychopathology but a question of life quality.

Life Conditions for the "New-born Family" in Denmark

We now present information on the situation in Denmark around a child's birth, which, inspired by John Lind (1975), is so often called the birth of a family. The information given in this section is mainly based on official statistics and publications, a list of which can be obtained from the authors.

Fewer and fewer children have been born in Denmark in recent years, and the number of births in 1979 was 59.464, the lowest in many years. The falling birth rate since the middle of the 1960s reflects the fact that more women have only one or two children, and many have their first child at a later point in their lives, while some do not have children at all. The more common use of contraceptives in the 1960s, and the right to legal abortion, which was introduced in 1973, make it possible for parents to choose how many children they want to have. It should also be mentioned that, since the law on free abortion was passed, the number of

Photo 3. (Source: Åse Rosing).

legal abortions has been more or less constant at about 25,000 per year, with a tendency toward a slight fall in recent years.

Infant mortality (i.e., the number of stillborns in relation to the total number of births) has, in the years from 1970 to 1979, decreased from 8.5 per 1000 births to 5.2. *Perinatal mortality*, defined as the number of stillbirths plus deaths in the first 7 years of life, is also reduced, from 17.9 per 1000 births in 1970 to 9.9 in 1979. *Neonatal mortality*, which refers to the number of deaths in the first 28 days after delivery, decreased from 11.0 per 1000 births in 1970 to 5.7 in 1979. Finally, mortality after the 28th day and up to 1 year of age (i.e., postnatal mortality) is relatively unchanged, from 3.2 in 1970 to 3.1 in 1979.

Turning to the age of the mother at delivery, 73% of infants delivered in 1974 were born to women between the ages of 20 and 29. The 30–34-year-olds gave birth to 16%, and only 5% of all children were born to teenage mothers. The number of teenage mothers has decreased from around 10,000 in 1963 to 3,600 in 1977. There is a clear tendency for the younger mothers to have less school education.

Until about 1970 the number of children born out of marriage was around 10%. Since the 1970s, however, this number has increased considerably, reaching a level of every fourth child in 1977 and every third child in 1979. It is important to note that this information concerns legal marital status and does not necessarily reflect the number of parents actually living together.

It is more and more common for young people to live together as traditional couples but without getting legally married in what is called a cohabitation, "relation without certificate." Many get married later on, often around the birth of the second child, so that births out of wedlock often should be considered as births before wedlock. The number of couples living in cohabitation has increased in the later years, from about 100,000 in 1974 to 170,000 in 1977. However, a rising number of children do grow up in families which are one-parent families, with 40,000 children from 0 to 6 years of age living with their mothers alone and about 1% of the same age group living alone with their fathers.

The size of the families is generally smaller than before. Many children grow up now in small families. Only a minority of younger children have more than one sibling. If we look at the 0–6-year-old group in 1976, only 5% had three or more siblings, 35% were only children, and 42% had one sibling. About 30,000–40,000 Danes chose to settle in collectives in the 1960s and 1970s. This way of life is most common among young people. In 1975, 10% of 18–24-year-olds lived in collectives, whereas this was true of only 4–5% of the 25–39-year-old. The number of children who are born in these collectives is unknown.

We shall now turn to the description of the care routines and services provided by the medical and social health systems in relation to the birth of a child. In Denmark consultations at the general practitioner, as well as hospital admissions and operations, are free of charge. During pregnancy women go to their general practitioner for prophylactic examinations, usually four times. They are also entitled to prophylactice health examinations by a midwife. The number of these examinations vary from five to seven, according to need.

Furthermore, birth preparation has been provided in Denmark, as in the greater part of Europe, since the 1930s. The method used is in the form of relaxation training and information for pregnant women, based on a Soviet and a British model. For many years psychoprophylaxis has been part of the posteducation of midwives and has, since the middle of the 1970s, been an obligatory part of their education.

No legislation regulates the birth preparation, and the pregnant woman is not legally entitled to such education, as compared to her right to birth aid and prophylactic examinations by general practitioner and midwife. However, in 1976 the Danish health authorities recommended that maternity wards offer birth preparations courses to pregnant women.

The number of pregnant women who do, in fact, receive birth preparation education is not known. According to the birth environment investigation, from 1976 to 1977 (Kamper-Jorgensen, Holstein, Osler, & Poulsen, 1979a, 1979b) 87% of the maternity wards offered such courses themselves. These are free of charge. The courses varied very much in length and content: 18% were short (i.e., under 10 hours' duration), 55% were between 10 and 19 hours duration, and 28% were long (i.e., 20 hours or more). The size of the class varies, but is most often 12 participants. In half of the places the father may participate in the entire course, and other persons may also participate. The most essential differences between the courses are connected with their length, the degree of the father's involvement, the psychological topics, and the form of education.

In Denmark deliveries can take place (a) in maternity wards, which typically are hospital departments with over 1,000 births per year; (b) in other hospital wards, with 100–500 deliveries per year; (c) in maternity homes, with approximately 500–1,000 deliveries per year*; or (d) at home. In 1979 the 59,773 births that took place in Denmark were distributed according to Table 3.

In a study encompassing the whole country (Birth Environment Study, Kamper-Jorgensen et al., 1979a, 1979b), information was collected with respect to several conditions regarding birth and delivery during the years 1976 and 1977. This study, which had a participation of 84% of the wards responsible for 83% of all births in Denmark during that period, gives an idea of how different hospitals of the country described their own neonatal care routines and services to parents. The study was conducted by three physicians and a sociologist in close cooperation with Denmark's largest consumers' organization in this field, "Foraeldre og fodsel" (Parents and Birth), which is a grass-roots movement of parents who were concerned and dissatisfied with the existing maternity ward routines.

---

* Maternity homes disappeared altogether in 1985, and almost all deliveries take place in a hospital setting now.

Table 3. Infants born in 1979 by place of confinement

	Maternity ward	Other hospital ward	Maternity home	At home	Elsewhere	Total
No.	42,770	14,723	1,949	286	45	59,773
%	71.6	24.6	3.3	0.5	0.1	100

Sundhedsstyrelsen: Medicinsk foedselsstatitik 1979. Copenhagen, 1982.

The questions that were asked in the study reflect the routines and practices which were considered problematic at that time from a consumer's point of view. We shall present below some of the information which was obtained, especially regarding practices about contact between the spouses, between mother and infant, and about breast-feeding. At the time this study was conducted, 13% of the mothers delivered babies in maternity homes, a figure which in 1979 was reduced to 3.3%. There is a high degree of uniformity in the practices used in the different wards throughout the country as regards allowing the presence of an accompanying person during delivery. Almost all wards give permission to the father or another person to be with the mother from the very beginning of admission. In most places, the mother may have another person than her husband during delivery. Only 10% of all wards accepted older children to attend delivery, and these were almost exclusively maternity homes.

As mentioned before, there had already been debate and much discussion on the question of mother–infant contact at the time when the Danish Birth Environment Study was conducted in 1976–77. Several Swedish studies (Lind & Jaederling, 1964; Greenberg, Rosenberg, & Lind, 1973) had already described the advantages of rooming-in with respect to the mother's feeling of self-confidence and competence in taking care of and understanding her infant. Women were intensively engaged in the question of a development towards unlimited contact between mother and infant after delivery in maternity wards throughout the country. In 1976–77, three-fourths of all the wards had no restrictions on early contact between mother and infant, though in some places infants delivered at night were removed at once to a separate nursing room.

In 1976–77, the average length of stay at the ward after delivery was 5–6 days for 80% of the respondents. In the majority of places (83%) the mother was the main person taking care of the child from the first day. In many places, there were special visiting hours for the fathers. In 91% of the wards it was possible for the father to be in close physical contact with his newborn baby. Certain places had prepared social written material to help the father in child-caring functions. In 73% of the places siblings were admitted for visits. However, they were not allowed to be in close contact with the newborn. This is one of the areas which recently has been changing.

Only 19% of the maternity wards that participated in the Birth Environment Study had neonatal departments at the same hospital. At the remaining maternity wards, the infants were transferred, in cases of necessity, to the nearest hospital with neonatal facilities. The procedures for transferring the mother, together with the infant, vary from hospital to hospital and is also a local political-economic question. One-third of the wards transferred the mothers quite often, one-third seldom, and one-third never, and 20% of the women whose infants were transferred to a neonatal ward were not able to visit them, as long as they themselves were at the maternity wards. This question is still being discussed, especially since recent budget reductions interfere with mothers being transferred to another hospital after delivery, if the infant has to be admitted to a neonatal ward.

Routines concerning breast feeding have been under debate and have changed in the last 10 years. As mentioned in connection with our study, about one-third of the mothers reported dissatisfaction with the rigid breast-feeding schedules they had to follow at the maternity ward in 1975. The mother's insecurity, however, often resulted in her acceptance of the ward's instructions regarding fixed feeding schedule as being "the only way," even though it did not suit her or her infant. In such cases, the ward's routines did not support the mother in seeing her infant as being active and capable of signalling his or her needs. Furthermore, these routines prevented the mother from establishing a sense of confidence based on understanding the infant's expressions and needs and her own capacity to relieve those needs.

In spite of the numerous studies which have clearly shown the advantages of self-demand feeding (Olmsted & Jackson, 1950; Illingworth, Stone, Iowett, & Scott, 1952; Egli, Egli, & Newton, 1961), the Danish maternity wards have been reluctant to change their practices. In a Danish study of 321 mothers who delivered in different places of the country in 1976, it was found that 80% had experienced scheduled breast-feeding at their maternity wards (Delholm, Mahneke, Mortensen, & Rasmussen, 1978). The information provided by the mothers in this study is not in accordance with the information provided by the maternity wards. In the Birth Environment Study, which has been referred to throughout this section, 84% of the country's maternity wards reported that they had the following routines concerning breast-feeding: 24% had fixed-schedule feeding, 20% had self-demand feeding, and 52% said that they had both routines and that it was up to the mothers to choose.

The routine which is generally followed in the wards with respect to breast-feeding seems to be related to attitudes regarding the regular use of supplementary bottle-feeding. As seen in Table 4, wards with scheduled breast-feeding hours gave extra bottle feedings more often than wards with self-demand feeding. There also seems to be a relationship between the routines concerning breast-feeding and the routines concerning mother–infant contact (i.e., in wards with self-demand feeding, the infant is with its mother all the time).

Kamper-Jorgensen et al. (1979a, 1979b) find that some wards, which they call "medical hygienic oriented," are more restrictive and follow strict rules regarding routines than wards, which are psychosocially oriented, less strict, and more

Table 4.   Breast-feeding principle in relation to selected other routines: Percentages (Kamper-Jorgensen et al., 1979).

	Breast-feeding principle	
	Fixed time schedule	Self demand
Mother is allowed to take the child herself from the crib for feeding	95	100
Night-time breast feeding allowed	89	100
The child will get routine supplementary feed:		
if hungry outside feeding hours	36	13
if hungry during the night	76	43
if mother has only little milk	95	60
Child with the mother all day	52	100

($N = 19$) ($N = 16$)

liberal in their routines. In the maternity ward the relationship between style of leadership, division of work, and responsibility on the one hand, and the attitude and routine of the staff on the other hand, was studied in a Danish project conducted in two different maternity wards (Guldager & Thorup, 1977). This study concludes that, in wards with a hierarchic staff organization and an authoritarian leadership, the procedures are generally strict and the attitudes toward the mothers reflect the type of administration. This seems in turn to affect negatively the mother's adaptation to her infant's rhythm. A more democratic organizational structure and a division of labor in the wards seem, however, to promote and facilitate the mother's preparation to the situation she will meet when discharged from the hospital.

Both of these studies suggest that, if the wards changed their attitudes towards contact between mother and child, breast-feeding, and so on, a change in the organizational structure of the ward would take place at the same time. The medical personnel's worries concerning the possible deleterious effects of changes of routines can be dissipated by studies such as that of de Chateau, Holmberg, and Winberg (1975), who showed that omission of extra bottle-feeding and control weighing (i.e., weighing the infant before and after breast-feeding) did not have negative effects on the infants during the period at the hospital, but had positive effects in the form of better psychological triving of the mothers and led to significantly more mothers breast-feeding after 2 weeks.

It has always been common in Denmark to breast-feed infants, and most studies on this subject show that about 95% of all infants are breast-fed after birth. However, the length of the period of breast-feeding has become shorter and shorter since the 1930s, with a slight raise around the Second World War but a continuous fall until the beginning of the 1970s. At the end of the 1930s, 60% of all infants born in wedlock in Copenhagen were exclusively breast-fed until 2 months of age, whereas in 1969 this figure was 26%. In the 1930s, 47% were still breast-fed at 6 months of age, versus 9% in 1969.

As seen in Figure 1, there has been a clear rise in the length of the breast-feeding period, from 9 weeks in 1950 to 13 weeks in 1976. According to newer studies (Rosenkrantz, Juul, & Gronenberg, 1982; Vogelius, 1982) with populations from Denmark's two largest cities, Aarhus and Copenhagen, the rate of breast-feeding is even higher now.

The sample from Aarhus consisted of approximately 2,000 women who gave birth from September 1977 to February 1979 and whose breast-feeding patterns were followed from 0 to 6 months. The sample from Copenhagen was of 753

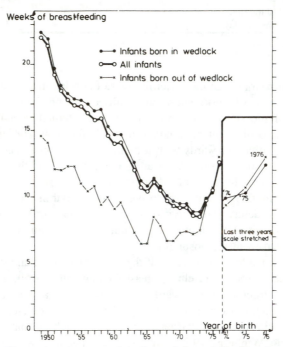

Figure 1. Average duration of breast feeding in Copenhagen 1949–76 according to infant health visitors' records. Data for 1949–72 based on exhaustive statistics; data for 1973–76 based on a sample. Each point represents between 243 and 7992 infants; the associated standard error is always less than 0.4 week.

From "Recent increase in breast feeding (Letter to the editor)," by F. Biering-Sørensen, J. Hilden, & K. Biering-Sørensen, 1978, *Acta Paediatrica Scandinavica*, *67*, 665–666. Copyright © 1978. Reprinted by permission.

women who delivered at Herlev Hospital from April 1978 to January 1979 and were followed in 9 months. The average length of breast-feeding period was 14 weeks in the Aarhus sample; and 24% were breast-feeding 6 months after delivery; and, in Copenhagen study, where the mothers were followed until 9 months, 20% were still breast-feeding at that time.

Among other results from both studies, a positive correlation was found between the length of the breast-feeding period and the amount of time elapsed between the delivery and the first breast-feeding. In average the breast-feeding period was 4 weeks longer for women who had had the infant at the breast immediately after the delivery than for women who had to wait 7 hours or more. In both samples, a positive correlation was found between length of the breast-feeding period and regular bottle feeding in the period of initiating breast feeding.

After discharge from the maternity ward, health of the infants is followed by a public health nurse who visits them in their home. Every community in Denmark is under legal obligation to provide health counseling in the form of home visits by a public health nurse free of charge. This counseling is more intensive for children with special needs, a group which would be called "high risk" in English-speaking countries, and which consists of premature infants and infants with birth complications, and infants who are retarded in their physical or psychological development, have nervous symptoms, or have social adjustment difficulties for their living conditions.

Almost all children in Denmark under 1 year of age receive the visit of a public health nurse. The number of visits in each home is around 10 per year. In addition to the public health nurse's visits, four preventive medical examinations are scheduled at the family's general practitioner (in Denmark such examinations are not normally conducted by pediatricians) at the child's 5th week and 5th, 10th, and 15th month of age, at which time all the necessary vaccinations are also performed. The attendance at these examinations is almost 100%. Both public nurses' activities and preventive check-ups play an important role in relation to early detection of somatic, physical, or social problems.

Compared to the welfare system described in relation to health services, with regard to maternity leaves the legal system has been very unsatisfactory in Denmark until recently. According to the former rules, the mother had the right to a leave of absence with economic compensation for 14 weeks after delivery. The mother had also the right to a leave of absence 4 weeks before the expected date of delivery. From July 1984 the leave of absence was extended to 20 weeks, and from July 1985 to 24 weeks. The last 10 weeks can be shared between father and mother. At the same time, fathers will be given the right to 2 free weeks around the birth of the child. The new rules, which come closer to the Swedish system, constitute improvement in the Danish legal system concerning parental leave of absence.

The majority of mothers with children of ages 0 to 6 years of age work outside the home. Almost 90% of mothers with one child are employed. This is also true for 80% of mothers with two small children. Among mothers with three or more children the rate of employment is around 70%. The employment situation varies with the age of the youngest child. There seems to be a new pattern in the employment as mothers no longer always stop working when they have young children. Mothers of a child between the ages of 0 and 6 years had a higher rate of employment (86.6%) than mothers of children of school age (78.3%) in 1978. Part-time employment is quite frequent (about 50%) among mothers of young children.

Mothers seem to work for longer hours than they wish to. Only a few regard two full-time working parents as being ideal. In 1975 42% of mothers who worked for more than 25 hours per week said that they would prefer their husband to have part-time rather than full-time work. However, this is seldom the case. In 1976 almost 90% of all fathers with small children worked for at least 40 hours a week. Beyond the working hours, transportation (including leaving and fetching children from day-care institutions) took about 1 hour per day in 1976. Statistics on unemployment specific to parents of young children are not available.

A topic under lively discussion in recent years has been the participation of fathers in daily work at home. Generally, men in Denmark have taken more and more of their share of housework. We saw that, in 1975, in families with small children where mothers were employed for more than 25 hours per week, 25% of the fathers did not participate in any kind of housework, 60% worked between .5 and 2 hours per day, and 13% worked in the house for more than 2 hours per day.

According to another study, also from 1975, Danish men worked at household chores for an average .75 hour per day, against 10 minutes in 1964. The corresponding figures for married women showed a decrease in household work from 5 hours per day in 1964 to just 4 hours in 1975.

In a qualitative study (Christensen, 1980), based on young couples who were interviewed before and after the birth of their first child, it was found that women report that their husbands share a greater part of the household work than the men themselves report. At the same time it was found that women felt that it was their duty to get the men more involved in household work and experienced it as a defeat when they did not succeed. Christensen calls this "the woman's new burden."

Concluding Remarks

The growing interest in young children's living conditions, and in research in this area, is reflected in two major initiatives.

The first was a commission appointed in November 1975 by the Danish government. The purpose (Bornekommissionen/The Child Welfare Commission) was to analyze the conditions of life for infants (0–7 years) and to discuss whether these conditions were adequate for the infants' psychological, physical, and social growth, and at the same time make suggestions and proposals for improvements.

From the beginning, the commission wanted to have an open debate with the population and therefore arranged many meetings and discussions throughout the country. In August 1977, the commission sent out a draft for debate ("Infant in Denmark") in which some central problems were outlined, and in which everybody was invited to make proposals and offer ideas and the like to supplement the work. The feedback and the replies that the commission received from study circles and individual persons were published in 1979: "We consider . . . . about infants in Denmark."

The Child Welfare Commission finished its work in 1981 with four reports from different working areas and a general report from the entire commission. In the area of the neonatal period, the work of the commission has undoubtedly contributed to the improvement in maternity leave legislation, mentioned earlier in this chapter.

The second initiative came from the three research councils (humanistic, medical, and social) which are responsible for coordination of and economic support for research. In 1976, they established a working group to analyze the research situation relating to small children, and 4 years later, in 1980, the three research councils agreed upon a joint endeavor to initiate more research on infancy in Denmark. With a commissorium for 5 years, a committee (Udvalget vedrorende smabornsforskning) was appointed with the purpose of awarding grants and arranging workshops, seminars, and postgraduate courses.

The possibilities for research in Denmark in this area look promising for the near future, and we may hope that our knowledge of small children and their families will be increased and refined. Furthermore, it will be interesting to follow the developments which will occur as part of the multiple dialogue between involved professionals, parents, and politicians.

References

Biering-Sørensen, F., Hilden, J., & Biering-Sørensen, K. (1978). Recent increase in breast feeding (Letter to the editor). *Acta Paediatrica Scandinavica, 67,* 665–666.

Biering-Sørensen, F., Hilden, J., & Biering-Sørensen, K. (1980). Breast feeding in Copenhagen, 1938–1977. Data on more than 365,000 infants. *Danish Medical Bulletin, 27,* 42–48.

Boernekommissionen (1979). *Vi mener . . . om smaaboern i Danmark* [We believe . . . about preschool children in Denmark]. Copenhagen: Boernekommissionen.

Brazelton, T.B. (1973). *The neonatal behavioral assessment scale* (Clinics in Developmental Medicine, No. 50). London: William Heineman.

Brudal, L.F. (1979, January). En undersoegelse af psykiske forstyrrelser post partum med saerlig henblik på profylakse [A study of psychic disturbances with special consideration given to prophylaxis]. *Tidsskrift for Norsk Psykologforening.*

Christensen, E. (1980). *Foerste barn [First child]*. Copenhagen: Dansk Psykologisk Forlag.

de Charteau, P., Holmberg, H., & Winberg, J. (1975). Amningsfrekvens, viktutveckling, vaegnings- och tillmatningsrutiner på BB [Breast feeding frequency, weight development, weighing and feeding routines in maternity ward]. *Svenska Laekertidningen, 72,* 4388–4390.

de Chateau, P., & Wiberg, B. (1977a). Long-term effect on mother-infant behavior of extra contact during the first hour post partum, I. First observation at 36 hours. *Acta Paediatrica Scandinavica, 66,* 137–144.

de Chateau, P., & Wiberg, B. (1977b). Long-term effect on mother-infant behavior of extra contact during the first hour post partum, II. A follow-up at three months. *Acta Paediatrica Scandinavica, 66,* 145–151.

Delholm, J., Mahneke, T., Mortensen, H., & Rasmussen, P.B. (1978). Amning [Breast feeding]. *Maanedsskrift for Praktisk Laegegerning, 56,* 65–82.

Egli, G.E., Egle, N.S., & Newton, M. (1961). The influence of the number of breast feeding on milk production. *Pediatrics, 27,* 314–317.

Goetzsche, V., Lier, L., & Munck, H. (1979). *Graviditet, foedsel og det foerste leveaar* [Pregnancy, birth and the first year of life]. Stockholm: NU BIO.

Greenberg, M., Rosenberg, I., & Lind, J. (1973). First mothers rooming-in with their newborns: Its impact upon the mother. *American Journal of Orthopsychiatry, 43,* 783–788.

Guldager, E., & Thorup, H. (1977). *Barseldage. En undersoegelse af sygeplejen paa to barselsafdelinger* [Postpartum days. A study of the nursing care in two maternity wards]. Copenhagen: Dansk Sygeplejeraad.

Hwang, C.P. (1978). Mother-infant interaction: Effects of sex of infant on feeding behavior. *Early Human Development, 2*(4), 341–349.

Illingworth, R.S., Stone, D.G.H., Iowett, G.H., & Scott, J.F. (1952). Self-demand feeding in a maternity unit. *Lancet, 1,* 638–687.

Kamper-Joergensen, F., Holstein, B., Osler, M., & Poulsen, E.F. (1979a). Foedselsmiljoeundersoegelsen, I. Materiale, metode, graviditet, foedselsforberedelse [Childbirth environment study, I. Material, method, pregnancy, birth preparation]. *Ugeskrift for Laeger, 141,* 1179–1183.

Kamper-Joergensen, F., Holstein, B., Osler, M., & Poulsen, E.F. (1979b). Foedselsmiljoeundersoegelsen, III. Barselperioden, boern paa neonatalafdeling [Childbirth environment study, III. Childbirth period, infants in neonatal ward]. *Ugeskrift for Laeger, 141,* 1786–1790.

Kay, K. (1975, September). *Towards the origin of dialogue*. Paper prepared for the Lock Lomond Symposium, University of Strathelyde.

Lagercrantz, E. (1979). *Foerstfoederskan och hennes barn* [The primiparous woman and her infant]. Stockholm, Wahhlstroem & Widstrand.

Lewis, M., & Feedle, R. (1973). Mother-infant dyad: The cradle of meaning. In P. Pliner, L. Kramers, & T. Alloway (Eds.), *Communication and effect*. New York: Academic Press.

Lind, J. (1975). Familjens foedelse [The birth of the family]. *Svenska Laekartidningen, 72,* 1545–1548.

Lind, J., & Jaederling, J. (1964). The influence of "rooming in" on breast feeding. *Acta Paediatrica Scandinavica, 53,* 159–164.

Marner, L. (1980). *Det nyfoedte barn* [The newborn child]. Unpublished manuscript, Copenhagen.

Mirdal, G.M. (1976). *Det ufoedte barn—det nyfoedte barn* [The unborn child—the newborn child]. Copenhagen: Munksgaard.

Mirdal, E.M., & Munck, H. (1985). Foraeldre-barn binding [Parent-infant bonding]. In L. Kochler & J. Merrick (Eds.), *Barns haelsa och vaelfaerd. Nordisk laerobok i socialpediatrik* [The health and welfare of the child. Nordic textbook on social pediatrics]. Lund: Studentlitteratur.

Moss, H.A. (1967). Sex, age and state as determinants of mother-infant interaction. *Merrill-Palmer Quarterly, 13*, 19.

Moss, H.A., & Robson, K.A. (1968). Maternal influences in early social visual behavior. *Child Development, 39*, 401–408.

Munck, H. (1977). *Mor-barn interaction under amning* [Mother–infant interaction during breast feeding]. Unpublished manuscript, Copenhagen.

Munck, H. (1978). *Graviditet og tidligt moderskab: Krise—traume—udvikling?* [Pregnancy and early motherhood: Crisis—trauma—development?] Unpublished manuscript, Copenhagen.

Munck, H. (1983). Spaedbarnsforskning. In H. Munck, V. Goetzsche, & L. Marner (Eds.), *Nyfoedte og deres naere miljoe—teori, forskning og praksis* [Newborn infants and their near environment—theory, research and practice]. Copenhagen: Smaaboernsforskning i Danmark VIII [Infancy research in Denmark V III].

Olmsted, R.W., & Jackson, E.B. (1950). Self-demand feeding in the first week of life. *Pediatrics, 6*, 396–401.

Richards, M.P.M., & Bernal, J. (1972). An observational study of mother–infant interaction. In N.B. Jones (Ed.), *Ethological studies of child behavior*. Cambridge: Cambridge University Press.

Rosenkrantz, V., Juul, F.A., & Gronenberg, C. (1982). *Amning. En undersoegelse af ammeforloebet blandt 2000 moedre til nyfoedte boern i Aarhus amt* [Breast feeding. A study of the course of breast feeding among 2000 mothers of newborn infants in Aarhus]. Copenhagen: FADL.

Sullivan, D.A., & Beeman, R. (1981). Satisfaction with postpartum care: Opportunities for bonding. Reconstructing the birth and instructions. *Birth and the Family Journal, 8*(3).

Sundhedsstyrelsen. (1982). *Medicinsk foedselsstatistik 1979. Vitalstatistik, 1(1)* [Medical birth statistics. Vital statistics].

Thoman, E.B., Turner, A.M., Leiderman, P.H., & Olson, J.P. (1972). Neonate-mother interaction during breast feeding. *Developmental Psychology, 6*, 110–118.

Uddenberg, N. (1974). Reproductive adaptation in mother and daughter. *Acta Psychiatrica Scandinavica*, Suppl. 254.

Uddenberg, N., & Engelsson. (1978). Prognosis of post partum mental disturbance. A prospective study of primiparous women and their 4½-year-old children. *Acta Psychiatrica Scandinavica, 58*, 201–212.

Vogelius, J. (1982). *Resume fra undersoegelsen "Faktorer der paavirker ammeforloebet og ernaeringens indflydelse paa barnets sundhedstilstand* [Summary of the study "Factors influencing the course of breast feeding and the influence of nutrition on the health of the infant]. Copenhagen: Forebyggelsesraadet.

CHAPTER 7

Neonatal Behavior and Maternal Perceptions of Urban Mexican Infants*

Lucille C. Atkin
María del Carmen Olvera
Martha Givaudan
Gerarda Landeros

*Instituto Nacional de Perinatología,
Montes Urales 800
11000 México D. F., México*

The National Institute of Perinatology (*Instituto Nacional de Perinatología*—INPer), located in Mexico City, is a tertiary level, public research, teaching, and service institute dedicated to the study and prevention of perinatal risk. Its symbol, a drawing of the Mixtec Princess 3-Stone Knife at delivery, was chosen to represent the modern integrated concept of perinatal care on which the INPer is based (Jurado-García, 1980).

At the same time, it reminds us of the cultural context in which it is embedded. This combination of the ancient and the new is typical in many ways of Mexico City and its population, a mosaic of different cultural origins.

The largest part of Mexico City's population (as well as of the country as a whole) is considered *mestizo,* that is, descendents of the union between native and Spanish people. In many ways, the cultural characteristics of today's population are flavored by this particular mixture. The unique cultural amalgamation which resulted from the Spanish conquest can be seen in many traditions and

* We would like to express our appreciation to the following people for their help during different phases of this project: Esther Casanueva, Pedro Arroyo, Alfonso Hernández, and Josefina Islas. We are also grateful to the mothers and infants who participated in the study, as well as the personnel of the rooming-in service of the *Instituto Nacional de Perinatologia* for their cooperation and support.

Figure 1.   The Institute's emblem is a drawing of the Mixtec Princess 3-Stone Knife at delivery, taken from the Codex Nuttall (Jurado-García, 1980).

customs where the pervasive influence of superstitions and magical thinking is still evident.

However, the city's population is extremely heterogenous. Different sectors seem to live in completely different worlds. While wealthy families may live in luxury, the very poor still live in deplorable conditions. The degree of acceptance of diverse elements of the Mexican cultural heritage also varies considerably, generally, though not exclusively, along socioeconomic lines.

Mexican family life is also distinct in the different socioeconomic strata. However, in very general terms we can say that a woman's role is determined largely by her functions as a mother above all else. Mexican women are very dedicated to their children, often to the extent of self-abnegation. For most, their daily chores are very time-consuming, due to the inaccessibility of labor-saving devices. In many ways Mexican wives tend to be relatively subordinated to the authority of the husband, although the tasks of raising and educating the children are usually left to them. However, these patterns are not universal and, in fact, have been changing in recent years, favoring greater father participation and egalitarian relationships.

Social ties among members of the extended family are very important, providing a host of social, economic, and affective exchange functions. Even in the case of nuclear families who live separately, it is common to find that extended family members live nearby and visit each other frequently.

Serving such a heterogeneous population, the INPer provides highly sophisticated, modern perinatal care to women from diverse socioeconomic strata, but also dedicates a large part of its efforts to community education and to the study of diverse biological, psychological, and social aspects of the reproductive process and perinatal risk. Among its interests are ways of facilitating developmentally supportive mother–infant interaction through the hospital context itself where rooming-in (see Figure 2) is provided for all healthy neonates and breast-feeding is widely encouraged, as well as through educational interventions of diverse types. Research concerning mother–infant interaction and child development has been planned within the context of a conceptual model emphasizing the reciprocal influences among the infant's own characteristics, the quality of the postnatal environment, and the child's interaction with his or her family.

From the beginning of our work with neonates and older infants, we became aware of many folk beliefs and practices concerning health care and child rearing in the population served by the INPer. While not all of the women espouse these beliefs, many have heard about them and have received advice from friends and family based on them.

We found that, in some cases, the information we provided about early child development did not fit easily into the expectations and experiences of the woman with whom we were working. It became apparent to us that a better under-

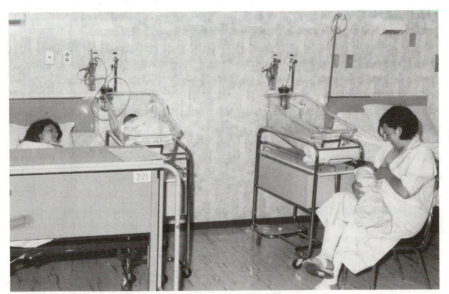

Figure 2. **Rooming-In at the *Instituto Nacional de Perinatología* provides 24-hour a day contact between mother and newborn.**

standing of the cultural milieu of child rearing in our population would help us to be more effective both as interveners and as researchers.

We therefore began several semiformal attempts to identify the most common beliefs relevant to infant care, since no references were available in this regard. We collected information obtained by the members of an interdisciplinary study group composed of nurses, pediatricians, and developmental psychologists, based on interaction with women attended to by INPer. We also conducted two pilot studies, in which trained undergraduate psychology students interviewed women in the prenatal out-patient clinic concerning a wide range of beliefs and practices.

The pilot studies showed us that it is very difficult to obtain information concerning folk beliefs and practices, through standard interview techniques, within the context of a hospital setting, where many of these traditional ideas are openly criticized. We did have considerable success when we interviewed women with whom we had previously established a positive relationship, especially when we interviewed them in their own homes. Furthermore, we found it to be very important to express our sincere interest in and respect for the information we were receiving, and to avoid attitudes of criticism and ridicule so common among health professionals.

In light of this experience, we are able to describe some of the beliefs and practices related to neonates and older infants which exist in the population attended in the INPer. However, we are not able to provide quantitative data concerning their prevalence or distribution within the different socioeconomic subgroups. While it is most probable that the mother's educational level largely determines the degree to which she espouses folk beliefs, we have a sense that there are other influences, such as family structure, that cross educational lines. In our experience, it is not so rare to find educated women who give credence to the traditional precepts, as well as poor, unschooled women who reject them in favor of more modern attitudes.

In general, the richest variety of folk beliefs are related to health issues concerning the causes of and cures for pathological conditions. In some cases, the beliefs reported are almost identical to those reported by the Spanish historians who recorded indigenous folk beliefs at the time of the Conquest. For example, Sahagún (1956) reports the following admonition:

A pregnant women should not look at the sun or moon when eclipsed or the creature she carries will be born without lips or nose or with its mouth open or crossed-eyed or so that they are not born as monsters . . . If she were to look at the eclipse, to prevent the effects she would put a black stone knife on her chest touching her flesh. (p. 34)

Even today, pregnant women are warned not to be outside during, or to look at, an eclipse, since if they were to do so, their child would be born with a cleft palate. Although they no longer carry obsidian knives, they are told to put a metal safety pin or scissors under their clothes to prevent the negative effects of the eclipse's powerful rays.

Among the great variety of traditional health-related beliefs we have identified, two are of special importance for the care of young infants: air (*aire*) and the evil eye (*mal de ojo* or just *ojo*). Many illnesses, especially conjunctivitis, are caused by *aire*, either brought in by the people who enter the house or contracted when the child is out of doors. The evil eye is caused by people with "strong vision" who admire the baby and, therefore, often unwillingly, cause him or her harm, producing inconsolable crying or, in extreme cases, leading to the infant's death. Fortunately, members of the immediate family are not able to give a baby the evil eye.

In line with this belief, some mothers try to limit the number of visitors who come to see the newborn and/or avoid taking the baby outside for the first month or two. While this may have beneficial effects by reducing contact with possible sources of infection, which are highly prevalent in the environment, other preventive measures and remedies prescribed are probably not as useful.

In order to avoid the *aire*, many babies are kept bundled up with a ubiquitous cap and several layers of clothing and/or blankets, even when the mid-day sun has warmed up an initially chilly day. A variety of amulets are placed on the children to avoid their being given the evil eye, and certain articles, including chilies, garlic, and assorted herbs, may be put under the baby's pillow or in the mother's pocket for the same purpose.

Once the child has become ill, however, several remedies are available. The most important one is a "cleansing" done with a whole raw egg, often accompanied by certain chilies held in a cross formation passed over the baby's body. This egg is then broken into a glass half filled with water to reveal the evidence of the *aire* or *ojo* which it has removed from the body.

Considering these folk beliefs, it is possible that our presence in the home to observe the baby with the BNBAS, at such an early age as 10 or 20 days, might be a source of alarm for some mothers. To our knowledge this was generally not the case, although one mother in the study we will describe further on expressed her concern and admitted that she had taken a variety of these precautions before, during, and after our visits.

In addition to such health care issues, we also explored folk beliefs and practices more directly related to infant behavior and to the kind of early experiences provided for babies. Here we will mention only those which specifically are relevant to the neonatal behaviors evaluated with the BNBAS, using five general divisions: orientation and alertness, irritability and state control, motor responses, autonomic regulation, and general impression.

Orientation and Alertness

When we initially proposed and described the use of the BNBAS, several colleagues suggested that the baby's visual alertness, and the possibility of eye-to-eye contact, would not be as important in our population as in the United States. Many women believe that the more a baby sleeps, the healthier he or she will be, and they do not express eagerness to interact with the infant.

However, we found considerable heterogeneity in this regard: some mothers wanting their babies to spend time in a calm, alert state, and others preferring the infant to awaken only to eat and be bathed. The important factor for some seems to be that the infant should make few demands for interaction, either by sleeping or by remaining quietly awake on a bed.

As far as visual capabilities are concerned, it is commonly considered that infants can only see shadows and cannot distinguish objects or people until 2 or 3 months of age. An important belief among some women is that if an infant looks at bright objects, especially lights, or if an object is suddenly moved in his or her visual field, the child will become cross-eyed and thereby possibly ruin his or her vision.

Irritability and State Control

Crying is considered the infant's primary form of communication. However, it is very common to hear that it is important not to pick up infants when they cry, or carry them in general, since they will become accustomed to arms and then soon they will demand too much attention. There is also the belief, though less frequently expressed, that by allowing the infant to cry, it will strengthen his or her lungs, as well as discourage "excessive" demands. Such beliefs usually appear to be related to the mother's need for time to do her housework and care for other children.

Furthermore, some women will attribute an infant's fussiness or frequent crying to the effect of *aire, ojo,* or other conditions or illnesses. In such cases, the child may be "cleansed," as previously described, or cured with a variety of remedies, mostly herbal, some of which are apparently quite effective. This does not mean, however, that most mothers will not take their baby to the doctor. In fact mothers who utilize the traditional cures may simultaneously seek and apply more scientific treatments.

Motor Responses

In this area, there are a variety of relevant beliefs which are relatively widespread, although by no means universal. Several prohibitions exist in relation to the infant's position, many stemming apparently from the belief that an infant's bones are still soft or weak, that is, not completely solidified at birth. Infants are not supposed to be held upright until they are 3 months old, since their cheeks will sag; nor are they to be stood up, since they will become bow-legged. Abrupt movements are to be avoided, as well as the sitting position (especially if pulled

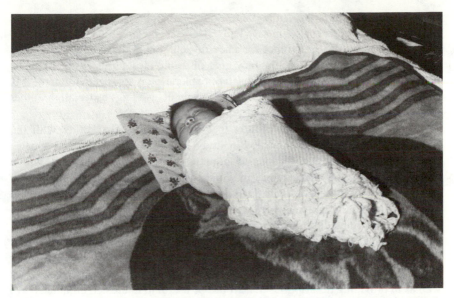

Figure 3.   Twenty-day-old infant, who lives in a *vecindad*, in the typical swaddled, supine position.

up, as is done in the BNBAS Pull-to-sit item), since this will cause the anterior fontanelle (*mollera*) to "fall." Infants are not to be placed in the prone position for long, since their chest bones might become deformed or they could possibly suffocate.

Swaddling is a relatively common practice. Some women believe it is necessary, since otherwise the infants frighten and/or scratch themselves due to uncontrolled arm movements. A related belief, mentioned by a few women, prohibits cutting the infant's fingernails to avoid such scratches, since it would supposedly interfere with a child's language or cognitive development. Swaddling is also considered useful so that the child does not grow up *tentón* (see Figure 3), that is, wanting to touch everything in sight.

Autonomic Regulation

Infants' startle reactions are commonly attributed to the baby having become frightened. Since such movements further frighten the infant, some mothers wrap up their babies like *tacos* (as mentioned before) with their arms at their sides in order to avoid this problem.

Tremors are consistently attributed to the infant being cold, even when the room temperature is quite warm. This is another reason given for keeping the baby well bundled up.

General Impression

Many mothers express preference for a healthy, quiet, non-demanding baby. This fits well with the description that they give of their "ideal child" as being well-behaved and docile. Although some active exploration is tolerated at home, it is important that the child should not be excessively demanding, especially in other settings or when visitors are present.

It was within this general context that we began our first study with the BNBAS. As a first step, we decided to study a small group of healthy neonates fairly intensively. Our primary long-term interest was to provide ourselves with a point of reference for later studies in which we planned to establish prognostic stratifications for infants of diverse risk characteristics, based on their behavioral evolution during the neonatal period.

On a more immediate level we wanted to describe the behavior of healthy Mexican babies from an urban population born in the modern hospital facilities that the INPer provides. We were interested in observing their behavior over repeated evaluations throughout the first month and a half of extrauterine life, as well as in providing descriptions that would be useful to interested clinicians. We also wanted to study the infants in their homes, once they had left the hospital, in order to learn more about the social and physical contexts in which they develop.

Likewise, we were convinced that an evaluation of maternal perceptions could be an important way of increasing the sensitivity of the neonatal behavioral evaluations, as well as providing information about the cultural relevance of the BNBAS in our particular setting. Although two relevant scales existed in the published literature at the time (Broussard & Hartner, 1971; Field, Dempsey, Hallock, & Shuman, 1978), we considered it necessary to adapt an instrument to our own circumstances and interests. We therefore developed an interview which we call the Inventory of Maternal Perceptions (*Inventario de Percepciones Maternas*—IPM) (Atkin & Ramos, 1980) which we will describe in greater detail in the following sections.

As an initial study using the IPM, we were interested in studying the perceptions of women relatively free of apparent psychological problems in relation to their normal infants' behavior. This would provide us with a point of comparison for later studies of mothers who themselves presented psychological risk and/or whose infants were atypical. Furthermore, the possibility of comparing the maternal perceptions with infant behavior, independently evaluated, offered an excellent external criterion of comparison for the IPM interview.

Study Population

Twenty-nine mother–infant dyads participated in our initial study of neonatal behavior and maternal perceptions. They were carefully selected so that the

Table 1.   Selection Criteria For Initial BNBAS-IPM Study

Maternal Characteristics	Infant Characteristics
Resident of Mexico City or vicinity	Singleton
Two or more prenatal visits in INPer	Full weight for gestational age
Free of pathology during pregnancy	APGAR $\geq$ 7 at 1' and $\geq$ 8 at 5'
No teratogenic drugs ingested	Silverman-Anderson value $\leq$ 2
Term pregnancy (37 weeks to 41 weeks 6	Arterial Cord Blood $p^H \geq 7.20$
days)	Stable condition in delivery room
Uncomplicated vaginal delivery with vertex	Admission to Rooming-In Service with in-
presentation	structions for normal healthy newborn care
Favorable psychological profile[a]	Free of major congenital malformations
—positive attitude towards pregnancy	No apparent neurological abnormalities
—positive family support	Continue free of any pathological state which
—no psychiatric history nor apparent psy-	could alter his or her behavior during the
chological problems	period of study
Sign Informed Consent Statement	

[a] According to data recorded in the Institute's Prenatal Psychological Study.

babies would be biologically healthy and free of risk characteristics. While the mothers were also healthy, they were from a variety of social backgrounds, as is typical of the INPer's population. However, they were screened so as to include only those who were positively motivated in relation to their pregnancy and baby, as well as being free of apparent psychological pathology. Table 1 lists the specific criteria we used to select the couples.

During a period of one year (April 1981 to April 1982), 54 dyads fulfilled these criteria and initially entered the study. However, 12 infants developed hyperbilirubinemia and needed phototherapy during their postnatal hospitalization, and four presented this condition once at home. These infants were consid-

Table 2.   Biological and Demographic Characteristics of the Mothers of the 29 Healthy Infants

Characteristics	Range	Median	Number of Women
Age	16 to 33	24	—
Gestations	1 to 5	2	—
Parity	1 to 4	2	—
Previous Miscarriages	1 to 3	—	5
Infant Deaths	1 to 2	—	3
Schooling (years completed)	3 to 19	10	—
Married	—	—	27
Living with Extended family	—	—	8
Without Epidural Block[a]	—	—	25

[a] Four women were administered an epidural block with Lidocaine and Epinephrine at 2%.

Table 3.   Biological Characteristics of the 29 Healthy Infants[a]

Characteristics	Range	Median	Mean
Gestational Age[b] (in weeks)	37.0–41.6	39.5	39.2
Birth Weight (in grams)	2625–3640	3140	3110
Capurro[c] (in days)	262–295	280	279
APGAR			
1 minute	7–9	8	—
5 minutes	8–10	9	—
Silverman-Anderson	0–2	1	—
pH			
Artery	7.20–7.48	7.30	—
Vein	7.25–7.53	7.35	—

[a]The group includes 15 females and 14 males.
[b]Gestational age according to date of last menstruation in weeks. The decimal indicates days.
[c]A clinical estimation of gestational age (S.D ± 15 days) derived from the Dubowitz Assessment based on physical and neurological parameters (Capurro, Konicheszky, Fonseca, & Calderyo-Barcia, 1978).

ered separately and are not included in the group of "optimal" newborns (Olvera, Givaudan, & Atkin, 1987). Five other infants were excluded from the study group due to the presence of nonoptimal conditions discovered after the initial evaluations (serious feeding problems in three cases, cranial asymmetry in one, and minor congenital malformations which produced important alterations in the mother–infant relationship in another). An additional four infants were lost to the study when their parents moved out of the Mexico City area. Tables 2 and 3 show some of the basic biological and demographic characteristics of the 29 dyads who remained in the study group.

Environmental and Evaluation Settings

Throughout the period of study we observed the infants and interviewed the mothers six times: twice while hospitalized in the Rooming-In Service, at 24 and 72 hours after birth (± 12 hours), and four times at home, when the infants were 10, 20, 30, and 45 days old (± 3 days). We included the 45-day evaluation in order to observe the evolution of those behaviors which had not reached optimal levels by 30 days. Except for the last evaluation, the BNBAS evaluations were performed without the mother being present. Meanwhile, she was being interviewed by another psychologist about her perceptions of her infant's behavior. At 45 days, after completing the IPM interview, the mother was invited to observe the evaluation and at that time we answered any questions she had concerning her child's development and the study itself.

The rooming-in environment provides considerable opportunity for the mother to begin to know her infant. Once the newborn's temperature is stable, he or

Table 4.   Housing Characteristics of the Families Studied

	Total	X̄ Inhabitants[a] per dormitory	No. Overcrowded[b]
Separate house	11	2.6 (1–4)	7
Apartment building	10	2.7 (1.6–4)	6
Vecindad or single-room dwelling.	8	3.9 (1.5–6)	7

[a]The numbers in parenthesis indicate the range.
[b]More than two persons per dormitory.

she is placed in a transparent, portable crib at the mother's bedside. Thereafter, the baby is with her 24 hours a day, and usually by the second day, the mother is actively participating in his or her care. While the nurses provide supervision and information about basic neonatal care and breast-feeding, they do not intervene in any systematic way to educate the mothers concerning their infant's behavior.

While the mother was interviewed at her bedside, the infant was taken to a special room on the same floor. The conditions were fairly optimal for the behavioral evaluation since the room was dimly lit, warm (between 24° and 26°C), and relatively isolated from external environmental noises.

The home settings were of course far more varied and offered a wide range of contexts for the infants' early development. As can be seen in Table 4, they included separate houses, apartment buildings, *vecindades* (dwellings which consist of various one or two-room housing units around a shared patio and characterized by common bath and washing facilities), and single-room dwellings. Most of these, however, were overcrowded in terms of the number of inhabitants per dormitory. In order to perform the evaluation, one of the psychologists took the baby to the most quiet and appropriate area of the dwelling, while the other psychologist interviewed the mother separately at times in the patio.

Inventory of Maternal Perceptions

In light of the wide range of educational levels among the women attended in the INPer, some of whom are completely or functionally illiterate, we decided to develop an interview rather than a questionnaire to evaluate the mother's perceptions of her infant. We were specifically interested in her perceptions of the kind of behavior evaluated in the BNBAS. However, we wanted to tap into her observations based on her spontaneous interaction with her infant, rather than establish specific situations as in the instrument developed by Field, Dempsey, Hallock, and Shuman (1978), the Mother's Assessment of the Behavior of her Infant (MABI). Our intention was to intervene as little as possible, in order to identify the mother's naturally occurring perceptions of her infant's behavior.

The interview consists of three major sections, as well as a summary of the mother's attitude observed during the session. The interview was pilot tested previously in order to assure acceptable phrasing and to determine the precoded response option categories. The first section includes the questions concerning the specific maternal perceptions with regards to behaviors similar to those evaluated with the BNBAS. Some of the questions were adapted from the MABI, while others were developed to identify naturally occurring situations which approximate those of the behavioral assessment. In some cases these are necessarily quite different (see Appendix).

The second section consists of comparisons between the woman's own baby and her subjective image of a "typical" baby at the same age. While similar to Broussard's method, we included different behavioral aspects and used a single comparative rating. The mother is asked whether her infant is better, the same, or worse than the average baby in terms of his or her characteristics in each of the following areas: sleep, alertness, orientation, strength, consolability, crying, feeding, sucking, "attractiveness," "smartness," and "easiness of care." In the third section we included several supplementary questions related to some of the mother's attitudes towards her baby's behavior as well as towards stimulation activities.

The interview took approximately 20 to 30 minutes to complete. Three psychologists were trained in its application and maintained an average interrater reliability level of .96 throughout the study. The same psychologist did not interview the mother on consecutive occasions so as to reduce any bias that might be introduced by her remembering the answers from the previous evaluation.

Neonatal Behavioral Assessments

Four psychologists, whose reliability in the BNBAS was certified by personnel from the Child Development Unit in Boston, performed the behavioral evaluations. Their interobserver reliability was checked periodically throughout the study and remained at an average level of .95. When possible, adjacent age evaluations were performed by different psychologists.

In addition to the original behavioral items, we also included the five scales proposed by the Kansas group (Horowitz, Sullivan, & Linn, 1978): Orientation Inanimate Visual and Auditory, Quality of Infant's Alert Responsivity, Examiner's Persistence, General Irritability, and Reinforcement Value of Infant's Behavior.

Results

The immediate objective of our study of healthy infants is to describe their behavior in terms that are useful to clinicians (such as pediatricians and nurses) who are interested in evaluating neonatal risk. We therefore have sought ways to present the data that would reflect their ordinal nature, yet still provide a clear description of the group's behavior at each age, as well as the changes over time.

We also want to describe to what extent the mothers of these infants, as a group, were aware of their infant's behavior, and in what ways their perceptions might be the same or different from what was observed by the psychologist using the BNBAS. In other words, what is the margin of discrepancy found between the behavior of healthy infants and their mothers' perception of these behaviors? This study was in fact one of the steps in the validation process which the IPM interview is undergoing. However, it is important to mention that, from the beginning, we did not expect a necessarily close agreement between the mothers' perceptions and the infants' behavior in all aspects. Rather, we anticipated that certain systematic differences would exist, and that these would be related logically to the kind of culturally determined beliefs and practices we have found to be common in our population.

In order to facilitate the presentation of the results, we will divide them into five sections: orientation and alertness, irritability and state control, motor responses, autonomic regulation, and general impression. In each we will first describe the infants' behavior alone and then discuss the relevant IPM items together with their related BNBAS scales.

We have grouped the BNBAS scores on each scale into several conceptually meaningful categories which correspond to the IPM responses. In the figures we have presented the proportion of infants who received scores in the most optimal category during the behavioral evaluations at each age. Likewise, for the related IPM items, we present the proportions of mothers who situated their infants in the equivalent categories. The statistical significance of the difference observed between these categories on the BNBAS and the IPM was tested using the Chi^2 for proportions.

While not presented graphically, the text makes reference to the proportion of infants and/or mothers in other categories, whenever this helps to give a more complete description of the results. Furthermore, in order to provide some contextual elements for these data, we will also mention the mothers' responses to the relevant supplementary IPM questions and to the "your baby–typical baby" comparisons. These will be described in terms of selected response categories which best illustrate the tendencies observed in the data.

Orientation and Alertness

In general terms, almost all the infants (.88 or more) responded in some way to each of the visual and/or auditory stimuli from the first day on; by 20 days, all of them did so. As can be seen in Figure 4, the proportion of infants in the best categories increases regularly throughout the first month of life in all the scales. In response to the visual stimuli (ball and face), one-third or less (.31 and .27) of

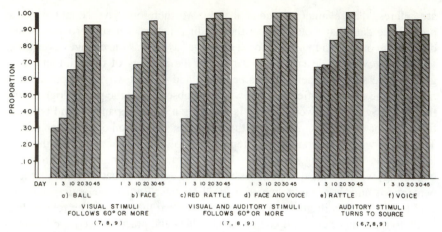

Figure 4.   Orientation responses: Proportion of healthy neonates showing optimal responses.

the infants responded optimally on the first day. The corresponding proportion at 30 days was .93 and .96, respectively. In the case of orientation to the examiner's face, this proportion diminished slightly at 45 days.

When the visual stimuli were combined with the auditory stimuli (red rattle and examiner's face and voice), the responses were even better, showing a similar tendency to increase throughout the period of study. From 20 days on, all the infants responded to the combination of the examiner's face and voice with visual following of 60° or more. However, it is important to mention that only some of the babies (.10, .39, and .68, at 20, 30, and 45 days, respectively) received a score of 9, smoothly following the stimulus horizontally, vertically, and in a circle.

The response to the auditory stimuli alone (the sound of the rattle and the examiner's voice) was very good from the first day on. Two-thirds or more of the group turned and looked for the stimulus (.67 to the rattle, and .77 to the voice) on the first day. While the response improved over time, this increase was less regular than with the other stimuli. By the 45th day, there was a slight decrease in the proportion of infants who received the best scores. In these evaluations several babies responded minimally, and others gave responses which were not included in the scale, such as smiling, increased activity, and rhythmic arm and leg movements.

In order for the babies to have responded to the orientation stimuli, it was, of course, necessary for them to have maintained an alert, quiet state, at least briefly. As can be seen in Figure 5a, from the very first evaluation, the predominant state of .59 or more of the infants was one of quiet alertness. However, in general, their periods of alertness were initially short (see Figure 5b), alternating with other states, including crying. At 10, 20, and 30 days, approximately one-

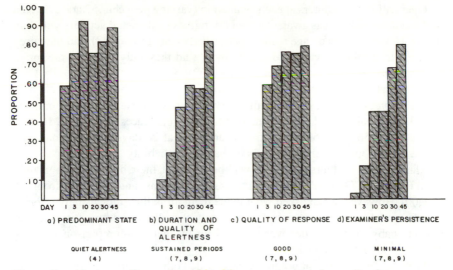

Figure 5.   Alertness: Proportion of healthy neonates showing optimal responses.

half of the infants presented sustained periods of alertness. However, it was not until 45 days that almost all of the group (.82) was able to do this.

After the first day, the quality of response during the periods of alertness improved dramatically (Figure 5c). The majority of the infants (between .59 and .79) showed modulated responsiveness and active participation in relation to the stimuli presented.

During the first week, the examiner had to be very persistent in order to elicit the orientation responses (Figure 5d). In many cases, especially on the first day, she had to use special techniques (such as vestibular stimulation, arm restraint, and/or swaddling) in order to observe the infants' capabilities. At 10 and 20 days, it was far less common to have to resort to these techniques. By 30 and 45 days, the infants responded easily, requiring only the presentation of the orientation stimuli in order to respond.

According to the IPM interview, most of the mothers reported that their infants were in a calm, awake state for a total of only 1 hour or less on the first day as well as on the third day after birth (.83 and .62, respectively). On the tenth day, the modal category was from 1 to 2 hours (.38 of the mothers); on the 20th day, from 2 to 4 (.55), and thereafter, more than 4 hours (.43 at 30 days, and .46 at 45 days). On the first three evaluations, half of the mothers were eager for their infants to spend more time calmly awake, although an almost equal proportion said they were satisfied with the situation as it was. On day 20, 30, and 45, fewer mothers (.28, .29, and .30, respectively) wanted their infants to spend more time than they did calmly awake; most were satisfied (.62, .64, and .63); and only two or three of them said they wished the baby would sleep more.

Over half of the mothers at each evaluation (varying between .57 and .79) said that when their baby was awake and not crying, they interacted actively with him or her. However, at each age some mothers (between .11 and .28) said they used the time to do their own chores, and others said they only watched the infant from a distance (varying between .04 and .32).

Almost all the mothers (.89 or more) said they believed their infant could hear at least voices and music from the very first day. However, fewer mothers thought their baby could see well enough to distinguish faces at 1, 3, and 10 days of age (.31, .55, and .69, respectively) and only at 20 days did the group as a whole (.89 or more) believe their baby had this capability.

Many of the mothers did, however, believe that their babies "recognized" them (between .72 and .79 on the first three evaluations, and thereafter from .96 to 1.00). However, when asked what made them think this, they usually referred to differential responses which did not imply visual recognition, for example, that the baby quieted better when picked up by them in comparison with the nurses or other family members.

When asked whether or not the babies needed other experiences in addition to obligatory care activities, the most frequent response (.48 to .55) was "love". Only at 30 days was it common (.61) to receive responses which could be categorized as stimulation, such as exercises and showing objects.

As far as verbal stimulation was concerned, all except one mother said it was important to talk to babies from the very beginning. At 1 and 10 days, the most frequent reason given was so the baby would get to know his or her mother (.62 and .59). By 30 days, however, it was more common (.64) for the mothers to mention facilitating the infant's development as a reason for talking to their baby.

Results of the three IPM questions that relate to specific BNBAS scales are shown in Figure 6. In relation to both the visual-auditory and the auditory-animate stimuli, the proportion of mothers who said their infant visually followed persons in movement (Figure 6a) and turned toward their voices (Figure 6b) increased over the period of study. However, especially in the first four evaluations, significantly fewer mothers perceived these specific abilities in comparison to the number of infants who actually presented similar behaviors on the BNBAS ($Chi^2(6) = 39.51$; 64.55, respectively, $p < .01$). Especially on day 1 and day 3, it was quite common for the mothers to report that they had not noticed if their infant could or could not do these activities.

The results for general alertness contrasted sharply with these differences on the specific behavioral items (see Figure 6c). The proportion of mothers who said that their infant attended visually for moderate to long periods of time at each age (except day 10) corresponded closely to the proportion of infants who were given the best scores on the BNBAS Alertness scale ($Chi^2(6) = 3.99$, N.S.).

Three of the comparisons which the mothers are asked to make between their infant and a "typical baby" were particularly relevant to the behavior we have included in this section: alertness, orientation, and "smartness." The proportion

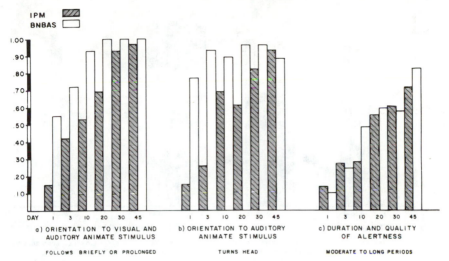

Figure 6.   Orientation and alertness: Proportion of best scores on IPM questions and BNBAS performance.

of mothers who considered their infant better than average increased steadily over the period of study (from .27 to .44 for Alertness, and .12 to .69 for Orientation). As in all the 11 comparisons included in the IPM interview, the category of "worse than average" was actually used, but infrequently (usually by 1 to 3 mothers). However, on day 3, six mothers (.21) said their baby was alert and quiet for less time than a typical baby, and four (.14) said the baby oriented less well than others. Nevertheless, the majority of the group considered their baby's duration of alertness and quality of orientation to be average. Only at 45 days did more than half of the mothers (.69) consider their infant to have exceptionally good orientation responses.

Although the definition of "smartness" was purposely left to vary at the mother's discretion, the infant's visual and auditory alertness was usually mentioned as a key component. When asked how smart their baby was, all except one mother (on day 3) said their infant was average or better than average. As with Alertness and Orientation, the proportion responding better than average increased over time, from .33 to .64.

Irritability and State Control

In general, this group of babies was not very irritable. No infant was bothered by all eight aversive stimuli, and only a few by six or seven (see Figure 7a). Even on the first day, one-third (.31) of the infants showed a low level of irritability, being bothered by three stimuli or less. In the later evaluations, approximately half of

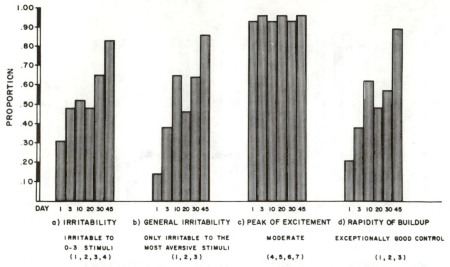

Figure 7.   Irritability: Proportion of healthy neonates showing optimal responses.

the babies showed low irritability. By 45 days it was rare to find a baby who responded negatively to more than three of the aversive stimuli.

In terms of general irritability (one of the Kansas additions to the original BNBAS), the same tendency can be observed (Figure 7b). The proportion of infants who showed low irritability on this item, crying only to the most aversive maneuvers of the evaluation, increased regularly during the period of study. Correspondingly, the proportion of infants who cried easily, that is, to even the most positive stimuli, decreased from .24 on day 1 to .07 on day 45.

Almost all of the babies studied received favorable scores in the moderate range, in terms of their peak of excitement (Figure 7c). In this category we have included infants who were predominantly in state 4 or 5, as well as those who cried but self-quieted or were easily consoled. This last group (i.e., a score of 7) was included since we considered it optimal under certain circumstances, especially in their first week. It was actually quite frequent, accounting for .69, .65, .31, .55, .39, and .14 of the total group at each age, respectively.

The proportion of infants who did not cry, or who did so only at the end of the assessment, in response to the most aversive stimuli (Figure 7d), increased over the period of study. The most common response during the first two evaluations (.61 and .52) was for the infants to start crying in the middle of the assessment, that is, scores of 4, 5, and 6. Even on the first day, few infants (.17) cried near the beginning of the session (scores of 7 or 8), and thereafter this was even less frequent (between .10 and .03).

The infant's irritability is highly related to his or her overall state lability. During the first week there were a few infants (six on the first day and four on the

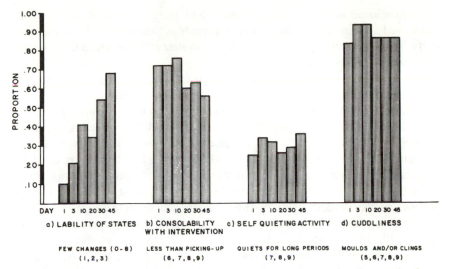

Figure 8.   State Control: Proportion of healthy neonates showing optimal responses.

third) who presented very frequent state changes. However, by the 10th day, .97 or more showed moderate or good state control. As can be seen in Figure 8a, the proportion of infants who made few state changes during the evaluation increased steadily with age.

These infants, when they did cry, were easy to quiet (Figure 8b). On the first three evaluations, three-quarters of the group quieted without being picked up, either with the examiner's face and voice or with the hand on the chest and/or by restraining the arm movements.

On the last three evaluations, this proportion had decreased slightly, although over half of the babies still responded easily. Although not shown in the figure, in almost all cases (.94 to 1.00) the greatest intervention needed was to pick up and /or to rock the baby. No infant was inconsolable. It is also important to note that the group does not present a tendency to improve its consolability with age. At each evaluation some infants could be calmed by the examiner's voice (varying between .38 and .48), some by touching them and/or restraining their arms (between .16 and .38), and some by being carried (between .19 and .40).

Almost all these infants, once crying, made attempts at self-quieting, and many (ranging from .72 to .86) succeeded, although briefly. As can be seen in Figure 8c, at each age approximately one-third of the group self-quieted for sustained periods. As in the case of consolability with intervention, there was no tendency toward more or less self-quieting over time.

As can be seen in Figure 8d, almost all of these healthy babies molded and relaxed when held. Although only a few infants actually clung to the examiner, it is important to mention that none, at any age, resisted being held.

As mentioned in the previous section, the mothers reported that their infants maintained an alert, quiet state for longer periods as time went on throughout the study. This information parallels the increase in state stability which these infants presented during the BNBAS evaluations.

Almost all of the mothers referred to their infant, in general terms, as calm rather than irritable, attributing his or her crying to specific needs. When we compare the number of reasons mentioned by the mothers (from a pre-established list of eight) with the number of aversive stimuli that provoked crying on the BNBAS, significant differences appear (see Figure 9a). On the first three evaluations, the proportion of mothers who reported that their baby cried for three or fewer reasons was higher than the corresponding proportions according to the BNBAS. In later evaluations, the proportion of infants who cried to three or fewer of the BNBAS aversive stimuli continued to increase. However, the proportion of mothers who mentioned three or less reasons decreased. At the ages of 20, 30, and 45 days, more mothers referred to a greater number of reasons, although this usually did not exceed 4 or 5 ($\text{Chi}^2(6) = 17.04$, $p < .01$).

In this regard, it is important to note that the stimuli listed in the IPM question are necessarily quite different than those listed in the BNBAS item. The three reasons most frequently mentioned by the mothers were hunger, heat or cold and wet or dirty diapers. These, of course, are not evaluated in the BNBAS. However, the similarity lies in the fact that both the IPM question and the BNBAS item attempt to evaluate irritability by identifying how many events, from a fixed list appropriate to each situation, made the infant irritable or actually cry.

Most of the mothers also reported that their infant was relatively easy to console (see Figure 9b). No one said her baby was inconsolable, and very few (three or less) said the baby would only quiet by being fed. At each evaluation, between .71 and .82 of the mothers said that their infant could be quieted by talking to and/or patting him or her; in other words, without having to be picked up. These proportions are similar to those that correspond to scores 6, 7, 8, and 9

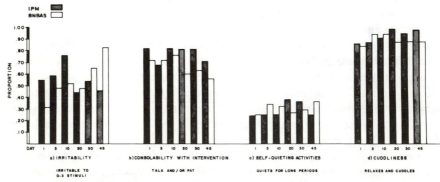

Figure 9.   Irritability and state control: Proportion of best scores on IPM questions and BNBAS performance.

on the Consolability with Intervention scale of the BNBAS, which include the examiner's face, voice, hand on chest, and/or restraining the baby's arms ($Chi^2(6) = 6.72$, N.S.).

Consistently throughout the period of study, one-quarter to one-third of the mothers had observed that their baby was able to self-quiet for prolonged periods (see Figure 9c). These proportions were similar to those based on the number of infants who were observed to self-quiet repeatedly during the behavioral evaluation ($Chi^2(6) = 2.79$, N.S.). Although not shown in the figures, the proportion of mothers who said their infant could not self-quiet at all, at each evaluation (.04, .27, .04, .14, .07, and .11, respectively), was lower, except on day 3, than the corresponding proportion of infants who did not succeed during the BNBAS evaluation (.11, .21, .20, .19, .33, and .27, respectively).

Almost all of the mothers said that their baby responded to being held by relaxing and cuddling, and in some cases, by clinging (Figure 9d). The proportions were very similar to those based on the infants' behavior ($Chi^2(6) = 5.49$, N.S.). Since the pilot data have suggested that it was difficult for the mothers to distinguish between a baby's needing help or not to cuddle, our IPM response categories did not make this distinction. Therefore, we cannot compare the degree of cuddliness perceived by the mothers with the BNBAS scores. Rather, the comparison is in terms of whether or not the infant responded positively to being held. Very few mothers (between .04 and .14) said that their baby remained passive, and only one said their baby actually resisted this kind of physical contact.

Four of the comparisons between "your baby" and a "typical baby" are relevant to these data: sleep, crying, consolability and "easiness of care." The proportions corresponding to better-than-average, in relation to how well the infant sleeps and the amount of crying, are quite variable. Almost all the mothers (except one or two) said their baby slept as well or better than the average baby, without showing any tendency towards improvement over time. Only on day 10 did the majority of the mothers (.72) consider that their infant was better-than-average in terms of crying; that is, he or she cried less. At each evaluation, a few of the mothers (from one to four) felt their baby was worse than most in this regard.

In terms of the infant's relative consolability, a large proportion of mothers (between .68 and .79) considered their infant to be easier to console than the average baby. When asked how easy it was, in general terms, to care for their baby, this same image emerged; over half of the mothers felt that their baby was easier than average to care for.

Motor Responses

The predominant tone of the infants studied was always good (see Figure 10a). On the first day, only one baby showed a tendency towards hypotonicity, while, on the 30th and 45th days, a different infant was slightly hypertonic. The major-

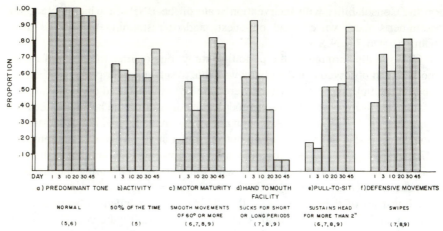

Figure 10. Motor responses: Proportion of healthy neonates showing optimal responses.

ity of the infants showed a moderate level of motor activity, in terms of both spontaneous and elicited movement. At each age evaluated, a small proportion of infants showed slightly less activity and others slightly more. However, it is important to emphasize that no infant presented extreme activity, neither below a score of 3, nor above a score of 7 (Figure 10a).

In relation to motor maturity, these infants initially presented restricted movements, especially of the upper extremities, with occasional jerkiness; for example, .56, .38, and .52 having scores of 4 and 5 on days 1, 3, and 10, respectively. However, as time went on, it became more common to observe infants with smooth movements and arcs of 60° or more (see Figure 10c). On the third day this was seen in over half of the group. Although on the 10th day, which was the first home evaluation, the corresponding proportion was much smaller; thereafter, well over half of the group continued to show smooth, wide movements.

From the very first day, over half of the babies showed good hand-to-mouth facility (Figure 10d). This was especially marked on the third day of life, when almost all of the infants (.93) showed actual insertions and sucking attempts. Nevertheless, this behavior was observed less and less frequently from 20 days onward. On the last two evaluations, only two infants (.07) showed this behavior. At these same evaluations, the majority of the infants (.52 and .71) made no attempts at hand-to-mouth contact during the evaluation.

In the pull-to-sit item (Figure 10e), few infants were able to maintain their head erect once seated, even briefly during the first week of life. At 10, 20, and 30 days, half of the group were able to achieve this, although most could only do it for less than 10 seconds. It was only at 45 days of age that almost all of the infants (.89) could maintain their head erect, although even at this age only .43 received scores of 8 or 9.

In response to a cloth placed over their eyes, almost all of the babies presented some kind of defensive movements. Except on the first day, the most common response was to make swipes of the arms either directed or nondirected (Figure 10f). Although only one or two of the infants actually succeeded in removing the cloth, it is also important to note that only one or two remained quiet and did not "defend themselves" from such an aversive stimulus.

Figure 11 shows the comparison of the IPM questions with selected BNBAS motor scales. In all five of these comparisons, there were differences between what the mothers observed and how the babies performed on the BNBAS.

Almost all of the mothers considered that their infant's tone was usually very good, referring to it as "relaxed yet firm" (see Figure 11a). This is similar to the proportion of infants who were scored optimally (i.e., 5 or 6) by the psychologist. Even though only one or two of the mothers at each age considered their baby a bit too stiff, and one mother, at 20 days, considered her baby a bit too floppy, differences between the IPM and BNBAS proportions reached statistical significance (Chi^2(6) = 13.49, p <.05).

In relation to the infant's level of activity there is considerable discrepancy between the proportion of mothers who referred to their infants as moderately active and the proportion of infants who scored in this category on the BNBAS (Figure 11b) (Chi^2(6) = 16.12, p <.05). The decrease in moderate activity perceived by the mothers is due to an increase in the number of infants considered as highly active after the first week.

Related to these IPM-BNBAS comparisons is an IPM question concerning how strong or weak the mother considers her baby. The proportion of mothers who considered their infant to be strong increased steadily from .41 on the first day to .86 on the 30th day. Few mothers considered their infants fragile or weak (5 on the first day, 3 on the third, and only 0 or 1 thereafter). When asked to compare her baby with a "typical baby" in terms of strength, all except one

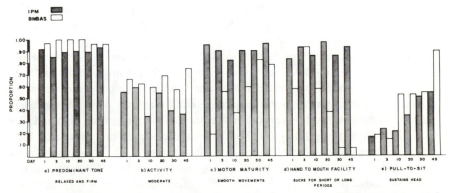

Figure 11. Motor responses: Proportion of best scores on IPM questions and BNBAS performance.

mother considered their infant average or better than average, with the latter category increasing steadily in frequency over time, from .34 on day 1 to .68 on day 45.

Returning to the IPM questions that relate to specific BNBAS items, Figure 11c shows the comparison for motor maturity. Here it is quite apparent that the mothers did not observe the same behavior that the psychologists were registering (Chi^2(6) = 67.0, p <.01). In fact, almost all the mothers considered that their infant's arm movements were smooth, without any jerkiness, from the very first day. The IPM best response category shown in the figure includes "limited" and "wide" arcs, the primary criteria for inclusion being a lack of jerky movements. Actually the mothers were usually not very sure of the amplitude of the movements, whereas they were more positive about the presence or absence of jerky movements. Only on day 10 did any of the mothers (and even then, only two) report frequent jerky movements. At each evaluation, a few of the mothers (.14 to .04) had observed occasional jerkiness, although the corresponding proportions according to the BNBAS were consistently higher (ranging from .56 to .15).

Another area in which there was considerable discrepancy between the mothers' perceptions and the behavior observed during the behavioral evaluation was in the area of hand-to-mouth facility (Figure 11d). Although many infants did not demonstrate this skill during the evaluations, especially during the last three sessions, almost all the mothers consistently reported that they did have this ability (Chi^2(6) = 109.23, p <.01).

Related to hand-to-mouth facility, though at the same time quite different, is the infant's nutritive sucking and feeding behavior. Approximately half of the mothers compared their baby favorably to a "typical baby" in terms of the quality of feeding behavior. The proportions ranged from .48 to .64 without showing any age trend. Only one or two mothers during the first four evaluations considered their baby worse than average.

In relation to the quality of the infant's sucking, all except one mother on the first day considered her baby to be average or better than average. From 10 days on, more than half of the group perceived their baby's nutritive sucking as exceptionally good.

The pull-to-sit item was one of those which, from the beginning of our experience with the BNBAS, we found to be stressful for many of the mothers. In the IPM interview, we asked the mothers what their baby did when the pediatrician pulled him or her to a sitting position as part of the neurological examination performed during the hospital stay. A low proportion (.16 and .23, at 1 and 3 days, respectively) of those who had observed this event said their infant had some head control once seated (see Figure 11e). These proportions were similar to those based on the infant's actual performance. However, once at home, we asked the mother if she had sat her infant up in a similar way, and if so, to what extent had the baby been able to hold up its head. On the first evaluation at home, half of the mothers (15) said they had not sat their infant up. Even at 45 days, six mothers said they still had not done so. Considering this reluctance to pull the baby to a sitting position, it is not surprising that the proportion of mothers who were aware that their infants could maintain relatively good head control once seated was consistently lower than the corresponding BNBAS proportions (Chi^2(6) = 17.1, p <.01).

Autonomic Regulation

As can be seen in Figure 12a, in four out of six of the evaluations, the majority of the infants did not receive optimal scores since they had presented some tremulousness in active and quiet alert states. However, the tremors these infants showed were relatively minor. Only two infants on day 1 presented tremors repeatedly in various or all states observed (scores 8 and 9). No infant received these scores on any subsequent evaluation.

With respect to the startles observed during the evaluation (Figure 12b), it was only on day 1 that a considerable proportion of infants (.44) presented more than two startles. Even at this age, only one baby presented seven or more. Thereafter, startles were quite infrequent. In fact, almost all the babies (between .82 and .93) presented a maximum of two during each evaluation. Considering that one of these corresponds to the Moro evoked by the examiner, this level can be considered quite low.

Finally, in Figure 12c, one can observe that the proportion of infants who showed few skin-color changes (scores 2, 3, and 4) increases slowly during the

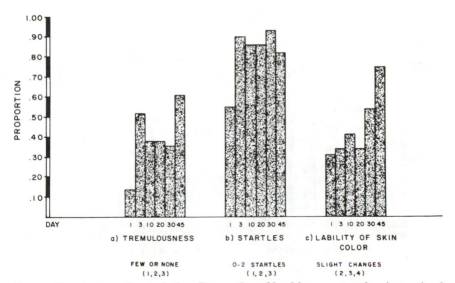

Figure 12. Autonomic regulation: Proportion of healthy neonates showing optimal responses.

period of study. Actually, moderate color changes (on chest and/or whole body) were the most common during the first four evaluations (.65, .65, .59, and .65, respectively) and somewhat less so by 1 month of age (.47 and .36 at 30 and 45 days, respectively). It is important to add that only one infant on the first day showed extreme color changes with slow recuperation. This was never observed on subsequent evaluations. Furthermore, no infant presented an absence of color changes (score 1) at any evaluation.

On the two IPM questions related to Autonomic Regulation, important differences appear. The mothers and the psychologists seemed to have been observing very different behaviors. Almost half or more of the mothers reported that they had not observed any tremulousness in their baby (Figure 13a). At each age, except at 45 days, this proportion was higher than for the corresponding BNBAS category (Chi$^2(6)$ = 19.45, p <.01). In other words, during the first month the mothers perceived fewer tremors than the babies had actually presented during the behavioral evaluation. The next highest proportions on the IPM question were for mothers who observed tremors when the infant was motorically active or crying (ranging from .17 to .38). Fewer mothers had observed tremors while the baby was in a quiet, alert state, and only one (on the 1st, 30th, and 45th days) in several different states.

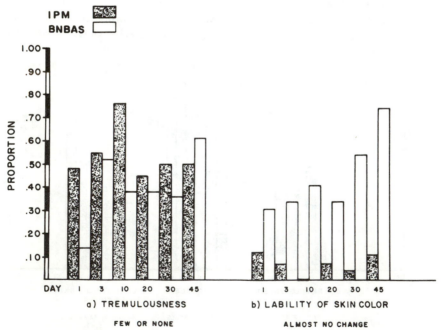

Figure 13.   Autonomic regulation: Proportion of best scores on IPM questions and BNBAS performance.

In terms of skin color lability, very few mothers considered that their baby's skin color showed little change when crying and/or when undressed (Figure 13b) (Chi^2(6) = 70.52, p <.01). Almost all the mothers said that their infant's face or whole body changed color considerably, but returned to normal quickly. No real age trend was discernable, although half of the mothers referred to changes in the extremities on the first three evaluations (.52, .62, and .64, respectively), while they more often mentioned changes in the entire body at 20, 30, and 45 days (.50, .54, and .44, respectively). Apparently, this was due to their initial reluctance to uncover the infant, thereby limiting their opportunity to observe changes on the chest.

General Impression

In order to obtain a general image of these infants, it is useful to describe their behavior on three additional BNBAS scales: Social Attractiveness, Need for Stimulation, and Reinforcement Value of the Infant's Behavior. On all three, the result was a predominantly positive image which improved over the period of study (see Figure 14).

In terms of Social Attractiveness, no infant was scored as very stressed (0) during the evaluation. The proportion of infants who showed brief periods of organization and stability (1) decreased rapidly from .48 on day 1 to .04 on day 30 and .00 on day 45. Both good organizational stability (2) and sustained responsiveness (3) were observed frequently, with the latter increasing over time to .75 at 45 days.

Most of these infants (ranging between .62 and .90) were well organized

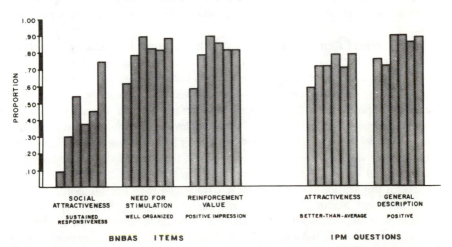

Figure 14.   General impression: Proportion of best scores on BNBAS items and IPM questions.

without, but improved with, stimulation (score 2 on Need for Stimulation). In most cases, the examiners were left with a positive impression of them (scores of 7, 8, or 9 on Reinforcement Value), even from the first day (between .59 and .90). Only one infant left a slightly negative impression on day 1, and another infant an ambivalent reaction on day 3.

Although not planned to relate exactly to these BNBAS scales, two IPM questions provided information about the mother's general impression of her baby. A similar favorable image of the group emerged. On the comparison between "your baby" and a "typical baby" in relation to the infant's "attractiveness," more than half of the mothers (.59 to .79) considered their baby more attractive than average. Only one mother consistently compared her infant negatively in this regard.

When asked to give a general description of their infant at the beginning of the interview, most of the mothers used terms that were scored as positive. The corresponding proportions ranged between .72 to .90. All the other mothers gave replies that were considered as ambivalent or neutral, except on days 30 and 45 when one mother described her baby in terms that were scored as negative.

Discussion

The infants studied were selected for having been born and having coursed their neonatal period in favorable biopsychosocial conditions. The behaviors they presented concur with these perinatal characteristics. As a group they presented a positive and relatively consistent image: They showed a progressive adaptation during their first month and a half of extrauterine life, demonstrating capabilities which allow for a growing and favorable interaction with their postnatal environment.

Their mothers were selected for having had a normal pregnancy as well as certain favorable characteristics in terms of their attitude towards the pregnancy, social supports, and psychological/psychiatric history. However, they came from a wide variety of educational and socioeconomic backgrounds, as is typical of the INPer's population. Their general perceptions of their infants were quite positive, probably reflecting both their own favorable attitude as well as the infants' behavior. Although they considered their babies as good as or better than average on a variety of behavioral dimensions, they actually underestimated or overestimated various aspects of their behavior.

Several implications arise from these data which have been important in our work, both with health professionals and parents of healthy babies. Among the orientation stimuli included in the BNBAS, the combination of the examiner's face and voice was the most powerful, in that it produced the best responses from the very first day. This, of course, is common knowledge to individuals versed in recent child development literature. However, in our context it is quite surprising to many people. These data have helped us show that healthy newborns are in fact capable of responding from the first day to the social overtures of their mothers and/or other caregivers.

After the first week, the orientation responses as well as the quality and duration of the babies' alertness improved consistently. In addition, the examiner needed to use less and less intense and persistent forms of manipulation in order to achieve a favorable social interaction. Together, these patterns translate into a progressive improvement in the neonate's capability and facility to participate in his or her environment throughout the first month and a half of life.

However, many of the mothers initially underestimated the babies' specific orientation abilities. While they were aware of and interested in the babies' general alertness and wakefulness, they were not aware of the babies' ability to distinguish contrasts, visually track, or to turn towards a voice. Only by the end of the first month were they able to accurately describe their babies' behavior.

Nevertheless, the repeated exposure to the IPM interview may actually have made them more aware of their infants' visual capabilities than they would have been without it. We found that after one or two interview sessions the mothers spontaneously reported that, due to our questioning, they had looked for possible orientation abilities which they otherwise would not have noticed. In fact some mothers who had previously said their baby could not see or could only see shadows remarked with surprise that our questions alone had made them realize that their baby "appeared to" be able to distinguish and/or follow faces. This implies, of course, that the interview itself, although it provided no direct information or feedback as such, actually served as an intervention, increasing, to some extent, the mother's awareness of some of her infant's capabilities.

These same BNBAS results, especially in relation to the examiner's persistence, also show clearly the importance of helping the newborn organize his or her responses, particularly during the first week of life. In our cultural context, however, parents and health professionals are often not aware of certain simple techniques that can be used to facilitate interaction with small babies. The information provided by our study of healthy newborns, as well as demonstrations of the BNBAS, have been helpful in this regard. Caregivers can easily be taught to take advantage of the baby's spontaneous periods of alertness, however brief these may be. They can be shown specific techniques, such as those used by the examiner during the BNBAS, which help to optimize the infant's behavior as well as their own enjoyment of their baby through such pleasurable early interaction.

Over the period of study, the group of babies also presented greater state stability and less irritability. Their mothers considered them as easy to handle and generally not irritable. Their perceptions concerning the babies' consolability and attempts at self-quieting were quite similar to the behavior observed during the evaluations. Apparently, these behaviors were highly salient for the mothers and were viewed quite favorably by them.

The discrepancy between the psychologists' and the mothers' views of the babies' irritability is probably due to the nature of the irritability itself as well as the context in which it is evaluated. On the BNBAS item, one is assessing the infant's reactivity to aversive stimuli, some of which are quite uncommon for the baby. The decrease in BNBAS irritability may reflect, in part, the infants' greater state stability and acceptance of physical manipulation.

The increase in the number of reasons mentioned by the mothers probably reflects different processes. The IPM question focuses on the baby's typical ways of expressing his or her demands and modes of response to important daily situations. Furthermore, the mothers were probably becoming more aware of their infants' signals as they got to know their babies. The babies themselves may have also been expressing their needs in a more intentional and specific way towards the end of the first month.

In relation to their motor responses, these infants presented a generally favorable image. However, their head control in pull-to-sit was relatively poor. Many of these babies were not able to keep their head up once seated for more than 2 seconds, until the very last evaluation. This observation is especially important in light of one of the common baby-care practices in Mexico, that of not placing an infant in vertical or inclined positions, including sitting up, during the first few months. Some authors (e.g., Bell, 1974; Lester & Brazelton, 1982) have suggested that certain traditional child-care practices may have developed as a response to the babies' own characteristics and abilities. The practices, in turn, may reinforce the initially low level of performance by limiting some of the babies' opportunities to exercise these abilities.

The mothers' perceptions of the babies' motor abilities and autonomic regulation were quite different from the babies' actual behavior. The discrepancies that existed in tone, motor maturity, pull-to-sit, and tremulousness suggest that the mothers may not have had much opportunity to observe the infant's behavior in these areas. The widespread use of swaddling, and the mothers' reluctance to sit her baby up, may partially explain this lack of awareness of the quality of the baby's behavior in these areas.

In regard to activity level, part of the discrepancy is probably due to the fact that the mothers seemed to equate higher activity with greater strength and motor abilities, which the infants, of course, presented at the later ages. In order to avoid this confusion, we have modified this question and the response alternatives in the IPM interview we are presently using.

The discrepancy in terms of hand-to-mouth facility probably reflects the fact that the mothers observed their infant's sucking attempts under a variety of conditions, such as hunger and drowsiness, states which the psychologist tried to avoid when performing the BNBAS evaluation. The decrease at 20, 30, and 45 days in the number of infants who demonstrated their hand-to-mouth facility during the behavioral assessment probably reflects the infant's diminished need rather than lack of ability. The infants cried less during these later evaluations, and when they did cry, they used other behaviors (such as visual fixation) to calm themselves, providing little opportunity for the examiner to observe their hand-to-mouth ability. The mothers, of course, continued to have ample opportunity to observe their baby's finger- (or hand-) sucking ability, and seemed to have been quite tuned into this behavior (although not always showing approval).

Whereas the infants showed lower skin color lability towards the end of the study period, most of the mothers were still reporting marked color changes, especially when their babies cried. This overall difference may have been due, in part, to the context of the observations. The infants cried less frequently during the later BNBAS evaluations. At home the babies most likely still cried more and harder at times then they did during the behavioral evaluations, providing their mothers with the continued opportunity to observe greater color changes.

Furthermore, there was even an increase in the number of mothers who reported whole body changes as time went on. During the first three evaluations some of the mothers who reported changes only on the face and extremities said they had not noticed changes on the chest since they did not like to uncover the baby. When asked at later evaluations, they had more opportunity to observe color changes and therefore reported changes on the whole body.

Taken as a whole, the BNBAS-IPM comparisons are quite congruent with the popular beliefs common in the INPer's population. We cannot, however, claim direct relationships, since the information was obtained from independent sources. Nevertheless, the similarities are worth noting.

Irritability and state control seem to be the most salient areas for the mothers. Their infants are relatively calm and easy to console, similar to the cultural ideal. Although mothers repeatedly mentioned that they did not want to accustom their babies to being carried, it is difficult to know how this actually relates to their behavior. Obviously, the mothers studied carried their babies sufficiently to have perceived their good cuddliness, which, by the way, they usually referred to as quite gratifying.

In the area of orientation and alertness, we observed an important under-estimation on the part of the mothers. This seems to reflect their lack of knowl-edge concerning neonatal capabilities, which is shared by many health profes-sionals. Since they did not expect to observe organized visual or auditory responses, they did not engage in those behaviors which would elicit them. However, indications in this regard are usually received enthusiastically by par-ents, although often skeptically by professionals.

The beliefs concerning posture and movement seem to be the most pervasive and resistant to change. In some ways, they are reinforced by the infants' own behaviors as well as the mothers' living conditions and expectations. The motor abilities that healthy babies present, and the variability among them, do not appear very relevant to these mothers.

These group behavioral patterns raise a variety of questions, which we hope to be able to answer through several projects which are underway. Two of the most important issues are the individual patterns within the group and the predictive value of these indicators.

The group results themselves make clear the importance of exploring the individual patterns which the babies, their mothers, and the dyads present. For example, several BNBAS items, including Consolability with Intervention, Self-Quieting Activities, Cuddliness, and Activity, showed similar group proportions in the different response categories at each age. Whether or not these represent consistent temperamental differences can only be answered by the analysis of individual evolution curves.

Similarly, it is important to identify individual trends among the mothers, as well as the interrelations among their responses on the IPM interview. Although the mothers as a group were well motivated towards their babies, a few can be considered less optimal in their attitudes expressed over the study period. In some cases, these mothers account for the more discrepant values observed in the group.

We are also interested in analyzing the correlations between the BNBAS and IPM results on an individual basis, within mother–infant dyads. In what way does the impression the psychologist obtains from the complete evaluation relate to that provided by the mother by means of the interview? How discrepant can they be without having to be interpreted as a warning sign of problems at some level?

The predictive significance of these data require they be compared to values obtained on high-risk groups, both of infants and mothers, who are then followed longitudinally. Several projects that are underway have already demonstrated their utility in the short run, but only the follow-up results can identify their prognostic validity in our population.

For example, we evaluated the behavior of the 12 jaundiced infants who originally had entered the study of healthy babies. Consistent differences were observed at 3 days of age (before the diagnosis) and at 10 days (after phototherapy) in comparison to the behavior of the infants who did not develop hyperbilirubinemia (Olvera, Givaudan, & Atkin, 1987). The discriminant analysis used produced consistent factors which discriminated between the two groups to a significant degree. However, it would be very risky to make predictions for other infants, due to the small number of subjects on which the factors are based.

We have found the BNBAS very useful in the evaluation of high-risk neonates, referred to the Growth and Development Department by other Services. In a preliminary analysis (Landeros & Atkin, 1983), we have compared the scores of a group of infants, who were in an early stimulation program based on a neurodevelopmental model of physiotherapy, to the behavioral profiles we have developed based on the scores of the group of healthy babies. Out of 24 of these infants evaluated with the BNBAS, 23 had discrepant scores (i.e., less optimal than .90 of the healthy babies) in motor responses, 12 in orientation and alertness, 11 in state control and irritability, 6 in autonomic regulation, and 16 in

Figure 15.   Two years later: One of the boys from the study and his mother.

general impression. Furthermore, the evaluation situation permitted us to identify qualitative alterations in the infants' behavior which were not directly registered in the BNBAS scores. It should be possibie to systematically register these and other "alarm signs" in conjunction with the behavioral evaluation.

Finally, we have been using both the BNBAS and the IPM with infants who were attended to in our ICU. This population will, of course provide far greater variability in terms of infant behavior. Considering the extent to which the perceptions of the mothers of healthy infants were discrepant from the actual behavior, the question arises whether or not the mothers of high-risk infants will observe their nonoptimal behavior when it occurs.

Since separate psychologists perform the IPM and the BNBAS evaluations, we have been able to confirm informally that the impressions obtained independently are often quite similar. Apparently the mothers do describe their infant in more negative terms when in fact the infants' behavior is more highly disorganized.

In summary, we have tried to situate the behavior of a group of healthy neonates within the context of their mother's perceptions of their behavior as well as of the cultural beliefs and practices surrounding them. While interesting in and of itself, the impact of this combination of factors on the child's future development can only be identified over time. The predictive value of each instrument within our setting, which may depend to some extent on the particular interrelations among these elements, can only be tested through longitudinal follow-up. Meanwhile, in the short run, this combination has proved to be highly productive. It has provided us with the basis for a better understanding of the women we are serving, as well as new perspectives for research and educational programs.

References

Atkin, L.C., & Ramos, G.T. (1980). *Inventario de Percepciones Maternas*. Unpublished manuscript. (Available from Dr. Lucille C. Atkin, Departamento de Crecimiento y Desarrollo, Instituto Nacional de Perinatología, Montes Urales 800, México.)

Bell, R.Q., (1974). Contributions of human infants to caregiving and social interaction. In M. Lewis & L.A. Rosenblum (Eds.), *The effect of the infant on its caregiver*. New York: Wiley.

Broussard, E.R., & Hartner, M.S.S. (1971). Further considerations regarding maternal perception of the first born. In J. Hellmuth (Ed.), *Exceptional infant: Studies in abnormalities* (Vol. 2). New York: Brunner Mazel.

Capurro, H., Konichezky, S., Fonseca, D., & Caldeyro-Barcia, R. (1978). A simplified method of diagnosis of gestational age in the newborn infant. *Journal of Pediatrics, 93,* 120–125.

Field, T.M., Dempsey, J.R., Hallock, N.H., & Shuman, H.H. (1978). The mother's assessment of the behavior of her infant. *Infant Behavior and Development, 1,* 156–167.

Horowitz, F.D., Sullivan, J.W., & Linn, P. (1978). Stability and instability in the newborn infant: The quest for elusive threads. In A.J. Sameroff (Ed.), *Organization and stability of newborn behavior: A commentary on the Brazelton Neonatal Behavior Assessment Scale. Monograph of the Society for Research in Child Development* (Serial No. 177), *43*(5–6).

Jurado-García, E. (1980). Perinatal care in Mexico. In S. Aladjem, A.K. Brown, & C. Sureau (Eds.), *Clinical perinatology* (pp. 560–595). St. Louis, MO: C.V. Mosby.

Landeros, G., & Atkin, L.C. (1983, November). *Niños canalizados a fisioterapia.* Paper presented at the General Clinical Session of the Instituto Nacional de Perinatología, México City.

Lester, B.M., & Brazelton, T.B. (1982). Cross-cultural assessment of neonatal behavior. In D. Wagner & H. Stevenson (Eds.), *Cultural perspectives on child development* (pp. 20–53). San Francisco, CA: W.H. Freeman.

Olvera M.C., Givaudan, M., & Atkin, L.C. (1987). Estudio comparativo de la conducta de neonatos hiperbilirrubinémicos y sanos a través del primer mes de vida. *Boletín médico del Hospital Infantil de México, 44*(7), 396–401.

Sahagún, F.B. (1956). *Historia General de las Cosas de la Nueva España* (Tomo II). México: Editorial Porrúa.

Appendix
Correspondence Between BNBAS Items and IPM Questions

BNBAS Items[a]	IPM Questions
Orientation and Alertness	
1. Orientation Animate Visual and Auditory: follows 60° or more (7, 8, 9)	1. How much does your baby watch or follow persons who move around him or her?: follows briefly or prolonged
2. Orientation Animate-Auditory: head turns to stimulus and search with eyes (7, 8, 9)	2. If you talk to your baby from the side (without being seen) what does he or she do?: turns head to look at mother
3. Alertness: sustained periods (7, 8, 9)	3. During the time your baby is awake, how often is he or she observing and responding to what is going on around him or her?: moderate to long periods of attention
Irritability and State Regulation	
4. Irritability: cries to 3 or less stimuli (1, 2, 3)	4. Which of the following reasons make your baby cry? (8 options) 0–3 reasons
5. Consolability with Intervention: Less than picking up (6, 7, 8, 9)	5. What is the least you have to do to calm your baby when he or she is crying?: talk and/or pat.
6. Self-Quieting Activity: (7, 8, 9)	6. If your baby is crying, is he or she able to calm himself or herself?: prolonged periods
7. Cuddliness: molds and/or clings (5, 6, 7, 8, 9)	7. When you hold your baby, what does he or she do with his or her body and arms?: relaxes and cuddles, possibly clings

(*continued*)

Appendix *(continued)*

BNBAS Items[a]	IPM Questions
Motor Responses	
8. Predominant Tone: good tone (5, 6)	8. When you move the baby's legs and arms (when he or she's not crying), how does his or her body feel?: relaxed and firm
9. Activity: moderate spontaneous and elicited (5)	9. How active do you consider your baby?: moderately active
10. Motor Maturity: smooth movements (6, 7, 8, 9)	10. When your baby is not crying and moves his or her arms, how does he or she move them? smooth movements, no jerkiness
11. Hand-to-mouth Facility; several insertions and/or sucking (7, 8, 9)	11. Have you seen if your baby puts his or her hand in his or her mouth? If yes describe.: sucks for short and/or long periods
12. Pull-to-sit: sustains head (6, 7, 8, 9)	12. (Day 1 and 3) Have you seen the doctor sit your baby up? (At home) Have you sat your baby up as the doctor did? (demonstrate) what does he or she do with her head?: sustains head, at least briefly
Autonomic Regulation	
13. Tremulousness (1, 2, 3)	13. Have you noticed any tremulousness in your baby's hands, legs or chin?: none or only when asleep or being manipulated.
14. Lability of skin color: slight changes (2, 3, 4)	14. When you undress your baby or when he or she is crying, how much does his or her color change?: almost no change.

[a] Best responses are listed after the item or question. The corresponding BNBAS scores are indicated in parenthesis.

PART III

CULTURAL PERSPECTIVES ON THE HIGH-RISK INFANT AND FAMILY

CHAPTER 8

Working Toward a Humanized Neonatal Care System in Naples, Italy: Interactions Between Parents, Infants, and Health Care Personnel

R. Paludetto, G. Mansi, P. Rinaldi, P. Margara-Paludetto

Neonatal Unit Second School of Medicine
Naples, Italy

M. Faggiano-Perfetto

Mental Health Center
Naples, Italy

Over the last 30 years, perinatal care has undergone many changes. In most industrialized countries, children are now usually born in a hospital, and remarkable progress has been made both in obstetrics and neonatal care.

The introduction of sophisticated technology in the fields of obstetrics and neonatal care has placed an enormous onus on health care personnel (Marshall, Kasman, Cape, 1982; Paludetto, 1977). In addition, the creation of large units designed for the intensive care of pregnancies and newborns with problems compounds the difficulties of personnel. Staff is often under great stress; they have to deal with emergencies, with the death of the fetus or newborn, and with grief-stricken parents. This is obviously fertile ground for the growth of relational problems both among health care staff, and between staff and parents (Klaus & Kennell, 1976, 1982; Marshall et al., 1982; Paludetto, Faggiano-Perfetto, Asprea, Margara-Paludetto, & De Luca, 1980; Paludetto, Faggiano-Perfetto, Asprea, De Curtis, & Margara-Paludetto, 1981).

In the United States, Klaus and Kennell (1976) pioneered a more humanized perinatal care. The result was that women began to have their husband or a relative present during the delivery, and they spent longer time with their baby after it was born. Moreover, neonatal special care units (NSCUs) encouraged parents to enter and interact with their newborns.

Italian Experience

In Italy, unfortunately, this inversion of tendency did not occur. In 1978, only 13% of Italian hospitals allowed rooming-in, and in 42% of hospitals, the first breast-feeding occurred after the first 24 hours (S. Nordio, personal communication, June 6, 1980). Visiting is allowed only during prefixed periods during the day, and a relative cannot be present during the delivery. In NCSUs, parents are allowed to take care of their infants only when the babies are nearing discharge from the hospital.

It is difficult to pinpoint the reasons for this resistance to change. Generally speaking, it cannot be attributed to a lack of information. The positive aspects of a more humane policy have been widely publicized, together with experiences showing that these changes do not enhance the risk of epidemy if simple hygienic precautions are taken (Klaus & Kennell, 1976). There is evidence that health care personnel are somewhat resistant to change (Paludetto, Faggiano-Perfetto, Asprea, De Curtis, & Margara-Paludetto, 1982). Hence, attempts should be made to analyze feelings of medical personnel in order to obtain their cooperation in implementing changes.

Here, we describe our experiences in the NSCUs of the Second School of Medicine, University of Naples, which was one of the first in Italy to allow parents to enter. We evaluated the attitudes of parents and health care personnel towards these changes with a structured research program.

Neapolitan Experience

The Second School of Medicine of Naples is a large, fairly recent University Hospital with 2000 beds (Figure 1). In the Obstetrics Department, about 3000 deliveries take place each year. People come from Naples and the provinces, but pregnancies at risk come from all over the Campania region. An idea of the type of population that comes to the Obstetrics Department is given by the data of a polycentric investigation performed on a sample of 2305 infants born between August 1, 1977 and July 31, 1979 in Naples (Bertulessi et al., 1983). In this group, more than 10% of the women had less than four medical examinations during the pregnancy, and less than 5% followed birth preparation classes. The incidence of babies of low birthweight (<2500g.) was 8.3%.

A nursery began to function in 1975, and an NSCU with intensive care at the beginning of 1976. The nursery and the Obstetrics Department are in one build-

Figure 1.   The University Hospital of the Second School of Medicine of Naples.

ing, and the NSCU in another: a long corridor connects the two buildings. There
are three delivery rooms and two surgery rooms. Women are usually in labor in a
room with other women. During hospitalization, newborns were in the nursery,
far from the mothers' rooms. Normally, 50 newborns were present in the nursery
each day. Five or six nurses were present throughout the day. Most of the staff
had no previous experience, and, during the first 2 years the Unit was opened,
internal organization and personnel training were given priority. At the beginning, our main efforts were to assure the presence, at every delivery, of one
neonatologist and one nurse.

When the nursery began to function, the situation was not unlike that of other
Italian hospitals. The mother is normally in labor with other women and without
the comfort of a relative. She saw the baby for a short time after delivery, after
which it was taken to the Nursery where it remained for the first 12 hours. After
that, the newborns were taken to the mothers every 3 hours for feeding. Altogether, babies were with their mothers about 3–5 hours a day.

To assess the feeling of parents towards delivery and their interaction with
their newborn during hospitalization, we interviewed 32 couples of parents of
healthy-term newborns (Paludetto et al., 1980).

All the interviews reported in this chapter follow the indications described by
Cesa Bianchi (1970) and Galtung (1967). Anonimity was guaranteed to all sub-
jects. A psychoanalyst (M.F.P.) conducted the clinical interviews individually.
The interviews were nondirective and lasted an average of 35–45 mins. Subjects

were allowed to cope with the different topics in the way, and for as long as they liked. Codification, grouping of answers in clusters, and interpretation of results were performed with homogeneous criteria by whole team through group work.

The 32 couples replied to questions concerning the following aspects: (a) hospital accommodation and personnel, (b) needs and fears during gestation and delivery, (c) problems concerning the newborn. Sixteen mothers were primiparae, 16 multiparae. Table 1 shows the main characteristics of the 32 couples. Table 2 shows the replies to questions about the pregnancy and how the women prepared for the delivery. Although Italians have access to public welfare assistance, 21 mothers preferred private care; only three mothers attended birth preparation classes, and, strikingly, 17 mothers out of 32 thought that these were useless.

We then asked: "Were you afraid during the delivery? If so, what were you frightened by?" (Table 3). Interviews with obstetricians had shown that fear was one of the most important issues of delivery (Asprea, Faggiano-Perfetto, Orzalesi, & Paludetto, 1978).

Table 1.   Main Characteristics of 32 Couples of Parents of Healthy-at-Term Infants

		Mother	Father
Age	20	4	—
	21–25	7	15
	26–30	8	2
	31–35	9	9
	36–40	3	3
	>40	1	3
Education	Illiterate	—	—
	Elementary	15	10
	Secondary	9	12
	High School	6	7
	Degree	2	3
Occupation	Unemployed	—	—
	Worker	1	14
	Farmer worker	3	—
	Housewife	18	—
	Office worker	5	9
	Tradesman	—	4
	Craftsman	—	4
	Private profession	3	1
	Home worker	2	—

		Couples
Resident In:	Naples	14
	Province	14
	Other	4

Table 2.   Data on Birth Preparation of 32 Mothers of Healthy-at-Term Infants

	N=32
Programmed pregnancy	24
No	8
Medical visits during pregnancy	
Private medicine	21
Welfare assistance	10
No visit	1
Psychoprophylaxis	
Yes	3
No	29
Usefulness of the birth preparation classes	
Yes	9
No	17
I don't know	6

I would like to open a parenthesis on the Italian public welfare system and on women's rights during and after pregnancy. In Italy, everyone, including the unemployed, is entitled to public welfare. By law, employed women (but not housewives or homehelps) stop work from 2 months before to 3 months after the delivery (there are exceptions to this rule: nurses cease to work from 3 months before to 3 months after, because hospital work is considered dangerous for the mother and baby). During this period, the mother receives 80% of her salary.

Table 3.   Answers of 32 Couples of Parents of Healthy-at-Term Infants to the Question:

"Were You Afraid During the Delivery?"

	Mothers (32)	Fathers (32)
No	9	19
Yes	16	13
Not answered	7	—

"What Were You Frightened By?"

	Mothers (16)	Fathers (13)
Fear in general	9	—
Fear of the unknown, of the unexpected	5	8
Fear of pain	1	—
Fear of death	1	—
Anxiety for the baby	—	1
Anxiety for the wife	—	4

Table 4.   Answer of 32 Mothers of Healthy-at-Term Infants to the Question:

"What Routines During the Delivery Would You Change?"

	Mothers
A relative present	5
A relative present and private room to have more privacy	7
A private room	3
More participation and interest in the needs of the woman	2
More personnel/more care	1
Nothing	10
I do not know	4

After that, during the first year of life of the baby, the mother can stay at home for 6 months (the salary is 30%). If the baby is sick during the first 3 years of life, the mother or the father can stay home for any length of time without pay and he or she cannot be fired.

Of the 16 mothers who answered yes, 14 were generally frightened, or were frightened by the unknown. Going on with our questions we asked: "What routines during the delivery would you change?" (Table 4). Seventeen would like more privacy, more interest in their needs, and a relative present. The next question was: "Did you wish someone near you during the delivery? Who?" (Table 5). Of the 15 women answering affirmatively, only three would have liked to have the husband; the other 12 wanted the mother or a female relative or any relative. Moreover, the women who did not want the husband explained that they felt "ashamed" or that they did not want to make the husband "worry." Finally, 15 of the 32 men said they wanted to be present during the delivery.

The last section of the interviews concerned the mother–infant relationship and how the mothers viewed the child when they first saw it (Table 6). Most of the mothers (18) thought the baby nice, pretty, and beautiful. Interesting data

Table 5.   Answer of 32 Mothers of Healthy-at-Term Infants to the Question:

"Did You Wish Someone Near You During the Delivery?"

	N=32
Yes	15
No	11
I don't know	6

"Who?"	**N=15**
Mother	6
Husband	3
A female relative	3
Any relative	3

Table 6.   Answer of 32 Mothers of Healthy-at-Term Infants to the Question:

"How Did the Baby Seem to You the First Time You Looked at It?"

	N=32
Nice, pretty, beautiful	18
Normal	3
Fragile, weak	2
Ugly	7
I didn't feel what I expected	1
I didn't feel it mine, until I started to breast-feed it	1

come from the answers to the questions concerning whether the mother wanted to stay with the child for a longer period immediately after the delivery, and whether the child should remain in the room during the stay in the hospital. Sixteen mothers out of 32 would like to have the child longer after delivery to touch and look at him or her. On the contrary, 24 mothers out of 32 were content to have the child only for 5–6 hours a day.

Before planning changes in hospital routine we investigated the opinion of 15 obstetricians (Asprea et al., 1978). Only two of the 15 obstetricians said that the presence of the husband could be considered after appropriate modification of the organization. Similar answers were given by midwives interviewed about 6 years later: 17 of 20 midwives said that relatives's presence in the delivery room would create "confusion and discomfort," and only one said that there would not be any problem (Paludetto, 1984, unpublished data).

In view of the resistance of the obstetricians to the presence of the relative in the delivery room, we introduced other modifications to promote a good relationship between parents and child from birth.

Effects of Changes on Breast Feeding

From January 1978, instead of carrying the baby to the mother only at feeding times, we left the newborns with the mothers from morning to late evening and we began to encourage self-demand breast feeding. With this modification, the frequency of exclusive breast feeding increased significantly, from 36% to 55% at discharge, from 31% to 46% at 1 month, and from 19% to 29% at 3 months of life. From May 1978, we replaced the formula supplement with 5% glucose solution, and exclusive breast feeding reached 71% at discharge, 52% at 1 month, and 27% at 3 months of life (Mastropasqua et al., 1980).

At the end of 1979, we introduced a specifically trained social worker to encourage breast feeding. We assessed the effects of three visits to the mothers during hospitalization, during which she listened to problems, helped the mother to breast feed the baby, and gave theoretical and practical information (Paludetto et al., 1981).

The population studied consisted of 204 primiparae, 102 of whom received visits from the social worker. The two groups were similar for paternal and maternal age, type of job, education, type of delivery, newborn's sex, Apgar score, weight, and gestational age. The exclusive breast feeding at discharge was 78.5% against 70.5% of the control group (n.s.), 67% against 52% ($p < 0.05$) at 1 month, and 43% against 39% at 3 months of age.

Reaction to Rooming In

Mothers

To monitor the introduction of rooming-in, we asked the 102 mothers who had the social worker's support their opinion on having the baby with them all day (Figure 2). Half of the mothers were satisfied with the period of contact with the child (12–14 hours a day), and 37% would like to have him also during the night (Paludetto, 1984). In view of the fact that the majority of prerooming-in mothers were satisfied with the 5–6 hours a day, it appears that, in Italy, the user does not question hospital procedure. To the last question: "Do you think it is useful to have the child with you during the day and why?", 84% of the mothers thought it was a good idea, emotionally speaking; of this 84%, 13% said that the nurses do not help them very much, and another 12% thought it was a good idea but unhygienic.

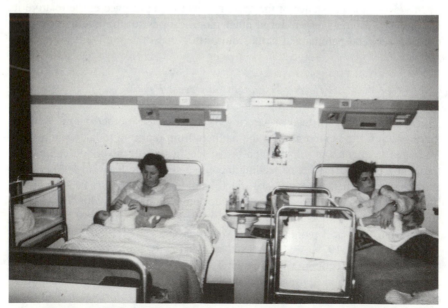

Figure 2.   Rooming-in at the Second School of Medicine in Naples.

Table 7. Main Characteristics of Nursery Caregivers

		N=21
Age	20	—
	21–30	16
	31–40	3
	>40	2
Marital status	Married	6
	Unmarried	15
	Divorced	—
Children	0	17
	1	4
	2	—
Resident In:	Naples	20
	Province	1
	Other	—

Nurses

To gauge the opinion of our health care personnel about rooming-in, we interviewed 21 of the 36 staff members on roll in the nursery (Paludetto et al., 1982). The interview covered: (a) acceptance of rooming-in; (b) motivations, problems, and gratification; and (c) relationship with patients and colleagues. Table 7 shows the main characteristics of the nursery caregivers.

Table 8 report replies to the question: "Should the mother and the infant share the same room?" Fifteen answered affirmatively; three answered yes, but only in rooms with 1 or 2 beds. But when we asked: "What are the major problems involved in keeping mother and infant together?" six said that it entailed more work because the mothers call them too often, four mentioned problems of hygiene and crowding, three that the mother is more anxious and tired, and eight said that there were not any problems.

Table 8. Answers of 21 Nursery Caregivers to the Question:

"Should the Mother and Infant Share the Same Room?"	N=21
Yes	15
Yes, But only in Rooms with 1 or 2 Beds	3
No	2
I Don't Know	1

"What Are the Major Problems Involved in Keeping Mother and Infant Together?"	N=21
No problem	8
Greater problems for personnel	6
(The mothers call staff too often)	
Hygiene and crowding	4
The mother is more anxious and tired	3

It should be mentioned that the mothers' rooms are located on different floors to the nursery, and that the personnel were not increased when the rooming-in was implemented.

We had the impression that the change to rooming-in decreased the nurses' self-esteem. The increased calls from the mothers for support and suggestions on the care of the newborn is not seen by our nurses as qualified work. Several meetings and discussions improved the nurses' attitudes towards intervening in physiological phenomena like the first parent–infant interaction, breast feeding, and other, similar issues. However, much still needs to be done to achieve optimal results.

We felt that knowledge of the potentialities of the newborn would lead to a greater interaction between staff and infant, and so to more gratification for staff, and a better parental/infant relationship. We used the Brazelton Scale (Brazelton, 1973) to evaluate the behavior of the infants in our nursery. After a self-training in the use of the scale of about 1 year, Dr. Roberto Paludetto and two psychologists, Patrizia Rinaldi and Giuseppina Mansi, had 2 weeks of training on reliability with Dr. Elena Frusi, who got the reliability in Boston. We then had the opportunity of working and comparing the methodology with Dr. Fabrizio Ferrari in Modena, Dr. Helen Ross from the University of California in San Diego, and Patricia L. Linn in Cleveland, Ohio. Finally, Dr. Roberto Paludetto recently got the reliability in Boston.

The introduction of the scale in the nursery was first viewed with curiosity, and some of the personnel were rather skeptical about these women with bells and balls working around the rooms. However, the skeptics soon became converts when they realized the amazing abilities of the newborns.

It also appeared that performing the scale is a useful support intervention, and often personnel asked to show parents how their baby could see and follow.

Behavioral Evolution of Jaundiced Newborns

Nurses and doctors indicated that jaundiced infants treated with phototherapy behave differently to other infants. To investigate this, we studied 60 infants selected from the nursery of our university. Criteria for selection were: (a) a healthy uneventful pregnancy; (b) normal spontaneous labor; (c) no medication or anesthesia during delivery; (d) vaginal delivery without complications; (e) single birth; (f) no congenital malformation; (g) Apgar >7 at 5 minutes; (h) full-term infants weighing at least 2500g; (i) breast feeding; and (j) no perinatal complication other than clinically visible jaundice. We evaluated treatment and compared subjects' performance three times: on the 3rd day of life, 24 hours after the first observation, and at 1 month of age (Paludetto, Mansi, Rinaldi, De Curtis, & Ciccimarra, 1983).

Treatment Group (N = 30)

Six hours of phototherapy was the minimum time required to be enrolled in the treatment group, and the infant had to be in the third day of life at the time of the first examination. Phototherapy was administered in the nursery. During the period of the study special blue light was used. Mothers came to the nursery and fed their babies approximately every 3 hours.

Comparison Group (N = 30)

When an infant was identified as a suitable treatment subject, a comparison subject matched for sex, mother's age, and father's profession was chosen. In the comparison group, bilirubin determinations for clinically visible jaundice was performed at the time of the first observation in 16 infants. These subjects had rooming-in after the first 12 hours of life. Table 9 indicates the main characteristics of the two groups.

The scores of the Brazelton examination at the 3rd day of life of the two groups are reported in Table 10. For 6 of the 26 items we found higher values in the comparison group (Wilcoxon's test): inanimate visual, animate visual, visual and auditory, alertness, pull-to-sit, and cuddliness. The first four items belong to the orientation cluster, and, in this cluster, visual items appear to be the most impaired. One item (pull-to-sit) belongs to the motor performance cluster, and one (cuddliness) to the regulation of state cluster. On the 4th day of life, all infants were reexamined. Fourteen infants had terminated phototherapy. The mean lapse of time since suspension of treatment in these infants was 9.9 hrs. (range 2–27.5). The mean length of treatment had been 39 hrs. (range 22–58). We compared these 14 subjects with their 14 matched comparison group sub-

Table 9.   Main Characteristics of the Two Matched Groups of Newborns

	Treatment Group (N=30)		Comparison Group (N=30)	
Male	22		22	
Female	8		8	
Gestational age (mean and range), weeks	39.3	(37–41)	39.2	(37–41)
Birthweight (mean and range), grams	3317	(2520–4170)	3385	(2700–4110)
APGAR score, 1 minute (mean and range)	8.3	(3–10)	7.7	(4–9)
Hours since birth (mean and range)	71	(46–89)	60	(44–73)
Total bilirubinemia at the time of observation (mean and range) mg/100 ml	13.3	(8.4–17.5)	9.6	(3.5–14.3)*
Hours of continuous phototherapy (mean and range)	24	(6–45)		

*In the 16 comparison subjects only where bilirubin level was determined for clinically visible jaundice.

Table 10. Comparison of the 26 Behavioral Items of the Brazelton Scale between the Phototherapy Treated Newborns and Controls (N=30)

Cluster	Item	Phototherapy Group Median (Range)	Control Group Median (Range)
Habituation	Light	6 (3–9)	7 (4–9)
	Rattle	8 (2–9)	6 (2–9)
	Bell	6 (2–9)	7 (2–9)
	Pinprick	3 (2–9)	3 (2–6)
Orientation	Inanimate visual	3 (2–8)	5 (3–8)*
	Inanimate auditory	5 (2–8)	6 (4–9)
	Animate visual	3 (2–7)	5 (3–9)**
	Animate auditory	5 (4–7)	6 (4–7)
	Visual and auditory	4 (2–8)	5 (3–8)***
	Alertness	4 (1–6)	5 (2–8)***
Motor performance	Tonus	6 (2–6)	6 (5–6)
	Maturity	4 (3–8)	5 (3–7)
	Pull-to-sit	5 (1–7)	6 (4–8)**
	Defense	4 (1–8)	5 (1–8)
	Activity	4 (2–5)	4 (3–5)
Range of State	Peak of excitement	3 (2–5)	4 (2–5)
	Rapidity of buildup	2 (1–6)	3 (1–6)
	Irritability	6 (1–6)	6 (1–6)
	Lability of state	4 (1–5)	4 (2–5)
Regulation of state	Cuddliness	4 (3–5)	5 (3–9)**
	Consolability	6 (2–9)	5 (2–9)
	Self-quieting	7 (1–9)	5 (1–8)
	Hand-to-mouth	2 (1–9)	4 (1–9)
Autonomic regulation	Tremors	8 (2–9)	8 (1–9)
	Startles	8 (4–9)	8 (3–9)
	Skin	6 (3–7)	5 (2–7)

*p < 0.05
**p < 0.01
***p < 0.005
Wilcoxon's signed rank test

jects. The comparison infants continued to score better in the orientation cluster and particularly in visual orientation. At 1 month of age, 12 posttreated infants and 12 matched comparison subjects were available for examination. Infants treated with phototherapy still showed significantly poorer performances on two items of orientation. These data resemble those of other groups (Telzrow, Snyder, Tronick, Als, & Brazelton, 1980; Nelson & Horowitz, 1982).

Finally, we compared behavior on the 3rd day of life between 20 comparison subjects whose peak total bilirubin before or at the time of observation was <10 mg/100 ml, and 10 comparison subjects with peak total bilirubin >10 mg/100 ml. The behavior did not differ between the two groups. However, we were dealing with relatively low levels of bilirubinemia. As currently practiced, phototherapy entails separation. Separation is itself a complex variable that means a lack of the normal visual, verbal, and tactile experiences that nonseparated infants are subject to receive. Separation and phototherapy also induced stress in parents and effected interaction with their infants.

Attempt to Minimize the Effect of Phototherapy

Investigation on the poorer performance of infants receiving phototherapy have been limited. In an attempt to ascertain whether covering the eyes accounts for their poorer performance, we evaluated whether an opaque screen over the head of the bassinet (Figure 3), instead of the normal patch, improves the behavioral organization of jaundiced but otherwise healthy term infants treated with phototherapy (Paludetto et al., 1984).

Thirty-eight matched infants were randomly assigned to have a patch or a

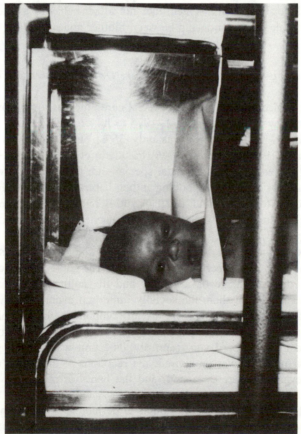

Figure 3.   Screen to cover the eyes of the newborn in phototherapy.

screen. Serum bilirubin at the time of observations was 11.2–17.5 mg/100 ml (x = 13.7, patch) and 9.4–16.4 mg/100 ml (x = 13.4, screen). Nineteen infants of whom eleven were jaundiced (6.2–14.3 mg/100 ml, x = 10.3) served as control subjects. The infants were examined with the Brazelton scale on the 3rd day after birth when the patch subjects had been under blue light from 6 to 45 hrs. (x = 23.9) and the screen subjects from 6 to 61.5 hrs. (x = 22.6).

Our data confirmed the poorer short-term orientation performance of jaundiced infants treated with phototherapy, but do not indicate that covering the eyes with an opaque screen improves behavioral organization. Mothers and nurses did not encounter any difficulties in feeding or taking care of the newborn using the screen method to shield their eyes. On the contrary, they expressed a preference for this method, which permits the newborns to keep their eyes open and their mothers to see the babies eyes throughout treatment.

We think it important to gather more data on other samples, to extend the assessment period, and to investigate the effect of differences in the behavior of jaundiced infants treated with phototherapy on infant–caregiver interaction. It is possible that, although the screen does not affect behavior as measured by the Brazelton scale, the relationship between mother and infant might be affected.

Opening the Neonatal Special Care Unit with Intensive Therapy

The major concern in the neonatal special care unit was to improve the survival of the sick baby. From November 1, 1975 to July 10, 1977, survival of very low birthweight (<1500g.) babies was only 36%, but it improved to 53% from November 1, 1977 to June 30, 1980 (Paludetto et al., 1982).

During the early 1970s, neonatal special care units in Italy were absolutely closed. Parents could be seen looking at their babies through a window. This kind of care seemed to be cruel and, as Klaus and Kennell (1976) suggested, probably iatrogenic. Therefore, we decided to open our neonatal special care unit to the parents.

Many colleagues, and some of the hospital managers, were skeptical about performing such an "experiment" in Naples. The socioeconomic conditions of the town, the percentage of illiteracy, and the cultural background in which friends and neighbors share the socially important event of delivery and, even more, the newborn hospitalization, are all components that promise a traumatic relationship with health care personnel. The high rate of infectious diseases in Naples led us to proceed very carefully. The unit was opened gradually. The problem of infection was monitored, the reactions of the health care personnel and of the parents were evaluated, and the behavior of the newborns was assessed.

In the first period, after a few months of periodical staff meetings, the mother was allowed to enter the intensive care unit only for feeding times, and the father only in the afternoon. No relatives were allowed to enter. Despite this limited

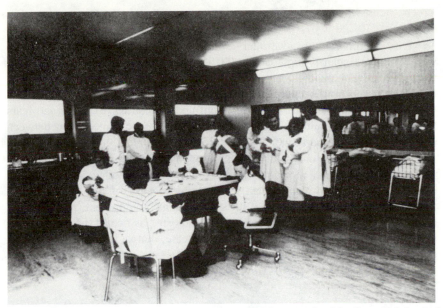

Figure 4.   Group of parents in the neonatal special care unit of the Second School of Medicine in Naples.

"opening," nurses and doctors felt "observed" and not free to do their job. Therefore, we intensified meetings to solve organization and clinical problems. One year later, we established the practice that, with few changes, we follow today.

The father is often the first member of the family to enter our unit. He first speaks with one of the two head nurses who now are involved in the parents' support program, and then he is given a written set of rules governing the unit. The father is required to wear a gown and to carefully wash his hands before touching the baby. The same rules apply to the mother, but she receives more support because of her physical problems and her normally greater involvement in the care of the baby (for example, breast feeding). As other authors have pointed out (Harper et al., 1976), the anxiety upon entering the Unit is naturally very great. The environment and the equipment of intensive therapy are rather frightening at first, but, slowly, with the help of the health care personnel, the anxiety is overcome and it becomes easy for the parents to touch, take care of, and feed their baby, even if it still in incubator.

Many parents integrate so well in the organization of the unit that they can give valuable suggestions to improve our care routines. Sometimes, spontaneous groups develop, thus partially recreating an embryo of the cultural traditions and the sociality that surrounds home delivery and that the hospital has suppressed (Figure 4).

Reactions of Parents to "Opening" the NSCU

To verify our impressions, we interviewed 30 couples of parents of low birth-weight infants (mean 1700g., range 1100–1980) 10 days or later after admission to the NSCU. The main characteristics of the sample are given in Table 11. The interview covers four sections: (a) the pregnancy and the delivery, (b) contact between the couple and the obstetrical staff and structures, (c) needs and fears following the birth, and (d) parent–infant interaction and interaction between parents and medical personnel (Paludetto et al., 1981).

Here we report responses only to the fourth point. To the first question: "What was your first impression of your child?" (Table 12), 13 mothers and 18 fathers said that they had an "unpleasant impression, because of the smallness and frailty of the infant and because of the surroundings" (equipment, phleboclysis, etc.). This confirms what had already been indicated as one of the problems to bear in mind when programming "open" type care, that is, anguish of parents at the sight of their infant and what surrounds it (Harper, Sia, Sokal, & Sokal, 1976; Klaus & Kennel, 1976). However, after the first impact and with help of

Table 11.   Main Characteristics of 30 Couples of Parents of Preterm Infants

		Mothers	Fathers
Age	<20	2	2
	21–25	9	14
	26–30	10	7
	31–35	4	4
	36–40	5	3
Education	Illiterate	1	1
	Elementary school	13	3
	Secondary	5	13
	High school	6	9
	Degree	5	4
Occupation	Unemployed	—	1
	Worker	1	4
	Farm worker	2	2
	Housewife	21	—
	Craftsman	—	5
	Tradesman	—	4
	Office worker	5	11
	Free-lance	1	2
	Entrepreneur	—	1

		Couples
Resident in:	Naples	14
	Province	12
	Other	4

Table 12.   Answers of 30 Couples of Parents of Preterm Infants to the Question: "What Was Your First Impression of the Infant?"

	Mothers	Fathers
Very beautiful	4	2
Nice, sweet	9	7
Small, but nevertheless resembling a member of the family	2	1
General comments (colour of eyes, hair, etc.)	1	2
Unpleasant impression due to smallness, fraility, phleboclysis, equipment	13	18
I did not feel it belonged to me	1	—

the care personnel and of other parents, our subjects are able to cope with the situation quite well.

In fact, 27 mothers and 16 fathers interviewed 10 or more days after admission to the NSCU replied affirmatively to the question: "Have you touched, fondled your child?" Twenty-six mothers and 11 fathers fed the baby, even though it was still in an incubator. The question: "Do you change your child now?" showed that 16 mothers changed the baby, while, up to this point, only very few fathers did so and one of them declared that changing the baby was not his job (Table 13). I would now like to open a parenthesis on the father, because, in our experience and also from the interviews, it is evident that the preterm father's involvement is particularly deep (Figure 5), and that it is very different from that of fathers of healthy newborns (Paludetto et al., 1980). This type of behavior does not correspond to the cultural model of the father in the South of

Table 13.   Answers of 30 Couples of Parents of Preterm Infants to the Question: "Have You Touched, Fondled Your Child?"

	Mothers	Fathers
Yes, immediately	17	13
Yes, after a few days	5	1
Touched for a few seconds	5	2
No	3	14

"Do You Feed It Now?"

	Mothers	Fathers
Yes	26	11
Just once	—	1
No	4	18

"Do You Change It Now?"

	Mothers	Fathers
Yes	16	3
Just Once	—	1
No	14	25
No, It is not my job	—	1

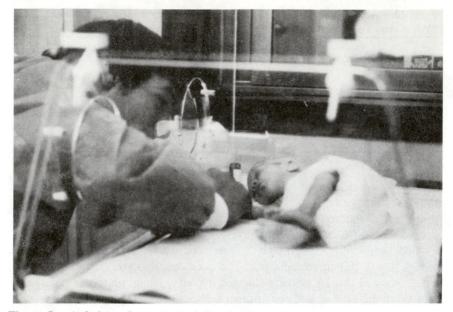

Figure 5.   A father of a preterm infant in the neonatal special care unit of the Second School of Medicine in Naples.

Italy. In fact, the rule is that the mother, often with two grandmothers, takes care of the baby. The father is often excluded from this activity, as though the mother would like to have the prerogative of caring for the baby.

It is possible that this unusual paternal behavior of our fathers occurs because they are the first family member to enter the unit and they inform the mother of the infant's progress when she is unable to come, and/or because other members of the family are excluded from the unit.

Many fathers expressed their satisfaction at having had the possibility to take care of their baby, and some others during clinical follow-up reported that in that period they felt important and indispensable to their baby.

Parents generally achieved a good relationship with the staff, and, to the question: "What is most reassuring in the unit?", the most frequent reply was the medical and nursing staff, their willingness to listen, and their availability 24 hours a day.

We had the impression that the mothers were more involved in the care of their babies than were mothers in some units visited in the United States. Unlike Dell' Antonio, Rosini, Argese, and Lombardi, (1979), who investigated a traditional unit with very restricted parental visits, we did not observe in our subjects any progressive decline of interest in the baby towards the time of discharge from the NSCU (Paludetto, Dell' Antonio, De Curtis, De Vito, & De Vita, 1983). Confirmation of this comes from the frequency of parents' visits to our NSCU. Ninety-eight couples of parents were interviewed by the social worker upon discharge from the Unit. Only one couple had never seen the baby before discharge. Ninety percent of the mothers and fathers entered the unit at least once a day. Thirty-four percent of the mothers, and 11.5% of the fathers, saw their baby at least four times a day. The mean duration of the visits was between 30 and 60 minutes for the majority of our parents. For 30% of the mothers and 16% of the fathers, the mean duration was more than 1 hour (Paludetto et al., 1982). The frequency of visits is clearly very intense. Ninety percent of the babies are inborns, and, hence, during the first days of hospitalization, most of the mothers are still in the obstetrical division. However, the intensity of visits remains high, even after the mother has been discharged from hospital, and parents often make long, arduous journeys to see their babies.

Neonatologists

The neonatologists in our department greeted the new "open" policy with various degrees of enthusiasm, and they gradually integrated into the new system. In fact, 9 out of 15 had a good relationship with fathers, and 12 of 15 with mothers, while such valid relation has not been found with the mothers and fathers of healthy-term newborns (Asprea et al., 1978).

Health Care Personnel

Our health care personnel deserves particular consideration. They bear the major burden of opening the unit to the parents. Health care personnel have a 24-hour contact with parents, and, generally speaking, parents feel more free to express their anxieties and perplexities to the nurses rather than to the neonatologist. Nurses provide support to worried parents and serve to contain their anguish.

To evaluate the reactions of health care personnel to the "open" policy, we interviewed 30 of the 34 nurses on rolls (Paludetto, Faggiano-Perfetto, Asprea, De Curtis, & Margara-Paludetto, 1982). The main characteristics are reported in Table 14. All the subjects interviewed gave an affirmative answer to the first question: "Are you sure about the usefulness of allowing mothers into the Unit?" (Table 15). The following reasons were given: it establishes a better relationship with the child, and mothers may feed their child and mothers help health care personnel. Twenty-five agreed on the usefulness of the father's presence, and for the reasons somewhat similar to those listed above. Three subjects pointed out the help and support the father can give the mother, and six subjects maintained that the father "should be involved." On the whole, the presence of parents in the unit is considered useful but, differences arise regarding restrictions of visiting times. Data on suggested restrictions for mothers and fathers, and the relative

Table 14. Main Characteristics of Health Care Personnel in the Neonatal Intensive Care Unit

		N=30
Age	20–25	15
	26–29	10
	30–35	2
	36–39	3
Marital status	Married	4
	Unmarried	25
	Divorced	1
Children	0	26
	1	2
	2	2
Resident in:	Naples	24
	Province	6
	Other	—

Table 15. Answers of Health Care Personnel of an "Open" Neonatal Intensive Care Unit to the Questions:

"Are You Sure About the Usefulness of Allowing Mother into the Unit?"

	N=30
Yes	30

"If So, Why?"

The mother accepts her child better	22
For breast feeding and for the good of the child	2
For the good of the child	4
To help health care personnel	2

"Are You Sure About the Usefulness of Allowing Father in the Unit?"

	N=30
Yes	25
Less sure in comparison with the mother	3
Not always	1
No	1

"If So, Why?"

	N=29
To establish a good relationship with child	20
The father should be involved	6
To support the mother	3

Table 16.   Answers of Health Care Personnel of a Neonatal Special Care Unit to the Questions:

For the Mothers
"Would You Restrict the Admittance of the Parents to the Unit?"

	N=30
Yes	15
No	15

"If So, How?"

Admittance at feeding time only	11
Depending on routine work	2
Not during the night	2

"Why Would You Place Such Restrictions?"

	N=15
Mothers often fuss and interfere with personnel's work	8
Mothers easily get upset	2
Admittance during the day is sufficient	2
Mothers gossip, criticize and control the work of the unit	2
Mothers get too attached to their children	1

For the Fathers
"Would You Restrict the Admittance of the Parents to the Unit?"

	N=30
Yes	25
No	5

"If So, How?"

	N=25
Admittance at feeding time only	6
Prefixed times (from 1 to 3 times a day)	16
Between feeding times	3

"Why Would You Place Such Restrictions?"

	N=25
Fathers interfere with personnel's work	12
Fathers are not so important as mothers	4
Mothers may not feel at ease when they feed the baby	2
Fathers get bored	2
Fathers gossip and control the work of the unit	1
Fathers are easily upset	1
Fathers get too attached to their children	1
I do not know	2

motivations, are reported in Table 16. Half of the subjects did not suggest any restrictions for the mother, while, of the other half, 11 suggested letting mothers in during feeding time only; two during the day only; one always, except during therapy; and one depending on routine work in the unit. The reasons for such restrictions are the following: mothers may hamper work routines and cause confusion; they may hamper the work of the unit, criticize, or gossip.

Greater restrictions were suggested for the fathers. In fact, 25 nurses would limit the father's presence. It is difficult to find the motivation underlying these replies. Certainly, stress and hard work (Marshall et al., 1982), together with the feeling of being watched, play a big role. The fear of making mistakes, and the competitive role with the parents, can be an important issue. Our findings have been discussed in small groups, and nurses have gradually become more able to deal with difficult situations. Two doctors are on call 24 hours a day to discuss problems, immediately when necessary, and to back up the nurses when necessary.

Finally, and this is important, in accordance with the experience at other units which started this policy, there was no increase in the rate of infection as a result of "opening" the Unit (De Curtis et al., 1979; De Curtis, 1980).

Perception and Feeling about the Preterm Infant

The interpersonal relationship is one of the most difficult aspects of the work of NSCU personnel, but it can also be one of the most gratifying. It is interesting, therefore, to ask what kind of relationship the personnel can have with the preterm infant, who is believed to have a very limited ability to interact with the environment.

In reply to the question: "Aesthetically, what is a preterm infant like?" (Table 17) most subjects said he or she is "nice," and there were no negative remarks about the smallness and fraility of the child when compared to full-term infants. To the following question: "Do you think a preterm infant is aware of what is happening around him?", "Can he see?", "Can he hear?", 22 of the caregivers believed that the infant is aware of the environment; 25 answered that he or she can hear, while only 12 think he or she can also see (Paludetto et al., 1982).

The difference noted between the infant's auditory and visual capabilities is interesting. During intensive care, the newborn seems to react more to sounds than to changes in illumination or to the appearance of faces. Reactions to frequent noises, such as the shutting of incubator panels, or to bangs on the incubator during emergencies, are fairly obvious, while it is necessary to focus attention very carefully on the infants' eyes to note any change in vision. On the other hand, however, the difference in these sensory capabilities was confirmed with the Brazelton scale (Paludetto, Rinaldi, Mansi, Andolfi, & Del Giudice,

Table 17. Answers of Health Care Personnel of an "Open" Neonatal Special Care Unit to the Questions:

	N=30
"Aesthetically What is a Preterm Newborn Like?"	
Nice	17
Nicer than the fullterm newborn	1
Some are nice, some are not	2
Just like any other newborn	2
Rather small	2
Ugly, but only at birth	2
Rather ugly	4
"Do You Think a Preterm Infant is Aware of What is Happening Around Him?"	
Yes	18
Hazily, in his own way	2
Not immediately, maybe later	1
Some are, Some are not	1
No	8
"Can He See?"	
Yes	11
Hazily	1
Maybe	2
I do not know	1
No	15
"Can He Hear?"	
Yes	23
A little	2
No	5

1984). This kind of knowledge of the personnel is important and can be very useful if shared with the parents.

Table 18 reports the answers to the question: "Does the preterm newborn realize that he is petted?", 27 caregivers replied affirmatively. The other question in Table 18 regards the caregiver–preterm newborn relationship more directly: "Do you talk to the preterm baby?" and if so, "do you think he can respond?", all subjects spoke to the infant, and, more important, 90% maintained that the infant is in some way capable of answering. To the question, "In your opinion, does the preterm infant suffer?", all subjects answered that he or she does and some indicated the cause of suffering, i.e., treatment and diagnostic procedures.

To the question: "Does the preterm newborn need affection?" all subjects answered affirmatively and frequently added, "He needs more love than other

Table 18. Answers of Health Care Personnel of An "Open" Neonatal Special Care Unit To the Questions:

	N=30
"Does the Preterm Newborn Realize That He is Petted?"	
Yes	24
Yes, Indeed	3
No	3
"Do You Talk to the Preterm Newborn?"	
Yes	21
Very much	1
A little, sometimes	7
I communicate without speaking	1
"If So, Do You Think He Can Respond?"	
Yes, indeed	22
In his own way, yes	4
Sometimes	1
I do not know	1
No	2
"Do You Think a Preterm Suffers?"	
Yes	29
More Than Other Newborns	1
"Do You Think the Preterm Newborn Need Love?"	
Yes	18
More than other newborns	11
Like all others	1

newborns." The awareness of caregivers regarding the infant's response to their behavior increases the interaction between caregiver and infant. This aspect can help to avoid burn-out in NSCU staff, and it can help the staff in their day-to-day work of supporting parents.

Early Behavioral Development of Preterm Infants

Our new "open" policy demanded a better knowledge of the behavioral development of preterm infants. This would help us in structuring programs and enable us to inform nurses and parents about the behavior of preterm infant at different postconceptional ages.

Behavioral studies had focused primarily on isolated sensory and motor behaviors, and it was not known whether the behavior of preterm infants progresses smoothly in each area towards full-term behavior, or how the various areas interrelated.

The Brazelton Neonatal Behavior Assessment Scale (Brazelton, 1973) was used to evaluate the early development of behavior among 30 preterm infants from 35 to 44 weeks postconceptional age (Paludetto et al., 1984). The infants were chosen from our Unit between January 1979 and October 1981. Criteria for inclusion in the study were: (a) gestational age less than 35 weeks; (b) birthweight appropriate for gestational age (according to Lubchenco, Hansman, Dressler, & Boyd, 1983); (c) not a multiple birth; (d) gestational age in agreement with clinical evaluation, performed by the method of Dubowitz, Dubowitz, & Goldberg (1970); (e) no malformation; (f) no mechanical ventilation; (g) no convulsion or other abnormal neurological signs for more than 4 days; (h) maximum total bilirubinemia below 16 mg/100 ml; and (i) breathing room air at the time of observation. The main characteristic of the 30 infants are shown in Table 19.

At 35 weeks the Brazelton evaluation of 28 infants was performed in the unit, and two were evaluated in the follow-up clinic; at 38 weeks, 13 were evaluated in the unit and 17 in the follow-up clinic; and at 40 and 44 weeks, all the infants were evaluated in the follow-up clinic.

For description of data, we used the conceptual organization of items into the clusters indicated by Lester, Als, Brazelton (1982). We also analyzed the changes with age of single items (see Table 20). Moreover, we used the raw data rather than recoded data, because we were interested in the direction of the performance (e.g., hypotonic or hypertonic), even for the seven items for which Lester and colleagues suggest that extremes in both directions be given the same score (tonus, activity, peak of excitement, rapidity of build-up, irritability, lability of state, skin). We considered all the behavioral items of the BNBAS, except the

Table 19.   Main Characteristics of the 30 Preterm Infants Considered in the Study

Boys	17
Girls	13
Gestational Age (W.) (Average and Range)	20.7 (27–34)
Birthweight (G.) (Average and Range)	1545 (750–2020)
Type of Delivery Spontaneous	23
Cesarean section	4
Vacuum extraction	3
APGAR score on 5 min (average and range)	7.4 (1–10)
Total maximum bilirubinema mg./100 ml (average and range)	11.9 (7.2–15.9)
Hours of continual phototherapy (average and range)	126 (24–264) (27 subjects)
Days in Incubator (average and range)	37.1 (14–70) (29 subjects)
Days in unit (average and range)	46.5 (23–76)

Table 20.   Median Scores on Brazelton Examination Items of 30 Preterm Infants at Different Postconceptual Age

Scale Items	35 Weeks		38 Weeks		40 Weeks		44 Weeks	
ORIENTATION:								
Inanimate visual	3	(1–7)	4	(2–7)	4	(2–8)	6	(3–9)***
Inanimate auditory	6	(3–8)	6	(3–7)	5.5	(3–8)	6	(4–8)
Animate visual	3	(1–7)	3	(2–6)	4.5	(2–7)	5	(2–8)***
Animate auditory	5	(3–7)	6	(3–7)	6	(4–7)	6	(4–8)
Animate visual and auditory	3	(1–7)	4	(3–6)	5	(2–8)	5	(2–9)***
Alertness	3	(2–7)	4	(2–6)	5	(2–8)	5	(2–8)***
MOTOR:								
Tonus	5	(3–6)	6	(4–6)	6	(4–7)	6	(5–7)***
Maturity	3	(2–5)	3.5	(2–7)	4	(2–6)	4	(2–6)**
Pull-to-sit	3	(2–7)	5	(3–8)	5.5	(3–8)	6.5	(4–8)***
Defense	5	(1–8)	6	(2–8)	6	(1–8)	6.5	(4–8)**
Activity	4	(2–7)	4	(1–7)	5	(1–9)	5	(3–8)**
RANGE OF STATE:								
Peak of excitement	4	(3–7)	7	(4–8)	7	(3–8)	7	(3–8)**
Rapidity of buildup	3	(1–8)	5	(1–8)	5.5	(1–8)	4	(1–7)
Irritability	2.5	(1–7)	5	(1–7)	4.5	(1–9)	4	(1–8)*
Lability of state	3	(1–7)	4	(1–6)	4	(1–6)	3	(1–7)
REGULATION OF STATE:								
Cuddliness	4	(3–7)	4	(3–7)	4	(4–6)	5	(2–6)***
Consolability	7	(2–9)	7	(2–9)	6	(2–9)	7	(2–8)
Self-quieting	9	(3–9)	5.5	(2–9)	5	(1–9)	6.5	(2–9)***
Hand-to-mouth	1	(1–7)	1	(1–8)	1	(1–8)	1	(1–7)
AUTONOMIC STABILITY:								
Tremors	3	(1–9)	4	(1–8)	4	(1–8)	1	(1–7)
Startles	3.5	(2–8)	2	(2–6)	2.5	(2–7)	3	(2–8)
Skin	5	(2–6)	5	(2–6)	4.5	(2–6)	2	(2–7)

*p < 0.05
**p < 0.01
***p < 0.001 (Friedman Test)

decrement items, which in many cases could not be evaluated, particularly at 40 and 44 weeks. In particular, it was difficult to start the examination in the follow-up clinic with the infant in a sleep state, and, when it was possible, they frequently changed from one state to another, making it impossible to administer these items. However, of the 22 items analyzed, 13 showed a statistically significant variability with postconceptional age (Table 20).

Orientation

Changes suggesting improvement with increasing postconceptional age were found in four of six items: inanimate visual, animate visual, auditory, and alertness. However, we did not find a similar trend for auditory responses; response to a rattle was high at 35 weeks and remained essentially the same up to 44 weeks postconceptional age. Response to a voice followed the same pattern.

Motor

Scores for all five items suggested improvement with postconceptional age. For the tonus item, it appeared that hypotonic scores diminished with increasing age, and for the activity item there was a trend towards more activity with increasing age.

Range of State

For the peak of excitement item, an overall increase in the amount of motor and crying activity was observed during the whole examination as postconceptional age increased. A similar trend was observed for irritability.

Regulation of State

In this cluster, we did not test the cuddliness item at 35 weeks on 13 infants in incubators, because it was not considered safe to remove them. The other 17 infants showed improvement in response to being cuddled by the examiner, or held upon her shoulder, with increasing postconceptional age. The consolability item measures the number of the examiner's activities necessary to interrupt a fussing state and to induce the baby into a quieter state. The examiner intervenes if the infant has been actively fussing or crying for 15 seconds. It was not possible to score this item for 13 infants at 35 weeks, five at 38 and 40 weeks, and six at 44 weeks, because they did not become sufficiently upset during the examination. With this limitation, however, no difference in this item was found with increasing postconceptional age.

The self-quieting item measures the baby's activities in a fussing state which are observable efforts to quiet himself. Success is measured by a state change lasting for at least 5 seconds. We found a statistically significant change with increasing age, but in the opposite direction: scores decreased with age. However, this may be explained by the fact that our infants frequently did not become very upset during the examination, particularly at 35 weeks. For the hand-to-mouth item, all the infants had very low scores at each examination.

Autonomic Stability

No statistically significant change was seen in this cluster with increasing post-conceptional age.

There was a general trend for the BNBAS clusters to progress from 35 to 44 weeks postconceptional age. On the whole, the motor performance and orientation clusters showed better behavioral evolution than other clusters. In the orientation cluster we found a statistically significant improvement with age in animate and inanimate visual responses. We compared our findings with data collected previously for healthy-term infants (Paludetto et al., 1982); our preterm infants at 40 to 44 weeks postconceptional age scored on visual responses in the medium range of term infants. With regard to auditory orientation, our preterm infants' scores on the inanimate and animate auditory items were in the same range as those of our healthy-term infants from 35 weeks postconceptional age, which suggests that this behavior is well established early in life (Parmelee, 1981). In the regulation of state cluster there was very little ability to bring the hands to the mouth between 35 to 44 weeks. This was not so with our term infants (Paludetto et al., 1982). One of the reasons for this difference could be the posture of term babies in an incubator.

Moreover, the preterm infant is often restricted in movement by respiratory or other intensive therapy, which does not favor bringing the hand to the mouth (Figure 6). These considerations and other recent results which suggest the usefulness of nonnutritive sucking (Bernbaum, Pereira, & Watkins, 1983; Field, Ignatoff, & Stringer, 1982), induced us to study the relationship between sucking and respiration. It appeared the nonnutritive sucking does not decrease oxygena-

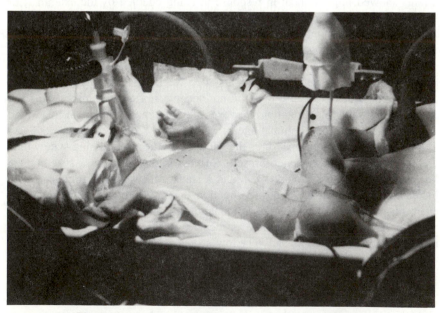

Figure 6.   A preterm infant during assisted ventilation.

tion, but, on the contrary, provides a modest increase in infants between 32 and 35 weeks postconceptional age (Paludetto, Robertson, Hack, Shivpuri, & Martin, 1984).

One of our most interesting observations is the lack of coherence in the behavioral evolution of preterm infants. Some features develop faster than others; this is particularly evident for auditory compared with visual responses. We need to understand better how and why different brain functions do not mature simultaneously in those young infants, and what the implications are for optimal social interaction with the caregiver.

These studies suggest that the infant is able to respond from an early age to auditory communication. Moreover, they indicate the usefulness of nonnutritive sucking, and, hence, should encourage postures that can facilitate bringing the hand to the mouth.

Conclusions

In summary, the changes introduced at the Second School of Medicine of Naples intended to achieve a greater humanization of neonatal care have been appreciated by parents and by the majority of the health care personnel.

The health care personnel working in the Neonatal Special Care Unit accepted these changes better than personnel working in the nursery. This difference between personnel working with healthy and those working with sick newborns can be attributed to various causes. The longer stay in hospital permits a greater interrelationship between parents and staff. The work in intensive care unit is more stressing but requires more motivated and specialized caregivers. Last but not least, physicians focused particularly on the care of the sick newborn. The behavior evaluation of the newborn contributes to understanding the abilities of the newborn, and also serves to stimulate the interaction of personnel and parents with the baby.

We did not have any great organizational difficulties, and fears that the Neapolitan parents were not "prepared" for these changes turned out to be unfounded.

Unfortunately, in Italy, these "new routines" are not yet generalized. However, we hope that, following our experience and those of other units, this policy will soon become the normal rule for our hospitals.

References

Asprea, A.M., Faggiano-Perfetto, M., Orzalesi, M., & Paludetto, R. (1978). Problematiche relazionali nell'ambito dell'assistenza perinatale. Risultati preliminari di un'Indagine sugli Operatori Sanitari (Ostetrici e Neonatologi). *Rivista Italiana di Pediatria, 4,* 531–569.

Bernbaum, J.C., Pereira, G.R., & Watkins, J.B. (1983). Nonnutritive sucking during gavage feedings enhances growth and maturation in premature infants. *Pediatrics, 71,* 41–45.

Bertulessi, C., Bevilacqua, G., Rossi, A., Caccamo, M.L., Corchia, C., Cortinovis, I., Cuttini, M., DeMattia, D., De Scrilli, A., Mansani, F.E., Paludetto, R., Stormi, M., Vegni, C., Zuliani, G., & Zuppa, A.A. (1983). L'Indagine Perinatale (Rapporto no 2). Consiglio Nazionale delle Ricerche. Indagine Progetto Finalizzato di Medicina Preventiva. Sub Progetto Medicina Preventiva Perinatale MPPI. Ricerca Policentrica Ostetrico-Pediatrica. Il Pensiero Scientifico (Ed.) Roma.

Brazelton, T.B. (1973). *Neonatal Behavioral Assessment Scale* (Clinics in developmental medicine No. 50). London: S.I.M.P.

Cesa Bianchi, M. (1979). Orientamenti attuali nella metodologia psicologica. *Totus Homo, 2,* 2.

De Curtis, M., Galasso, V., Barone, R., Cipollone, I., Di Mita, U., Paludetto, R., & Orzalesi, M. (1979). Incidenza, mortalità ed eziologia dell sepsi batteriche in un Reparto di Patologia Neonatale nel biennio 1976–77. *Rivista Italiana di Pediatria, 5,* 73–80.

De Curtis, M. (1980). Lettera al direttore. *Rivista Italiana di Pediatria, 6*(2), 270.

Dell'Antonio, A., Rosini, M.P., Argese, G., & Lombardi, F. (1979). Prematurità come fattore di disturbo nel rapporto madre-bambino. *Età Evolutiva, 4,* 69.

Dubowitz, L., Dubowitz, V., & Goldberg, C. (1970). Clinical assessment of gestational age in the newborn infant. *Journal of Pediatrics, 77,* 1.

Field, T., Ignatoff, E., Stringer, S. (1982). Nonnutritive sucking during tube feedings: effects on preterm neonates in a NICU. *Pediatrics, 70,* 374–381.

Galtung, J. (1967). *Theory and methods of social research.* London: Allen-Unwin.

Harper, R., Sia, C., Sokal, S., & Sokal, M. (1976). Observations on unrestricted parental contact with infants in the Neonatal Intensive Care Unit. *Journal of Pediatrics, 89*(3), 441.

Klaus, M.H., & Kennel, J.H. (1976). *Maternal–infant bonding.* St. Louis, MO: Mosby Co.

Klaus, M.H., & Kennel, J.H. (1982). *Parent–infant bonding.* St. Louis, MO: Mosby Co.

Lester, B.M., Als, H., & Brazelton, T.B. (1982). Regional obstetric anesthesia and newborn behavior: a re-analysis towards synergetic effects. *Child Development, 53,* 687–692.

Lubchenco, L., Hansman, C., Dressler, M., & Boyd, E. (1963). Intrauterine growth as estimated from liveborn birth weight data at 24 and 42 weeks of gestation. *Pediatrics, 32,* 193.

Marshall, R.E., Kasman, C., & Cape, L.S. (1982). Coping with caring for sick newborns. Philadelphia, PA: W.B. Saunders Co.

Mastropasqua, S., Esposito, D., Mazzarella, V., Budetta, L., Pugliese, A., Paludetto, R., & Rubino, A. (1980). Effetti di un parziale rooming-in sull'incidenza dell'allattamento al seno. *Rivista di Pediatria Sociale, 30*(4), 459–461.

Nelson, C.A., & Horowitz, F.D. (1982). The short-term behavioral sequelae of neonatal jaundice treated with phototherapy. *Infant Behavior and Development, 5,* 389–399.

Paludetto, R. (1977). Rapporti interpersonali nell'ambito dell'assistenza perinatale [Editoriale]. *Rivista Italiana di Pediatria, 3,* 431–436.

Paludetto, R., Faggiano-Perfetto, M., Asprea, A.M., Margara-Paludetto, P., & De Luca, T. (1980). Il parto in ospedale visto dagli utenti. *Rivista Italiana di Pediatria, 6,* 595–601.

Paludetto, R., Palazzo, C., Margara-Paludetto, P., De Curtis, M., Scarcella, A., & Ciccimarra, F. (1981). Effetti dell'informazione e del supporto nei primi giorni dopo il parto sulla frequenza dell'allattamento al seno. *Rivista Italiana di Pediatria, 7,* 527 A.

Paludetto, R., Faggiano-Perfetto, M., Asprea, A.M., De Curtis, M., & Margara-Paludetto, P. (1981). Reactions of 60 parents allowed unrestricted contact with infants in a Neonatal Intensive Care Unit. *Early Human Development, 5,* 401–409.

Paludetto, R., Faggiano-Perfetto, M., Asprea, A.M., De Curtis, M., & Margara-Paludetto, P. (1982). Accettazione dell'introduzione del rooming-in diurno da parte del personale paramedico. *Rivista Italiana di Pediatria, 2,* 159–162.

Paludetto, R., Taurisano, M., Del Giudice, G., Andolfi, M., De Curtis, M., Cascioli, C.F., Rinaldi, P., Mansi, G., Magli, A., & Ciccimarra, F. (1982). Evoluzione nel tempo della prognosi immediata ed a distanza nel neonato di peso alla nascita <1500g. *Rivista Italiana di Pediatria, 8,* 532.

Paludetto, R., Margara-Paludetto, P., Tasco, M.C., Rinaldi, P., Mansi, G., Ariola, P., De Curtis, M., & Ciccimarra, F. (1982). Visite dei genitori al neonato ricoverato in un Centro di Terapia Intensiva Neonatale. *Rivista Italiana di Pediatria, 8,* 607–608.

Paludetto, R., Faggiano-Perfetto, M., Asprea, A.M., De Curtis, M., Margara-Paludetto, P. (1982). Attitudes of health care personnel of an "open" Neonatal Intensive Care Unit towards parents and preterm infants. *Rivista Italiana di Pediatria, 8,* 279–285.

Paludetto, R., Mansi, G., Rinaldi, P., De Curtis, M., Corchia C., De Luca, T., & Andolfi, M. (1982). Behavior of preterm newborns reaching term without any serious disorder. *Early Human Development, 6,* 357–363.

Paludetto, R., Dell'Antonio, A., De Curtis, M., De Vito, P., De Vita, G. (1983). Evolution of mother-infant relationship in an open Neonatal Intensive Care Unit. Comparison with a traditional Unit. *Rivista Italiana di Pediatria, 9,* 27–33.

Paludetto, R., Mansi, G., Rinaldi, P., De Curtis, M., & Ciccimarra, F. (1983). The behavior of jaundiced infants treated with phototherapy. *Early Human Development, 8,* 259–267.

Paludetto, R., Rinaldi, P., Mansi, G., Andolfi, M., & Del Giudice, G. (1984). Early behavioral development of preterm infants. *Developmental Medicine & Child Neurology, 26,* 347–352.

Paludetto, R., Robertson, S.S., Hack, M., Shivpuri, C., & Martin, R. (1984). Transcutaneous oxygen tension during nonnutritive sucking in preterm infants. *Pediatrics, 74,* 539–542.

Paludetto, R., Mansi, G., Rinaldi, P., Saporito, M., De Curtis, M., & Ciccimarra, F. (1984). Effects of different ways of covering the eyes on behavior of jaundiced infants in phototherapy. *Biology of the Neonate, 4,* 1–8.

Paludetto, R. (1984). Epidemiologia e promozione dell'allattamento al seno. In G. Bucci,

M. Mendicini, & G. Marzetti (Eds.), *Neonatologia*. Roma, Italy: Il Pensiero Scientifico.

Parmelee, A.H. (1981). Auditory function and neurological maturation in preterm infants. In S.L. Friedman & A. Sigman (Eds.), *Preterm birth and development*. New York: Academic Press.

Telzrow, R.W., Snyder, D.M., Tronick, E., Als, H., & Brazelton, T.B. (1980). The behavior of jaundiced infants undergoing phototherapy. *Developmental Medicine and Child Neurology, 22*, 317–126.

CHAPTER 9

Newborn Behavior and Development in Indonesia*

Patricia W. Piessens

Boston University School of Nursing

Our understanding of the many factors that influence behavior and development of neonates is incomplete. Current knowledge of this topic is derived from anthropological, psychological, nursing, and medical studies on middle-class infants in developed countries, mainly because they are readily accessible as study subjects. However, as is stated by Goldberg (1972), in order to make generalizations about the infant population of the world, it is imperative that the behavior of infants of other cultures be studied. Only then will it become possible to determine which variables universally affect infant behavior, and which ones are unique to a given culture.

Lester and Brazelton (1980) proposed a psychobiological model for the cross-cultural study of the organization of infant behavior. According to this model, neonate behavior reflects the phenotypic expression of the interplay between genetic (presumably universal), and environmental (presumably culturally specific), variables. To test the validity of this model, we studied newborn behavior in Indonesia using a method designed to evaluate the effects of prenatal, delivery, and birth variables on behavior, Brazelton's Neonatal Behavioral Assessment Scale (BNBAS; Brazelton, 1973).

The aim of our study was to obtain normative behavioral data on a homogeneous native Asian population, carefully controlling for optimal intrauterine and perinatal experiences. This information was then used to determine whether the behavioral characteristics of normal Indonesian neonates, as measured by the

---

* This study was supported (in part) through funds provided by the Department of Health and Human Services, Public Health Service, Health Services Administration: Bureau of Community Health Services, Project 101.

BNBAS, are similar to those reported for normative samples of Caucasian infants.

Indonesia: Its Geography, History, People, Economics, Health

Indonesia consists of 13,000 islands stretching more than 3,000 miles across the equator, lying entirely within the tropics. Its climate is determined by the rainfall, and this, in turn, is governed by two predominant trade winds. From a geological point of view, Indonesia is a restless area with almost daily volcanic eruptions and minor earthquakes shocks.

Where an adequate water supply, or irrigation, exists, rice is grown. The *sawah* (wet rice cultivation) is the most intensive form of agriculture and coincides with the greatest density of population. Apart from petroleum reserves, which are estimated at 10 billion tons, Indonesia is moderately rich in minerals. Against these resources stands an unevenly distributed population of approximately 151 million concentrated in the fertile areas, sometimes reaching a density of 5,000 people per square mile (in Jakarta, for example). About 65% of the inhabitants live on Java.

The sea has determined the nature of Indonesian history. It separated the islands and gave each one the opportunity to develop its own character. Hence, there are immense differences among the 350 ethnic groups in terms of language and customs. Indonesia was finally recognized as an independent state in 1949 after years of bitter struggle with the Dutch (Tas, 1974). Java has, over a period of 1500 years, seen Indians, Arabs, Chinese, Portuguese, and Dutch come and go. It has one of the world's densest population and a high development of the arts.

Indonesia's health situation and problems are similar to those of other Third World countries: high infant and child mortality rates, parasitic diseases, communicable diseases, malnutrition, poor sanitary and environmental conditions, illiteracy, and poverty. Health centers, polyclinics, maternal and child health clinics, private practitioners, and indigenous healers are the sources of health care. Utilization studies of government health services in rural areas show that one-third of the "felt need" of the population is being met (Maglacas, Hammad, & Djojoingto, 1976), even though only 2.8% of the general government expenditure was on health in the early 1970s.

Statistical health data obtained from 1961 to 1971 show that there were approximately 627,000 deaths among infants less than 1 year old, and another 335,000 deaths among children ages 1–5. Infant mortality rate is estimated at about 140 per 100 live births. In 1972, the child mortality rate was estimated at about 215 per 1,000 children ages 1–4. These compare to rates in the United States of 12 and 70, respectively. Similarly, maternal mortality rates are significantly higher than those found in the West. Estimated rates vary between 50 and

800 deaths per 100,000 live births, as compared to 5–20 in Western nations (United Nations Fund for Population Activities, 1979). UNICEF has estimated that about 30% of the children under the age of 6 suffer from chronic moderate calorie malnutrition, and that 3% have *kwashiorkor* or *maramus*. In addition, iron, iodine, and Vitamin A deficiencies have been reported.

Traditional Customs of Childbearing in Indonesia

Ritual Protections for Infants. The Javanese see development to maturity as a series of stages of steadily decreasing vulnerability to attack or entry by evil spirits. A person who is psychologically whole can withstand the onslaught, but the defenses of an infant or child are still undeveloped. The fetus is said to be "mediating spiritual matters" (*tapa,* the mystic's withdrawal from the world), fasting, and going without sleep within "the cave of his mother's womb for 9 months in preparation for his emergence into the disturbing world." While this is the period of highest vulnerability, especially the first 7 months, the period immediately following birth is not much safer. The first 5 days, until the umbilical cord stump falls off, and the *pasaran* ritual meals, at which infants are given a name, are the most dangerous. For the next 30 days, infants are kept in the house to deter various evil spirits from entry. The next recognized stage is marked by the seventh-month *slametan,* or ritual meal, at which the child is allowed to touch the ground for the first time. Prior to this ritual, children are vulnerable to spirits which find it particularly easy to enter people through their feet.

If this happens to children it is called *sawanen.* The symptoms range from nightmares and hysterical weeping, to extreme lassitude and sickness, to convulsions, in short, any inexplicable childhood disease. Additional protection against *sawanen* is provided by a salve made of crushed onion mixed with coconut paste. This is applied on the fontanel (another extremely vulnerable port of entry for spirits) every day for the first 35 days after birth and whenever needed during the next 6 months. This salve, called *pupuk lempujang,* is a symbol of infancy.

Traditional Customs of Pregnancy and Childbirth. A Javanese woman with many children is envied; a barren woman is pitied. At the first sign of pregnancy, women desire extremely peppery food, *rudjak.* This is served in beverage form to neighbors and friends at the ritual meal celebrating the seventh month of pregnancy. Even Javanese who do not follow the animistic ritual meal observance will not omit serving *rudjak* at the seventh month, though they serve it casually.

Even though the series of ritual meals are the best safeguards against dangers to mother and fetus, other taboos are observed to prevent two great dangers: a difficult birth and a deformed baby. Therefore, the mother should not eat certain foods, for example sugar cane, or at birth "the baby will start to come out, stop, start again, and stop." *Kepel,* a fruit with lines running horizontally, is avoided because, if eaten, the baby will be born sideways. One of the shadow puppet plays, *Wayang,* is about the birth of Ganesha, the god with the head of an elephant, whose mother was frightened by an elephant when pregnant.

Besides observing the pregnancy taboos, the husband shares responsibility in the birth process. The traditional family calls in a *dukun baji,* or midwife to whom knowledge of magic has been transmitted by an older woman. A mat is spread on the floor or wide-sized bench, and the wife sits on it. The husband sits behind his wife, supporting her between his legs as she leans back straining to push her baby out. The midwife says the proper magical spells for the protection of the paturient woman and baby, and firmly massages the woman's legs, thighs, and abdomen.

If labor is difficult, the mother-to-be is encouraged to chew a paste of young banana leaf and salt; this mixture is then drawn down her body from the center of her chest to the vagina. At this point, she also can ask pardon from her husband. This "begging the pardon" of relatives in situations of extreme distress has, according to Geertz (1961), the purpose of restoring the relationship. Equilibrium and calmness of mind in facing pain will come with its restoration.

After the baby is born, the midwife waits for the descent of the placenta before cutting the umbilical cord, as it is the supernatural "younger brother" of the baby. Together with the spirit of the amniotic fluid, which is seen as the "older brother," it will mysteriously guard the individual through his or her lifetime. These two spirits are called upon frequently in spells and prayers. Cutting the child free is a magical, delicate task, performed only by the midwife with a special bamboo knife. Turmeric is then rubbed on the stub of the umbilical cord. The placenta is buried in a traditionally prescribed manner outside the door, and further incantations are made by the midwife so that the power of afterbirth will be kept under control and not cause sickness to the infant.

An important difference between the traditional birth attendant, the *dukun baji,* and the medically trained midwife, the *bidam,* is their effect on the roles of other family members. When the *dukun baji* comes, the husband has an important, active role in actual birth, and relatives are often present, including older children who may watch. But the medically trained *bidam* dismisses all these interferences, in effect robbing the extended family of their sense of responsibility and participation.

Traditional Treatment of Mother and Neonate. After birth, infant and mother are bathed and massaged. The midwife comes every day for 35 days to continue treatment. The baby must be massaged twice a day for 5 days. The purpose is to shape the body properly and to exercise it so it is soft and not stiff. The mother is also massaged, but not so frequently.

The Javanese have a highly developed lore of home remedies made from leaves, roots, and fruits. In urban environments, these remedies are purchased even by Indonesians who have adopted Western styles of living. Interestingly enough, these remedies are not taken during pregnancy. Following delivery, however, new mothers usually take two potions. One is to make the mother feel good and cool (*dingin*), and contains about 20 ingredients, including ginger, garlic, roses, sugar, and pepper; the second is a similar drink to make her milk taste good and flow copiously. The babies are salved and then covered with rice-flour powder, which gives them a rather gray look. The latter practices persist among city dwellers.

Traditional Infant Care. The Javanese believe that a baby is extremely vulnerable, especially to sudden shock (*kajet*) that can lead to sickness or death. All their customs of infant care can be seen as attempts to ward off danger. Babies are handled in a relaxed, completely supportive way by their mothers, who provide nurturance, unconditional emotional support, and love. As a result, infants seldom cry and are consoled immediately when this happens. When the mother is not immediately available, other members of the extended family, regardless of age and sex, will attempt to console the baby.

Infants spend most of their time cradled on their mother's hip by means of a long narrow shawl, a *slendang*. This is looped over one shoulder and down over the opposite hip, giving a firm place for the baby to sit, conveniently adjacent to the breast. The *slendang* offers complete security, and most children are carried rather than left to run around. When a child is sick, up to the age of 8, mothers will take them in the *slendang* rather than leave them lying on a bed. Although infants are breast fed for at least 1 year, whenever they fret or appear hungry, mother's milk is not usually considered sufficient. Infants are given supplementary feedings of mashed banana and rice paste, but never forced to eat.

Many of the traditional Javanese practices related to pregnancy and infant care persist among the "Westernized" inhabitants of large Indonesian cities, even though most deliveries now occur in hospitals and/or birth clinics and are performed by medically trained midwives. However, while infant formulas have supplanted more traditional forms of dietary supplements, Javanese babies are still handled with the same respect and gentleness as they have been for centuries.

Pregnant women from affluent, Westernized classes now seek and receive modern prenatal care but continue to follow traditional Javanese customs such as the necessity for ritual meals and the avoidance of *Jamu* preparations. Thus, knowledge and understanding of the traditional ways of Javanese is an essential factor to be considered in the analysis of studies on infant behavior in this society. The foregoing material has either been adapted, or quoted directly, from Geertz (1961).

Setting of the Present Study

St. Carolus Hospital is a large general hospital centrally located in Jakarta, the capital of Indonesia (population approximately 9 million people). This institution has several small inpatient units located in various areas of Jakarta; special clinics are held in the main hospital. It supports a school of nursing as well. A home delivery program, staffed by midwives, is available for families who live adjacent to the hospital.

The hospital is immaculately maintained, well equipped, and well staffed: 367 nurses are employed here, and 60 of them are midwives. Approximately 4,000 infants are delivered yearly at St. Carolus, mostly by midwives. The daily census of infants in the nursery averages 68. The nursery is spacious and airy, with wooden cots designed for phototherapy. Some infants with jaundice are treated by exposing them to direct sunlight. A vehicle designed to hold eight infants is used to transport them to sunlit areas for treatment, and to their mothers for scheduled feedings.

Adjacent to the main nursery are three smaller rooms: two are used for handling of low-weight (LBW) babies; one room is reserved for "septic" infants. There are no respirators, but heated incubators are available. All babies examined were carried from the main nursery and placed in a cot in one of the adjacent rooms, where there were two or three LBW infants at any given time. Although the room was dark, room temperature was constant at 85 degrees F. An atmosphere of quiet permeated the entire institution.

All of the mothers in this study delivered in the same large 4–5-patient bedroom. Operating facilities for Caesarean sections are available if needed. Only those mothers who attended prenatal clinic are allowed to deliver at St. Carolus. Their initial clinic visit usually occurred in the first trimester of pregnancy and was followed by monthly return visits. Obstetricians care for families who are in class 1 (see description below), but midwives provide the obstetrical care for mothers in three other classes. Fathers can be present at delivery with prior permission from the hospital administrators, but none of the fathers in this study chose to observe the delivery process.

After delivery and exam of the infant, midwives swaddle and place the infant inside a wooden cabinet with a glass door next to the mother's bed. Then, both are transferred to the maternity ward which contains two or three private rooms, and two 4-bed and three 10-bed wards. If the mother's and child's hospital course is normal, hospitalization lasts 5 days. Approximately 85% of the mothers at St. Carolus breast feed their infants. Infants remain swaddled for several hours following delivery and are covered at night, but, for the most part, are dressed in diapers only, as the ambient temperature never drops below 85 degrees F. Except for the feeding, the nurses are the primary caregivers for infants at St. Carolus, although a rooming-in policy is being considered.

The cost of obstetric inpatient services at St. Carolus is based on the families' economic status. There are four classifications of fee per day. The fee schedule according to economic class is as follows:

Class I: 15,000–16,000 rupiah
Class II: 7,500–10,000 rupiah

Class III: 2,000–5,000 rupiah
Class IV: 200–500 rupiah

(At the time of this study, 617 rupiah equalled 1 U.S. dollar.) The fee includes labor and delivery costs, and hospitalization including three meals a day. Delivery of a male infant costs slightly less than delivery of a female infant.

Methodology

Sample

The present study was carried out at St. Carolus Hospital, Jakarta, Indonesia. Based on a daily review of all hospital records of mothers and infants, 60 newborns were selected according to the following criteria:

1. Family listed their religious practice as Islamic.
2. Family was of Malay (nonwhite, non-Chinese) ethnic stock.
3. Mother achieved a score of 85% or higher on Parmelee's Obstetrical Complications Scale (Littman & Parmelee, 1974).
4. Mother's prenatal hemoglobin was 9.0 or greater.
5. Delivery assistance was provided by midwives (*bidan*) only.
6. Delivery was spontaneous and vaginal.
7. No medications were administered to the mother during labor and delivery.
8. Gestational age was 37–42 weeks, as assessed by the pediatrician at St. Carolus.
9. Infant was defined as clinically healthy after physical examination by the attending pediatrician at St. Carolus.
10. Apgar scores were 7 or above at 1- and 5-minute intervals, as assessed by assisting midwives (Apgar, 1953).
11. Weight of infant was 2500 gms or more.

Data Collection Tools

Parmelee's Obstetrical Complications Scale. Information for Parmelee's OCS (maternal obstetrical history, labor and delivery, and immediate postnatal events of mother and neonate) was obtained from hospital chart reviews or inquiry of hospital nurses. This scale was used to select the mothers for the study.

Demographic Data. The following information was recorded:

1. Infant's sex, age in hours, date of birth
2. Mother's height and weight before and after delivery
3. Parent's age, occupation, education, and religion

4. Number of children, adults, and servants in household
5. Mother's attendance at prenatal clinic
6. Mother's last menstrual period
7. Delivery by physician or midwife
8. Antenatal medications
9. Type, amount, and timing of medications given to mother during labor and delivery
10. Type and frequency of infant feeding
11. Time infant last fed
12. Infant's weight in grams on day of delivery, Day 1, Day 3
13. Infant's Apgar scores

Anthropometric Measurements of Newborns. The following measurements were made on Days 1 and 3:

1. Head circumference was measured with a steel tape and recorded in centimeters.
2. Weight of infant was measured on a balance scale and recorded in grams.
3. Length of infant was measured as crown–heel length, with infant placed in tonic neck reflex position and recorded in centimeters using a steel tape.

Rohrer Poderal Index (PI). The PI, a weight-for-length ratio, was used to determine fetal nutrition. Unlike birthweight, the PI in full-term babies has not been shown to be confused by race, sex, fetal age, or parity of mother when defining nutrition (Miller & Hassanein, 1973). A low PI indicates thinness, and a high value indicates obesity. The reliability of this measure is dependent on the crown–heel length measurement. For accuracy, the tonic reflex position was used to overcome the natural tendency of newborns to maintain a flexed position. The PI calculated as:

$$\frac{\text{Birthweight in grams} \times 100}{\text{Crown-to-heel length in centimeters 3}}$$

Brazelton Neonatal Behavioral Assessment Scale. The administration of the BNBAS involves a series of observations of the infant in sleep, alert, and crying states. The latter are induced with the presentation of the following stimuli: light, bell, rattle, cloth cover over the newborn's head, uncovering, undressing, five pinpricks to the heel, a neurological reflex exam, and the examiner's voice, face, touch, and handling. Aversive stimuli are used to alter the infant's state in order to assess habituation, and to assess ability of self-consoling or response to examiner's maneuvers to console.

The reflex items are scored on a 3-point scale as low (1), medium (2), or high

(3); asymmetry and absence are noted as well. The 26 behavioral items are rated on a 9-point scale, with the midpoint of the scale, for most items, denoting the expected behavior of a normal 3-day-old infant. Each infant was examined on Days 1 and 3 of life. All newborns were examined in the same quiet location of the nursery. They were all in a sleep state at the beginning of the exam and as close to midway between feedings as possible. Anthropometric measurements were collected after the BNBAS exam, when the infant was returned to the main nursery.

Data Analysis

The mean scores of Indonesian infants on 20 reflex and 26 behavioral BNBAS items were analyzed to detect differences between examinations on Days 1 and Day 3. The reflex scores of this sample were then compared to mean reflex scores of Brazelton's (1973) normative sample. The behavioral mean scores were compared to Als, Tronick, Lester, and Brazelton's (1979) normative sample of 54 infants. Because reliability in scoring the behavioral items is defined as giving the same or adjacent scores, only differences greater than one full point of the mean are considered significant for the purpose of this comparison. Following this analysis, the 20 reflex and 26 behavioral item scores of Indonesian sample were summarized into six behavioral and one reflex clusters. The recording and analysis of cluster scores were done as recommended by Lester, Als, and Brazelton (1982).

These summary cluster scores were examined by analysis of variance (ANOVA) to compare behavior on Days 1 and 3 of the Indonesian sample. Pearson correlation coefficients we calculated by using summary cluster scores on Days 1 and 3 as dependent variables, and parity of mother, maternal age, mother's hemoglobin, paternal occupation, OCS, PI, and gestational age as independent variables. Differences in scores on Days 1 and 3 and correlations between independent and dependent variables were considered significant when $p \leq 0.05$ as determined by the appropriate statistic.

Characteristics of the Indonesian Study Population

Family Data

The religion of all families studied was listed in the hospital record as Islamic. Nurses or families confirmed that family names were Indonesian. Of the families selected, 75% were in Class III, 13% were in Class II, and 11% were in Class IV (see Table 1). Thus, most families studied belong to the lower economic class according to the criteria used by St. Carolus Hospital to calculate hospitalization fees.

Table 1.   Hospital Class of Families

Hospital Class	Hospital Cost in Rupiahs/Day*	No. Families
I	15,000–16,000	0
II	7,500–10,000	8
III	2,000–5,000	45
IV	200–500	7

*One dollar U.S. is equivalent to approximately 617 rupiahs.

Table 2 shows the occupations of the infant's parents, all of whom were married. Of the mothers, 72% were housewives, whereas 28% were employed in occupations ranging from sales clerks to laborers. Of the fathers, 35% were employed as sales clerks, 25% were government employees, 11% were laborers, and 10% were pushcart vendors. The fathers' ages ranged from 20 to 44 years.

Obstetrical History

Obstetrical data are summarized in Table 3. The mothers' ages ranged from 17 to 38 years. In our sample, 47% of the mothers were primiparae, while 28% were pregnant for a second time. Hemoglobin levels in the last week of pregnancy averaged 10.9. All mothers received prenatal guidance and follow-up by midwives from the first trimester on. No prenatal complications occurred in 81% of the mothers; 18% of the women developed vaginal infections that were treated with vaginal suppositories. One mother was treated with ampicillin for a urinary tract infection in her second trimester.

The average duration of labor was 8.4 hours. No medications were given during labor and delivery. All but two of the mothers (97%) had no labor complications. One mother showed signs of preeclampsia, and another had a

Table 2.   Occupations of Mothers and Fathers

Mothers	No.	Fathers	No.
Housewife	43	Sales Clerk	21
Sales Clerk	4	Government Employee	15
Government Employee	1	Teacher	1
Teacher	3	Shoemaker	2
Nurse	2	Laborer	7
Secretary	2	Pushcart Vendor	6
Shoemaker	1	Student	1
Laborer	1	Taxi Driver	3
Student	2	Driver	3
Unknown	1	Unknown	1
Total	60	Total	60

Table 3.   Maternal and Obstetric Characteristics

Maternal Characteristics	Mean	S.D.
Age	24.6	3.9
Gravida	1.9	1.1
Parity	1.8	1.0
Abortion	0.1	0.3
Hemoglobin (gms/dl)	10.9	0.9
Length of Labor (hours)	8.4	5.8

Prenatal, Labor, and Delivery Characteristics	No.
Prenatal complications	
None	48
Vaginal Infection	11
Urinary Tract Infection	1
Labor/Delivery Medications	
None	60
Labor Complications	
None	58
Preeclampia	1
Other Illness	1
Types of Delivery	
Spontaneous Normal Vaginal	60

chronic illness (leprosy) that did not interfere with labor and delivery. All deliveries were spontaneous, vaginal, and assisted by midwives.

Infant Data

Of the 60 infants in this sample, 62% were males and 38% were females. Average gestational age was 39.4 weeks, as assessed by midwives and confirmed by a pediatrician. Midwives based their estimates on the mother's last menstrual

Table 4.   Indonesian Infant Characteristics

Infant Characteristics	Mean	S.D.
Gestational Age	39.4	1.6
Apgar		
1 Minute	9.0	0.6
5 Minute	9.6	0.4
Weight (gms)		
Day 1	3040	349
Day 3	2976	328
Crown-to-heel Length (cms)	47.7	2.0
Head Circumference (cms)	34.0	1.5
Ponderal Index	2.8	0.3

Table 5. Mean Values of Selection Criteria for Indonesian and Caucasian Samples

Selection Criteria Items	Indonesian Mean	Caucasian Mean
Mother's Age (years)	24.6	27.2
Gravida	1.9	1.8
Parity	1.8	0.7
Length of Labor (hours)	8.4	7.8
Gestational Age (weeks)	39.4	39.8
Weight (kgs)	3.0	3.4
Apgar Score: 1 minute	9.0	8.5
5 minute	9.6	9.2

Table 6. Comparison of Reflex Scores on Days 1 and 3 of Indonesian and Normative Caucasian Samples

Brazelton Exam Reflex Item	Indonesian Sample				Normative Sample[a]
	Day 1		Day 3		Day 3
	Mean	S.D.	Mean	S.D.	
Plantar Grasp	2.0	0.0	2.0	0.0	2
Hand Grasp	2.0	0.0	2.0	0.0	2
Ankle Clonus	0.03	0.2	0.03	0.2	0,1,2
Babinski	2.0	0.0	2.0	0.0	2
Standing	1.6*	0.7	1.7*	0.7	2
Automatic Walking	1.4*	0.8	1.6*	0.7	2
Placing	1.9	0.3	1.9	0.3	2
Trunk Incurvation	2.0	0.2	2.0	0.1	2
Crawling	1.8*	0.5	1.8*	0.4	2
Glabella	2.0	0.0	2.0	0.0	2
Tonic Deviation of Head and Eyes	2.0	0.0	2.0	0.0	0,1,2
Nystagmus	1.9	0.4	1.9	0.3	0,1,2
Tonic Neck Reflex	2.0	0.3	2.0	0.2	2
Moro	2.0	0.2	2.0	0.2	2
Rooting (Intensity)	2.0	0.0	2.0	0.0	2
Sucking (Intensity)	2.0	0.0	2.0	0.1	2
Passive Movement					
Right Arm	2.0	0.2	2.0	0.2	2
Left Arm	2.0	0.2	2.0	0.2	2
Right Leg	2.0	0.2	2.0	0.2	2
Left Leg	2.0	0.2	2.0	0.2	2

[a]From Brazelton, 1973. Indonesian scores identified by asterisks differ from those of the normative sample.

period, with conception being predicted 10–14 days later. Pediatricians calculated gestational age by method of Dubowitz, Dubowitz, and Goldberg (1970).
Apgar scores were within upper limits of normal (see Table 4). The mean for Day
1 was 9.0 at 1 minute and 9.6 at 5 minutes.

Table 4 also shows that the mean weights of infants studied was 300 grams on
Day 1 and 2976 grams on Day 3. The Indonesian standard birthweight is 3000
grams (personal communication from the chairman of University of Indonesia's
Child Development Unit). The mean crown–heel length was 47.7 cms. Head
circumference mean was 34.0 cms, with a range of 30–37 cms. Mean Ponderal
Indices obtained on Day 1, and shown in Table 4, are above the 90th percentile
based on Rohrer's formula.

In Tables 5 to 7, the behavioral characteristics of Indonesian infants are
contrasted with a normative Caucasian sample of 54 infants also examined on
Days 1 and 3 of life (Als et al., 1979). Mean scores on selection criteria for both
samples are compared in Table 5. It is evident that both samples represent highly
selected healthy newborns whose mothers had uncomplicated obstetric histories
and deliveries.

Behavioral Characteristics of Indonesian Infants

BNBAS Reflex Scores

Table 6 presents the item-by-item comparison of Day 3 reflex scores of our
Indonesian sample and of Brazelton's normative sample. (For most reflex items,
scores between 1.9 and 2.1 are considered within normal limits.) Indonesian
infants have mean scores of 2.0 on most of the reflex items on both Day 1 and 3.
As a group, however, their reflex responses to items of automatic walking,
crawling, and standing are lower than the reflex responses of the normative
Caucasian sample. The Indonesian mean scores for the items are, respectively,
1.4, 1.8, and 1.6 on Day 1, and 1.6, 1.8, and 1.7 on Day 3 (see Table 6).

BNBAS Behavioral Scores

Indonesian mean scores on behavioral items are compared to Caucasian American normative sample mean scores in Table 7. For ease of presentation, the
behavioral items are grouped in four a priori clusters. As was noted earlier, mean
scores must differ by greater than one point to be considered significant (Horowitz et al., 1976). Indonesian and American infants obtained similar overall
scores, but several differences in scores on individual items are worth noting (see
Table 7).

On items indicating motor and tone capacity, the overall response of infants in
both samples was similar, but hand-to-mouth facility was better among the

Table 7.   Means ± Standard Deviations on BNBAS Items for Days 1 and 3 of Indonesian and Caucasian (a) Sample

Behavioral Test Items	Indonesian Sample (b)		Caucasian Sample (c)	
	Day 1	Day 3	Day 1	Day 3
Dimension 1: Interactive Process				
Orientation Inanimate				
Visual	6.5 ± 1.1	6.9 ± 1.0*	5.6 ± 1.4	5.4 ± 1.5
Auditory	6.5 ± 0.7*	6.9 ± 0.8*	5.5 ± 1.1	5.8 ± 0.8
Orientation Animate				
Visual	6.8 ± 1.1	7.3 ± 0.9	6.3 ± 1.2	6.5 ± 1.1
Auditory	7.2 ± 0.8*	7.5 ± 0.8*	5.5 ± 1.3	5.8 ± 1.9
Visual/Auditory	7.4 ± 0.9	7.6 ± 0.7	6.6 ± 1.1	6.9 ± 0.9
Alertness	7.0 ± 0.8*	6.8 ± 0.8	5.6 ± 1.0	5.5 ± 1.9
Cuddliness	6.9 ± 0.8	6.8 ± 0.8	5.6 ± 1.0	5.8 ± 1.2
Consolability	5.8 ± 1.1	5.6 ± 1.0	6.4 ± 1.7	6.2 ± 1.4
Dimension 2: Motor Process				
General Tonus	5.0 ± 0.7	5.1 ± 0.7	5.3 ± 0.9	5.4 ± 1.0
Activity	3.9 ± 1.0	4.1 ± 1.0	3.9 ± 0.8	4.6 ± 0.9
Motor Maturity	4.7 ± 0.7	4.9 ± 0.6	4.2 ± 0.6	4.7 ± 0.9
Hand-to-mouth Facility	6.5 ± 1.3*	7.1 ± 1.2*	4.9 ± 2.2	6.0 ± 1.8
Defensive Movements	4.5 ± 1.6	4.9 ± 1.7	4.9 ± 2.4	6.9 ± 1.3
Pull to Sit	4.6 ± 0.9	4.9 ± 1.0	5.6 ± 1.2	5.8 ± 1.3
Dimension 3: Control of State				
Response Decrement				
To Light	6.5 ± 1.0	6.1 ± 0.9	6.3 ± 1.6	7.1 ± 1.5
To Rattle	6.5 ± 1.2	6.2 ± 1.0	6.7 ± 2.1	6.8 ± 1.8
To Bell	6.2 ± 1.1	5.9 ± 1.0*	6.9 ± 2.1	7.1 ± 1.8
To Pinprick	4.1 ± 1.1	4.3 ± 1.0	4.4 ± 1.5	4.2 ± 1.2
Rapidity of Build-up	4.2 ± 1.1	4.1 ± 1.0	3.5 ± 2.2	3.6 ± 1.8
Peak of Excitement	5.8 ± 1.1	5.6 ± 1.1	5.4 ± 1.3	5.8 ± 1.3
Irritability	3.8 ± 1.1	4.0 ± 1.0	4.1 ± 1.5	4.0 ± 1.5
Self-Quieting	5.3 ± 1.5	5.4 ± 1.2	5.2 ± 1.6	5.1 ± 1.5
Lability of State	4.1 ± 1.0*	4.1 ± 1.0*	2.7 ± 1.2	2.8 ± 1.1
Dimension 4: Response to Stress				
Startles	3.2 ± 0.7*	3.2 ± 0.4*	4.5 ± 1.8	4.3 ± 1.6
Tremulousness	3.4 ± 1.3*	2.9 ± 1.2*	5.0 ± 1.7	4.4 ± 1.8
Lability of Skin Color	4.0 ± 0.4	3.9 ± 0.3	4.4 ± 1.4	4.1 ± 1.2

(a) From Als et al., 1979.
(b) N = 60; for Response Decrements, N = 53 on Day 1; N = 49 on Day 3.
(c) N = 54.
*Indonesian scores are different from the corresponding scores of the Caucasian sample.

Indonesian infants on both days. For those items addressing the neonate's capacity to attend and respond socially, Indonesian infants were generally more alert than their American counterparts on Days 1 and 3, and oriented better to vocal stimuli on both days. On Day 3, the Indonesian infants were also more responsive to the red ball and bell. Likewise, scores on the behavioral item indicating cuddliness were better on Day 1 in the Indonesian group.

The response to items representative of infants' ability to control their states of consciousness was virtually the same for the two groups, except for lability of state and habituation to bell. Indonesian infants experienced more state changes on both days then the American sample. They habituated less well to repeated auditory stimuli of the bell on Day 3.

The most significant differences in scores were seen in the a priori cluster that assessed physiological response to stress. On both Days 1 and 3, Indonesian infants showed fewer signs of stress during the examinations than the American group, as indicated by lower mean scores on items of startle and tremulousness.

Thus Indonesian infants scored lower on reflex response of automatic walking, crawling, and standing than the normative sample. Other reflex responses were the same. Mean scores on most behavioral items were also similar for the two groups. Indonesian infants alerted more than their American counterparts and exhibited fewer signs of stress.

Summary Cluster Scores

This system combines 26 behavioral items into six clusters and uses the 20 reflex responses to generate a seventh cluster. Each cluster is qualitative, with higher scores indicating better performance, except in the reflex cluster, where higher scores indicate poorer performance (Lester et al., 1982). Table 8 shows the mean summary cluster scores of our sample on Days 1 and 3. Indonesian infants scored above-average to high on orientation, regulation of state, and autonomic stability both days. They received average scores on items of habituation, range of state,

Table 8.   Comparison of BNBAS Summary Cluster Scores of Indonesian Infants on Day 1 and Day 3

Cluster	Summary Score (mean ± S.D.)		F Value
	Day 1	Day 3	
Habituation	5.80 ± 0.75	5.61 ± 0.68	2.32
Orientation	6.90 ± 0.80	7.27 ± 0.73	7.15*
Motor	4.49 ± 0.62	4.75 ± 0.62	5.38**
Range of State	4.53 ± 0.38	4.51 ± 0.35	0.10
Regulation of State	6.13 ± 0.64	6.22 ± 0.65	0.58
Autonomic Stability	6.79 ± 0.44	6.98 ± 0.44	5.39**
Reflexes	0.70 ± 1.15	0.68 ± 1.20	0.02

*$p < .01$.
**$p < .05$.

and motor capacity. Reflex scores were low, indicating normal reflex behavior overall.

To ascertain whether neonatal behavior on Day 1 differs from that on Day 3, analysis of variance was used to compare summary cluster scores. Table 8 lists the partial F tests. Significant differences were found by day of exam for the orientation cluster ($F_{1,118} = 7.15$, $p < .01$), for the motor cluster ($F_{1,118} = 5.38$, $p < .05$), and for the autonomic stability ($F_{1,118} = 5.39$, $p < .05$). No difference in scores on other cluster items were noted between Days 1 and 3. It is of interest to note that, in all the cases where scores did change, the infants performed better on Day 1 than on Day 1.

Pearson correlation coefficients were calculated to examine whether scores on the seven cluster items on Days 1 and 3 were influenced by the sociocultural variables of parity of mother, maternal age, mother's hemoglobin, paternal occupation, OCS, infant's Ponderal Index, and gestational age. Table 9 shows the result of this analysis.

Table 9. Pearson Correlation Coefficients for Summary Cluster Scores and Sociocultural Variables for Indonesian Sample by Day 1 and Day 3

Day 1						
Habituation	−.06	−.05	.05	−.33*	.20	−.07	−.02
Orientation	.05	−.04	−.23	.14	.19	.00	.01
Motor	.14	.12	−.01	.11	.14	−.06	.08
Range	.05	−.01	−.01	.13	−.09	.05	.04
Regulation	−.23	.02	−.05	−.06	.14	−.15	.06
Auto. Stability	−.09	−.12	.02	.16	.09	−.18	−.03
Reflexes	−.02	−.08	.24	−.05	−.27**	.00	.03

Day 3						
Habituation	−.06	−.06	.18	−.09	−.05	.01	−.02
Orientation	−.04	.05	−.07	.11	.40*	.02	.13
Motor	.08	.17	.02	.21	.25**	−.08	.15
Range	−.25**	.08	.24	−.09	.10	−.12	.03
Regulation	.04	.29**	−.14	−.11	.17	.09	.05
Auto. Stability	.12	−.01	−.16	.11	−.11	−.02	.06
Reflexes	.08	.04	.03	−.05	−.22	−.23	−.25**

*$p < .01$
**$p < .05$
(a) Abbreviations used are as follows:
PA = Parity of Mother
MA = Maternal Age
HG = Hemoglobin of Mother
Po = Paternal Occupation
OC = Obstetrical Complication Scale
PI = Ponderal Index
GA = Gestational Age

Parity of Mother. Infants of multiparae had lower scores in the cluster assessing range of state on Day 3. With this single exception, parity of mother had no effect on test results.

Maternal Age. No correlation between the seven cluster scores and maternal age was found on Day 1. However, regulation of state was positively correlated with maternal age on Day 3.

Hemoglobin of Mother. There was no correlation between mothers' hemoglobin and infants' cluster scores on either day.

Paternal Occupation. Paternal occupation correlated with Habituation scores on Day 1 only. Lower habituation scores were associated with fathers who were employed as clerks or government employees.

Obstetrical Complications Scale. Three significant correlations were noted between OCS and the seven cluster summary scores. On Day 1, a high OCS score was associated with lower reflex scores. In contrast, infants on Day 3 scored higher in motor and orientation clusters if mothers had a high OCS score.

Ponderal Index. There was no relationship between mean ponderal indices with cluster scores on Days 1 and 3.

Gestational Age. Lower reflex scores we correlated with higher gestational age on Day 3. No other relationship was found between gestational age and the cluster scores.

In summary, analysis of summary cluster scores of the Indonesian sample yields the following results. First, orientation, motoric, and autonomic behavior improved significantly between Day 1 and Day 3. Second, among the sociocultural variables examined, several were found to affect scores on the BNBAS, but, in general, a given variable influenced at the most only three of the seven cluster scores. Lastly, the low Pearson correlation coefficients indicate that the effect of individual sociocultural variables on infant behavior is weak, albeit statistically significant.

Discussion

According to the psychobiological model for the cross-cultural study of the organization of infant behavior, the behavior of newborns is influenced, not only by biological factors, but also by psychological and sociological variables. To test this hypothesis, 60 healthy, full-term, Indonesian neonates, carefully selected for optimal intrauterine and perinatal experiences, were examined on Day 1 and Day 3 of life with Brazelton's Neonatal Behavioral Assessment Scale. The behavior of these neonates, all of whom are normal by Indonesian standards, was then compared with samples of normal Caucasian infants in order to identify sociocultural factors unique to Indonesia that influence neonate behavior.

The first section of this discussion analyzes the effect of those variables included in the psychobiological model that could be examined in the Indonesian study population. Next, we compare the behavior of our normative sample of Indonesian infants to that of similar groups of Caucasian neonates. In the next section, the results of the present study are compared with those of other studies on infant behavior in different cultures. Finally, sociocultural and other variables that affect behavior in Indonesia are discussed.

Sociocultural and Economic Variables

Wolff (1977) considers that genetic factors contribute to cultural difference, and that these must be taken into account when biological variations and cultural diversity among groups are stressed. In order to evaluate a genetically homogeneous group of infants, only the offspring of families of the Islamic faith with Indonesian (Javanese) surnames were included in the present study. This effectively eliminated infants of ethnic Chinese or mixed (Dutch-Javanese) origin.

It was difficult to determine the exact socioeconomic status of the families we studied. St. Carolus' fee-for-service scale is based on the family's perceived economic status. Of the 60 families we studied, 75% were listed as Class III in the hospital ledger. Our sample, therefore, probably is not representative of the lower socioeconomic status trend to use the government-sponsored hospital and clinics that are less expensive than St. Carolus Hospital (personal observation).

The occupations of the fathers reflect those of the heterogeneous urban population of developing countries. Many were sales clerks or government employees. The traditional role of the Indonesian woman is reflected in our study population; that is, 72% were housewives.

Obstetrical History

The age range of the fathers in this study was 20–44 years; mothers' ages ranged between 17 and 38 years. Of the 60 mothers, 47% were primiparas. All mothers attended prenatal clinic in the first trimester and were followed monthly until the last trimester, when visits became weekly. The average hemoglobin level immediately antepartum was 10.9, a normal value by Indonesian and Caucasian standards. According to the criteria of weight-for-height and hemoglobin level, the mothers were nutritionally healthy.

Of the 60 mothers, only 12 had prenatal complications, consisting of 11 vaginal infections treated with vaginal suppositories and one urinary tract infection treated with ampicillin. Only two mothers experienced labor complications. All mothers delivered vaginally without labor medications, anesthesia, or forceps. Midwives assisted all of them during labor, which lasted, on the average, 8.4 hours. Mothers, in this sample, achieved a mean score of 144 out of 160 on the Obstetrical Complications Scale.

It is evident that newborn behavior can be influenced by events that occur prenatally while the fetus is developing in utero. The obstetrical experiences of the mothers in our sample are generally considered optimal. Hence, it is unlikely that prenatal events adversely influenced the behavior of infants we studied.

Infant Characteristics

The 60 infants (37 males and 23 females) we studied are clinically healthy and full-term. Their growth measurements were within normal Indonesian standards, and their Apgar scores are high at 1- and 5-minute intervals. Based on these data, intrauterine development of the infants we studied was optimal. It should be pointed out that growth measurements of our Indonesian sample are similar to those of full-term U.S. infants (Cloherty & Stark, 1980).

Caregiving Environment

Except for feeding, nurses provided most caregiving to the infants during their stay in the hospital. Feeding was scheduled on a 4-hour basis. All infants were breast fed, remaining approximately 30 minutes with their mothers. Families were allowed to view infants through the nursery window during scheduled visiting hours.

After discharge, infant caregiving changes dramatically. Infants are carried in *slendangs,* a practice that facilitates close body proximity between caregiver and child. They are breast fed on demand, although there is a recent trend towards bottle feeding: 15% of the mothers currently opt for this method at St. Carolus, but none of the mothers in this study bottle fed their infants. In a population with a high infant-mortality rate, child-rearing customs like these represent adaptive behaviors organized around the goal of infant survival rather than behavioral development (LeVine, 1979).

Behavioral Characteristics of Indonesian Infants

Reflex Behavior

The scores of Indonesian infants in reflex items were the same as those of Brazelton's (1973) normative sample, except for three items. Indonesian reflex responses of autonomic walking, crawling, and standing were lower than their American counterparts on both Days 1 and 3. Prechtl (1967) also found that neurological responses of autonomic walking and crawling were difficult to elicit during the first 2 or 3 days of human life.

Freedman (1971) noted similar findings on reflex behavior of Navajo infants. He suggested that these findings represented characteristics of passivity, and that, both physically and temperamentally, Navajo infants are more suited for the practice of cradle boarding than more active infants would be. The practice of carrying infants in a sling persists in Indonesia even among city dwellers. Hence, the low response to these reflex items in the Indonesian group is conducive to this child-rearing practice.

Behavioral Characteristics

In order to highlight the behavioral characteristics of 60 Indonesian infants, their mean scores on 26 behavioral items were compared to mean scores of a normative sample of 54 Caucasian-American infants (Als et al., 1979). It should be emphasized that both samples had comparable obstetrical and birth histories.

Indonesian infants were similar to the Caucasian normative sample on most behavioral items indicating motoric capacity and organizational capacity to control their state of consciousness. On items that address the infants' capacity to attend and respond socially, there were many similarities and some differences between the two groups. The major difference in the behavior of the two groups is in the area of physiological response to stress.

Indonesian infants generally came rapidly to an alert state that was maintained for extended periods. This prolonged alertness was accompanied by a high level of responsivity to inanimate visual and auditory stimuli on Day 3. On Days 1 and 3, Indonesian infants oriented better to animate auditory stimuli than their American counterparts. De Casper and Fifer (1980) noted that newborns are able to discriminate between the voices of their mothers and other speakers. Others have found that newborns are sensitive to rhymicity, intonation, frequency variation, and phonetic components of speech (Condon & Sander, 1974; Eisenberg, 1976). Interestingly, Indonesian infants habituated less well to the inanimate stimulus of a bell on Day 3 than the Caucasian sample, but responded better to items of cuddliness on Day 1.

The ability to attend to auditory cues together with an extended state of alertness conceivably could prolong the period of interaction between caregiver and infant. This, in turn, could explain why Indonesian infants are willingly handled by all members of their extended family, a striking phenomenon in Indonesia (personal observation). The Indonesian neonates' ability to follow and make eye contact with this investigator was impressive (see Figure 1). We believe that this may result, to a large extent, from the fact that these infants have no erythema or edema of the eyelids, as the prophylactic eye drops instilled at birth consist of a more diluted silver nitrate solution than is used in the United States.

Both groups responded similarly on motoric items, although hand-to-mouth facility was better among Indonesians on both days of testing. In the item of defensive movements, when a cloth was placed firmly on part of the infant's face, infants in both samples responded similarly on Day 1. However, on Day 3, the American sample struggled to remove the cloth, whereas Indonesian infants lay impassively with few overt motor responses. Freedman and Freedman (1969) noted these same differences in their comparison of Chinese-American and Euro-

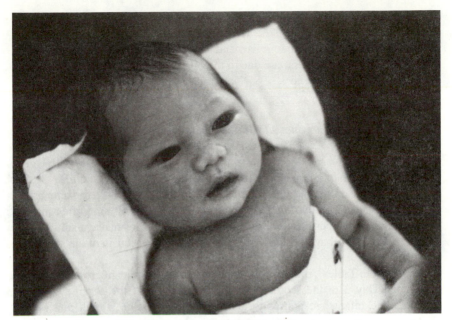

Figure 1.   6-hour-old Indonesian neonate

pean-American infants. This response, like the low reflex responses of automatic walking and crawling, may reflect difference in temperament. The Indonesian infants seem more imperturbable than the Caucasian group and may accommodate to external stimuli better. Whether this kind of response is representative of Asian infant populations in general remains to be seen.

Both samples were able to control their states of consciousness in similar ways. The Indonesian group manifested more state changes than Caucasian infants. Indonesian infants generally took longer to reach higher states of arousal but quickly returned to alert or lower states. Many of them were predominately in state 4 and never reached an insulated crying state during the BNBAS exam. This is another example of imperturbable behavior in Indonesian neonates' toleration of external stimuli.

Other behavioral responses of the Indonesian sample that differed from those of the American group were related to items of physiological stress. Indonesian infants rarely startled during the exam and were nontremulous. However, their Moro response was easily elicited. Repeated startles or overreaction to external stimuli are thought to interfere with performance of North American infants on the BNBAS (Lester & Brazelton, 1980). Lack of startles and tremors could also account for better performance of Indonesian infants on orientation items.

It should be pointed out that many mothers included in the Caucasian normative sample had received medications during labor and delivery. At first, this was considered to minimally affect infant behavior (Tronick, Wise, Als, Adamson, Scanlon, & Brazelton, 1976). Hence, it is possible that some of the behavioral differences between Indonesian and Caucasian neonates, such as startle, tremulousness, and alertness, are due to the effects of drugs rather than to sociocultural or genetic differences.

Sociocultural Variables of the Psychobiological Model and Infant Behavior in Indonesia

To assess changes in behavioral performance between Day 1 and Day 3 after birth, individual reflex and behavioral items by the BNBAS were summarized into seven clusters, as advocated by Lester et al. (1982). This simplifies analysis of the quality of the performance of neonates: Better performance results in high scores in the six behavioral clusters, and in low scores on items in the reflex cluster.

As shown in Table 8, analysis of variance reveals significant changes between Day 1 and Day 3 in the scores of neonates on three of the seven assessment clusters. The infants' responses to animate and inanimate stimuli and overall alertness increased. Some improvement was also noted in their ability to integrate motoric stability also was better on Day 3. There was no difference in the four other summary cluster scores on Days 1 and 3.

To determine which factors included in the psychobiological model for the cross-cultural study of the organization of infant behavior affected the performance of Indonesian infants, correlational analysis of the data was performed. We determined Pearson correlation coefficients between parity of mother, maternal age, OCS, PI, gestational age, mother's hemoglobin (taken as an indicator of nutritional status during pregnancy), paternal occupation (taken as a reflection of the family's socioeconomic status), and scores on each of the seven summary cluster scores. Few significant correlations were observed, but some of these deserve mention, because they may reflect the traditional Indonesian view of child rearing.

Infants of multiparous mothers had a lower range of state scores on Day 3 than infants of primiparous mothers. This relationship may reflect the caregiving experience of multiparous mothers: It suggests that they were able to decrease irritability and lability of state of their infants better than the primiparous mothers.

Infants' regulation of state on Day 3 was positively correlated with higher maternal age. The score items of cuddliness, consolability, self-quieting, and hand-to-mouth activity included in this cluster likewise could reflect the caregiving experience of older mothers. These observations are consistent with the concept that changes in neonatal behavior are due to a reciprocal feedback system between the infant and caregiving environment (Lewis & Rosenblum, 1975; Als, 1977; Brazelton & Als, 1979).

Three significant correlations were noted between OCS and the seven cluster scores. A high OCS score was associated with low reflex scores on day 1, high neonate performance on motor cluster on Day 3, and good orientation of infants. In other words, mothers who had no or minimal obstetrical complications delivered more neurologically, motorically intact and alert infants. Lower reflex scores on day 3 were also associated with higher gestational age. This relationship underscores the importance of full-term fetal growth in utero as it relates to neurological development.

No other significant correlations were noted in the Indonesian sample between the seven summary cluster scores and biomedical and sociocultural variables of the psychological model for the cross-cultural study of the organization of infant behavior. It is of interest to note that no significant differences could be demonstrated between raw item scores obtained on Day 1 and Day 3, yet some cluster scores, which are based on recoded item scores, differed on these 2 days of testing.

Finally, it should be pointed out that, while statistical analysis of our results revealed several significant associations between some variables of the psychological model, the impact of some of these variables on infant behavior is rather small. Indeed, Pearson correlation coefficients tended to be low for all the variables tested. Thus, the biological significance of these statistically significant associations remains in doubt.

Comparison of the Behavior of Indonesian Newborns with That of Infants of Other Ethnic Groups

A detailed comparison of the results of this and other cross-cultural studies reveals some striking similarities as well as differences. Twenty years ago, African infants were noted as learning motor skills earlier than American and European infants (Geber & Dean, 1957). Innate racial differences were assumed to be the cause (Geber & Dean, 1957; Jensen, 1973). Other studies attributed the findings to traditional methods of child care (Goldberg, 1972), or to more subtle differences, such as social class (Geber, 1958), or mother's attitudes and anxieties during pregnancy (Geber & Dean, 1958).

Because of the methodological problems in the studies, Warren (1972) was unable, in review, to conclude that African infant precocity existed. Using the Bayley Scale in a later study of 64 Kipsigi infants, Super (1976) found that motor skills of sitting and walking, which Kenyans acquired early by American standards, are specifically taught by the caregivers. However, the Kipsigi infants were not advanced in skills that were not taught or practiced. These results suggest that motor development can be accelerated if the infant is constantly stimulated by its environment. The degree of such stimulation varies among different ethnic groups, and it is tempting to speculate that the low scores of

Indonesian infants on some reflex items of the BNBAS reflects this phenomenon.

Differences in temperament were noted in Freedman and Freedman's (1969) comparative study of Chinese-American and European-American infants. The Chinese-American babies were less changeable, less perturbable, and habituated more readily. They were also able to console themselves and were consoled more easily than their American counterparts. The authors suggested that temperament may affect the kind of caregiving that is practiced in different ethnic groups.

The striking similarities in behavior of Chinese-American and Indonesian infants was replicated in Freedman's (1971) comparison of Japanese, American, and Navajo Indian infants. The pattern of behavior of the Oriental group was as formally described. The Navajo infants were unique in that they tended to become red when excited. They also showed less resistance in motor tone and no walking or stepping movements. Kluckholm and Leighton (cited in Lester, 1980) believed that the unique behavior of Navajos is due to cradle boarding during infancy. Freedman suggests, however, that it is due to passivity and imperturbable temperament characteristics. Whatever the true explanation, these observations are consistent with the idea that infants promote their own caregiving and survival by contributing to the development of unique adaptive cultural practices (Lester, 1980).

Coll, Sepkowski, and Lester (1979) compared 24 2-day-old Puerto Rican, Black, and Caucasian American infants. Significant differences in BNBAS scores were found among all three groups. Blacks and Caucasians scored higher on habituation items. Puerto Ricans performed better on social responsiveness and were more capable of controlling their physiological response to stress; they came rapidly into alert states, were highly responsive to stimulation, and showed much physical activity. Black infants scored significantly higher than other groups on motoric dimension.

These findings were obtained on groups of infants selected to meet standard biomedical criteria (maternal obstetric conditions, Apgar scores, gestational age, and ponderal indices) of healthy full-term infants. Hence, this study suggests the existence of innate, perhaps genetic, factors that influence the behavior of "normal" newborns of different cultures. Our own observations are consistent with this hypothesis.

From the studies reviewed above, several conclusions can be drawn. Measurable differences exist between the behavioral patterns of distinct ethnic groups. However, conclusions can be drawn from cross-cultural studies must remain speculative for several reasons. First, most studies compare "normal" Caucasians infants with neonates from other cultures selected for a particular variable with an anticipated negative effect on behavior or development (e.g., nutrition). It stands to reason that studies of this design are bound to reveal differences between the "study" and the "reference" groups. Whether these differences are due to innate or extraneous influences cannot be assessed, however, because of the multiplicity of uncontrolled-for factors that mar this approach.

The second reason is of a more general nature. Implicit in cross-cultural evaluations of infants is the supposition that a norm established for sheltered Caucasians is applicable to other populations. This is not the case. For example, if rice contained an as-yet-unknown inhibitor of growth hormone, then half the infant population of the world would be abnormal by a standard developed in a non-rice-consuming society.

A more fruitful approach to further our understanding of what influences neonatal behavior is to focus on a given homogeneous population, in order to determine the effect of a single controllable variable. Studies of this nature have identified two variables that are likely to affect all infant's behavior and early development: nutritional status of the mother, and child-rearing practices. The role of socioeconomic status per se remains unsettled.

Conclusion

Implicit in the psychological model for the cross-cultural study of the organization of infant behavior is the assumption that the behavior of neonates results from the interaction between two different types of variables. Physical and biomedical factors are thought to affect infants of all races in a similar fashion. In contrast, the unique genetic, social, and cultural makeup of different societies should affect only those infants born into a given environment.

Using the BNBAS, several investigators have documented differences in the behavior of infants of different cultures. With few exceptions, cross-cultural studies have focused on the impact of adverse pre- and postnatal conditions on infant behavior, and have compared test scores of infants in underprivileged societies with those of one or another normative sample of well babies born into mostly middle class Caucasian families. Results of such studies have been used to support the tenet that differences exist in the behavior of newborns of different ethnic background. However, as is pointed out by Rebelsky and Daniel (1976), this conclusion must remain tentative until normative data are available for homogeneous groups in ethnic populations.

The present study describes the norm of behavior in a group of infants of a homogeneous sociocultural background. All neonates studied were born into families of Javanese stock, Islamic faith, and lower-middle-class status that make up the majority of urban dwellers in Indonesia. All were selected because their pre- and postnatal status was normal by Indonesian and, indeed, by American, standards.

In most respects, the behavioral characteristics of Indonesian infants were similar to those of their American counterparts. However, some notable exceptions were observed that may, we believe, reflect the unique genetic and/or sociocultural background of the Indonesian sample population. Alternatively, such differences in behavior could be construed as adaptive, in that they would favor the perpetuation of traditional child rearing practices in Indonesia. For example, Indonesian infants, like the Navajo (Freedman, 1971), scored low on reflex scores of walking, crawling, and standing. Such behavior would be most conducive to carrying infants strapped in a sling, a practice that persists in Indonesia even in an urban setting such as Jakarta.

On the other hand, compared to their American counterparts, Indonesian infants scored better in the area of orientation to their environment by "alerting" for long periods of time. This capacity, in turn, captivated their caregivers. Indonesian infants were especially proficient at responding to external stimuli with nontremulous, startle-free behavior. Rather than overreact to offensive stimuli, they exhibited evidence of imperturbable temperament considered by many to be characteristic of other Asian populations.

Because of its design, the present study documents the behavior of a "normative" group of Indonesian infants. As such, it establishes a local standard that can be used to measure the impact of suspected adverse factors on neonates of the same ethnic background. This will eliminate some of the problems of interpretation that mar other cross-cultural studies of infant behavior.

References

Als, H. (1977). The newborn communicates. *Journal of Communications, 27,* 66–73.

Als, H., Tronick, E., Lester, B.M., & Brazelton, T.B. (1979). Specific neonatal measures: The Brazelton Neonatal Behavioral Assessment Scale: In J.D. Osofsky (Ed.), *Handbook of infant development* (pp. 185–215). New York: John Wiley and Sons.

Apgar, V. (1953). A proposal for a new method of evaluation of the newborn infant. *Current Research in Anesthesia and Analgesia, 32,* 260–267.

Brazelton, T.B. (1973). *Neonatal Behavioral Assessment Scale.* London: Spastics International Medical Publications.

Brazelton, T.B., & Als, H. (1979). Four early stages in the development of mother-infant interaction. *The Psychoanalytical Study of the Child, 34,* 349–369.

Cloherty, J.P., & Stark, A.R. (1980). *Manual of neonatal care.* Boston: Little, Brown and Co.

Coll, C., Sepkowski, C., & Lester, B.M. (1979). Differences in Brazelton Scale performance between Puerto Rican and mainland Black and Caucasian infants. *Infant Behavior and Development.*

Condon, W.S., & Sander, L.W. (1974). Neonate movement is synchronized with adult speech: Interactional participation and language acquisition. *Science, 183,* 99–101.

De Casper, A.J., & Fifer, W.P. (1980). Of human bonding: Newborns prefer their mother's voices. *Science, 208,* 1174–1176.

Dubowitz, L.M.S., Dubowitz, V., & Goldberg, C. (1970). Clinical assessment gestational age in the newborn infant. *Journal of Pediatrics, 77,* 1.

Eisenberg, R.B. (1976). *Auditory competence in early life.* Baltimore, MD: University Park.

Freedman, D.G. (1971). Genetic influences on development of behavior. In G.B.A. Stoelinga & J.J. Von Der Werff Ten Bosch (Eds.), *Normal and abnormal development of behavior* (pp. 208–236). Leiden: Leiden University Press.

Freedman, D.G., & Freedman, N.C. (1969). Behavioral differences between Chinese-American and European-American newborns. *Nature, 224,* 1227.

Geber, M. (1958). The psychomotor development of African children in their first year and the influence of mother behavior. *Journal of Social Psychology, 47,* 185–195.

Geber, M., & Dean, R.F.A. (1957). The state of development of newborn African children. *Lancet, 272,* 1216–1219.

Geber, M., & Dean, R.F.A. (1958). Psychomotor development in African children: The effects of social class and the need for improved tests. *Bulletin of the World Health Organization, 18,* 471.

Geertz, H. (1961). *The Javanese family: A study of kinship and socialization.* New York: The Free Press.

Goldberg, S. (1972). Infant care and growth in urban Zambia. *Human Development, 15,* 77–89.

Horowitz, F.D., Ashton, S., Culp, R., Yaddis, E., Levin, S., & Reichman, B. (1976). *The effects of obstetrical medications on the behavior of Israeli newborn infants and some comparisons with other populations.* Mimeo, University of Kansas.

Jensen, A. (1973). *Educability and group differences.* London: Methuen.

Lester, B.M., Als, H., & Brazelton, T.B. (1982). Regional obstetric anesthesia and newborn behavior: A reanalysis toward synergistic effects. *Child Development, 53,* 637–692.

Lester, B.M., & Brazelton, T.B. (1980). Cross-cultural assessment of neonatal behavior. In H. Stevenson & D. Wagner (Eds.), *Cultural perspectives on child development.* San Francisco, CA: W.H. Freeman and Company.

LeVine, R.A. (1979). Child rearing as cultural adaptation. In P.H. Leiderman, S.R. Tulkin, & A. Rosenfeld (Eds.), *Culture and infancy* (pp. 15–27). New York: Academic Press.

Lewis, M., & Rosenblum, L.A. (1975). *The effect of the infant on its caregiver.* New York: John Wiley and Sons.

Littman, B., & Pamelee, A.H. (1974). *Manual for obstetrical complications.* Los Angeles, CA: Department of Pediatrics, University of California Medical Center.

Maglacas, A.M., Hammad, A.E.B., & Djojoingto, W. (1976). Nursing education: The changing patterns in Indonesia. *WHO Chronicle, 30,* 461–463.

Miller, H.C., & Hassanein, K. (1973). Fetal malnutrition in white newborn infants. *Pediatrics, 52,* 504–512.

Prechtl, H.F.R. (1967). Neurological findings after pre- paranatal complications. In J. Jonxis, H.K.A. Visser, & J.A. Troelstra (Eds.), *Aspects of prematurity and dysmaturity* (pp. 303–321). Springfield, IL: Charles C. Thomas.

Rebelsky, F., & Daniel, P.A. (1976). Cross-cultural studies of infant intelligence. In M. Lewis (Ed.), *Origins of intelligence* (pp. 279–297). New York: Plenum Press.

Super, C.M. (1976). Environmental effects on motor development: 'The case of African Infant Precocity'. *Developmental Medicine and Child Neurology, 18,* 561–567.

Tas, S. (1974). *Indonesia: The underdeveloped freedom.* New York: Bobbs-Merrill Co.

Tronick, E., Wise, S., Als, H., Adamson, L., Scanlon, J., & Brazelton, T.B. (1976). Regional obstetric anesthesia and newborn behavior: Effect over the 1st ten days of life. *Journal of Pediatrics, 58,* 94–100.

United Nations Fund for Population Activities. (1979). *Draft report of the UNFPA Needs Assessment.*

Warren, N. (1972). African infant precocity. *Psychological Bulletin, 78,* 353–367.

Wolff, P.H. (1977). Biological variations and cultural diversity: An exploratory study. In P.H. Leiderman, S.R. Tulkin, A. Rosenfeld (Eds.), *Culture and infancy* (pp. 357–381). New York: Academic Press.

CHAPTER 10

Parental Attitudes and Mother–Infant Interaction in Mothers From Maghreb Living in France*

Serge Stoleru

Chargé de Recherche
INSERM
Unité 292
France

Martine Morales-Huet

DEA de Psychologie Clinique
Psychologue Clinicienne
Dept. de Psychopathologie Clinique
Biologique et Sociale de l'Enfant et de la Famille
Université Paris Nord

This study will describe clinical aspects and cultural features of motherhood in women of Maghreb living in a Parisian suburban area.

The Situation of Maghrebian Immigrants in France

Historical, Demographic, and Socioeconomic Data. The migration of Maghrebian workers to France is associated with the period of intense economic growth that followed World War II. The losses of the two world wars, and the demographic stagnation caused by the sharp decrease of natality in France,

---

* We wish to thank Marie-France Grinshpoun, who carried out the content analysis involved in the assessment of parental attitudes.

considerably diminished the supply of manpower at a time when economic development needed a large population of workers. For these reasons the most industrialized European countries, including France, were led to look for manpower where it exceeded the opportunities for employment, which was the case in the Maghrebian countries (Centre International de l'Enfance, 1974). Maghreb is the northern part of Africa and is comprised of Morocco, Algeria, and Tunisia. Most of its people are Arabic. All these countries were once colonized by the French.

In 1982, 850,000 Algerians, 460,000 Moroccans, and 200,000 Tunisians were living in France. This flow of immigration has tended to become more and more a familial migration and not the migration of manpower. The birthrate in Maghrebian families is much higher than in the French families. They contribute a growing proportion of the natality of the country. In 1970 it was estimated that 10% of the births were foreign births, that is, children of at least one parent with foreign nationality. This percentage was much higher than the percentage of the foreign population in the general population, estimated to be 6%.

The children of the Maghrebian families form the second generation of the Maghrebian peoples living in France. Some are children, some are adolescents, and some are adults who have young children.

This second generation experiences a variety of conflicts related to the fact that they belong to two very different cultures. Frequently, this generation is split between these cultures. The differences manifest themselves also as a conflict between the two generations, the generation gap being markedly widened. A typical illustration is the conflict between Maghrebian fathers and their adolescent daughters, who would like to live as their French peers do. Maghrebian fathers generally do not accept their daughters' demands for more freedom, and these conflicts often have dramatic results, such as adolescents' suicide attempts.

Young Maghrebians of the second generation often experience other conflicts. Not only do they commonly feel rejected by the French community, but they do not perceive themselves either as members of their community of origin; as a result, they experience continually a sort of hesitation and a tension in their sense of cultural identity.

The socioeconomic status of Maghrebian families is, on the average, much lower than the SES of French families; for example, a large proportion of Maghrebian workers occupy positions that French workers did not accept at least at a time when unemployment was not a major issue. A study on infantile mortality during the first year of life applied to infants born between 1966 and 1970 showed the following figures: 18 French infants out of 1,000 legitimate births; 31 Algerian infants out of 1,000 legitimate births. The study also found that the mortality rate of Algerian infants was much higher after the first month of life, which may indicate that external causes of mortality (accidents, infection, etc.) have more effect than internal factors (hereditary diseases, congenital malformations, etc.). During recent years, the economic crisis and the rise of unemployment have tended to become sources of tension and conflict between the French and Maghrebian communities. The policy of the last two governments has been to reduce drastically the flow of immigrants and also to encourage their return to countries of origin.

Clinical Setting and Research Procedure

The subjects of our study were referred to us by a team of 10 midwives with whom we collaborate. This team is part of the personnel of the Direction Departementale de l'Action Sanitaire et Sociale du Departement de la Seine-Saint-Denis. They are employed by a public agency in charge of public health in one of the Departements. The work of the midwives takes the form of home visits, and an important aspect is the prevention of prematurity by prenatal care. Out of the total number of women cared for in 1981, French patients were a minority—38% were of Maghrebian extraction and 18% belonged to other ethnic groups. Each midwife calls the Faculte de Medecine Experimentale when she thinks that the psychopathological problems of patients need a specialized intervention, and the cases referred are generally severe. These patients experience psycho-pathological disturbances along with problems related to their low socioeconomic status. They are frequently "hard-to-reach" families, for whom a classical clinical approach involving appointments in a specialized clinic is very often unsuccessful. Collaboration with the midwives makes the first clinical contact with patients possible. For as long as the patients are pregnant, the midwives come with us for the home visits and take part in the interviews, which allow for the establishment of a clinical relationship between the patient and the team. At the end of the interviews the midwives make the appropriate gynecological examinations and prescriptions, and, shortly after the birth of the babies, they end their participation in the home visits. Our collaboration with the midwives also includes a monthly seminar during which the problems of a new case are discussed. Because of the large proportion of Maghrebian and Black African patients, several seminars focus on cultural issues.

Our clinical aim is first to provide psychotherapeutic help to the pregnant women referred to us. After the baby's birth we continue this therapeutic work with the patient, but at this stage the psychotherapy is not only directed toward the mother but also toward the mother–infant interactive dyad. Three to seven days after the birth of the babies, we systematically pay a visit to the women in the maternity ward, and the newborn babies are assessed by use of the Brazelton Neonatal Behavioral Assessment Scale (Brazelton, 1973). The mothers attend this assessment, which is used as a clinical tool illustrated by the two cases outlined.

We have been developing a clinical instrument for the evaluation of parental attitudes (Stoleru, Reigner, & Morales, 1984). The subjects are presented with a series of 20 photographs showing infants and toddlers in various situations (playing, feeding, etc.) or representing parent–child dyads. The examiner asks each subject to express thoughts and feelings evoked by the pictures, as well as a story that may account for the scene observed. Furthermore, after every spontaneous response to the last 10 pictures, participant and examiner can talk freely and investigate some aspects evoked by the pictures in more detail. The presentation of the pictures and responses are videotaped. The analysis of the responses is made on the basis of the recordings. Two types of analyses are performed. The first one is clinical and qualitative; the second one is made by a researcher who does not know the clinical cases and who uses a method of quantitative content analysis for the study of the responses. A list of various categories of content elements has been established. Each occurrence of a single content element (later called "reference") is coded.

In the sixth month of the baby's life a sequence of free-play interaction between mother and baby is videotaped. This sequence takes place in a room where baby and mother are not in the presence of an observer. The tape is made by cameras equipped with a system of remote control, and after the sequence the mothers observe the videotape and can offer comments and information important for understanding the interaction.

Aspects of the Traditional Maghrebian Culture

To understand the situation and experiences of Maghrebian women living in France, it is necessary to take into account the traditional mode of organization of the Maghrebian family and, in particular, the parental roles and the interaction of parents and infants. In Maghrebian communities, families usually comprise three generations living in the same house, and the number of children per parental couple is usually high. In Algeria there is an average of eight siblings per family (Abdelkader, 1982). As a result, young children are generally cared for by their mothers, their paternal grandmothers, their aunts, and their sisters.

As emphasized in several studies (Dachmi, 1982; Jamai, 1980; Zerdoumi, 1982), the male and female roles are very differentiated. "The North-African society is a patriarchal society with a patrilinear transmission. The patriarch, chief of the family, embodies the law and the authority. For the Moslem man, it is impossible to rebel against this authority without exposing himself to be cursed" (Jamai, 1980, p. 21). The father, the uncle, and the elder brother share the power according to a well-defined hierarchy.

After puberty, the separation of males and females follows strict rules. Girls must wear a veil on their faces. During feasts and meetings men gather in one part of the premises, whereas women are in a different place with the children (impuberal boys and girls). Sexual relationships are strictly prohibited before marriage. A husband may repudiate his bride if she is not a virgin. After the first night a female relative will publicly demonstrate the former virginity of the bride by exhibiting a blood-stained sheet to the wedding guests. A corollary of this tradition is that Maghrebian girls living in France have been reported as asking for or obtaining operations to "recover" their virginity before their weddings.

The woman's role is limited to her domestic work, to procreation, and to the care of children. She is usually modest, reserved in her opinions, and would seem to be resigned to the constraints of her condition (Zerdoumi, 1982). It may appear that she is essentially a subordinate under the authority of her husband. R. Berthelier (cited in Jamai, 1980, p. 26) describes the status of Maghrebian women: "Socially women are nothing; as an individual, she is impure as is evidenced by her menses; as a wife, she is only a sexual object and not a marital partner." However, when she becomes a mother, and particularly the mother of a boy, she recovers powers, roles, and the consideration of her relatives. "Women, once they are mothers, become idealized by men . . . for every adult, the mother—his or her mother—is an infinitely loved and respected figure that is listened to" (Jamai, 1980, pp. 30–31). And the older she gets, the more she is respected. Fertility therefore assumes a crucial importance for young women, because it is a means of improving their social and familial status. The infertile woman is seen as cursed: The husband, whose sense of virility and honor is damaged by her infertility, may repudiate her. Women live usually through a succession of pregnancies, with short intervals between children, and this is generally seen as positive, since each pregnancy improves their status.

However hidden they may be, a mother's powers are many: "In many families, it is the mother who chooses . . . the wife for her son. She also inquires about her daughter's future husband. She consults her husband or elder relatives . . . when the affair has already been started. The father intervenes in order to arrange with the father of the future bride the amount of the marriage portions that the husband must bring to his future wife six months before the ceremony. Neither spouse can choose his or her partner; if they have not known each other earlier, they see each other for the first time on the night of the consummation of the marriage" (Zerdoumi, 1982, p. 38). Once married, they live with the husband's family.

Maghrebian families experience the birth according to its sex in different ways. Dachmi (1982, p. 128) writes about "the disappointment of the mother who delivers a girl whereas all the waiting and the ideal image of the newborn were focused upon the arrival of a boy." Several studies emphasize the extreme closeness—physical and psychological—of mother–infant interaction, particularly in the case of male babies. Because tradition and mores dictate, the mother makes a slave of herself for her infant; she belongs totally to her baby (Zerdoumi, 1982). She will often carry the baby swaddled and attached to her with a shawl. During the night the baby sleeps by her, and often for much longer than the first months of life.

The mother hears every cry as a signal of danger and first of all will try to soothe the baby by breastfeeding it. The episodes of breastfeeding are therefore frequent and easily elicited by the infant. The percentage of breast-fed babies in the northern part of Algeria was estimated to be 86% (urban zones) and 88% (rural zones) as compared with an estimate of 37% in France (W.H.O., 1982). Weaning is often late, compared to French standards. A study carried out in Algeria found that 63.9% of the babies were weaned between 12 and 18 months, and 19.3% between 18 and 24 months (Zerdoumi, 1982).

We have tried to outline some aspects of the cultural background of motherhood and mother–infant interaction in Maghreb which influences the beliefs, expectations, and ideals about family organization, sex roles, and patterns of childrearing, as well as related behaviors and feelings. Migration to France obviously has had a profound impact on these cognitive, affective, and behavioral aspects. The following clinical cases illustrate our clinical approach, as well as some phenomena occurring at the interface between two cultural milieus.

Clinical Cases

Houria

Houria, a 25-year-old Tunisian woman, had come to France 6 years ago. She had been pregnant for 35 weeks when we made the first home visit. The midwife referred her to us because of this patient's preoccupation that her baby, once born, would not be able to survive. Two of her previous babies had died in their first month of life.

The midwife accompanied us on our first home visit. The midwife's participation in the first interview greatly facilitated the establishment of a psychotherapeutic relationship. Houria knew that the aim of our intervention was to help her cope with her emotional turmoil, but the midwife had also told her that we might be helpful to her in her wish to find another apartment—a wish related to the fact that she had stayed for several days by the body of her dead baby in her present apartment.

Before she told us her story, Houria started a tape-recorder. She explained that she wanted her husband to hear the interview, but also that her baby would be able to listen to this narrative after it was born. She experienced great pleasure in making this recording. This was the first manifestation of a marked aspect of Houria's personality: the transformation of life into a stage, the dramatization of major or minor events, and the pleasure she took out of this.

She told us that the first pregnancy had taken place in Tunisia, had been uneventful, and that a healthy female baby, Ayate, now 7, had been born. However, 2 years later, a second baby girl died from a heart malformation. "I was shocked," said Houria, words she was to repeat again and again in the following part of the interview. The third pregnancy resulted in the birth of a healthy boy, Abdelkarim, now 3. A short time before his birth, Houria's father died of heart disease. The next child, another boy named Abdallah, died after a month of an unknown cause (Sudden Infant Death Syndrome). When she talked about this pregnancy and the death of the baby, Houria again repeated, "I was shocked." Houria's fifth and current pregnancy started 2 months after Abdallah's death, at a time when she was still in mourning. She expressed her overwhelming anxieties about the baby to be born and her doubts about her capacity to care for him or her. Her anxiety precluded any other expectations or daydreams about the baby. She thought often of the death of the previous baby, and her anxieties led her to wake up Abdelkarim every night to check that he was still alive. Houria's struggle against guilt feelings and depression seemed to us to be both intense and constant.

The Prenatal Assessment of the Patient's Parental Attitudes Through a Projective Method. Three weeks before the baby was born, we showed Houria the pictures used for the evaluation of parental attitudes. Firstly, we studied clinically her responses to the pictures. Some themes were expressed frequently and had never been manifested with such consistency in our other patients. Houria saw the children in many of the photographs as being exposed to dangers or risks. Frequently, she saw the children as being ill. In our other pictures, she saw the children as neither ill nor at risk. However, even then Houria wished to know whether the child in the picture was "normal" or not. Figure 1—one of the photographs—elicited the response, "Oh, this is beautiful, but there is also the pillowcase—he may be smothered by it—he may put it into his face."

Figure 1.   One of the pictures used to study parental attitudes. (Petit Format, Almasy)

Often when the child was seen as being exposed to a risk, Houria saw this as some fault committed by the mother. In particular, she responded to two different pictures by saying that the baby was at risk of falling because it was not properly held by the mother. We felt that she unconsciously applied the same rigor in her judgments about her behavior with her own babies, and that her guilt feelings could be related to a feeling that she might have been responsible for the death of two of her babies. The quantitative analysis of the responses to the pictures was carried out by an independent researcher. The results showed that Houria emphasized the dangers and risks to the children in the photographs in 28 references out of a total of 112 references (25%). She saw risks existing after birth, but also before, as malformations. References to normality were fairly frequent (12 instances, or 10.7%) and seemed to be related to the mother's anxieties about various illnesses or handicaps. Houria expressed her needs to be reassured about the future of the unborn baby (eight instances, or 7.1%). The child must receive tenderness and every stress must be avoided (nine instances, or 8%). A lack of attention and of care for the child was particularly reprehensible (eight instances, or 7.1%). For example, the child that was left alone, abandoned by his or her parents, was in danger. The child must be cared for (eight instances) and as a result would make his or her mother happy (five instances).

A Visit to Hatem and His Assessment Through the BNBAS. Houria gave birth to a full-term 3,510-gram boy. However, when bradycardia was discovered, the pediatric staff prolonged the baby's hospital stay. On our next home visit, 8 days after the baby's birth, Houria was very anxious because of what seemed a confirmation of her fears about the baby's life, but she was somewhat reassured by the intensive monitoring of her baby. She had chosen Hatem as his first name and explained it meant "the last one."

We felt that there was a risk that Houria's attachment to the baby might not fully develop because of this separation and her anxieties and depression. We therefore suggested that she and her husband, who also participated in the interview, should come with us to the hospital to see the baby and take part in the BNBAS assessment. We found the baby sleeping and connected to a cardiorespiratory monitor. Houria did not dare to take him in her arms nor to wake him up before we encouraged her to do so. When she held him in her arms, finally, she looked at his face a long time, smiled, rocked him, gently caressed his neck and feet, talked to him in a low voice, and whispered: "My love. . . ." The baby woke up and, hearing his mother's voice, turned his head toward her. A few moments later he started crying. Houria looked helpless, made a few unsuccessful attempts to soothe him, and then, as if she felt completely unable to comfort him, put him on his bed without saying a word.

The baby appeared skinny and sickly; moreover, his head had been shaven and his scalp was somewhat cyanotic. The BNBAS led to the following findings. The baby's lability of states was fairly high and his alertness (state 4) was replaced by episodes of crying (state 6) when he was slightly disturbed, for instance, by a passive mobilization. These crying episodes were frequent (peak of excitement scored 7) and were, along with state 4, one of the two predominant states. However, the baby demonstrated his ability to be consoled when taken in arms and also when stimulated in order to assess his orientation responses (consolability scored 5). The use of the criteria for a priori clustering of behavioral processes of the newborn (Als, Tronick, Lester, & Brazelton, 1977) found the performance of this baby to be "adequate" for three of the dimensions (Interactive Processes, Motoric Processes, Organization Processes: State Control) and "good" for one dimension (Organization Processes: Physiological Response to Stress).

One of the team did not assess the baby but observed the parents' reactions as they watched the examination. At each crying episode, pain appeared on the father's face. Houria had stepped backwards behind her husband and looked almost petrified. Later she told us that, in these moments, she was invaded by thoughts, images, and feelings related to her dead baby and not to her present baby. The mental images of the dead baby were like a screen between her and the newborn baby. When the examiner laid the baby in a prone position to elicit his crawling reflex, Houria suddenly burst into tears. At this sight, she explained later, the image of her previous baby when she had found him dead had flashed in her mind. She was not yet aware of her newborn baby's competence, particularly his orientation responses to the examiner's face and voice.

After the assessment, the examiner encouraged Houria to take the baby in her arms, which she did after some hesitation. She was able to put an end to her distress, all the more as the baby fell asleep peacefully once in his mother's arms. Although sensitive to his baby's cries, the father did not seem to be as disoriented in reaction to his anxiety. He came every day to see his baby despite the long distance between his home and the hospital. The father's behavior thus appeared as a favorable factor. On follow-up, 5 years later, when we asked Houria how useful she found our one-year-long psychotherapeutic intervention had been, she said: "Very useful, especially when you performed the examination of my newborn baby!"

The Development of the Mother–Infant Relationship. On our next home visit 2 weeks later, Houria told us she had been to the hospital five more times. Her attachment to the baby, then 23 days old, seemed to have developed. She told us that the baby was beautiful and that she was worried by the fact he had not gained weight since he was born. She thought he recognized her and her husband, as he cried when they left. However, she added that the dead baby was more beautiful. Among the Arabs, she explained, it is said that infants who are to die are the more beautiful. The pleasure and the pride experienced in the emerging relationship with the newborn therefore mixed with sadness and regret and memories of the dead baby.

The perpetuation of the memory of the dead baby might be seen as a part of a normal mourning process. However, it also seemed that Houria tended to cling to these recollections, perhaps as an effect of her guilt feelings about the baby's death, preventing her from experiencing feelings of joy. This was reinforced by the Arabic belief expressed before. Despite these restrictions, Houria's attachment to the baby developed after—and perhaps in part as a result of—our visit to the hospital, during which she had seen her new baby and had been able to overcome her fears by looking at and holding him.

During the home visit, Houria talked about her wish to find another apartment. She felt the current apartment to be a cause of evil. She feared the arrival of her baby, as if the next evil would be his death. She kept saying to herself that she would become mad if she continued to live there. Among the Arabs, she explained, there was a belief that evil could be brought by a house. She had already changed her doctor and the hospital she had gone to, because of a similar belief.

However, her anxieties about her apartment seemed also to be related to the fact that her mother was to go back to Tunisia 2 weeks later. This seemed to indicate that her preoccupations with her housing might represent a way to express her difficulty in separating from her mother and her regret not to be able to go back with her to Tunisia. When the date of the mother's departure arrived, Houria, in a fit of despair, broke down and told us that she did not feel like living in France any more and that she had not found, with her husband, the loving relationship she had experienced with her mother.

The idea that an object or a person can magically cause evil is frequent among patients of Maghrebian origin and often takes the form of the belief in the evil eye. On the day when Hatem was brought home, we noticed he wore an amulet on his chest as a protection against the evil eye. The father said it served as a protection against a potential threat from an enemy of the family but did not elaborate on this. It was his parents who had recommended the use of the amulet, which was a little bag made by Houria's mother. Its contents had been sent from Tunisia.

Casting the evil eye is generally a trait of envious persons. "The woman who has a very beautiful child, boy or girl, is particularly afraid of the evil eye. She is especially afraid of strangers who visit her, of neighbours and even of close relatives, she fears those who like children as well as those who are jealous. The eye of those who love is said to be hard. 'The eye of affection is more noxious as the eye of anger' says an Arabic proverb" (Zerdoumi, 1982, pp. 150–151). Houria and her husband told us about another belief: two women giving birth at the same time must not visit each other for 40 days, especially if the two babies are of the same sex. Houria said that a year before, just before her baby's death, she had been visited by a friend who had recently given birth, and that she thought the loss of her baby was connected to this visit. Houria's mother left for Tunisia on the fortieth day of the baby's life, a time when the baby is believed to be less vulnerable. So, in this cultural setting, the infant was perceived as exposed to risks involving magic and supernatural influences. The risks were counteracted with rituals and objects that were themselves loaded with magic and supernatural powers.

The marital relationship was also influenced in several respects by cultural factors. Houria had been married at 16 to one of her brother's friends, a time, she said, when she was not thinking of marriage at all. Several times she stated their relationship was good and said: "He is the man I love." The husband was a 32-year-old locksmith. We appreciated his patient and understanding way of responding to his wife's anxieties. However, as mentioned earlier, Houria did not seem to have succeeded in separating from her mother and in compensating her loss with a strong and deep marital relationship. On one occasion, we heard Houria complaining to her husband about their apartment and reproaching him for bringing her to France, a country "where it is cold" and where, according to her, they suffered racism and rejection. At other times, Houria felt guilty of complaining and wondered whether she was altering her husband's love for her.

Migration to France induces basic changes in the organization of the Maghrebian family which help to explain Houria's feeling of solitude. In the traditional cultural setting, families are large units, usually consisting of three generations. Houria said that her brothers were still living with her mother after their marriage, in accordance with tradition. "They do not want to come out of my mother," she commented. She emphasized how hard it had been for her to leave her parents. The risk of being alone with her children in the apartment of a building of a Parisian suburb was part of the Western way of life. However, we never found her alone, since, after the departure of Houria's mother, her husband's sister came to live with the family so she should not be alone with her baby.

As the weeks passed, the mother–infant interaction developed in a harmonious way. On one home visit when the baby was 7 weeks old, we observed that Houria responded consistently and without delay to her baby's cries in taking him on her lap, and she was usually able to soothe him. When the baby was 11 weeks, we noticed that he observed attentively the faces of persons around him and had developed full smiling responses. Many were addressed to his mother, and we saw them engaged in prolonged episodes of eye-to-eye contact and mutual smiling. Houria was much more confident than before. Her mood was much less depressed.

This considerable and lasting improvement was upset when ventricular extrasystoles were found in the baby. The parents had been preparing for a trip to Tunisia for several months, as two ceremonies were to take place: Hatem's circumcision and the wedding of the sister of Houria's husband. Hatem's circumcision could not now take place; as she was telling us about Hatem's cardiac abnormalities, the patient broke down. This was the occasion on which she said that she did not want to live in France any more and she had not found with her husband the loving relationship she had with her mother.

Postnatal Presentation of Photographs. On the postnatal presentation of the photographs, we used a different set of pictures. The clinical, nonquantitative study of Houria's responses showed that, as on the first presentation, in a large percentage of instances she saw the babies as exposed to risks. In other pictures, she eventually felt the babies were safe, but first she wanted to know if they were in danger, normal, or abnormal. The frequency of these fears led us to hypothesize that they might mask aggressive feelings which Houria felt might produce disastrous results.

In response to the picture of a breast-fed baby, Houria said that her baby, when he was older, would still suffer from an initial lack (he had not been breast-fed) and that he would think of it. She saw him as almost wearing a label for life. The fact that breast feeding is the norm in Maghreb probably aggravated these feelings.

Houria's responses clearly showed she associated the happiness and the health she tried to bring to her children with the love she felt her mother had given her. However, her separation from her mother, and her marriage, were associated with ill health for her and her children. Houria mentioned that her aggressive feelings—she spoke of murderous impulses "against somebody who would do harm to her"—were a consequence of the loss of her mother's love and her resulting irritability. One of her responses indicated that part of her aggression was directed against her mother, probably as a consequence of their separation.

The quantitative content analysis yielded the following report: the expressions of worries and preoccupations were a dominant theme, representing 20 references in a total of 110 references (18%). Illness (12 references, or 10.9%) was the major source of Houria's anxieties. These anxieties were also expressed as fears about deaths of children (six instances, or 5.4%), or as the perception of risks or dangers threatening them (seven instances, or 6.3%).

She would have been reassured if her need to be loved and to give love (six instances, or 5.4%) had not been frustrated. She felt sad, disappointed, and irritable (seven instances, or 6.3%). These feelings were frequently projected on the children, who were perceived as alone, deprived of love, and ill treated (five instances, or 4.5%). Possibly as an attempt to compensate for this situation, Houria saw some mothers as attentive to their babies (six instances, or 5.4%), particularly in the way they held them.

Observation of the Mother–Infant Interaction in a Semistandardized Situation. Houria agreed to be filmed as she interacted with her baby. Hatem was 5.5 months old. Immediately after the sequence was taped, we watched the recording with her. We could see how Houria's anxieties about Hatem were expressed in her interaction with him. Two sequences illustrated this: (a) Houria holds a rattle and shakes it before the baby's eyes—he reaches for the toy—Houria does not give the rattle to him. When she observed the sequence, Houria explained that she had been afraid the baby would strike his head with the toy. (b) Hatem holds a rubber giraffe and sucks one of its legs—Houria pulls it out of his mouth. (She commented later that she feared Hatem would vomit.) Houria holds out the giraffe to Hatem, who is lying on his back—he grasps it—Houria pulls on the giraffe in an attempt to have the baby sit up. She commented later that this was a game she had seen her husband and the baby play the previous night.

Thus, 6.5 months after the beginning of our intervention, Houria's anxieties about the baby's health remained considerable and were reinforced by actual organic problems. Her interaction with the baby was sometimes playful, and her husband's interaction with the baby was occasionally used by her as a model for her own behavior. The therapeutic relationship with Houria continued. One of the home visits was very informative about her position in the two cultures she was confronted with. She and her husband had come back from Tunisia 1 week before. Hatem was with them, after a separation of 2 months, when he had been in a French nursery.

During this home visit, Houria seemed to be joyful and free of many of her worries. She had been reassured by Hatem's weight gain, as she had feared he would not eat without her. As for the baby, he had a somewhat inexpressive face, rather dull vocalizations, and was animated only in response to stimulations from his brother and his sister.

The dramatic change in Houria was probably related to several factors, but clearly her trip to Tunisia had been most beneficial; she wanted to go back to live in Tunisia in not more than 2 years, whatever her husband's decision would be. She told us that, in her town, she did not feel alone, as everyone knew and tried to help each other and it was there that she wanted to live with her children.

On follow-up, 5 years later, Hatem, as assessed by the Achenbach Children Behavioral Checklist (Mother and Teacher Report forms), had no significant behavior disturbances. The family was still living in France; Houria followed Islamic traditions even more closely than before.

Nefiza

Nefiza was 23 years old and belonged to the second generation of Algerian immigrants. She had been pregnant for 37 weeks when we met her for the first time. She lived in her mother's apartment, was single, and had already two children. Her midwife had requested our intervention because of the overt psychological disturbances in this young woman. Nefiza had violent impulses and emotions, experienced herself as dangerous, and feared she would "become mad" after the end of her pregnancy. For instance, the midwife reported a recent clash when Nefiza had threatened her mother with a knife.

She was the eldest of five siblings. Her parents, both of Algerian origin, separated at the time her first child was born and her father had returned to Algeria. When we met her, she was living with her mother, her brothers and sisters, and her 5-year-old son, in a four-room apartment located in a low-income Paris suburb.

It was in the grandmother's home that our first home visit took place. We were welcomed warmly, and this first interview—which touched very personal matters—took place in the living room, with Nefiza's mother and siblings. This atmosphere and this setting might reflect traditional interpersonal relationships in Maghrebian families, but other elements contrasted markedly. There was no patriarchal organization, Nefiza's mother had a professional occupation, and Western influences were apparent to a large degree. This was evidenced by their clothes and the furniture. There was no sign in the apartment of a connection with Moslem religion or the Koranic tradition.

Nefiza's story, particularly of her relationships with men and of her successive pregnancies, reflected her cultural identity conflicts. In the first interview she referred to her own culture—using deprecatory and rejecting terms. This attitude was expressed in an intergenerational conflict, particularly with her father. As an adolescent, she had rebelled against him, describing him as attached to cultural traditions, and she refused to marry the man he had chosen for her. She left her parents and studied in a boarding school, but her father decided that she would not go to a university as she had hoped.

At that time there were also violent conflicts between her parents. She said she derived some pleasure from these conflicts, because she could not accept sharing her mother with her father. The generational tension reached a crisis when she got pregnant at the age of 18. The father of the baby, an Algerian, left her when she was still pregnant. A short time after Ryad, her son, was born, her parents divorced and her father returned to his native country. Nefiza came back home and left her baby to the care of her mother, whom she was determined to change into a liberal and emancipated woman. Whereas her mother had always followed traditions, Nefiza wanted her to adopt the Western way of life. She also wanted her siblings to receive a much more liberal education. She was much less involved in the care of her infant. It seemed to us that having the first child had not made her a "mother"; she saw this identity and function as belonging to her mother.

Two years later, she had a girl, Sheherazad, whose father, also Algerian, had recently immigrated to France and who recognized Sheherazad as his child. Nefiza had a better relationship with him than with the father of her first child, and their relationship, although conflictual, was still continuing when we met her. After Sheherazad's birth, the couple came to live with Nefiza's mother, and for a few months Nefiza cared for the baby and felt that she was really becoming a mother as she had not done with Ryad. But conflicts arose between the couple and the grandmother, and Nefiza, her friend, and Sheherazad had to leave. Then the father wanted Sheherazad to go back to Algeria and live with his parents. When this happened, Nefiza tried to persuade herself that her baby was dead in order to forget her. "It is as if I had buried her," she said about her attempt to mourn the loss of her baby.

We saw this loss as both an object loss and a profound narcissistic wound, since Nefiza's identity as a mother was again shattered. She felt intensely guilty.

Her perception of herself as a "bad" mother was reinforced by the traditional cultural system of ideals and of models, such as the prohibition of sexual relationships before marriage and the idealization of motherhood. We were impressed in the first interview by her strong guilt feelings and by her doubts about her maternal capacities. She wanted, apparently, to demonstrate to us her lack of "maternal instinct," by talking aggressively and crudely of her feelings of rejection about Ryad.

She was pregnant for the third time when the interview took place. She had wished to have another child but was anxious about her capacity for attachment to her future baby. She was preoccupied as well about the physical condition of the baby right after delivery. It seemed that she experienced a genuine state of primary maternal preoccupation (Winnicott, 1958), and that this pregnancy represented an attempt to fill the loss of her daughter.

The Prenatal Assessment of the Patient's Parental Attitudes Through a Projective Method. The clinical analysis of the responses to the pictures indicated narcissistic conflicts. Beauty and ugliness were predominant themes. Pregnancy was seen as a threat to the beauty of the woman's body and as a threat to her capacity of seduction. In this way, we summarized that the narcissistic cathexes were competing with the cathexes of the baby to be born. Nefiza emphasized her repulsion to pictures of children she saw as ugly. A photograph showing a baby yawning with a wide open mouth evoked for her the picture of a monster. Ugliness seemed to be the factor that might impair her bonding to a child. Her responses showed sadistic impulses directed against children, resulting in deep feelings of fear, guilt, and depression. As a consequence, she tried to avoid thinking about the child she was bearing.

As an attempt to solve her conflicts between what we analyzed as objectal and narcissistic cathexes, it seemed to us that Nefiza experienced the mother–infant dyad as a unit invested with narcissistic cathexes. Then the infant was only perceived as a part of herself. When she saw the infant as a distinct entity, however, she felt rejected. For example, she considered a sleeping baby as withdrawn and reluctant to interact with his or her mother. Nefiza responded to a picture representing a mother feeding her baby by pointing to the bad way in which the mother was holding the infant, seeing her avoidance of skin contact and mutual gaze as the mother's inability to interact with the baby and to experience warm feelings towards him or her.

One of the main points in this series of responses was that the children were much more often seen as sources of displeasure than pleasure. Their look, perceived as suffering and accusatory, caused Nefiza's feelings of guilt to arise and made her feel like a totally inadequate mother. She projected her own feelings on children represented on the pictures. For example, she gave specific meanings to their facial expressions and attributed to them her own aggressive tendencies. Several responses indicated that the mother–child relationship excluded the father and, we felt, pointed to Nefiza's latent homosexual trends.

Some of Nefiza's perceptions were related to the status of immigrants in France and were expressed in response to the picture of a black baby. This evoked a recollection about her own past, and she talked about the depressing experience of the children of immigrants. This experience was related to their inability to speak another language, to communicate with others, and to have their needs met. As a result they felt helpless, vulnerable, and narcissistically hurt.

The quantitative content analysis indicated that the patient perceived negative affects in children as well as in parents (25 references, or 12.7%). She related these affects to a miserable socioeconomic status (20 references, or 10.1%). A poor communication between children and parents (16 references, or 8.1%), aggression (eight references, or 4.0%), as well as a lack of attention to the children (16 references, or 6.6%) were perceived. Children's abnormalities and handicaps (12 references, or 6.0%) appeared as further burdens for the family (six references, or 3%). Mothers were characterized as anxious (13 references, or 6.6%) and repulsed by ugliness in children (31 references, or 15.7%).

Maternity Visit. Nefiza gave birth to a healthy, 2970-gram girl and called her Nargiss. In a phone conversation preceding our visit, she said she was disappointed about having a girl and that she was afraid of the baby's physical "failure." We found her beautifully dressed, make-up on her face, with a joyful beaming expression. Her mother was present and held the baby, but she left a few minutes later, following Nefiza's advice to take care of her health. The grandmother had taken some days off at the time of the birth, and she was now complaining of asthenia. Nefiza said she felt as if this child was her first one and she had never had children before. She said she was very happy, and that she felt she was experiencing unique moments with her daughter, but that she knew they would soon come to an end. The father had not yet seen or recognized his baby, and Nefiza thought she would start working so as to raise her infant by herself. She gave the impression that she wanted to lock herself and her daughter in a closed world and to exclude both the baby's father and her mother from this narcissistic dyad. Then she thought about Sheherazad and said that her newborn was a "substitution" through which she would no longer have to think of her girl exiled in Algeria. We felt that her joy was somewhat compromised by her thoughts about Sheherazad, and that she tried to defend against them by her statements.

During this visit, Nefiza breast-fed her baby often. The first time this happened, the baby sucked vigorously, then sank into drowsiness. Nefiza looked at her from time to time but was much more involved in her interaction with us. Each time the baby cried, Nefiza would take her and feed her. It seemed to us that she could not stand her baby's cries; her immediate and invariable response was to feed her. We wondered whether she would later let her baby quiet down herself.

Nefiza said she had chosen the name Nargiss to fit her daughter's personality. This name is also reminiscent of the name of a flower, the narcissus, which is itself derived from a mythic character. She saw a narcissus as a flower "that opens and closes." She considered her baby as an autonomous being already endowed with an inner world and individuality, and her image of a flower, alternatively opened and closed, seemed to us to be meaningful, as it referred to an interactive pattern Nefiza was attributing to her infant through a projective mechanism. For example, she believed this type of interaction took place between Nargiss and the examiner during the BNBAS examination, as the baby oscillated between periods of alertness and periods of withdrawal from the stimulations. Of course, the baby's availability and need for interaction was really following a cyclic pattern, and it is quite possible that Nefiza had correctly interpreted this pattern. However, it seemed to us that she was loading this phenomenon with projected meanings related to her own narcissistic conflicts.

Nargiss appeared as a rather small but well-proportioned infant. Her face was quite red at the beginning of the examination, which was confirmed by the high lability of her skin color (scored 7). She had just been fed and was initially in a drowsy state. However, she rapidly reached a state of alertness which she maintained for a prolonged period. Then she demonstrated very good capacities to orient toward stimuli, especially visual ones. In the second half of the assessment, however, the baby was seldom alert, frequently cried, but was always easy to console. The use of the criteria for a priori clustering of behavior processes of the newborn infant (Als, Tronick, Lester, & Brazelton, 1977) showed the performance of this baby to be "adequate" for three of the dimensions (Interactive Processes, Motoric Processes, Organization Processes: State Control) and "good" for one dimension (Organization Processes: Physiological Response to Stress). Nefiza was very attentive to her baby during the BNBAS assessment. Her comments showed she was sensitive to her baby's competences, and enjoyed to see them. She was struck by the way her baby had put her head and hand on the examiner's shoulder. She hinted it had been important for her that the examiner was a male. Clearly, she had not expected a man to interact with her baby, or her baby with a man. But it may be that cultural factors played a role at this point, as, traditionally in Maghreb, the men do not usually interact with their children until they are about 3 years of age. However, Nefiza had always been very reluctant to share her children with their fathers, and this may be an individual rather than a cultural trait.

Nefiza found it difficult to tolerate Nargiss's cries during the examination. It was the first occasion she had heard her cry for some time without feeding her as an immediate response. She said she had never been able to tolerate a child's cries, and that they gave her a headache. As this visit ended, Nefiza asked to see us again "until the end," but she could not explain what she meant by this expression.

The First 6 Months of Life: Nefiza and Her Relationship with Nargiss.
Nefiza came back to live with her mother and her siblings. We made a home visit each week. Twice she accepted our proposal to see her in an office at the

university, but she did not actually come until the third time. Her inability to meet us outside her mother's home was one of many evidences to us of her difficulties in separating from her mother. On the first home visit following Nargiss' birth, we found the baby in the grandmother's arms. Nargiss had just been fed, but as soon as she started crying, Nefiza took her and started feeding her again. Some moments later she said she still could not tolerate her baby's cries, because she felt that those meant that "she, Nefiza, was unjust and bad." Her response to the cries was invariably to put the baby to her breast.

As mentioned earlier, this pattern of response is typical in Maghrebian culture, where a mother will try to soothe a baby "first by putting it to the breast at any time and with no measure" (Zerdoumi, 1982, pp. 90–91). However, this cultural factor did not fully account for Nefiza's breast-feeding behavior. She was no longer expressing the same pleasure and joy as in the clinic. The crying baby, she said, "got on her nerves." Struggling with her guilt feelings, she responded immediately by feeding the baby. She had the feeling that Nargiss was mocking and dominating her through her cries. Baby and mother seemed to us to be engaged in a symbiotic relationship, where the mother was still using projective mechanisms which made her see Nargiss as an aggressive and tyrannical baby.

As soon as the feeding was over, Nefiza gave Nargiss to her own mother, and the latter then cared for the baby and changed her diapers. This indicated to us how much the patient continued to feel it difficult to be a mother in the presence of her mother. At the end of this visit, she told us that her mother was accusing her of being responsible for the mother's divorce. We wondered whether her guilt feelings vis-a-vis her mother had not unconsciously led Nefiza, as a measure of reparation, to deliver her children into her mother's care, and had perhaps played a role in her own difficult relationships with men.

Nefiza's relationship with Nargiss' father, although very tense, was continuing irregularly. He was away from the Paris area at the time of the baby's birth. A few weeks after he came back, Nefiza wanted to live with him and their baby in a small apartment, though she was unclear about this move, just as it was unclear for her whether she could separate from her mother and live with a man. She came back to her mother's house after a few weeks.

Later, Nargiss's father found a job which entailed frequent trips to Algeria, and his relationship with his baby became uncertain. Nefiza described him as violent, immature, unstable, and a "bad" father. She said he was an alcoholic, and that he had once been admitted to a psychiatric hospital, the reason he gave for not meeting us. Like Nefiza's father, he opposed her wishes to resume her studies. Nefiza emphasized that Arab men could not tolerate a woman having a liberated professional life, and that this was equated with being a "loose woman". While she described these difficulties with Nargiss's father, it seemed to us as though Nefiza chose her partners as if she was driven by a repetition compulsion and as if they were revivals of her Oedipal love object.

We saw a number of changes occur during the first months of the baby's life.

For example, the grandmother was present less and less during the interviews, and Nefiza tried gradually to gain some distance from her. Her attitude to her son, Ryad, became less crude and aggressive. She accepted him more easily when he stayed close to her and was more and more attentive to, and even anxious about, his physical and emotional condition, for example, when she talked about his nightmares.

This change seemed to be related to the way she accepted motherhood and her identity as a mother in her current situation. She enjoyed her interaction with her baby more and more. Her inability to stand the baby's cries persisted, but Nefiza's sadistic impulses in her relationship with Nargiss lessened as she recognized the capacity for a reciprocal attachment. We observed, in her description of the first time Nargiss found her own way to the breast, that she also had changed her way to give the breast and that feeding had now become an experience of mutual pleasure.

Nefiza said she had "true conversations" with her baby and that she had two ways of addressing Nargiss, either babbling with her or talking to her as an adult. Nargiss stayed more and more on her mother's lap during the interviews, and not only when she was fed. We saw playful sequences between mother and infant. Nargiss had become a beautiful baby, with delicate facial features and easy smiling responses, and was an obvious source of pleasure for her mother. When the baby was 5 months, Nefiza told us she wanted to wean her, but that this appeared to be difficult because Nargiss refused the bottle. However, she stated also that, during breast feeding, she experienced an intimacy with her daughter that no one else could share. She said, "The bottle is cold, it is impersonal. It is just milk. But the breast is a bond. . . I did not know that a baby was able to express so much tenderness. Often she gazes at me and gets my head in her little hands." Nefiza seemed to be "discovering" her breasts and her capacity of attachment to her baby. In referring to the difficulties of weaning Nargiss, we felt she was also expressing how difficult it was for her to give up this kind of intimacy with her baby.

At the same time, she was struggling against her wish to withdraw with her infant into a closed dyadic relationship. She often asked friends to care for Nargiss for a while and enjoyed the moment the baby recognized her when she returned. "When she smiles at me, I am surprised, she is so happy to see me again. She looks at me with hungry eyes." When one of the therapists pointed out to Nefiza her own "hunger" for the baby, she answered, "I do not know what my eyes look like in these moments. If I had a double, I mean a mirror, I could see them." We were struck by this, as we had noticed Nargiss looked like a small replica of her mother. This impression was also conveyed by the clothes Nefiza chose for Nargiss which were like her own. One of the important aspects of the therapy was that Nefiza was helped to consider how she behaved with her baby and "to see herself as she was looking at her baby."

As her relationship with her infant developed, changes were apparent in

Nefiza. Her conversation about the baby was less crude and more moderated. She was beginning to be able to contain her aggressive impulses and was less afraid of them.

The Postnatal Assessment of the Patient's Parental Attitudes Through a Projective Method. When the baby was 6.5 months old, the qualitative clinical analysis of her responses to the photographs confirmed the changes that had occurred since the first presentation. The most important point was that the baby was seen as a source of pleasure for the mother. Also, the maternal figure represented a unique source of affective and libidinal gratification that no other caregiver could replace. Nefiza responded to a picture of a mother nursing her infant by saying that this situation was an intimate experience of mutual pleasure, and she stressed the importance of tactile sensations and of skin-to-skin contact. She perceived this interactive modality as the one most able to convey to the baby the mother's love for him or her.

Nefiza referred still to the ugliness of newborns right after delivery, but this perception was now overlaid by feelings of tenderness. In several responses, Nefiza underscored the children's capacities to fight for their survival. This seemed to be connected to her greater ability to contain her aggressive impulses and to her realization that the children had their own ways to cope with stress. Simultaneously, she used less projective mechanisms and tried to consider the children's needs and wishes in their own right. However, she persisted in tending to exclude the father from the mother–daughter relationship.

The quantitative content analysis of the patient's responses indicated that she appeared uncertain and was carefully looking for objective, meaningful elements about the time, place, age, sex, and personality of the characters (23 references, or 16.2%). A particularly important place was reserved for eye-to-eye contact, as the eyes appeared as the reflection of affects (16 references, or 11.2%). The baby's gaze helped the mother to meet his or her needs, to calm and comfort the baby (nine references, or 6.3%) as he or she was anxiously confronted with unfamiliar objects or persons (six references, or 4.2%). The infant reacted to these situations through his or her own coping mechanisms (nine references, or 6.3%). When nursed, the baby experienced a sensuous pleasure as he or she was in contact with his or her mother and could smell her (14 references, or 9.8%). The infant could then develop without difficulty. The patient was very attentive to the personality of the growing child (eight references, or 5.6%). She was anxious about the future of a child in a violent world (seven references, or 4.8%), and she refused toys related to war.

Observation of the Mother–Infant Interaction in a Semistandardized Situation. Nargiss was 6.5 months old when a sequence of mother–infant play was videotaped. At the very beginning of this sequence, Nefiza encouraged her baby to crawl away from her by placing a toy out of her reach. However, she then tried to reduce the distance between them and used a variety of strategies to attract her. One of these was to put a teddy bear against her chest and to pretend to nurse it.

When Nefiza watched the tape, she said that it reminded her of an instance when she had taken a doll in her arms, as if she was nursing another baby, so as to elicit envy in Nargiss.

At another point of the sequence, Nargiss was playing alone at some distance from her mother. Nefiza appeared sad and not involved. Then, suddenly, she bent towards her daughter and touched her. Later, she explained that she often needed to touch her infant so as to get rid of her depressive thoughts. The whole sequence swung between moments when Nefiza tried to put some distance between her and Nargiss, and moments when she attempted to get her baby's attention and to have the infant close to her.

Nefiza said she did not like to see how "far" from her baby she sometimes was. She made efforts, particularly when we were with her, to be more patient and more tolerant with Nargiss, for instance, when she cried and could not be soothed. She tried to offer us the best picture of herself as a mother, in accordance with the changes in her ideals and with the identificatory processes that were taking place in the therapeutic relationship.

On follow-up, 5 years later, Nefiza had succeeded in separating herself from her mother and had married a French man. Nargiss, as assessed by the Achenbach Children Behavior Checklist (Mother and Teacher Report forms), had no significant behavior disturbances.

Summary

These two case studies illustrate the interplay between cultural factors and individual psychopathological factors in Maghrebian mothers, and its influence on the psychological environment of their infants. After the death of her two babies, Houria, a Tunisian immigrant, was overridden by anxieties about the physical condition of her newborn infant, but these anxieties were intimately related to her nostalgia for her native country, and to the separation from her mother, a separation she equated with physical and mental illness for her and for her children. Immigration appeared to have precipitated the development of psychopathological disturbances that regressed after the patient returned to her country and her familial environment. Her baby was involved in this situation, as he was confronted with a depressed mother who was overanxious about his condition. When he was 6 months old, he experienced a significant separation from his parents when they left for Tunisia for 2 months.

The second patient, Nefiza, belonged to the second generation of Maghrebian immigrants. There was an interplay between her adolescent conflicts with her father and her rejection of her culture of origin. These conflicts played a considerable role in her parents' divorce. After the divorce, in Nefiza's relationship with her mother she became the authoritative figure and tried to convert her mother and siblings to the European way of life and cultural values. As a result of this, she left her first baby to the care of her mother; the next baby, a girl, was sent to Algeria to live with her paternal grandparents, and Nefiza was at last able to be the actual caregiver of her third baby.

References

Abdelkader, H.F. (1982). *Approche en psycho-sociologie et en psychopathologie du milieu Algerien et de ses mutations.* Unpublished doctoral thesis, University of Paris 6.

Als, H., Tronick, E., Lester, B.M., & Brazelton, T.B. (1977). The Brazelton Neonatal Behavioral Assessment Scale (BNBAS). *Journal of Abnormal Child Psychology, 5,* 215–231.

Brazelton, T.B. (1973). *Neonatal Behavioral Assessment Scale* (Clinics in Developmental Medicine, No. 50). London: William Heinemann Medical Books.

Centre International de l'Enfance. (1974). *Les enfants de travailleurs migrants en Europe.* Paris: ESF.

Dachmi, A. (1982). *Approche clinique du corps-à-corps mère-enfant Marocain en milieu rural.* Unpublished doctoral thesis, University of Paris 13.

Jamai, M. (1980). *Structure familiale Maghrébine et organisation de la personnalité.* Unpublished doctoral thesis, University of Bordeaux 2.

Stoleru, S., Reigner, M., & Morales, M. (1983). A projective technique for investigating parental attitudes: A preliminary report. In J.D. Call, E. Galenson, & R.L. Tyson (Eds.), *Frontiers of infant psychiatry* (Vol. 2). New York: Basic Books.

W.H.O. (1982). The prevalence and duration of breast-feeding: A critical review of available information. *World Health Statistics Quarterly, 2,* 92–116.

Winnicott, D.W. (1958). Primary Maternal Preoccupation. In *Collected papers. Through pediatrics to psycho-analysis.* London: Tavistock; New York: Basic Books.

Zerdoumi, N. (1982). Enfants d'hier. *L'éducation de l'enfant en milieu traditionnel algérien.* Paris: Francois Maspero.

CHAPTER 11

Fetal Nutrition: A Study of its Effect on Behavior in Zulu Newborns*

Brigitte H.E. Niestroj

Psychologisches Institut WE 3
Freie Universität Berlin

Man has no nature; all he has is a history.—Ortega

In the last decade, the psychology of early infant development has been going through an almost revolutionary shift of emphasis attended by a swift shift in the philosophy of the human newborn. The conference on the "Origins of the Infant's Social Responsiveness" was introduced by Marshall H. Klaus as coming "at the beginning of a scientific revolution" (1979, p. xi). The human newborn is rediscovered as a competent being. More recent theories of human development have greatly profited from the interdisciplinary research and are categorized by a multidimensional approach. In the theories of psychology, the human being has long been believed to be a tabula rasa, implying that the development of any person is the product of external influences outside the individual's control.

Behaviorism has for decades dominated psychological research with the assumption that any child can be conditioned to performing and developing the desired behavior provided the correct steps are taken by the caretaker. In this

---

* I am grateful to Professor Ronald Albino, who invited me to conduct the study, to Professors Allie Moosa and Bert Touwen, and to Dr. Kevin Nugent for familiarizing me with procedures for examining newborns. Dr. Heidelise Als and Professor Allie Moosa remained a constant source of information throughout the study. Professors Bert Touwen and Heinz F.R. Prechtl enhanced my knowledge about newborn behavior by discussing the assessment method in a very constructive and eye-opening way with me. Dr. Lilly Dubowitz helped me more than she is aware of in making sense of my findings. My thanks is due to Professor R.H. Philpott, of the Department of Obstetrics and Gynaecology, and the Medical Superintendent of King Edward VIII Hospital, for permission to study their patients.

theory, the child has nothing to contribute to his or her own development and is seen as the passive receiver of outside forces and stimuli rather than being an influential participant in his or her own development. Furthermore, conditioning a human infant is strongly related to controlling any behavior the child might be exposed to. In being able to control and manipulate the child's behavior, the caretaker has, not just to control his or her own behavior, but also that of the child's further environment. In this theory, spontaneity is seen as an interfering variable in the process of conditioning. In 1928, Watson and Watson published the book *Psychological Care of Infant and Child,* in which they emphasize the process of conditioning and the control of behavior of all persons involved and interacting with the infant. The influence, even decades after its publication, of this book on American middle-class child-rearing practice cannot be underestimated.

In 1935 another important and influential book appeared: *La Naissance d l'Intelligence,* by Jean Piaget. The biological-psychological equipment of the human newborn becomes the central aspect of his work. In this theory, infant development is strongly related to the activity of the human newborn, which has its source in biology. The biologically influenced activity of the infant is seen as the motor of further development. In this philosophy, the human newborn is a 'doer' rather than a passive being. Developmental psychologists have focused on the importance of the biological-psychological equipment of the human newborn for cognitive development, which has been believed to be internal.

This has led to another dichotomic assumption in developmental psychology. Cognitive development has been seen as organismic in origin, whereas social development has been believed to be more external and dependent on learning processes such as imitation and conditioning. Piaget, however, demonstrates the interplay between cognitive and social development and between biology and psychology. The relationship of biology to psychology in human behavior is raised more clearly in very early human development. Questions of an *'either* biology *or* environment' type have turned out to be of little help for describing and explaining early human behavior and development. The pure biological and the pure behavioristical approaches have had the same effect. They seem to remove the human being from control of development, and shaping and manipulating behavior.

Ethologists as well as biologically oriented developmental psychologists have long emphasized that the human newborn is equipped with behavior enabling the education of all those responses from the caretaker which are needed for survival and for facilitating development. The human organism is equipped with behavior of highly adaptive purposes. The perceptual, effector, and signalling equipment of the newborn enables him or her to interact socially and manipulatively with caretaker and environment. This interactional activity with the animate and in-animate environment assures the differentiation of the somatic, social, and cognitive potentiality and capacities of the human newborn. The behavioral equipment based on organismic systems is highly dependent on the active interaction with the environment for any further development. The interplay, however, of biology and environment in its broadest meaning is far from clear, and our comprehension of the processes involved is incomplete.

Ethologists and developmental psychologists have used the human behavioral repertoire and equipment as the basis for theoretical assumptions in which the great variability of human newborn behavior has seldom been accounted for, although the bewildering array of potential behaviors (Hofer, 1981) in human newborns has been known for a long time. Human newborn behavior has been described in very general terms, reflecting the aim of scientific research to look for the most generalizable principles. It is only in the last decade that a shift has taken place from the general to the particular which might lead to a new integrating theory of human infant development.

Cross-cultural and cross-sectional studies of human newborns have demonstrated the great variability of behavior. Many factors have to be considered to explain those differences in newborn behavior found in cross-cultural as well as in cross-sectional groups around the world. One factor which has been found to influence newborn behavior is intrauterine growth, as indicated in birth weight. Many studies have shown that birth weight has consequences for newborn behavior and can differentiate newborn groups with varying birth weight. Intrauterine growth shapes behavior.

Intrauterine Growth–Birthweight–Behaviour

Birthweight is a well recognized index of intrauterine growth. It seems still to be the most widely used single clinical measurement of growth in intrauterine and postnatal life. Although a nonspecific measurement of growth, since it represents the sum of increments of different body components, it is still an important measurement and is believed to be, in the short-term, a more sensitive index of ill health and poor nutrition than either length or head circumference (Davis, 1981). As an index of nutrition, growth is still a yardstick of the health of individuals and populations, "perhaps the best there is" (Tanner, 1976). The rate of intrauterine growth can be influenced by ethnic, geographical, sociocultural, socioeconomic, and sociomedical factors such as status, education, workload, diseases, use of tobacco, drugs, weight gain during pregnancy, maternal age, weight, height, and the obstetrical experience of the mother as expressed by birth order and number of previous deliveries, duration of labor, placental factors, or fetal abnormalities, either biochemical or genetic (Urrusti et al., 1972; Bergner & Susser, 1970; Mata, 1978).

It has been shown (Mata, 1978) that the maternal environment and immediate surroundings are fundamental to a satisfactory understanding of many characteristics of growth and survival of the newborn. *Maternal environment* includes physical, physiological, pathological, and obstetrical characteristics, as well as environmental influences affecting the mother and thereby the fetus. Physical, biological, and sociocultural factors interact and determine fetal growth and development.

Birth weight varies greatly both within and between populations. The rate of intrauterine growth in full-term newborns can range from 2400 grams (New Guinea), to 3880 grams (Anguilla and Nevis, in the Carribean), mean birth-weight (Davis, 1981). The wide variation in birth weight of term babies has been attributed to many specific factors already mentioned. However, the variation in birth weight of non-Western babies which is likely to be less of those of Western newborns is assumed to be largely due to poor nutritional status of non-Western women (Hollingsworth, 1965; Meredith, 1970). Intrauterine growth, of which birth weight is an outcome, and its variations are relevant in the context of this study, because it has an impact on the survival, the behavior, and the further development of the infant. Although low birth weight is known to be a world wide problem affecting the lower socioeconomic classes, it has a much greater impact in developing countries (Mata, 1978).

Low birth weight has been associated with neonatal death, impaired physical growth, immune competence, and intellectual and interactional performance. Generally, it has been accepted that the newborn infant brings with him or her an innate capacity or readiness to adapt to the culture into which he or she is received. Innate potential for growth, for learning, for relationships, however, can be greatly decreased when the newborn has suffered fetal growth retardation. An underweight newborn can be lethargic, withdrawn, inattentive, and thereby limited in his or her capacity to act on his or her environment. Differential behavioral features in underweight-for-dates and underweight-for-length new-borns have been reported in a number of studies. In a study by Lester, Emory, and Hoffman (1976) of the behavior of low-birth-weight and small-for-dates (SFD) newborns, it was demonstrated that birth weight was the best single predictor of the attention-orientation factor, and items relating to attention were found to differentiate low-birth-weight from full-birth-weight babies; newborns who were small-for-dates, so it was concluded, may be particularly at risk for developmental deficits.

Als, Tronick, Adamson, and Brazelton (1976) assessed the behavior of small-for-dates and full-birth-weight newborns with the Neonatal Behavioral Assessment Scale (NBAS). In addition to low birth weight, they employed another measure of fetal growth and nutrition: Rohrer's ponderal index (PI), which is a ratio of birth weight (in grams) $\times$ 100/the cube of crown–heel birth length (in centimeters). The ponderal index has been used in diagnosing fetal malnutrition, and it is assumed to be relatively independent of the sex, race, and parity of the newborn and the physical size of the mother (Zeskind & Ramey, 1978).

The typical underweight White newborn is described by Als et al. as being apathetic, unresponsive, and, hence, rather poor on interactional items. The babies made hardly any use of stimulation and received low ratings of attractiveness, which is a measure of interactive responsiveness, combined with the ability to overcome state disorganisation and physiological interference. A brief face-to-face interaction exhausted these babies, and, when wide awake, they were unable to process incoming information, thus remaining unavailable to the outside world. The results of those studies are in line with other, almost universally reported findings that fetal malnutrition, low birth weight, and the newborn's performance are strongly associated (Brazelton, Tronick, Lechtig, Laski, & Klien, 1977; Lester, Klein, & Martinez, 1975).

Als et al. mention other important implications the behavioral differences might have for the small and thin infant. They interviewed the mothers of those underweight babies informally at a later date. The majority of the mothers reported having problems with their babies, who were described as easily overstimulated, intense, and generally highly reactive. Some women even questioned whether they could ever cope with having another child. Small-for-dates babies seem also more likely to be put up for adoption, as Miller and Hassanein (1973) report. The development of those undernourished newborns might, however, proceed normally when they benefit from a supporting environment and from extra stimulation (Zeskind & Ramey, 1978, 1981).

Very often fetal malnutrition and environmental deprivation act synergistically to isolate the infant from the inputs necessary for normal development. This is especially true for developing countries in which under- and malnourishment is part of the human experience and existence. Lester (1979) speculated that the poor eliciting behaviors of underweight newborns could exacerbate the effects of malnutrition. He assumes that a poorly organized infant who has difficulty interacting with the environment and is a poor elicitor of maternal responses might not receive the kind of caregiving patterns necessary for his or her recovery, especially when the caregiver is also already stressed and nutritionally depleted.

The behaviors of the newborn are an outgrowth of prenatal life, of which nutritional status is one important factor influencing somatic and behavioral development of the infant and, in turn, the caretaker's behavior toward the child. In addition, child-rearing practices may affect both nutritional status and interactional processes between caretakers and newborns. Fetal growth and nutrition is not merely determined by biology but also by the cultural and social context in which it occurs, so that, even in the earliest stage of biological development, the genetic make-up of the embryo is influenced by many environmental interactions (Hofer, 1981).

It is assumed (Brazelton, 1977; Lester & Brazelton, 1982) that behavioral diversity and cultural differences are not determined exclusively by environmental factors, and that biology contributes towards certain patterns of child-rearing practices and social interaction, since one factor involved in shaping the early environment of the child is the biological equipment of human infants, which has now been found to vary across human groups. A newborn has already been shaped by the environment, since intrauterine conditions such as nutrition influence the growth of the fetus. It is now generally accepted that the interplay between biology, universal processes of human development, and the cultural milieu shapes the newborn and infant behavior as well as the caretaker's social interaction.

A multicultural approach might help to come to a more comprehensive understanding of this phenomenon. Theories of infant behavior and development which are based on multidimensional models (Lester & Brazelton, 1982) will also benefit from theories, assumptions, and findings obtained in fields like developmental biology, nutrition, ethology, pediatrics, anthropology, psychology, and the behavioral sciences. This intellectual conglomerate may lead to a better understanding of human development and behaviour. My own study on Zulu newborn behavior forced me to look into other research fields.

One purpose of this study was to compare performance on the NBAS in one ethnic group between different full-term newborn groups with varying fetal nutritional status, as indicated by birth weight. I had several goals in mind. First, I wanted to find out if birth weight is a factor influencing behavior. I attempted to partially replicate the Als et al. findings, but in an environment where the incidence of underweight newborns is known to be very high. The second objective was to provide a description of the behavioral features of those newborn groups as a basis for future studies of cultural antecedents of infant–caregiver interaction. My study has turned out to be more exploratory than hypothesis testing.

Social and Cultural Context

The study was conducted in Durban, an important habour city located on the southeastern African coast of the Indian ocean. Durban is part of Natal province and is mainly populated by English settlers, Africans, and Indians. English is the main language. Although the Zulus are to be found all over southern Africa, a large number live in Natal between the escarpment of the Drakensberg and the sea. Natal is mountainous, wooded, and grassy. When rainful allows, cultivation of the land is possible and harvest can be profitable; however, southern Africa has been effected by severe drought, and Natal is one of the worst-effected areas. Today, the Zulu comprise some 4.5 million of the estimated 21 million Black Africans in South Africa. The main language is Zulu. Cattle and agriculture formed the basis of subsistance, but today only the cultivation of some land has remained significant for the rural home economy.

In Natal's rural areas, domestic settlements are still found consisting of individual homesteads situated at a distance from one another. Small villages consist of a group of homesteads. Although larger towns can also be found in the area, they are less characteristic. A homestead usually is occupied by a man and his wife or wives and children. Married sons and unmarried daughters also used to live in their parent's home (Preston-Whyte, 1974). The family was, historically, an extended polygamous unit, but today the nuclear family is much more common, as are "broken" homes and families, as male friends and husbands work far away from home. The mud-walled, thatched-roofed huts are occupied mainly by women, children, and old men. Most adult males, but also younger women, are absent throughout the year working in the towns. It is assumed that the disproportionate sex ratio in the urban and rural areas has led to ever-increasing illegitimacy and a weakening of family ties.

Children are, as in most African societies, highly valued, and they seem to be very important for every woman, especially as a Zulu marriage will be confirmed by pregnancy and birth and will only be considered complete when the woman has borne at least one child. In a study on unplanned pregnancies among urban Zulu schoolgirls (Craig & Richter-Strydom, 1983) boys did seem to consider it important to marry a girl of proven fertility. Children have always been seen as property and as a great blessing, but the reason for having children might have changed with the transformation of culture and assimilation into White society and a very different economy.

In former times, the child was a valuable acquisition because it was an economic asset from an early age (van der Vliet, 1974). Girls became nursemaids for younger siblings or kin and helped their mothers in the household chores. Boys helped herd cattle, sheep, and goats and were expected to provide security for their parents in their old age. Although girls in rural areas may still take over the same tasks, boys are more likely to leave the home early to find work elsewhere, as cattle herding has decreased. The difference in expectations that European and African parents have regarding their children (LeVine, 1977) may not be so significant anymore. With a changed economy and with a growing formal school system, the child may be no longer able to contribute labor to the domestic productive unit or to support aging parents.

Zulu women talked to me about their child in terms of affection, enjoyment, emotional satisfaction, and love, but they also said that they expect this much more from girls than from their sons. Sons are expected to go their own way, whereas girls are expected to become supportive to their mothers. In the traditional extended homestead, all women and children would take an interest in the child, and the father later on. The infant would have many to mother him/her. However, many women now live in townships and only the immediate family, sometimes with males absent, will provide the care for the child.

This also implies a changing function for women in their role as mothers. A new mother, having giving birth, can still take delight in her child and also satisfaction with herself, but this might not take place anymore in a circle of greatly pleased and highly approving close kin. Many women live alone with their children under socioeconomic and psychological stress. For women in the rural area of Natal a pregnancy will still be seen in the context of reassuring the marriage, and the child will have a definite function in securing and stabilizing the woman's position in her husband's family. The 'meaning' attached to a child in a given cultural context will also influence the relationship between mother and child.

When a woman gives birth to her first child she might return to her parent's home in the last months of pregnancy. During delivery and after her mother will help and care for both the newborn child and the new mother. As is the custom in most southern African societies, birth is strictly a woman's affair. Sometimes a close relative, usually an older woman past child-bearing age (for instance, mother or grandmother), will supervise the delivery, which takes place in the woman's living hut. In the first few days, approximately 10, the woman and the newborn are surrounded only by the close female relative, and no one else, especially men, may enter the hut until the infant's cord has dried and fallen off.

The new mother is not supposed to leave the hut during that period of strict confinement but takes time to recover from the delivery and to be in intimate contact with her infant. Usually the mother does not need to participate in any task. The infant is handled and cleaned by the child's grandmother, who also introduces her daughter to early childcare practice. The attendent cares for child and mother. If available, food will be offered in plenty to put on weight. Food restrictions during pregnancy are well known (Richards, 1964; Cassel, 1955; Larsen, Msane, & Monkhe, 1983a,b). Zulu traditional birth attendants who might be called to assist the delivery will advise against the use of meat or milk, or the eating of eggs. Alcoholic beverages seem to be strictly forbidden to pregnant women. Those taboos and avoidances are believed to protect the child and to ease pregnancy and labor.

The first period of confinement is characterized by spoiling the new mother and enabling her to be in direct contact with the infant without long interruptions. It is only when the cord has fallen off that the mother can go outside the hut, mostly in the morning when the infant might also be taken and carried about for a little while, but avoiding exposure to intensive sunlight. The father, if present, may see and handle the infant; however, in some areas it is only after 4 or even 12 weeks that the man may see the child. Confinement to the hut usually lasts for 3 months. It also has the function of keeping the environment hygienic; hence the restriction of visitors, the almost ritual cleaning of spoons and plates that the mother was supposed to eat from, and infant care that was limited to one or two women. It is easy to imagine that, in such an environment, the survival of the newborn was secure.

Although we do not know much in detail about early infant care in an African community, we usually assume that, from the moment of birth, the African infant is surrounded by an unrestricted and unlimited nurturing environment and by direct body contact. The confinement period makes it likely that the southern African mother is able to indulge her infant's wishes and needs related to feeding, cleaning, sleeping, and physical closeness. It contributes also to an important cultural difference in child care practice within African societies. Mothers in other African societies seem to carry the newborn and young infant almost immediately on the back or on the side (Konner, 1972; Ainsworth, 1967); hence the newborn is used to an upright position in all states, including sleep. During the confinement period, the newborn is very likely to be either in the supine or prone position and rarely put in the upright position, although our knowledge of infant handling during that period is rather sparse. The upright position of the newborn is supposed to have a great influence on the motor precocity of African infants and has been discussed as one explanation for it.

It is not known if confinement is still practiced in urban Black communities, since it involves the constant presence and support of at least one other woman. This support will not always be available, as urban African women, including mothers, with a meagre earning capacity have to return to their jobs (Longmore, 1954). In some cases, the mother may even give the child to relatives.

In Bophuthattsawana, the urban Black community has confinement, with the exception that the baby has probably been born at a hospital or clinic (Richardson, Sinwel, Rantsho, Bac, & Moatshe, 1983). But the life of many is characteristized by poverty, desertion, and unwanted children. A young woman working in the town might return to her mother to deliver the child, remain for a couple of months, and return without the child to a place where work can be found and cash be earned. The woman might have her child by a man who denies fatherhood, who has his own family to support, or she might have a husband or male friend who is supportive for a while and sends money to her so that she can care for the child/children. Quite often, however, the woman is forced to leave her child behind with someone else and try to find work in towns to be able to support her child at home. In such circumstances motherhood is more a stressful situation leading to resentment, hopelessness, and deprivation than a delight to indulge in.

Breast feeding is common in most African societies, and only in exceptional circumstances would the infant be exclusively bottle- or spoon-fed. Among the Zulus it was and still is the custom to offer additional food, usually watery porridge, in the early months of life, introducing the baby gradually to other foods so that it is accustomed to an adult diet from an early age (van der Vlient, 1974; Richards, 1964). However, the Tswana of Botswana seem to breast feed their infants for a much longer period without offering supplementary food, and in Tanzania it was also the custom to give additional food to the very young infant (Raum, 1967). The reasons for these differences are not clear but may indicate differences in attitudes toward the human body, its essential needs, and also towards the function of breast milk.

A study on breast-feeding practices in KwaMashu (Ross, Van Middelkoop, & Khoza, 1983), a large urban African township in the greater Durban area, and in selected areas throughout Natal/Kwazulu, demonstrates that, in urban as well as in rural areas, women started to offer supplementary feeding several hours after birth and, with increasing age of the infant, there was a rapid increase in supplementary feeding. Of 221 women interviewed, 50% indicated the reasons "not enough milk" or "baby not satisfied" for introducing supplementation quite early. A further 22% of women had to return to work.

Formula feeding seems to be accepted as a satisfactory and safe alternative to breast feeding, although breast feeding practice has increased compared with several years ago. Women who were unsuccessful in previous pregnancies, or ambivalent about breast feeding, were less likely to breast feed their newborns. It was also found that babies delivered in hospital and breast fed immediately were significantly more likely to be fully breast fed for a longer period of time than hospital-delivered infants suckled later on the day of birth. Traditionally, newborns are not put to the breast for 12 to 24 hours, while the colostrum is expressed and thrown away, it being regarded with revulsion. Instead, the baby is given a mixture of sugar and water to clear its bowel of meconium (Larsen et al., 1983a,b).

Health conditions among the Natal Zulu have been extremely poor for many decades (Cassel, 1955). In 1940 a rural infant mortality rate of 276 per 1,000 live births was reported. In 1980 it was estimated that, in rural areas, African infant mortality was almost as high as in 1940: for every 1,000 live births, 240 children would not reach the age of 2, and those who survived had a 50% chance of being malnourished. For urban African areas, infant mortality rates of 69 per 1,000 live births were reported. In a community survey of 85% rural Zulu women who had given birth to a total of 361 children in home delivery, infant survival rate was 79.5%.

Malnutrition reached near-crisis proportions in 1980. In addition to poverty and a high unemployment rate among Africans, the lasting drought contributed to the problem of food supply. Infants and children under 5 years of age suffer most from mal- and undernutrition, hunger, and growth retardation, and from protein-calorie deficiency diseases such as *kwashiorkor* and *marasmus*. Rural areas in Natal have been more affected than urban areas, and the already nutritionally stressed situation of the people is made worse by the uncultivated land.

The Zulu population, together with other Black and Colored South Africans, is characterized by poor nutrition, low socioeconomic status, overcrowded living conditions, limited resources and education, limited health services, a high birth rate, and a large proportion of low-birth-weight newborns. The female population is further characterized by small and underweight mothers (Woods, Malau, De V. Hesse, & Van Schalkwyk, 1979). Colored primigravidas were found to be significantly smaller, lighter, and thinner than White mothers (Woods, De V. Hesse, Davy, & Van Schalkwyk, 1978), suggesting an inadequate energy intake before and during pregnancy. Although the relationship between maternal nutrition and intrauterine growth retardation, as reflected in birth weight, is not yet well understood, it is assumed that maternal size is an important determinant of fetal growth.

Data on newborns from the Baragwanath Hospital in Johannesburg, which serves the Soweto township population, revealed an exceptionally high incidence of low-birth-weight newborns. Of 18,000 newborns annually, 3,500, or 19.5%, weigh less than 2500 grams (Stein & Ellis, 1974). A detailed study of 250 underweight babies showed that the majority of the low-birth-weight infants (73%) had experienced intrauterine growth retardation and were small for their gestational age. It has been established that most growth-retarded newborns are born to mothers belonging to the underprivileged urban African population (Stein, 1975). However, birth weight data from newborns born in rural areas is more difficult to obtain (Richardson et al., 1983).

The development of those many small-for-dates infants is unknown. It has been established that low-birth-weight newborns born into a underprivileged community and suffering from endemic malnutrition have an increased mortality rate up to their fourth birthday (Mata, 1978). Infant survivors who are born underweight and are badly fed in the first 2 years of their lives might suffer brain damage through malnutrition (Stoch & Smythe, 1963). It is also known that there is a synergistic relationship between undernutrition and disease. Malnutrition can increase susceptibility to disease as much as disease can contribute to malnutrition.

The Hospital Setting

The study was carried out in Durban's King Edward VIII Hospital, which serves African patients from a very large area in Natal, sometimes coming from more than 100 miles away. The labor ward is, with that of the Baragwanath Hospital in Johannesburg, one of the busiest in the country. Women are asked to contribute to the fees, but the hospital services are available when the patient is unable to pay. The labor ward is a specialized ward, and surrounding clinics may send pregnant women to the hospital when difficulties during pregnancy or labor are anticipated. Many healthy pregnant women made use of the hospital and had a uneventful course of pregnancy and a normal vaginal delivery. Attached to the hospital was a medical school which trained Africans, Indians, and Coloreds. The midwives and nurses were almost exclusively Black South Africans, whereas the teaching staff in the medical school and the doctors in the hospital came from various parts of the world. As in most clinics and hospitals, the staff/patient ratio was low.

The hospital served urban and rural populations as well as different socioeconomic groups. The overall sample was highly heterogeneous, though within certain limits of demographic variables such as income level, occupation, place of residence, degree of modernization, housing, marital status, educational level, living conditions, health and nutritional status, life styles, value orientation, religious background, and family formation. Some women may have come from families composed of mother, father, and siblings, some from extended families with various combinations of relatives, or from fragmented families. Some women may have been alone with their child/children, divorced, or separated from their husbands or friends, as it is estimated that about 85% of bread winners live away from home. Some women may have come to Durban to be near their male friends or husbands who might have found work in the city without being able to take their family with them.

The sample was ethnically homogeneous in respect to ethnic origin. The women were not interviewed, although this would have contributed to an understanding of women and motherhood as much as of early child-rearing practices. In order to be able to approach people in a foreign culture and to ask them questions that will allow them to express the reality of their experience, social and cultural participation is needed and there was not enough time for this. However, unsystematic observations were made of the handling of the newborn.

Since King Edward VIII Hospital is a teaching hospital, deliveries were monitored throughout the day and obstetricians were available at any time. Normal deliveries were managed by the highly experienced staff midwives, and medical backup was obtained if needed, as doctors were present almost constantly. Family members were not allowed to attend the women during labor or in the immediate postpartum period, though this seemed to be possible in smaller rural clinics. Nonetheless, the nurses and midwives created an almost homey and warm atmosphere despite the constant and demanding workload in the ward. Silence was a characteristic of the labor ward. A quiet, soundless, labor is part of the African tradition, and the woman is asked to be courageous during her labor. Vocal expressions during these hours are believed to influence the newborn child in a negative way.

The delivery procedure was Western. When the child was born, its umbilical cord was cut and tied almost immediately, and mother and child were separated a few minutes after birth. The child then was examined neurologically, and the Apgar scores were assessed by the midwife, usually at 1 and 5 minutes. The baby was weighed, wrapped in towel, and put in a crib in the labor ward for a time while the mothers were attended by the midwives.

Every 2 hours a nurse collected the healthy babies and took them to the reception room, a central nursery for normal, healthy babies, where they were bathed, cleaned, equipped with a diaper, wrapped into a warm towel, and put together with other newborns in a huge, moveable cot which easily had space for eight babies. This provided the newborns with additional warmth and some physical contact which they seemed to enjoy. They looked comfortable and content. The newborns would remain in the reception room until the nurse found time to distribute them to their mothers on her return to the maternity wards.

While the babies were cared for by the nurse, the mothers were looked after by the midwife. Shortly after delivery of the placenta, and if no stitching was necessary, the woman would have time to rest in the delivery room, which provided bed space in a separate corner of the room. Mothers were given something to eat, usually a hot soup. Dependent on the workload in the labor ward, the women were taken to the lying-in rooms after 2 hours. It was only then that the babies were taken to their mothers and roomed-in, which could be after 3 to 8 hours or more, as about 50 normal newborns were delivered per day. But from that time onwards the babies were with their mothers, either at their bedside or sharing the bed space, cared for by the mothers, fed by them, and sent home the following day. Healthy mothers and babies were discharged 12 to 24 hours after delivery.

Although this early discharge was also due to the crowdedness in the maternity and labor ward, women seemed to be prepared to go home even sooner. In some other clinics visited in Southern Africa, women delivered under medical supervision but walked home with their child very soon after they had given birth. When newborns needed to be kept in the special-care unit, mothers were able to usually to remain in the hospital and stay as long as the condition of the child required it. During most of this time mothers cared for and fed the infant. In the nurseries mothers continued to be intimately involved in the care of their infants (Wayburne, 1983). Small and premature babies were only left alone in the hospital if mothers had other children to look after and had no neighbor or friend available to be with them, or when the woman had to secure her job, which could be at risk when absent for too many days or weeks.

Method

Subjects

Initially, 90 newborns were selected according to birth weight. The aim of the study was to assess the neurobehavior of growth-retarded or small-for-dates (SFD), appropriately grown (appropriately-for-dates—AFD), and large-for-dates (LFD), healthy full-term Zulu infants, in order to compare their behavior and learn more about immediate consequences birth weight might have on those babies. The study's objectives coincided with the interest of pediatricians in obtaining more information about the behavior of small-for-dates infants. At the onset, three newborn groups ranging in their birth weight from 2000 to 4450 grams were selected. The underweight newborn group ranged in their birth weight from 2000 to 2500 grams, the medium and, according to the hospital records the average/expected, birth weight from 2550 to 3500 grams and the babies who were regarded as large ranged from 3550 to 4450 grams.

All infants were free from gross complications of pregnancy and delivery and were pediatrically and neurologically regarded as normal. The obstetric history and the labor process of the woman was recorded in her file, so that it was possible to exclude all babies who might have been born under too much medication given to the mother and in cases in which the placenta showed any sign of abnormality. Very little or no medication was used in labor of those newborns included in the study. Selection criteria was a normal, spontaneous vaginal delivery without any pathological lie (e.g., breech, face to pubis) of the baby and a gestational age of 38 to 42 weeks.

All newborns had an APGAR score of 7 and higher at 1 minute, and of 9 and above at 5 minutes. Those 90 newborns included 30 first-borns (17 belonged to the underweight newborn group, 10 to the medium, and three to the high birth weight group); 17 second-borns; and 14 third-borns, of which two were in the underweight and eight in the high birthweight group. Parity ranged from 0 to 8, and maternal age from 17 (eight mothers) to 44. In the underweight newborn group, 26 of the mothers were under 25, whereas in the high birthweight group only 11 were under that age. Labor was longest for the underweight group (8.07 hours), shortest in the high birth weight group (6.42 hours), and medium (7.02 hours) for the average birth weight newborns. The mean birth weight of all 90 newborns was 3060 grams; females (46) had an average birthweight of 2976 grams; males (44), 3149 grams; and first-borns, 2652 grams (see Tables 1 and 2).

The small-for-dates newborns had the youngest mothers, the lowest birth order, and the highest number of first-borns. Large-for-dateness was associated with a high birth order and older mothers.

Table 1.   Birth Data (Biomedical Data)

Birth Data	Low PI Group $N = 15$		High PI Group $N = 14$		Low BW Group $N = 14$		High BW Group $N = 17$		Normal BW Group $N = 23$	
	X̄	SD	X̄	SD	X̄	SD	X̄	SD	X̄	SD
Birth weight grams	2.400	255	3.600	298	2.370	125	3.880	267	2.980	292
Apgar scores										
1 minute	8.5	.9	8.6	.9	8.8	.8	8.8	.9	9.0	.8
5 minutes	9.9	.2	9.9	.2	9.8	.2	9.9	.2	9.9	.2
Crown–heel length (cm)	48.2	2.6	49.7	1.2	45.8	1.0	53.4	1.2	49.3	1.5
Head circumference (cm)	33.6	1.2	35.8	1.4	33.0	.7	36.5	1.1	35.3	1.
Infant's age at testing (hour)	4.13	2.1	4.20	1.7	6.30	3.3	5.40	4.8	5.20	4.
Length of labor (hour)	9.35	5.2	6.38	4.4	8.00	6.0	7.00	3.6	6.10	3.5
Mother's age (years)	22	5.3	28.1	3.8	23.3	6.8	25.4	4.6	22.9	5.2
Birth order	2.2	1.7	4.2	1.9	2.7	2.2	3.2	1.6	2.6	1.9
Ponderal Index	2.13	.1	2.87	.4	2.47	.1	2.54	.1	2.48	.1

Table 2. Distribution of female/male newborns and birth order

	Low PI Group N = 15	High PI Group N = 14	Low BW Group N = 14	High BW Group N = 17	Normal BW Group N = 23
	N	N	N	N	N
Females	10	7	8	6	11
Males	5	7	6	11	12
First child	9	0	7	3	9
Second child	1	2	1	4	5
Third child	2	6	0	3	2
Fourth child	1	2	5	2	4
Fifths child and over	2	4	1	5	3

The medium birth weight group was randomly selected, as many healthy, full-term newborns were available during a period of about 4 months. The healthy underweight newborns, however, had to be included as they arrived. This was due to the conditions for the project. Although many underweight newborns were born, not many met the criteria of having only one "at risk" factor, namely, a low birth weight. This indicates that the healthy small-for-dates newborn was a rather rare occurrence, at least during the period of the study and in this population. The newborns in the higher birth weight group were again randomly selected, although newborns above 4000 grams were less likely to be born than those below. Several (7) newborns were later excluded: one small baby had a head circumference of less than 32 cm, one large baby had a head circumference of more than 38 cm (both are "at risk" factors); one large newborn had a low PI, and three of the small-for-dates a PI of above 2.8, indicating obesity; and one large baby had a PI over 3, which has to be considered clinically different.

As all healthy newborns and mothers were discharged the following day, the infants were tested during their first 12 hours of life and before their first feeding. The infants were examined in the reception room, which turned out to be appropriate and convenient, being quiet and where light was adjustable, with an average room temperature of about 29 C. The babies were tested before being returned to their mothers. The only food they had received was some sugar water routinely given in the reception room to all healthy newborns. The time of testing was the most appropriate which could be decided upon. The huge maternity wards were almost always overcrowded, so that testing would not have been possible without removing the newborn again from the mother. I always went to see mother and child again in the morning before they were discharged, checking the obstetric file of the mother, which was attached to her bed, and seeing the child, sometimes demonstrating to the mother parts of the examination.

Procedure

The 90 newborns were assessed with the Neonatal Behavioral Assessment Scale (1973), but it was not differentiated within the full-term range of 38 to 42 weeks. Prechtl and Beintema's (1976) manual for assessing the mature newborn neurologically was used when appropriate, although the scoring system of the NBAS was kept. I measured head circumference (cm) and length (cm) of the infant. Usually, I brought the sleeping infant to an adjacent cot-like table, which was divided into several small compartments, and waited for several minutes before starting with the examination. As it was rather warm in the room, the newborns were dressed only in a diaper (see Photograph 1).

For the decrement Habituation, the baby was kept in the horizontal position, and a soft foam cushion with a hole in the middle was used for keeping the infant's head in the midline (see Photograph 1). The Orientation items were assessed when the infant was put back to the supine position, therefore not necessarily giving the infant's best performance (discussed later), but keeping the examination procedure as standardized as possible so that all infants were kept in a similar position in respect to the eliciting procedures and helping the infant to come to an alert state and remain there for some time.

Although the data was initially analyzed according to the birth weight groups, I eventually divided those 90 newborns into five different categories, using the ponderal index as a criteria in addition to birth weight. This resulted in three different groups; the low PI group consisted of 15 newborns (mean PI 2.13) who were proportionately lower in weight than height, indicating thinness. Of those 15 low PI newborns, 10 were females and 9 were first-borns, supporting evidence that, during the latter part of pregnancy, females seem to have a lower rate of growth than males (McKeown & Record, 1954), and any group of babies that is small-for-dates is likely to be biased in favor of females (Ounsted, 1968; Stein & Ellis, 1974). In this group, the average age of the mother was the lowest of all (mean age: 22), which was to be expected, as 60% of the infants were first-borns.

A separate group comprising 14 newborns with a birth weight of 2000 to 2500 grams and an average ponderal index (mean 2.47) were identified as belonging to the official clinical underweight newborns. Newborns with a high birth weight but an average ponderal index were also collected in a group, since low birth weight and high birth weight, regardless of the ponderal index, have to be treated as a separate category (Stimmler, 1970). Newborns in the high ponderal index group (mean PI 2.87), indicating obesity, were of the highest birth order, and they were born to mothers in the highest age group.

Results

As a whole, the five newborn groups scored very low on alertness, peak of excitement, rapidity of buildup, and lability of states, all socially important

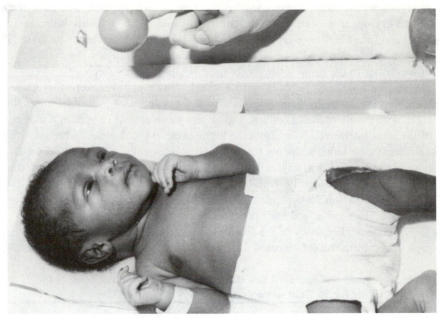

Photograph 1.   Zulu newborn.

behavioral dimensions. Their overall arousal level was low. The low level of alertness is also reflected in their Orientation scores, which remained within the first half of the scoring range, although several newborns received rather high Orientation scores. Head movements following the red ball were rare, but the newborns followed in a fairly attentive way with their eyes. Although they hardly attempted to turn their heads to follow the ball or to search for the sounds, the overall impression they gave was one of "interested" alertness but with little motor activity.

The Orientation responses to auditory stimuli were, surprisingly, slightly better than to visual stimuli. This might be an effect of the low alertness level, as the infants might have experienced the auditory stimuli as stronger. Their low arousal level limited their ability to respond to, and interact with, their environment. None of the infants had jerky movements, and no tremor was observed during the time of testing or in between. Most infants lay quietly on the table-cot, with controlled and smooth limb movements. The general activity level and motor activity was low. Most infants habituated rather quickly to disturbing stimuli, their responses were mostly localized, and neither the limbs or whole body were activated frequently.

The high ponderal index group differed in its response decrement to pinprick from the rest of the group insofar as those newborns reacted either with withdrawing both legs or with gross motor activity involving the whole body. They rarely showed localized responses, as the other newborns did, and once they started crying, they were very difficult to console. Although they were easily upset and irritable, they were able, together with the other newborns, to shut out light stimulus easily. The newborns in the other four groups were hardly ever upset, either in the prone or in the upright position, when stepping movement, placing, and walking reflexes were elicited. However, even here they coped well, quickly returning their responses to the environment to a quiet and calm state, with excellent motor control, and no jerky movements or windmill motions of the arms interfered. Apart from the high ponderal index group, which entered a different state rather suddenly for no apparent reason (e.g., from state 2 to state 6 when the pinprick was applied), all other infants went from one state to another quite slowly and smoothly. Hardly any infants reached the crying state 6, but came briefly to state 5 or remained in a state of quiet and sometimes passive alertness. Their range and shift of states was low (see Table 3).

The statistical analysis of the five newborn groups with different intrauterine growth and birth weight revealed differences in Habituation (response to rattle),

Table 3. Means and standard deviations for the 26 behavioral items of the Brazelton Scale for 90 Zulu newborns (first day)

Behavioral items	$\bar{X}$	SD
Response decrement to light	6.26	2.1
Response decrement to rattle	7.17	2.0
Response decrement to bell	7.0	2.2
Response decrement to pinprick	4.72	2.4
Orientation inanimate visual	4.38	1.6
Orientation inanimate auditory	4.99	1.6
Orientation animate visual	4.53	1.7
Orientation animate auditory	5.54	1.6
Orientation animate visual and auditory	4.67	1.7
Alertness	2.94	1.5
General Tonus	5.56	.8
Motor maturity	5.32	.7
Pull-to-sit	4.43	1.0
Cuddliness	4.98	.7
Defensive movements	5.39	1.1
Consolability	4.07	.8
Peak of excitement	4.57	2.0
Rapidity of buildup	2.28	1.9
Irritability	1.94	1.6
Activity	3.12	1.6
Tremulousness	1.07	.6
Startle	4.28	2.4
Lability of skin color	2.93	.2
Lability of states	2.0	.5
Self-quieting activity	1.68	2.4
Hand-mouth facility	4.77	3.4

in Motor Performance (general tonus, activity level), Regulation of State (cuddliness, consolability, self-quieting activity), Range of State (peak of excitement, irritability, rapidity of build-up), and Autonomic Regulation (startles). Differences obtained in scores on the Orientation items, however, did not approach statistical significance in the five groups, though several mean scores differed in at least one point (see Table 4).

In addition to the statistical analysis of the five newborn groups using the Kruskal-Wallis Test, multiple comparisons were made, applying the t-test. In addition to the five birth weight newborn groups, three other groups were composed controlling the effect of "sex of infant," "time of testing," (newborns tested within 4 hours after delivery, and newborns tested within 12 but after 4 hours of birth), and "birth order" (performances of first-borns were compared with behavior of later-borns). Of these three groups, the most interesting findings were the differences between female and male newborns in Orientation behavior. The females scored significantly higher on all five orientation items and reached a significantly higher level of alertness and activity than males. Females also habituated more quickly to light and responded to the pinprick with less limb movements than males (see Table 5).

Later-born infants showed higher hand-to-mouth activity ($p<.09$), more startles ($p<.1$), were easier consoled ($p<.05$), were less alert ($p<.1$), and habituated slower to respond to pinprick ($p<.1$) than first-born infants. Newborns tested within 4 hours after delivery scored slightly lower on the orientation-inanimate auditory item ($p<.1$) as well as on the orientation-animate visual one ($p<.08$). They were also less alert ($p<.1$), and their activity level was reduced ($p<.03$), but they performed more hand-to-mouth activity ($p<.1$) than newborns tested within 12 but after 4 hours of birth.

Comparison of low PI, high PI, underweight, full-weight, and overweight infants on behavioral items clearly showed a relationship between newborn performance and differential intrauterine growth. The most marked behavioral features were found in organizational processes regarding control of state. The low PI newborns hardly ever reached their peak of excitement; their motor and crying activity was the lowest of all infant groups, followed by the high birth weight group. The high PI newborn, however, almost always showed some motor excitement. Although the scores for rapidity of build-up remained in the lower ranges for all groups, there were differences.

The high PI newborns demonstrated a reduced control over their state without showing much agitation, which is also reflected in their level of irritability. For most of the tested infants "aversive" stimuli, as mentioned in the NBAS, did not exist. Self-quieting activity was highest in the low PI group and lowest in the high PI group. However, the low PI newborns hardly ever cried, since they made an effort, mostly successful, to return from a fussing to a more calming state. They also made more use of putting their hand to their mouths, comforting themselves, and thereby maintaining a successful quiet state more easily. The

Table 4.   Comparison of low PI, high PI, underweight, full-weight, and overweight infants on items of the Brazelton Scale

	Low PI group N = 15		High PI group N = 14		High BW group N = 17		Low BW group N = 14		Normal BW group N = 23	
Behavioral items	**X**	**SD**	**X**	**SD**	**X**	**SD**	**X**	**SD**	**X**	**SD**
Decrement to light	6.4	2.0	7.3	1.3	7.1	1.3	6.1	1.2	6.1	1.6[1]
Decrement to rattle	7.8	1.2	8.0	1.1	7.7	1.3	6.9	1.5	7.3	1.3[2]
Decrement to bell	7.9	1.3	7.8	1.0	7.5	1.6	7.5	1.3	7.1	1.8
Decrement to pinprick	5.0	2.7	3.8	2.6	5.0	2.1	5.7	2.3	4.9	2.2
Orientation inanimate visual	4.9	1.8	4.4	1.2	4.0	1.6	4.4	1.2	4.3	1.8
Orientation inanimate auditory	5.8	1.9	5.1	1.2	4.7	1.8	5.4	1.3	4.7	1.5
Orientation animate visual	5.2	2.0	4.5	1.1	4.1	1.7	4.9	1.6	4.4	1.7
Orientation animate auditory	6.2	1.6	5.6	1.0	5.0	1.9	6.2	1.4	5.3	1.4[3]
Orientation animate visual and auditory	5.3	1.9	4.8	1.4	4.3	2.0	5.1	1.7	4.5	1.6

Level of significance
[1] decrement to light $p < .1$
[2] decrement to rattle $p < .04$
[3] Orientation animate $p < .1$ auditory

Kruskal-Wallis Test, one-way.

	Low PI group N = 15		High PI group N = 14		High BW group N = 17		Low BW group N = 14		Normal BW group N = 23	
Items	**X**	**SD**	**X**	**SD**	**X**	**SD**	**X**	**SD**	**X**	**SD**
Alertness (4 only)	3.5	1.5	3.	1.2	2.5	1.9	3.1	.9	3.1	1.7
General tonus (4,5)	5.3	1.1	6.	.1	5.1	1.	5.7	.7	5.7	.6[4]
Motor maturity (4,5)	5.5	.6	5.6	.8	5.2	.6	5.3	.8	5.1	.4
Pull-to-sit (3,5)	4.6	1.3	4.5	1.3	4.9	.8	4.6	.8	4.3	.9
Cuddliness (4,5)	4.6	.1	5.2	.7	4.7	.6	5.	.0	5.	.05[5]
Defensive movements (4)	5.5	.8	5.5	1.1	5.8	1.1	5.1	1.2	5.2	1.4
Consolability (6 to 5,4,3,2)	4.1	.1	4.1	.3	4.6	.9	4.	.1	4.	.06[6]
Peak of excitement (5)	3.7	1.6	5.5	2.1	4.	1.9	4.3	1.7	4.8	2.0[7]
Rapidity of buildup (1 to 6)	1.9	2.	3.	1.2	1.8	2.1	1.9	1.4	2.	1.3[8]
Irritability (3,4,5)	1.7	1.3	2.2	1.	1.6	1.9	1.5	.7	2.1	1.4[9]
Activity (alert states)	3.4	2.1	3.6	1.1	2.6	1.6	3.1	1.6	3.	1.3
Tremulousness (all states)	—	—	—	—	—	—	—	—	—	—
Startle (3,4,5,6)	4.2	2.2	3.8	1.8	4.2	1.9	4.1	2.3	4.7	2.6
Lability of skin color (1 to 6)	2.9	.2	2.9	.2	2.9	.2	2.9	.2	3.	.0
Lability of states (all states)	2.	.0	2.	.2	2.	.1	2.	.1	2.	.1
Self-quieting activity (6,5, to 4,3,2,1)	5.5	.8	2.1	.9	4.1	3.3	5.4	1.9	3.1	1.5
Hand-mouth facility (all states)	6.	3.0	4.5	3.	5.3	3.5	5.7	2.5	4.1	3.6

Level of significance
[4] General tonus $p < .03$
[5] Cuddliness $p < .07$
[6] Consolability $p < .000$
[7] Peak of excitement $p < .1$
[8] Rapidity of buildup $p < .01$
[9] Irritability $p < .06$

Table 5.   Comparison of Behavioral Performances in male and female Newborns

Brazelton Test Behavioral Items	male newborns No. 44		female newborns No. 46		Level of signi- ficance
	X̄	SD	X̄	SD	
Response decrement to light	5.69	2.42	6.78	1.62	$p \leq .01$
Response decrement to rattle	6.93	2.09	7.40	1.97	NS
Response decrement to bell	7.00	2.32	7.14	2.30	NS
Response decrement to pinprick	4.30	2.48	5.10	2.41	$p \leq .1$
Orientation inanimate visual	3.79	.91	4.91	1.98	$p \leq .001$
Orientation inanimate auditory	4.65	1.54	5.29	1.73	$p \leq .06$
Orientation animate visual	3.97	1.24	5.04	2.00	$p \leq .003$
Orientation animate auditory	5.18	1.57	5.87	1.61	$p \leq .04$
Orientation animate visual and auditory	4.32	1.61	4.97	1.89	$p \leq .08$
Alertness	2.53	1.03	3.31	1.79	$p \leq .01$
General Tonus	5.51	.85	5.59	.87	NS
Motor maturity	5.25	.79	5.38	.61	NS
Pull-to-sit	4.41	1.03	4.42	1.11	NS
Cuddliness	5.02	.70	4.93	.87	NS
Defensive movements	5.37	1.23	5.40	1.17	NS
Consolability	4.13	.35	4.00	1.06	NS
Peak of excitement	4.37	2.08	4.74	2.08	NS
Rapidity of buildup	2.25	2.04	2.29	1.79	NS
Irritability	1.81	1.57	2.06	1.64	NS
Activity	2.83	1.46	3.38	1.71	$p \leq .10$
Tremulousness	1.00	.00	1.12	.87	NS
Startle	4.58	2.22	4.00	2.54	NS
Lability of skin color	2.90	.29	2.95	.29	NS
Lability of states	1.58	.49	1.63	.52	NS
Self-quieting activity	1.62	2.57	1.72	2.41	NS
Hand-mouth-facility	4.58	3.42	4.93	3.45	NS

high PI newborn group demonstrated more resistance to passive movements than the other newborn groups, including the high birth weight group, and were slightly on the hypertonic side, evidencing greater tone.

Although differences in the orientation scores failed to reach statistical significance, several aspects are important. The low PI group showed a higher capacity for responsiveness, as indicated in their level of alertness and in their scores for Orientation. They received the highest scores of all groups for all five Orientation items, and, apart from the inanimate visual Orientation item, their scores differed in at least one point. The lowest scores were obtained by the high birth weight group, which also scored lowest on alertness. In general, higher scores on the Attention-Orientation items were associated with lower birth weight babies, infants of younger mothers, with parity, and with sex. Of 29 low birth weight newborns, including the low PI babies, 18 were females and 16 were first-borns. In the total sample, a much clearer picture emerged in respect to male–female

Orientation behavior. Higher scores on Orientation items were associated with sex of the infant.

Marked differences were also found when comparing the high PI versus the high birth weight newborns. Newborns with a high birth weight but with an appropriate body–length ratio habituated faster to the rattle and showed more responsiveness to the animate visual stimulus. Both groups showed evidence of taking longer to habituate, or they were disturbed by the stimulus and started to cry. The high PI group was more likely to be "unavailable to the outside world" and was agitated more often. This group was also more irritable than the high birth weight newborns ($p < .1$) and reached a higher peak of excitement ($p < .1$). Spontaneous and elicited startles were also observed more often in newborns with a high ponderal index ($p < .1$). Their self-quieting activity was very brief, and intervention was almost always necessary. The high birth weight group made more attempts to bring their hands to their mouths, compared with the high PI group.

When comparing low PI newborns with high PI infants, several differences emerged: The low PI newborns habituated quicker in all items, but this reached statistical significance only in habituating to light ($p < .02$). Tonus was slightly better in the low PI group ($p < .06$); startles occurred more in the high PI group, indicating a higher sensitivity to any disturbing stimulus ($p < .03$). High Pi newborns needed more consoling ($p < .07$). In comparison to the low birth weight newborns, the low PI babies had a slightly better tone ($p < .05$) and scored slightly higher on motor maturity ($p < .08$) than the low birth weight infants.

In general, the low birth weight and the low PI newborns were mature in appearance and in their behaviour. There were no apparent signs of dysmaturity, nor was their skin dry and peeling. This last was observed in some of the high PI and high birth weight newborns, usually indicating fetal undernutrition or postmaturity. None of the low birth weight and low PI newborns showed any jerky movements or snap-back of limbs. Their limb movements were mostly free and smooth. They habituated calmly and rapidly to repeated disturbances. Although they moved into higher states of arousal slowly, they demonstrated more vigor in these states than the other full weight and overweight newborns. They responded with a good muscle tone when handled. Many of the infants were predominantly in state 3 or 4 and never reached an insulated crying state throughout the entire administration of the scale.

Differences in reflex behavior were also pronounced. All newborns were similar in the completeness of the Moro reflex, but they were different in head control, on being pulled to sit, in their crawling, and in stepping movements. They differed in some ways from each other in placing, stepping, and grasping. Automatic walking was much easier to elicit in low birth weight newborns; grasping was more intense in the higher birth weight groups. Rooting and sucking was less frequent in the low PI and low birth weight groups. The low and normal birth weight groups performed reflex behavior which could be charac-

Table 6.   Means and Standard Deviations of Day 1 Reflex Scores of Zulu Newborns

Reflex behavior	Low PI group N = 15		High PI group N = 14		High BW group N = 17		Low BW group N = 14		Normal BW group N = 23	
	X̄	SD	X̄	SD	X̄	SD	X̄	SD	X̄	SD
Plantar grasp	2.	.0	2.1	.3	1.9	.4	2.	.0	2.	.2
hand grasp	1.8	.5	1.9	.3	1.8	.3	1.9	.3	1.7	.3
ankle clonus	2.	.1	2.	.0	1.8	.3	1.9	.3	1.9	.3
babinski	2.	.1	2.	.1	1.9	.3	1.9	.3	2.	.2
standing	1.9	.3	2.	.0	1.8	.3	1.8	.5	1.9	.3
automatic walking	1.5	.6	1.4	.6	1.3	.5	1.8	.8	1.3	.4
placing	2.	.6	2.	.3	1.9	.6	2.	.3	2.	.5
crawling	1.9	.4	2.	.3	2.	.7	2.	.6	2.	.3
glabella	2.	.0	2.	.0	1.9	.3	1.9	.3	2.	.0
tonick neck reflex A	1.	.0	1.	.0	1.	.0	1.	.0	1.	.0
moro	1.9	.3	2.	.0	1.8	.4	1.8	.4	2.	.2
rooting	1.5	.7	2.	.6	1.9	.6	1.6	.6	2.	.8
sucking	1.9	.5	2.1	.3	2.2	.5	1.9	.5	2.	.3
passive movements										
arms R	1.9	.3	2.1	.6	1.8	.3	2.	.3	1.9	.2
L	1.9	.3	2.1	.6	1.8	.3	2.	.3	2.	.2
legs R	1.9	.3	2.1	.2	1.6	.4	1.9	.3	1.7	.3
L	1.9	.3	2.1	.2	1.6	.4	1.9	.3	1.9	.3

Tonic deviation of head and eyes/Nystagmus: omitted.

terized as hypotonic, whereas the high PI and high birth weight groups had several hypertonic responses, particularly pronounced in high PI newborns' resistence to passive movements. A number of infants could not be stimulated to produce any automatic walking motions (see Table 6).

Discussion

In summary, these Zulu newborns showed low motor activity, were nontremulous, low in vigor, and without any "overshooting" or "overreaction." Uncontrollable motor activity hardly ever interfered with responses or handling. Spontaneous startles were rare and only observed in the high PI group, whose responses and behavior were more marked and pronounced than those of the low PI or low birth weight infants. Transition from one state to another was slow and smooth, without reaching intense crying, in all groups except the high PI group. Many newborns had difficulty in maintaining a quiet, alert state for long periods; the level of alertness was generally rather passive, a phenomenon which is well known in newborns (L. Dubowitz, personal communication, August 1983).

The apparent control of motor behavior and state in those Zulu infants was high, permitting repeated and prolonged responses to kinesthetic stimuli and handling, but responses to auditory and visual stimuli remained low. One explanation might be the horizontal position in which the Zulu newborns were kept while tested on the Orientation items; eye-opening and visual scanning seems to occur more frequently in newborns held upright (Korner & Grobstein, 1966). This difference in positioning newborns would have to be considered when in cross-cultural comparisons. Within the Zulu newborn groups, however, the position in which the baby was held cannot make any difference, since all newborns were kept in the horizontal position.

The low PI newborns received the highest Orientation scores. It would, however, be exaggerating to interpret the higher Orientation scores of the low PI group as indicating hyperexcitability or hypertonic behavior. The small-for-dates and low PI newborns did not give the impression that they were hyperexcitable. They seemed to be able to smoothly orientate and follow the offered stimuli for a brief period. It was found by Saint-Anne Dargassies (1969) and by Joppich and Schulte (1968) that SFD infants can either be characterized by hyperexcitability or by rather apathetic behavior. The Zulu SFD and low PI newborns do not seem to fit in any of those descriptions and categories.

Dubowitz, Dubowitz, and Goldberg (1982) assessed the behavior of small-for-dates newborns in Cape Town and in London. Both ethnic small-for-date groups showed an increase in visual and auditory orientation and in alertness. Stimmler (1970) assumes that those small-for-date newborns who are proportionately much more depressed in weight than height and have a wasted appearance could be active and alert at birth and might be a-reflexic. That low birth-weight newborns do not need to perform any "deviant" behavior was also reported by Brazelton (1977), who studied Zinacanteco newborns in southern Mexico. Their motoric processes, their capacity to organize and modulate state, their physiological organization, and their orientation responses were consistently excellent.

The behavior of SFD infants as described in the literature reflects the great neurobehavioral variety of those newborns, cross-sectional as much as cross-cultural. The cross-cultural variety might also be due to a shift in the mean birth weight since mean birth weight differs immensely from one ethnic group to another.

However, the question remains: Is growth retardation per se associated with neurobehavioral abnormalities (Dubowitz et al., 1982; Polani, 1974)? Newborn behavior which is shaped by intrauterine growth will also be influenced by the different factors leading to growth retardation.

Dubowitz et al. (1982) discuss the difficulty in comparing studies on SFD newborns, as the variables considered differ greatly. In some studies (Michaelis, Schulte, & Nolte, 1970) infants suffered fetal distress and were pediatrically not well; in others (Schulte, Schrempf, & Hinze, 1971), infants had toxemic mothers. The low PI infants in this study had a birth weight between 2000 and 2500 grams. Most underweight infants in the Als et al. (1976) study weighed between 2500 and 3000 grams. The exact cut-off point in weight still varies, and there is a lack of standardization of terminology (Dubowitz, 1974). It would be necessary, when comparing studies of newborn behavior, to use the same criteria of selection.

The Zulu SFD newborns did not perform any deviant motor behavior. The motor behavior of full-term, small-for-dates infants is expected to be similar to that of newborn infant of normal weight at term (Michaelis et al., 1970; Joppich & Schulte, 1968). The maturation of the central nervous system and motor development are more closely related to the actual conceptional age than to the age from birth or to birth weight (Thomson & Billewicz, 1976).

Females and first-borns were more in number in the low PI and underweight newborn. It is a fact that birth weight rises with birth rank (Bergner & Susser, 1970; Niestroj, 1983). In a study on birth weight in Botswana (Niestroj, 1983), including 7,000 birth weights from different regions and across time, birth weight was directly in proportion to parity for both female and male infants, lowest in the primigravidae, highest in the grand multipara. Birth weight was lower for females in all weight categories. As in this study, females had higher scores on the orientation items. A similar result was also reported by Lester et al. (1976).

The association of low birth weight, sex, and birth order seems to be extremely important when discussing behavior of low birth weight babies in relation to maternal responses and to social interaction. First-borns, often of lower birth weight than subsequent children, might also behave differently. Colgate (1981) studied the behavior of newborns in Cameroon and found that lighter infants had a significantly better Range of State but poorer Autonomic Nervous System Regulation, and that they were more available for interaction, as evidenced by their significantly lower organization for arousal level.

The birth weight of first-born infants in Colgate's study ranged from 2500 to 3000 grams. This indicates that lighter African newborns do not seem to perform the type of behavior described for White light newborns. In Lester et al.'s (1976) study, *lower* scores on the attention-orientation factor were associated with lower birth weight newborns and babies of younger mothers. In the Colgate (1981) and Dubowitz (1982) studies and in this study, *higher* scores on the attention-orientation items were associated with lower birth weight infants born to younger mothers. And in this study, lower scores were found in higher birth weight newborns born to older mothers and those of higher parity. The behavior of lighter African newborns seem to be characterized by some 'better' performances. Age of mother, sex of infant, and birth rank are all factors which seem to influence intrauterine growth and have an impact on newborn behavioral characteristics, and are also likely to have consequences for any mother–child interaction. We know that birth order effects maternal caretaking. LeVine (see Tulkin, 1977) observed that, in the Hausa culture, mothers had minimal interaction with their first-born children. The Hausa custom involved the extreme avoidance by mothers of their first-born children, starting at birth. LeVine reported systematic differences between the attachments of first- and later-born children. Although we can assume that a first-born child will be treated and perceived differently from later-borns, we still know very little about child-rearing practices in the first few months in African communities.

Maternal caretaking of boys and girls will also differ, but systematic studies need to be carried out to investigate the implications for further physical, social, and cognitive development of the child. Our knowledge about attitudes towards and the handling of small African newborns, especially when they are first-borns and female, is sparse. For several African societies it is still the custom that women reduce their food intake during pregnancy or in the last trimester of pregnancy. The explanation given by women is that they wanted to control their food intake in order to produce a small child, which would facilitate an easier labor and birth. Women who deliberately attempt to have a small child might respond to that child in a quite different way than a woman living in a cultural and social environment where higher birth weight is also believed to be better and healthier.

Suskind (1977) and Katz (1977) noted that smallness might not be a disadvantage for the child but might be more adaptive later in the human life cycle. Women who reduce their food intake in the last trimester of pregnancy while food availability is not a constraint (Kusin et al., 1981; Niestroj, 1983) may believe that they enhance their own survival as much as that of the fetus when this custom is associated with the hope of an easier labor. Whether Zulu women also try to reduce their food intake was not clear. Pediatricians in the Cape area (L. Dubowitz, personal communication, August 1983) found out that a mother of twins with different birth weights gave more care to the smaller, underweight twin, while the well-grown child was looked after by relatives. These chance observations can help researchers to provide questions which are basically part of the cultural setting in which the investigation takes place. The question "is bigger really better" has already been asked, but we also have to ask, "Is dynamic behavior really better than passive behavior?" (Leiderman, Tulkin, & Rosenfeld, 1977).

It is assumed that the interactive and dynamic dimension in the NBAS reflects the infants' ability to elicit responses from, and to give feedback to, his or her environment. Differences in this dimension are supposed to be an important predictor of both the infants' capacity to elicit necessary nurturing and the parents' perception of the infant (Brazelton, 1977). However, further cross-cultural studies must look at the "meaning" attached to certain types of behavior believed to be important in our own culture but which may not be treated with the same importance in another culture. The same behavior in different cultures will be associated with different meanings and will evoke various types of response behavior. The interactive and dynamic dimension we stress in our early mother–infant interaction research may not have the same significance in other cultures.

It is only when we try to look at behavior in its cultural context that we may be able to describe the child's development and social interaction.

> While we sense that there are certain minimal physical and psychological needs and conditions at birth that, if unmet or uncorrected, place any infant in developmental jeopardy, we do not yet know the limiting conditions, worldwide, nor do we know the extent to which infants "at risk" by standards developed in our society can survive, adapt, and develop normally as viewed by members of their own societies. We tend, for example, to view flaccid, passive infants and children as abnormal, retarded, or possibly diseased, but greater study of worldwide patterns of development reveals passivity frequently to be nonpathological and in fact modal in many societies in which children nonetheless grow up to be fully functioning members. (Leiderman et al., 1977, p. 603)

There is little known about the behavior and development of large-for-date infants in an African population. Usually, "hypertropic," or large-for-date, newborns are described as less irritable and relatively hypotonic (Dubowitz & Dubowitz, 1977; Saint-Anne Dargassies, 1969). The Zulu large-for-date and the high PI newborns were the more irritable compared with other newborns in the same ethnic group. Although the irritability scores were generally low in all five newborn groups, the high PI group scored highest. Self-quieting activity was also low among those infants who were unable to return to a quiet state easily, either by themselves or by being consoled. In the Zulu study the larger infants were born to older mothers with high parity. The relationship between those factors is not yet well understood.

In a study by Dixon, Tronick, Keefer, and Brazelton, (1982) on perinatal circumstances and newborn outcome among the Gusii of Kenya, infants of older mothers tended to be smaller and more irritable. Higher parity and age of mother was associated with lower birth weight. These infants did less well on orientation items, were consoled less readily, and had a less optimal "cuddliness" response. They also had significantly higher irritability and activity scores, demonstrated significantly more startles, were more excitable, irritable, and active, and did less well in social interaction. The behavioral description of the Gusii smaller infants born to older mothers of high parity is almost identical with behavior of the Zulu large-for-date infants who were born to mothers belonging to the highest age and parity group.

In general, Zulu infants were low on irritability and showed good motor performance, both of which might have contributed to the very easy handling of the infants. The level of irritability with less motor maturity would still be of utmost significance for handling and for any physical interaction between caretaker and child. The motor behavior of African newborns has been discussed in terms of precocity (Geber & Dean, 1957; Ainsworth, 1967) and its relation to environmental, genetic, and nutritional factors (LeVine, 1970). Although the concept of motor precocity has been questioned (Warren, 1972; Keefer, Tronick, Dixon, & Brazelton, 1982), recent findings of qualitatively different motor tone and greater motor maturity suggest differences in performance between European and African newborns who were tested in the very first days of life (Keefer et al., 1982; Brazelton et al., 1976; Colgate, 1981).

The Zulu newborns evidenced few startles and were nontremulous; their movements were smooth and cogwheel-free, indicating genetic and intrauterine environmental effects, as they were tested before any training or parental handling was operative. The relationship between level of irritability and motor behavior in newborns is not yet clear. Ganda infants (Ainsworth, 1967), Gusii newborns (Dixon et al., 1982), and Cameroon newborns (Colgate, 1981) were described as being less irritable than American babies. The presumably greater tolerance to stress in African newborns might be related to their motor maturity, although Ainsworth observed low irritability among Ganda infants even when motor maturity was not apparent.

The data discussed in this chapter was gathered in the context of a short term study of the effect of intrauterine growth on Zulu newborn behavior and was designed as an outcome study. The immediate shortcoming of the study lies in its "one-shot" assessment of newborn behavior on the first few hours of life, since newborn behavior is known to be rather unstable (Beintema, 1968), at least within the first 3 days of life. The NBAS is based on a dynamic model of the organization of neonatal behavior, taking into account the possibility of considerable changes in scale performance during the neonatal period (Lester & Brazelton, 1982).

In this context it is interesting to note that Gusii infants did not change in their behavior significantly over an observation period of 2 weeks, and no recovery curve, which is typical of U.S. babies, was observed (Dixon et al., 1982). The results obtained in this study have no predictive value, but they do provide a description of the behavior functioning of Zulu newborns at a particular point in time. The indicative nature of the findings can help to formulate questions for further, more detailed investigations.

References

Ainsworth, M.D. (1967). *Infancy in Uganda: Infant care and the growth of love.* Baltimore, MD: Johns Hopkins University Press.

Als, H., Tronick, E., Adamson, L., & Brazelton, T.B. (1976). The behavior of the full-term but underweight newborn infant. *Developmental Medicine and Child Neurology, 18,* 590–602.

Beintema, D.J. (1968). *A neurological study of newborn infants* (Clinics in Developmental Medicine, No. 28). London: S.I.M.P. with Heinemann Medical.

Bergner, L., & Susser, M.W. (1970). Low birth weight and prenatal nutrition: An interpretative review. *Pediatrics, 46*(6), 946–966.

Brazelton, T.B. (1973). *Neonatal behavioral assessment scale* (Clinics in Developmental Medicine, No. 50). London: S.I.M.P. with Heinemann Medical; Philadelphia: Lippincott.

Brazelton, T.B. (1977). Implications of infant development among the Mayan Indians of Mexico. In P.H. Leiderman, St.R. Tulkin, & A. Rosenfeld (Eds.), *Culture and infancy. Variations in the human experience.* New York: Academic Press.

Brazelton, T.B., Koslowski, B., & Tronick, E. (1976). Neonatal behavior among urban Zambians. *Journal of the American Academy of Child Psychiatry, 1*, 97–107.

Brazelton, T.B., Tronick, E., Lechtig, A., Laski, R.E., & Klien, R.E. (1977). The behavior of nutritionally deprived Guatemalan infants. *Developmental Medicine and Child Neurology, 19*, 364–372.

Cassell, J. (1955). A comprehensive health program among South African Zulus. In B.D. Paul (Ed.), *Health, Culture and Community.* New York: Russell Sage Foundation.

Colgate, S.H. (1981). *Midwifery, mothering and behavioral assessments of African neonates.* Unpublished doctoral dissertation, University of Chicago, Evanston, IL.

Craig, A.P., & Richter-Strydom, K.M. (1983). Unplanned pregnancies among urban Zulu schoolgirls. *South-African Medical Journal, 63*, 452–455.

Davis, D.P. (1981). Physical growth from fetal to early childhood. In J.A. Davis & J. Dobbing (Eds.), *Scientific foundations of pediatrics.* London: Heinemann Med. Books Ltd.

Dixon, S., Tronick, E., Keefer, C., & Brazelton, T.B. (1982). Perinatal circumstances and newborn outcome among the Gusii of Kenya: Assessment of risk. *Infant Behavior and Development, 5*, 11–32.

Dubowitz, V. (1974). *Size at birth* (Ciba Foundation Symposium No. 27). K. Elliott & J. Knight (Eds.). Amsterdam: Associated Scientific Publishers.

Dubowitz, L., & Dubowitz, V. (1977). *Gestational age of the newborn.* Reading, MA: Addison-Wesley.

Dubowitz, L., & Dubowitz, V. (1981). The neurological assessment of preterm and full-term newborn infant. *Clinics in developmental medicine* (No. 79). Lavenham, Suffolk: The Lavenham Press Ltd.

Dubowitz, L., Dubowitz, V., & Goldberg, C. (1982). A comparison of neurological function in growth-retarded and appropriate-sized full-term newborn infants in two ethnic groups. *South-African Medical Journal, 61*, 1003–1007.

Geber, M., & Dean, R.F.A. (1957). The state of development of newborn African children. *Lancet, 272*, 1217–1220.

Greene, L.S. (Ed.). (1977). *Malnutrition, behavior, and social organization.* New York: Academic Press.

Hofer, M.A. (1981). *The roots of human behavior.* San Francisco: W.H. Freeman and Company.

Hollingsworth, M.J. (1965). Observations on the birth weights and survival of African babies: Single births. *Annals of Human Genetics, 28*, 291–300.

Joppich, G., & Schulte, F.J. (1968). *Neurologie des neugeborenen.* Berlin: Springer.

Katz, S.H. (1977). Toward a new concept of nutrition. In L.S. Grenne (Ed.), *Malnutrition, behavior, and social organization*. New York: Academic Press.

Keefer, H.C., Tronick, E., Dixon, S., & Brazelton, T.B. (1982). Specific differences in motor performance between Gusii and American newborns and a modification of the Neonatal Behavioral Assessment Scale. *Child Development, 53*, 754–759.

Klaus, M.H. (1979). Foreword. In E.B. Thoman (Ed.), *Origins of the infant's social responsiveness*. Hillsdale, NJ: Erlbaum.

Konner, M.J. (1972). Aspects of the developmental ethology of a foraging people. In N. Blurton Jones (Ed.), *Ethological studies of child behavior*. Cambridge, England: Cambridge University Press.

Korner, A., & Grobstein, R., (1966). Visual alertness as related to soothing in neonates: Implications for maternal stimulation and early deprivation. *Child Development, 37*, 867–876.

Kusin, J.A., Van Steenbergen, W.M., Lakhani, Sh., Jansen, A.A.J., Renqvist, U., & Elvers, H. (1981). Food consumption of pregnant and lactating women in Machakos area, Kenya. In H.J. Diesfeld (Ed.), *Health and research in developing countries*. Aachen: Peter Lang.

Larsen, J.V., Msane, C.L., & Monkhe, M.C. (1983a). The Zulu traditional birth attendant. *South-African Medical Journal, 63*, 540–542.

Larsen, J.V., Msane, C.L., & Monkhe, M.C. (1983b). The fate of women who deliver at home in rural Kwazulu. *South-African Medical Journal, 63*, 543–545.

Leiderman, P.H., Tulkin, St.R., & Rosenfeld, A. (1977). Looking toward the future. In P.H. Leidermann, St.R. Tulkin, & A. Rosenfeld (Eds.), *Culture and infancy. Variations in the human experience*. New York: Academic Press.

Lester, B.M. (1979). A synergistic process approach to the study of prenatal malnutrition. *International Journal of Behavioral Development, 2*, 377–393.

Lester, B.M., & Brazelton, T.B. (1982). Cross-cultural assessment of neonatal behavior. In D. Wagner & H. Stevenson (Eds.), *Cultural perspectives on child development*. San Francisco: W.H. Freeman.

Lester, B.M., Emory, E.K., & Hoffman, S.L. (1976). A multivariate study of the effects of high-risk factors on performance on the Brazelton Neonatal Assessment Scale. *Child Development, 47*, 515–517.

Lester, B.M., Klien, R.E., & Martinez, S.J. (1975). The use of habituation in the study of the effects of infantile malnutrition. *Developmental Psychobiology, 8*, 541–546.

LeVine, R. (1970). Cross-cultural study in child psychology. In P.H. Mussen (Ed.), *Carmichael's manual of child psychology* (Vol. 2). New York: Wiley.

LeVine, R.A. (1977). Child rearing as cultural adaptation. In P.H. Leiderman, St.R. Tulkin, & A. Rosenfeld (Eds.), *Culture and infancy. Variations in the human experience*. New York: Academic Press.

Longmore, L. (1954). Infant mortality in urban Africa. *South-African Medical Journal, 28*, 295–298.

Mata, L. (1978). *The children of Santa Maria Cauque*. Cambridge, MA: MIT Press.

McKeown, T., & Record, R.G. (1954). Influence of pre-natal environment on correlation between birth weight and paternal height. *American Journal of Human Genetics, 6*, 457.

Meredith, H.V. (1970). Body weight at birth of viable human infants: A world-wide comparative treatise. *Human Biology, 42*, 217–264.

Michaelis, R., Schulte, F.J., & Nolte, R. (1970). Motor behavior of small-for-gestational age newborn infants. *Journal of Pediatrics, 76*, 208–213.

Miller, H.C., & Hassanein, K. (1973). Fetal malnutrition in white newborn infants: Maternal factors. *Pediatrics, 52*, 511–522.

Niestroj, B.H.E. (1983). *Birthweight in Botswana.* Unpublished manuscript, Gaborone-Cambridge, England.

Ounsted, M. (1968). The regulation of foetal growth. In J.H.P. Jonixs, H.K.A. Visser, & J.A. Troelstra (Eds.), *Aspects of prematurity and dysmaturity* (Nutricia Symposium, Groningen, Stenfert Kroese, Leiden).

Piaget, J. (1935). *La naissance de l'intelligence chez l'enfant.* Neuchâtel: Delachaux & Niestle.

Polani, P.E. (1974). Discussion: F.J. Schulte, Fetal Malnutrition and Brain Development. In *Size at birth* (Ciba Foundation Symposium 27). Amsterdam: Associated Scientific Publishers.

Prechtl, H., & Beintema, D. (1976). *The neurological examination of the full-term newborn infant* (Clinics in Developmental Medicine No. 12). London: S.I.M.P. with Heinmann Medical.

Preston-Whyte, E. (1974). Kinship and marriage. In W.D. Hammond-Tooke (Ed.), *The Bantu-speaking peoples of Southern Africa.* London: Routledge & Paul.

Richards, A.I. (1964). *Hunger and work in a savage tribe.* Cleveland, OH: World Publ. Co.

Richardson, B.D., Sinwel, R.E., Rantsho, J.M., Bac, M., & Moatshe, M. (1983). Birthweight of babies born at home in a black rural community of Bophuthatswana, southern Africa. *Archives of Disease in Childhood, 58*, 176–179.

Raum, O.F. (1967). *Chaga childhood.* London: Oxford University Press.

Ross, S.M., Van Middlekoop, A., & Khoza, N.C. (1983). Breast-feeding practices in a black community. *South-African Medical Journal, 63*, 23–25.

Saint-Anne Dargassies, S. (1969). L'essentiel de l'exploration neurologique clinique du nouveau-ne. *Gazette de Medicine de France, 76*, 1293.

Schulte, F.J., Schrempf, G., & Hinze, G. (1971). Maternal toxemia, fetal malnutrition, and motor behavior of the newborn. *Pediatrics, 48*, 871–882.

Stein, H. (1975). Maternal protein depletion and small-for-gestational-age babies. *Archives of Diseases in Childhood, 50*, 146–148.

Stein, H., & Ellis, U. (1974). The low birthweight African baby. *Archives of Diseases in Childhood, 49*, 156.

Stimmler, L. (1970). Infants who are small-for-gestational age. *Proceedings of the Royal Society of Medicine, 63*, 500–501.

Stoch, M.B., & Smythe, P.M. (1963). Does undernutrition during infancy inhibit brain growth and subsequent intellectual development. *Archives of Diseases in Childhood, 38*, 546–552.

Suskind, R.M. (1977). Characteristics and causation of protein-calorie malnutrition in the infant and pre-school child. In L.S. Greene (Ed.), *Malnutrition, behavior, and social organization.* New York: Academic Press.

Tanner, J.M. (1976). Population differences in body size, shape, and growth rate. A 1976 view. *Archives of diseases in childhood, 51,* 1–2.

Thomson, A.M., & Billewicz, W.Z. (1976). The concept of the "light-for-dates" infant. In D.F. Roberts & A.M. Thomson (Eds.), *The biology of human fetal growth* (Vol. XV). London: Tayler & Francis.

Tulkin, St.R. (1977). Dimensions of multicultural research in infancy and early childhood. In P.H. Leiderman, St.R. Tulkin, & A. Rosenfeld (Eds.), *Culture and infancy. Variations in the human experience.* New York: Academic Press.

Urrusti, J., Yoshida, P., Velasco, L., Frenk, S., Rosado, A., Sosa, A., Morales, M., Yoshida, T., & Metcoff, J. (1972). Human fetal growth retardation: 1. Clinical features of sample with intrauterine growth retardation. *Peadiatrics, 50,* 547–567.

Vliet, van der V., (1974). Growing up in traditional society. In W.D. Hammond-Tooke (Ed.), *The Bantu-speaking peoples of Southern Africa.* London: Routledge & Paul.

Warren, M. (1972). African infancy precocity. *Psychological Bulletin, 78,* 353–367.

Wayburne, S. (1983). The care of newborn infants in a developing community. In J.A. Davis, M.P.M. Richards, & N.R.C. Roberton (Eds.), *Attachment in premature infants.* London: Croom Helm.

Watson, J.B. (1928). *Psychological care of infant and child.* London: Norton.

Woods, D.L., De V. Heese, H., Davey, D.A., & Van Schalkwyk, D.J. (1978). Stature and weight of coloured primigravidas in Cape Town. *South-African Medical Journal, 54,* 776–777.

Woods, D.L., Malan, A.F., De V. Hesse, H., & Van Schlkwyk, D.J. (1979). Maternal size and fetal growth. *South-African Medical Journal, 56,* 562–564.

Zeskind, Ph.S., & Ramey, C.T. (1978). Fetal malnutrition: An experimental study of its consequences on infant development in two caregiving environments. *Child Development, 49,* 1155–1162.

Zeskind, Ph.S., & Ramey, C.T. (1981). Preventing intellectual and interactional sequelae of fetal malnutrition: A longitudinal transactional, and synergistic approach to development. *Child Development, 52,* 213–218.

Afterword

T. Berry Brazelton

This volume from around the world presents a wide diversity of topics and of approaches. Its very diversity is both challenging and enlightening. As in any volume containing the work of sensitive, skilled researchers and clinicians, there are more questions raised than hypotheses solved. My overall impression of these chapters is that of wonder and questioning. Haven't we learned a lot over the last 17 years since the Neonatal Behavioral Assessment Scale (NBAS) was first published? And haven't we to learn a great deal more? These chapters make me humble in the desire to answer the questions they raise. We have just begun to tap the surface of the complexity of the human newborn and of his effect on his environment—not to mention the age-old equation of the environment's effect on both his endowment and his future development. We can certainly be sure that not one of these researchers is left with the oversimplified questions of "Is it genetic or environmental?" Each of them recognizes the intrauterine effects of culture on the neonate's genetic behavioral endowment. Each of them recognizes the rapidity with which cultural practices and expectations influence change in the neonate's behavioral repertoire (by three days in most of these chapters). The controversy is no longer a controversy. It has become an attempt to reframe and reassess the relative contributions of each very powerful influence.

Cross-cultural work is a way to look at these relative influences. But it is fraught with both positive and negative conditions which must necessarily influence our findings and our interpretations. The most important influence underlies a major reason for doing cross-cultural research. The reason is that we hope to look at another culture with more objectivity than we can our own. But, very quickly, we become aware of the enormous biases we bring from our own culture which influence every aspect of our research—our ability to see, what we observe, how we influence our own observations, and how we measure—in both recording and discarding information. We have a Pygmalian or expectancy effect on those we observe which cannot be discarded or measured. It can only be accepted. The Whitings sent an African anthropology student to our house to observe our practices with our last baby. My wife and I were self-conscious, irritable, extremely aware of each maneuver and of its value in the observer's eyes. Our behaviors became distorted. They were probably characteristic, but they were loaded with significances which were not necessarily characteristic.

How do we handle these biases? We learn from them. As we recognize them, they become part of our repertoire. When we can, we can share them with our subjects and record their reactions. The slippage we will inevitably encounter in our work in another culture becomes a major source of data. When we have trained observers to reliability on the Brazelton Scale and before they leave for cross-cultural work, we ask to see them upon their return. We observe them carefully and record any differences in performance or scoring. These differences or slippages are seen not as evidence of unreliability, but as the inevitable changes which sensitive observers will make as they work with a uniform population of babies, or as they adjust to the observing eyes of a different culture. The observations can then be used as most sensitive markers to differentiate the study population.

The NBAS has a somewhat flexible structure. Its goal is to produce and measure the infant's capacities and style as he or she reacts to a trained observer. Its very flexibility can become an asset in gaining insight into the baby's style. When all babies in a study have qualitative differences, such as Keefer and her colleagues and Hopkins describe in the motor behavior of African babies, and as Atkins in Mexico and Piessens in Indonesia describe, they may be more significant than the scorable items of the original NBAS. As a result, we have modified the NBAS by adding nine additional items in the revised version (Brazelton, 1984). These items, first designed for fragile babies, are meant to capture more qualitative aspects of a baby's performance. There are three concepts contained in these nine items. First, the cost to the baby measures his or her fragility and might answer some of the questions raised by Niestroj in her study of undernourished Zulu families. Second, the cost to the examiner to achieve a baby's best performance can be a measure of the baby's own style as Piessens demonstrated in her work with the Indonesian babies. The irritable babies in the Grossmanns' study and in Van Den Boom's work might have been understood better with such items. Irritability can be an index of a highly sensitive baby, of inner disorganization and poor state control, or it can be seen in a baby who is responsive to external maneuvers and will learn organization from a sensitive parent. These babies are different from each other in their responsiveness to sensitive handling. The quality of a baby's best performance is the third window into his or her style and potential influence on his or her environment. Future investigators may be freer to record such subtle differences. I found the qualitative descriptions of the babies in each of these chapters most valuable. We should always use observations and descriptions in cross-cultural reports.

Through the NBAS, these authors provide a window into the childrearing values in each culture. In each chapter I felt I understood the country and its people differently after the authors described the parents and children they studied. The descriptions were made more incisive by the authors' attempts to pin down the many variables influencing their study. Our inability to control variables was mentioned often. Moreover, the interaction between identified and unidentified variables as they produced the neonate's behavior and were influential in shaping the mother's behavior were a rich source of data and of confusion. We need more complex models for entering variables and for recording their effect on the baby and on parents. A systems method of analyzing the different systems as they interact to produce neonatal behavior would be a real breakthrough. A systems approach to understanding the baby and his environment will lead us toward a more productive understanding of the nature-nurture equation. The intrauterine variables which influence neonatal behavior are not additive but are likely to be synergistic. We have been relatively unsuccessful in efforts to assess this synergism. Cross-cultural studies such as these may help us further such a model. The questions raised by the Grossmanns and Hopkins chapters are a start toward this.

We have learned so much in our research with the Neonatal Behavioral Assessment Scale. One assessment is too simple as a window into the baby's potential. We need several serial assessments to capture the infant's capacity to recover from labor and delivery and his or her ability to utilize subtle but powerful environmental cues. Atkins' observation that the Mexican babies' resistance to bright lights and to visual responses could be correlated with the mothers' handling and their belief in the evil eye is interesting in this regard. We need more observations to understand how such subtle cues can be transmitted to shape neonatal behavior so early.

Repeated measures with the NBAS give us an initial description of the subtle changes in the baby. They do not give us answers as to the etiology of these behaviors. In this vein, I was particularly struck by the fact that many chapters (Grossmann and Grossmann, Van Den Boom, Munck, Stoleru) raised the issue that irritable babies received more attention in certain cultures; quiet babies received more attention in others (Keefer et al., Atkins, Niestroj). It seemed that babies who didn't fit the stereotyped expectancy required more nurturing from parents who were ready and able to interact with them. Might this be used as a measure of sensitivity in nurturing as one assesses the parent–infant interaction? We need to match the NBAS with sensitive assessments of the parents. These, too, can be adapted to include and be sensitive to cultural differences.

In order to identify subtle differences, we need well-trained researchers. Reliability is absolutely necessary among observers of neonates, for we are dealing with organisms which are sensitive to the subtle differences in neonatal environments. The differences between Danish and Italian nurseries could affect the very neonatal behavior being measured. Can we use differences in behavior as reflections of the subtle influences in environments? In any study we need to develop the nursery practices which we know will influence scores on the NBAS.

I would like to suggest a model for prediction and for use in studying subtle nature-nurture interactions as they influence development. It is based on the assumption that there is a map of infant development. As the baby progresses from one change-point to the next, the researcher can predict the short-term outcome the baby's progress in developmental lines (cognitive, motor, affective, linguistal). Parental influences and parental change can also be predicted. At the next change-point, the outcomes of the predictions are confirmatory. A good researcher or a good clinician should be able to estimate the influences of the baby's contribution, as well as that of his environment. But the missed aspects of the predictions become the most interesting. For in the missed prediction is contained three forces which deserve to be a part of the study (Figure 1):

(1) The observer's own biases, as they shape his or her observations; (2) the strength of the defenses of the subjects, which made it possible for them to cover the forces that led to the prediction error; and (3) the strength (or weakness) of the observer-subject transference. Each of these can be subjected to scrutiny in the light of the missed predictions. Over time they should diminish in intensity, and the predictions will become more precise. Prediction from infancy to later childhood in any area should not be linear. To expect a linear prediction would ignore the marvelous plasticity of newborns, the powerful shaping influence of their environment, and the transition points that dominate their development. At each of these points, there is the potential and the opportunity for a shift in the energy in the systems measured. The shift can be constructive or it can be costly.

Transition points become the most valuable windows into the developing parent–infant system, as well as into the effect of the observer and the research on that system. In cross-cultural research, a systems approach to prediction such as this might uncover the subtle, important influences of cultural diversity. These chapters give us such fascinating windows into the diversity of parents and infants in other parts of the world.

Benjamin Predictive Model

Figure 1.

Author Index

Subject Index